THE WAY OF
wisdom

Bruce K. Waltke

J.I. PACKER &
SVEN K. SODERLUND

Editors

THE WAY OF wisdom

Essays in Honor of BRUCE K. WALTKE

ZondervanPublishingHouse

Grand Rapids, Michigan

A Division of HarperCollins*Publishers*

The Way of Wisdom

Requests for information should be addressed to:

ZondervanPublishingHouse
Grand Rapids, Michigan 49530

Library of Congress Cataloging-in-Publication Data

The way of wisdom: essays in honor of Bruce K. Waltke / J.I. Packer and
Sven K. Soderlund, editors.
p. cm.
Includes bibliographical references.
ISBN: 0-310-22728-3
1. Wisdom Literature. 2. Wisdom — Biblical teaching. 3. Wisdom — Religious aspects — Christianity. I. Waltke, Bruce K. II. Packer, J.I. (James Innell) III. Soderlund, Sven.
BS1455.W39 2000
223'.06 — dc 21 00-039266
CIP

This edition is printed on acid-free paper.

Printed in the United States of America

00 01 02 03 04 / ❖ DC/ 10 9 8 7 6 5 4 3 2 1

Contents

Bruce K. Waltke: A Tribute

This book is a mixed bag of essays, some exploring biblical texts, others digging into theological themes, but all related in one way or another to seeking and finding wisdom. Why the mix? Because all the writers are colleagues, associates, or former students of Bruce Waltke who have teamed up from their different disciplines to honor him with this collection on his seventieth birthday, August 30, 2000. The variety seems fitting for such a one as Bruce, a many-sided scholar in the Renaissance mold whose brilliance as a linguist, exegete, biblical and systematic theologian, preacher, teacher, and pastoral counselor has made its impact at many different levels. Insofar as Bruce's work has a single core, however, it is the exegeting and expounding of the Old Testament generally and Wisdom literature specifically, hence the focus of the present collection.

Bruce Kenneth Waltke, a man greatly beloved, is a humble, genial, unassuming believer in whom strength of mind, sweetness of character, deep devotion, and a bubbling sense of humor signally combine. His inflexible commitment to patient, persevering hard work and his equally persistent demand for large quantities of such work from his students make him an academic who strikes fear into faint hearts; on the other hand, his freshness of biblical insight and his silver-tongued fusion of head and heart have generated in most of those who know him a respect close to veneration. His learning is wide and is put to work by uncanny powers of concentration, which explains how, sitting at an airport gate one day, he managed to miss two flights home in succession, being so absorbed in a book that he did not hear the boarding call for either! Many of his peers would without hesitation rate him as one of the leading evangelical Old Testament scholars of our time.

Bruce was born in New Jersey in 1930 to parents (Mennonite Brethren in Christ) whose deep commitment to Christ was accompanied by a profound affection for their children. His upbringing was thus a healthy and happy one. Personally converted at age eleven and active as a Christian from then on, he graduated from Houghton College (Wesleyan); studied theology up to the doctoral level at Dallas Theological Seminary (dispensational); joined the Dallas faculty and taught in it for sixteen years, not counting two years spent gaining a doctorate at Harvard (liberal) and one as post-doctoral fellow in Jerusalem under the auspicies of Hebrew Union College (Jewish). He began his first spell at Regent College (transdenominational evangelical) in 1976, then spent five years teaching at Westminster Theological Seminary (confessional Reformed), and after that returned to Regent, where he is now Professor Emeritus while also holding an Old Testament chair at Reformed Theological Seminary, Orlando. He married Elaine, whom he met at Houghton, in 1953, and they have three children: Suzanne, Stephen, and Jonathan. Bruce acknowledges the justice of Elaine's view that she is the string linking him to the ground and stopping him from flying off, like a kite that has broken loose into the stratosphere of unearthed abstractions. Ah, the debt we academics owe our spouses!

In addition to his stellar teaching career, Bruce's pen has been constantly busy. His books range from the very authoritative *Introduction to Biblical Hebrew Syntax* (co-authored with Michael O'Connor) to the very pastoral *Finding the Will of God*, while major commentaries on Genesis and Proverbs are still on the way, along with a full-scale biblical theology. There have also been many dictionary and journal articles and much editorial work, not to mention almost three decades of sustained labor on the New International Version of the Bible. Bruce tells with glee how after Suzanne and a friend, both eleven, had gazed at him working on the NIV, the friend asked what he was doing. Suzanne replied, "Translating." Her friend's curiosity appropriately aroused, she inquired, "Why's he doing that?" to which Suzanne blithely replied, "He doesn't know how to do anything else!" In fact, Bruce has known how to do several other things. He could have gone to the Juillard School of Music and become a professional violinist; he has served as a pastor; and he almost missed his academic vocation by too hastily enlisting as a military chaplain. Providentially the government lost his papers before he was sworn in, allowing Bruce to discover his gift in teaching.

Thank you, Bruce, for being who you are and giving what you give. We think of you as seventy years young rather than old, and on behalf of all who have shared in this book and others with us, we wish you many more golden years in which to continue doing the things you do so well. Giuseppe Verdi, your favorite composer, went on producing masterpieces through his eighth decade, and our hope is that you will do the same. After all, your father is still virile at 103!

In keeping with the range of Bruce's own writing and teaching, some of the articles in this collection are technical, requiring a knowledge of Hebrew and

Greek, while others are of broader appeal. On the whole, but with a few exceptions, we have followed the style guidelines of *The SBL Handbook of Style* (Peabody, Mass.: Hendrickson, 1999). We thank Zondervan for taking on this project, Stan Gundry in particular for enthusing about it, Verlyn Verbrugge for keeping us on course, and the members of the Regent College team (TA's Matthew Anstey, Jude Fredricsen, Andrew Kirk, David Taylor, Marcus Tso; copy editor Jennifer Seidel; and layout artist Greg Reimer), who worked on the production side, for giving their time and skills to make it happen.

J. I. Packer
Sven K. Soderlund

Contributors

Walter E. Brown, Professor of Old Testament and Hebrew, New Orleans Baptist Theological Seminary

David A. Diewert, Associate Professor of Biblical Languages, Regent College

William J. Dumbrell, formerly Professor of Biblical Studies at Moore College, Sydney; Regent College, Vancouver; Trinity College, Singapore

Peter Enns, Associate Professor of Old Testament, Westminster Theological Seminary

Gordon D. Fee, Professor of New Testament Studies, Regent College

James M. Houston, Board of Governors' Professor of Spiritual Theology, Regent College

Karen H. Jobes, Associate Professor of New Testament Studies, Westmont College

Walter C. Kaiser Jr., President and Colman M. Mockler Distinguished Professor of Old Testament, Gordon-Conwell Theological Seminary

Elmer A. Martens, Professor Emeritus of Old Testament, Mennonite Brethren Biblical Seminary

David J. Montgomery, Associate Minister, Knock Presbyterian Church, Belfast

Contributors

Roger R. Nicole, Professor of Theology Emeritus, Gordon-Conwell Theological Seminary; Visiting Professor of Systematic Theology, Reformed Theological Seminary

J. I. Packer, Board of Governors' Professor of Theology, Regent College

Richard L. Pratt Jr., Professor of Old Testament, Reformed Theological Seminary

Iain W. Provan, Marshall Sheppard Professor of Biblical Studies (OT), Regent College

John H. Sailhamer, Professor of Old Testament and Hebrew, Southeastern Baptist Theological Seminary

Robert C. Stallman, Associate Professor of Bible and Theology, Central Bible College

Raymond C. Van Leeuwen, Professor of Biblical Studies, Eastern College

Jonathan R. Wilson, Professor of Religious Studies, Westmont College

Ronald Youngblood, Professor of Old Testament and Hebrew, Bethel Seminary San Diego

Abbreviations

AB	Anchor Bible
AfO	*Archiv für Orientforschung*
AnBib	Analecta biblica
ANET	*Ancient Near Eastern Texts Relating to the Old Testament.* Edited by J. B. Pritchard. 3d ed. Princeton: Princeton University Press, 1969
ANF	*Ante-Nicene Fathers.* Edited and translated by Alexander Roberts and James Donaldson. Revised by A. Cleveland Coxes. 10 vols. Grand Rapids: Eerdmans, 1974
ATD	Das Alte Testament Deutsch
BDB	Brown, F., S. R. Driver, and C. A. Briggs. *A Hebrew and English Lexicon of the Old Testament.* Oxford: Clarendon, 1907
BETL	Bibliotheca ephemeridum theologicarum lovaniensium
BETS	*Bulletin of the Evangelical Theological Society* (see *JETS*)
Bib	*Biblica*
BKAT	Biblischer Kommentar, Altes Testament. Edited by M. Noth and H. W. Wolff
BL	*Bibel und Liturgie*
BR	*Biblical Research*
BSac	*Bibliotheca Sacra*
BSC	Bible Student's Commentary
BWA(N)T	Beiträge zur Wissenschaft vom Alten (und Neuen) Testament
BZ	*Biblische Zeitschrift*
BZAW	Beihefte zur Zeitschrift für die alttestamentliche Wissenschaft

CBET	Contributions to Biblical Exegesis and Theology
CBQ	*Catholic Biblical Quarterly*
CBQMS	Catholic Biblical Quarterly Monograph Series
CC	Continental Commentaries
ChrLit	*Christianity and Literature*
CT	*Christianity Today*
DPL	*Dictionary of Paul and His Letters.* Edited by G. F. Hawthorne and R. P. Martin. Downers Grove, Ill.: InterVarsity Press, 1993
EHAT	Exegetisches Handbuch zum Alten Testament
EncJud	*Encyclopedia Judaica.* 16 vols. Jerusalem, 1972
ETL	*Ephemerides theologicae lovanienses*
ETR	*Etudes théologiques et religieuses*
EvQ	*Evangelical Quarterly*
FAT	Forschungen zum Alten Testament
FOTL	Forms of the Old Testament Literature
GKC	*Gesenius' Hebrew Grammar.* Edited by E. Kautzsch. Translated by A. E. Cowley. 2d ed. Oxford: Clarendon, 1910
HALOT	Koehler, L., W. Baumgartner, and J. J. Stamm. *The Hebrew and Aramaic Lexicon of the Old Testament.* Translated and edited under the supervision of M. E. J. Richardson. 4 vols. Leiden: E. J. Brill, 1994–1999
HAR	*Hebrew Annual Review*
HTR	*Harvard Theological Review*
HUCA	*Hebrew Union College Annual*
IBHS	*An Introduction to Biblical Hebrew Syntax.* B. K. Waltke and M. O'Connor. Winona Lake, Ind.: Eisenbrauns, 1990
ICC	International Critical Commentary
IDB	*The Interpreter's Dictionary of the Bible.* Edited by G. A. Buttrick. 4 vols. Nashville: Abingdon, 1962
Int	*Interpretation*
ISBE	*International Standard Bible Encyclopedia.* Edited by G. W. Bromiley. 4 vols. Grand Rapids: Eerdmans, 1979–1988
ITC	International Theological Commentary
JAOS	*Journal of the American Oriental Society*
JBL	*Journal of Biblical Literature*
JETS	*Journal of Evangelical Theological Society*
JNSL	*Journal of Northwest Semitic Languages*

Joüon	Joüon, P. *A Grammar of Biblical Hebrew.* Translated and revised by T. Muraoka. 2 vols. Subsidia Biblica 14/1–2. Rome: Pontifical Biblical Institute, 1993
JRT	*Journal of Religious Thought*
JSOT	*Journal for the Study of the Old Testament*
JSOTSup	Journal for the Study of the Old Testament: Supplement Series
LSJ	Liddell, H. G., R. Scott, H. S. Jones. *A Greek-English Lexicon.* 9th ed. with revised supplement. Oxford: Clarendon, 1996
NAC	New American Commentary
NCB	New Century Bible
NIB	*The New Interpreter's Bible*
NIBCOT	New International Biblical Commentary on the Old Testament
NICNT	New International Commentary on the New Testament
NICOT	New International Commentary on the Old Testament
NIDOTTE	*New International Dictionary of Old Testament Theology and Exegesis.* Edited by W. A. VanGemeren. 5 vols. Grand Rapids: Zondervan, 1997
NTS	*New Testament Studies*
OTL	Old Testament Library
OtSt	*Oudtestamentishe Studiën*
Presb	*Presbyterion*
Proof	*Prooftexts: A Journal of Jewish Literary History*
PRSt	*Perspectives in Religious Studies*
RB	*Revue biblique*
SBLDS	Society of Biblical Literature Dissertation Series
SBLSCS	Society of Biblical Literature Septuagint and Cognate Studies
SBT	Studies in Biblical Theology
SJOT	*Scandinavian Journal of the Old Testament*
SJT	*Scottish Journal of Theology*
StPB	Studia post-biblica
TDOT	*Theological Dictionary of the Old Testament.* Edited by G. J. Botterweck and J. Ringgren. Translated by J. T. Willis, G. W. Bromiley, and D. E. Green. 9 vols. Grand Rapids: Eerdmans, 1974–
ThTo	*Theology Today*
TJ	*Trinity Journal*
TOTC	Tyndale Old Testament Commentaries

TWOT	*Theological Wordbook of the Old Testament.* Edited by R. L. Harris. 2 vols. Moody Press: Chicago, 1980
TynBul	*Tyndale Bulletin*
UF	*Ugarit-Forschungen*
USQR	*Union Seminary Quarterly Review*
VT	*Vetus Testamentum*
WBC	Word Biblical Commentary
WC	Westminster Commentaries
WTJ	*Westminster Theological Journal*
WUNT	Wissenschaftliche Untersuchungen zum Neuen Testament
ZAW	*Zeitschrift für die alttestamentliche Wissenschaft*
ZBK	Zürcher Bibelkommentare
ZNW	*Zeitschrift für die neutestamentliche Wissenschaft und die Kunde der älteren Kirche*

Theology and Wisdom

J. I. Packer

I. What Is Theology?

"She's a rum 'un, is nature. Nature is more easier conceived than described." So declared Charles Dickens's dreadful creation Mr. Wackford Squeers, schoolmaster, pontificating on the world around him. And an observer today might well feel like saying something similar about theology as it goes on show at gatherings of what is nowadays called "the guild"—the professionals who teach theology in universities, seminaries, and a variety of schools and colleges, along with their pre- and postdoctoral apprentices and the people who write books and articles, edit journals, manage Web sites, and publish CD-ROMs of which theology is the announced theme. Here we confront a "rum 'un" indeed. Never before has the world or the church seen anything like the range of views about God and religion that is paraded at these meetings in papers read, discussions mounted, and books set out on publishers' display tables. What account of theology, we ask, will embrace all this? Common ground and agreed method seem to be lacking. Should we then echo Mr. Squeers's cop-out and say, in effect, that describing and defining theology is currently a task beyond us? Do we adopt this counsel of despair, or what?

Eventually I want to argue that true theology is essentially identical with God's gift of wisdom, but let us start where we are. The first fact to be faced is that during the past two centuries the word *theology* has been drastically secularized and de-doctrinalized among us. No longer does it signify, as it once did, the analysis and assertion of a dominant churchly orthodoxy. Theology has become simply the voicing and discussing of any and every notion about God and religion—good and bad, old and new, familiar and strange, conventional and eccentric, true and false—and it is clear that many institutions of the theological trade wish to keep it that way. The idea that the church should somehow oversee the study of theology or that there should be basically one theology for everybody is dismissed as naïve ecclesiastical primitivism, not to say atavism; and the concept of heresy is deconstructed as a kind of outdated and sordid power play. Following this path, we reach the four frames of a memorable Peanuts cartoon in which Lucy, with her habitual schoolmarmly pertness, delivers the following speech: "My topic today is the purpose of theology. When discussing theology we must always keep our purpose in mind. Our purpose as students is undeniably selfish. There is nothing better than being in a class where no one knows the answer." Lucy focuses very well the fundamental frivolity of much theology today.

To put it clinically (for it is in truth a pathological development), pluralism—that is, the acknowledging of plurality as totally right and entirely proper—has become the popular theological paradigm among the Protestants of what we may call the Old West (North America, Britain, continental Europe, and Australasia). Roman Catholics and Orthodox in their different ways still think of theology as a spelling out of the faith of the church within an essentially biblical frame. But for Protestants generally, theology has come to mean adjusting the faith more or less to the prevalent culture according to each adjuster's individual ideas, so that doing theology and having a theology of one's own becomes more important than any of the specific affirmations and denials one makes. These personal theologies are repeatedly redesigned as their creators continue to read and discuss. For such Protestants, the Bible is a historical testament of religion with which to dialogue rather than the abiding testimony of God from which to learn and before which to bow; and the supply of energy for their dialogical engagements and theological experiments with Scripture seems endless. So pluralism is evidently here to stay.

This present-day plurality of positions among purveyors of theology can be accounted for in various ways. In North America, at any rate, sociological pressures have had something to do with it. The sequence of events is quite simple and predictable: the academics who are promoted are those who publish; publishers naturally want to sell books; notoriety speeds sales; *ergo,* new ideas and way-out opinions quickly find their way into print. In turn, this cycle provokes fascinating academic discussions, reminding us of what the late Martyn Lloyd-Jones used to say, namely that discussing religion is always a delightful activity, for it makes us feel good without our needing to do anything except talk.

Again, for the best part of a century now, many theology-teaching institutions have employed instructors less for the orthodoxy of their views than for their technical prowess and their penchant for stabbing sleepy minds awake. Moreover, many of these teachers seem to have operated on the assumption that their students' education was best served by challenging whatever confessional, Bible-based certainties were brought into the classroom. This has had the knock-on effect of impoverishing churches, for though it is a truism that congregations want to hear their preachers' certainties rather than their doubts, this kind of theological education makes the proclamation of certainties impossible, thus undermining the morale of believers and churches alike.

Behind these sociological realities, however, stands a problem that is both convictional and methodological. During the twentieth century, a number of streams of thought converged to produce what we now speak of as the post-Christian mind-set. Among these were philosophical and scientific rationalism's claim of being the only way to knowledge; evolutionary theory's attempt to explain everything in progress terms; literary and historical criticism's challenge to the Bible's trustworthiness; and positivism's skepticism about any form of supernaturalism. These ideas stand in startling contrast to the view that they displaced. Up to the seventeenth century, Christians everywhere had assumed, more or less explicitly and clearheadedly, that theology was a true science and indeed the Queen of the Sciences, in the sense of its offering an account of God that determines where the other sciences fit in and how they should be practised. Christians believed that this theology constituted a cognitive apprehension—that is, actual knowledge—of the reality of God in Christ according to the Bible and the church's creeds and liturgies. By the same token, they also believed that the apprehension was not self-generated but was given by God through the means of grace that he provides in and via the church. They believed, moreover, that this apprehension was marked by three integrated characteristics: that as it was factually instructional, so it was devotionally relational and morally transformational. In other words, knowledge of God is as much communion with him and obedience to him as it is grasping facts about him; and theology—that is, the formulation of this knowledge in orderly speech—is real and authentic only to the extent that it embodies these three elements with biblical accuracy and then expresses them in worship and holy living. This was the intellectual paradigm of the whole Christian world for a millennium and a half.

II. Theology Deformed

Between the seventeenth and nineteenth centuries, however, under the influence of commanding thinkers in the Cartesian mold, this consensus view was shattered by an epistemological upheaval in the Protestant West. The concept of knowledge was itself secularized and shrunk, with the result that theology (already over-intellectualized in many circles after more than a hundred years of ceaseless debates) was subjectivized, a process that virtually guaranteed the hegemony of pluralism.

Theologizing—once an orderly, reverent, and heartfelt echo of biblical teaching, kerygmatic and catechetical, normative and edification-oriented, an extension indeed of preaching, evangelism, and pastoral care—turned into a scholars' second-level reflection on the primary levels of Christian existence. In this secondary process of reflection, peoples' thoughts, feelings, and declarations—both historic and contemporary—become the agenda prescribed for treatment in place of the message of Scripture as such; and constantly, in this kind of exploration, the academic quest for coherence has taken precedence over the properly Christian passion for faithfulness to what God has revealed. In former days, theology had been conceived in personal terms as the discerning doxological devotion within which a teacher's knowledge of the Bible, church history, and practical ministry would be set and linked up; now, however, theology appears as one leg of a fourfold syllabus for clergy education, alongside biblical studies, church history, and ministry skills. Edward Farley well describes the eighteenth- and nineteenth-century's reconceiving and academicizing of theology:

> In brief, this shift is from theology viewed as a *habitus*, an act of practical knowledge having the primary character of wisdom, to theology used as a generic term for a cluster of disciplines. Crucial to this shift is the definition of theology by its reference and not by the subject's act. This objectification of theology appears to be the outcome of the sectarian (Catholic and Protestant, Lutheran and Reformed, orthodox and heterodox) controversies of the sixteenth and seventeenth centuries. That is, dogmas, articles of faith (pure and mixed), the teachings of the church obtain a certain primacy. "God and the things of God" had always defined the reference and content of theology, but theology itself had always been a sapiential knowledge that attended salvation. When the step is taken to define theology by its reference, it becomes the doctrinal truths themselves.[1]

There is, however, more to the story than the narrowing effect of post-Reformation debates, though, as Farley says, the shift was possible, natural, and unnoticed at the time just because of these debates. More far-reaching, more damaging to anything called orthodoxy, and more directly pluralistic in its actual tendency was Renaissance reason, now seeking to shake free of church control. John Locke, who thought of himself as a conventional Christian, is actually the focal figure here. The combined effect of his *Essay Concerning Human Understanding* and his later essay *The Reasonableness of Christianity* was to spread the idea that all knowledge, as such, results from reason's ordering of experience and testing of truth-claims; that its proper object is things (facts and truths) rather than persons and personal values; and that faith, which for Locke meant taking the word of a God deemed trustworthy with regard to transcendent things, was an extension of knowledge thus conceived and was therefore to be confirmed by rational testing as far as possible. From this launchpad, it was no great distance to questioning whether alleged divine testimony to the supernatural really was such. Locke's legacy, then, was a view of reason as the decisive arbiter of reality, entitled to suspect and critique assertions of faith, while knowledge even of God was conceived impersonally and informationally, with no devotional or behavioral elements entering into it at all.

Kant took the next step, categorizing God as a postulate, on the basis that reason shows he is not and can not be an object of knowledge in any proper sense of that word, nor can theological notions be anything other than the products of our own minds. Thus Kant finally closed the door on the historic idea of theology as the doxological, devotional, and (to use the arresting language that the Orthodox Church still employs) deifying knowledge of God that individuals gain through the Bible, worship and prayer. Small wonder, then, that theology today should have revamped itself for the task that some theologians have explicitly given it, namely, to interpret in existential terms corporate Christianity's historic sense of God, to elaborate biblical utterances about God as so many symbolic expressions of spiritual selfhood, and to play catch-up to contemporary culture, thus simply adding a dimension of religious awareness to what is already believed—and disbelieved—outside the church. It is only to be expected that the conversational tracks that such theologians follow will be their own, distinct from those of others, just as their perception of the culture surrounding them is distinct. In this way theological plurality becomes inescapable, which in effect is where we are today.

So the question pressed upon us is, Has theology lost its way? If one measures today's practice by what the patristic and Reformational teachers thought their job was—if, to be specific, one assesses it by the teaching of such as Gregory of Nazianzus and John Calvin, both of whom earned the description "the theologian" from their peers—there seems reason to suspect so. Here I would refer to Ellen Charry's book *By the Renewing of Your Minds: The Pastoral Function of Christian Doctrine,*[2] with its electrifying dedication to the prisoner who killed his foster-mother. Complementing Farley with a wider, pastorally focused survey, Charry summarizes our situation by affirming that "the secularization, elevation and constriction of reason in the seventeenth and eighteenth centuries undercut" the sapiential (wisdom-bringing), aretegenic (virtue-engendering, goodness-inducing), and participatory (disciple-forming, communion-creating) aspects of theological work. She continues thus:

> The church had always insisted on right belief, but as we saw with Thomas' teaching on formed faith, it was right belief in the service of

> devotion. With the Enlightenment, reason was used to free theology from church control, not to lead believers to know, love, and serve God better. From the perspective of classical thought, today's theology is abnormal, shrunken and impoverished, because it is limited to science alone, whereas for Augustine science was preparation for sapience. From the perspective of modern thought, classical theology is imprecise, unscientific, and pre-critical because it fails to demarcate preaching from criticism, teaching from analysis, and guidance from systematization.[3]

Charry calls for theology to return to the world of personal formation and training in Christian spiritual life and moral character and, with that, to the world of pastoral care, guidance, and therapy in the church—a move that would evidently entail an intellectual return to the fountainhead of Christian doctrine as well. This is how, in her view, theology will get back on track. Her view resonates deeply with the sentiments of this essay.

Where do we go from here in our argument? The answer is, back to the Bible. But first let us recall where we have arrived in the development of our thesis.

III. What Is Wisdom?

We have begun to see that the word *theology* has been understood in different ways at different times since Christian thinkers in the West began using it as a keyword, that is, since the twelfth century. Previously Augustine's term *wisdom (sapientia)* had carried the twelfth-century idea. From the twelfth to the seventeenth century, theology *(theologia)* was conceived primarily as a personal quality or condition, "a *habitus*, a cognitive disposition and orientation of the soul, a knowledge of God and what God reveals."[4] Secondarily, from Thomas Aquinas onward, theology came to be thought of also as a theoretical and practical science *(scientia)*, being viewed now from the standpoint not only of the knower but also of the content known (*sacra doctrina*, the holy teaching).[5] In Reformation and post-Reformation times, the word carried overtones of the orthodoxy of whoever was using it. But since the seventeenth century the word has come increasingly to signify sharing one's own ideas about other people's ideas about God—basically a conversational agenda that often leads nowhere. Thus has theology trivialized itself, as we have already noted.

What we are now to see is the striking likeness between the *theologia* of the medieval and Reformational believer and the wisdom of the truly wise person as pictured in the Bible. To the Bible, then, and particularly to the Wisdom literature, we now turn.

When I was a student of theology, half a century ago, working through the

Bible in a critical-historical way as the syllabus required, O. S. Rankin's *Israel's Wisdom literature* (1936) was the only resource book in English that I could find for up-to-date help in that area. Since then, however, much solid work has been added—work, be it said, to which my honored colleague Bruce Waltke has already contributed significantly and is set to contribute more—and scholars are currently busy tracing out the Wisdom heritage in different parts of Scripture. Firm foundations have thus been laid for what we are now attempting to do.

Our account of wisdom will be built up in two stages. Here, first, is a general description of wisdom according to both Testaments.

What is wisdom? The first thing to say about it is that it begins with (derives from, is rooted in) *the fear of the Lord* (Ps 111:10; Prov 9:10; cf. Prov 1:7). It comes our way through reverence toward, dependence upon, humility before, worship of, and obedience to the God who presents himself in covenant to his people. He is the object of their faith, hope, love, and enjoyment, and he promises to fulfill for them the role of guide, benefactor, helper, and sustainer as they set themselves to meet his covenant claims upon them. To honor, adore, and trust God in this way, and to acknowledge in prayer that wisdom comes from him alone (Jas 1:5), is to be wise at the most basic level. For only God is wise in himself and always free of folly; and human wisdom is a gift of God every time, never an unaided human achievement. When theologians call wisdom one of God's communicable attributes, what they mean is that it is a divine character quality that God graciously reproduces in sinful human beings by his generous grace. He imparts the gift to all who sincerely seek it from him and are ready for the changes that its coming may bring. In the long poetic sequence of Prov 1–9 a wise man tells his son that seeking wisdom from God must be his life's priority (4:7; 8:11). To reinforce this perspective, personified Wisdom is introduced and allowed to speak for herself (1:20–33; 8:1–9:18). But the means (words of counsel) are not the source of wisdom; rather, wisdom is formed in us as the Holy Spirit opens the eyes of the mind and the heart, working with and through what is seen and said. This is how we become wise in the full biblical sense of being prudent, patient, and God-honoring in all we do.

The basic acts of wisdom—in humans as in God—are to choose good and praiseworthy goals along with honorable means of pursuing them. Believers who focus on God see his praiseworthy wisdom displayed in creation and providence, in the complex processes and variegated beauties of the natural order, as much in tiny lovely things as in huge, awesome things. Also they see God's wisdom displayed in the measure of justice found in this fallen world and in acts of what appears as divine kindness toward undeserving humanity in the flow of events. They see God's wisdom also, and supremely, in the plan of salvation: the eternal predestining of the Mediator; the long preparation for his coming; his incarnation, atonement, resurrection, and enthronement; the ministry of the Holy Spirit in individuals and churches; and the disciplines and delights of the Christian life. To acknowledge God's wisdom in this way is their own wisdom in action. At the same time, wisdom teaches them to set their own good goals, to devise positive means of realizing them, to steer clear of all forms of foolish and evil behavior, and to help others to do the same.

Furthermore, the wise are realists who adjust to the way things are. They develop skill at fitting in. As Cornelius Plantinga delightfully puts it, glancing at Proverbs and Ecclesiastes as he does so,

> The wise eventually learn and then accommodate themselves to such truths as these:
>
> - The more you talk, the less people listen.
> - If your word is no good, people will not trust you, and it is then useless to protest this fact.
> - Trying to cure distress with the same thing that caused it only makes matters worse.
> - If you refuse to work hard and take pains, you are unlikely to do much of any consequence.
> - Boasting of your accomplishments does not make people admire you. Boasting is vain in both senses of the word.
> - Envy of fat cats does not make them slimmer and in the end will rot your bones.
> - If you scratch certain itches, they just itch more.
> - Many valuable things, including happiness and deep sleep, come to us only if we do not try hard for them.[6]

Wise people know that accepting things that cannot be changed is the secret of contentment, and active goodwill toward others is the secret of sweetness. In all these ways they know how to live. It was, I think, Oswald Chambers who said of the Old Testament Wisdom literature that the Psalter teaches you how to pray and praise, Proverbs teaches you how to behave, Job teaches you how to suffer, the Song of Solomon teaches you how to love, and Ecclesiastes teaches you how to enjoy. This statement, which is itself wisdom in the sense of discernment, indicates something of the versatility and range of wise living according to the Scriptures.

Such then is wisdom in general, as a personal quality and style of life under the version of God's covenant of grace that Israel knew. But we who live under that covenant in its new form (see Heb 8–9) have more to say than this. The New Testament unfolds the fulfilling of God's eternal plan of redemption through the mediatorial ministry of Jesus the God-man who came to save, died for sins, rose to reign, sends the Spirit here and now, and will consummate world history by his return. The life of God's kingdom in heaven, which we shall enjoy in its fullness after Jesus' second coming, is ours in foretaste already. Those who believe know the reality of justification, adoption, regeneration, and the beginnings of transformation in the present; and their fellowship is already with the Father and the Son through the Spirit. God through Christ has changed the world by letting loose in it the powers of new creation. The supernatural society called the church lives in and through Christ by worship, love, and service, including the acceptance of suffering when faithfulness requires it. What *new covenant specifics,* now, should those who know these New Testament realities add to the general description of wisdom given above? The following four, at least:

An *epistemological* addition is needed first. It was said above that wisdom is at every stage and in every aspect God's gift, received through his word by the agency of the Holy Spirit. It should now be said specifically that the word that brings wisdom is the apostolic message about Jesus Christ, which the canonical New Testament sets before us. This message consists of historical facts plus a detailed theological explanation of those facts that presents them as, among other things, fulfilling Old Testament predictions and promises. Where this history and theology are not center stage, there is no true wisdom. Paul made that point when confronted by the Corinthian preference of the "wisdom" of flowery self-promoting rhetoric, whatever its religious content, over the plain, unvarnished, factual wisdom of the God-given cruciform gospel as he himself had preached it (see 1 Cor 1–3). This was "God's secret wisdom" (1 Cor 2:7), which turns all the world's alleged wisdom into foolishness. Modern scholars who dismiss the apostolic witness forfeit wisdom and embrace foolishness. Docility before God's revelation, which is what the apostolic witness is, is the only wise way.

Next a *christological* addition is needed. As was indicated above, the apostolic proclamation of God's wisdom in Christ is to be acknowledged in full. The following string of citations, culled almost at random, gives some idea of the ground that the wisdom of God in the person, place, and mediatorial ministry of Jesus Christ covers: "We preach Christ crucified . . . Christ the power of God and the wisdom of God" (1 Cor 1:23–24; cf. 1:18). "Christ Jesus . . . has become for us wisdom from God—that is, our righteousness, holiness and redemption" (1 Cor 1:30). "In [Christ] are hidden all the treasures of wisdom and knowledge" (Col 2:3). "In Christ all the fullness of the Deity lives in bodily form, and you have been given fullness in Christ. . . . God made you alive with Christ. He forgave us all our sins, having canceled the written code, with its regulations, that was against us . . .; he took it away, nailing it to the cross" (Col 2:9–10, 13–14). "Christ redeemed us from the curse of the law by becoming a curse for us" (Gal 3:13). "I have been crucified with Christ and I no longer live, but Christ lives in me. The life I live in the body, I live by faith in the Son of God, who loved me and gave himself for me" (Gal 2:20). "He was delivered over to death for our sins and was raised to life for our justification" (Rom 4:25). "We have now been justified by his blood" (Rom 5:9). Where any of these truths—divine incarnation, penal substitutionary atonement, the gift of justification, union with Christ in his death and resurrection, and a new personal life through faith in him—have fallen by the wayside, the wisdom that acknowledges God's wisdom is thereby lacking.

Third, a *soteriological* addition is needed. This flows from what has just been said. Salvation, by common consent, is the theme of the entire New Testament: salvation, that is, in the sense of rescue from the guilt and power of sin, from the present and future wrath of God, from all the evil that marks and mars this present world-order, from the dominion of the devil, and from the condition of being without hope, without help, and without any positive relation to God. The Holy Scriptures, Paul reminds Timothy, "are able to make you *wise for salvation* through faith in Christ Jesus" (2 Tim 3:15; cf. Rom 15:4; 1 Cor 10:11). It is the mark of wisdom to latch on to this and never lose sight of it.

Lastly, a *behavioral* addition is needed. Christians should "walk"—live their lives, behave—in wisdom, "not as unwise but as wise" (Eph 5:15; cf. Col 4:5). In Ephesians this admonition is reinforced by a reminder that "the days are evil," after which Paul begins a detailed presentation of Spirit-filled living and family ethics, all irradiated by the knowledge of God in Jesus Christ. This shows that "wise" here is being used in a fully theological sense, so as to imply a responsible living out of Christian conviction and discernment. Wisdom in the New Testament sense is a matter of learning to imitate Christ in selfless love and humility; to make and keep peace in all relationships; to serve the real needs of others; and to submit to pain, grief, and disgrace when circumstances inflict them. It is a mark of wisdom to aim at full Christlikeness in each of these respects.

Here, then, are four main ways in which New Testament wisdom moves beyond its Old Testament counterpart, building on it and extending it in the light of Jesus Christ.

IV. Theology and Wisdom

Now at last the key thought of this essay can be stated in a formal way: Putting theology back into its proper shape means recognizing that the older analysis of it was basically correct and that theology is essentially identical with God's gift of wisdom according to the Scriptures. To grasp this point we have to put behind us the modern reconception of theology as essentially a cluster of academic disciplines—historical, sociological, philosophical, and ethical—that include ideas of one sort or another about God, disciplines that can all be studied up to a level of expertise without involving or conferring either divine illumination of one's heart or divine transformation of one's character. Theology, or *theologia* as we shall from now on call it (using the original Latin word for the original Christian thing), draws on studies of this kind and would be hamstrung without them, but it is not to be equated with any of them separately or with all of them together. The classic idea of *theologia* is that it is wisdom coming from within, divine illumination animating our discernments, devotions, and declarations; in other words, it is a function of spiritual life expressing itself in thought, speech and decisions that are marked by divinely wrought understanding.

Such understanding assumes that one is anchored and drilled already in the "standard of sound teaching" that Paul told his deputies to enforce (1 Tim 4:6, 11–16; 2 Tim 1:13; 2:1–2, 23–25; 4:1–5; Titus 2:1–8, 15); when teachers like Julian of Norwich, John Calvin, Ignatius Loyola, and John Owen insist that understanding is the root and fruit of devotion, they are not reducing the importance of clear-headed orthodoxy. Their point, and Paul's, is rather that true notions should lead to wisdom by becoming a source of insight and of life-change through the Holy Spirit. When Paul prays that the Colossians might be filled with "the knowledge of [God's] will through all spiritual [i.e., Spirit-given] wisdom and understanding" (Col 1:9), he is asking God that *theologia,* as described, may increasingly become the mark of their lives. To be marked in this way demands more than becoming conscious of what action orthodox biblical beliefs would require, though that evidently is part of it (a part that pietists in the conservative evangelical tradition always did and still do assiduously maintain). But *theologia* should be conceived as the intellectual and moral dynamic animating the believer to work and worship, love and obedience, virtue and excellence, as he or she grips and obeys the revealed truth by which he or she has first been gripped.

So *theologia* is really an aspect of the reality of sanctification; it is a pointer to, and a benchmark of, the way the Holy Spirit uses the word of God to change people, making them more like Christ. In this process the Spirit operates intellectually, by imparting understanding of Christ and of all the Scriptures as witness to him; and motivationally, by engendering trust in Christ and sustaining within us a purpose of cleaving to revealed truth; and in addition behaviorally, by inducing the Christ-like pattern of action that flows from this state of the soul. When Augustine urged that theological *scientia* (cognitive acquaintance with the true and health-giving beliefs about God) has as its goal personal *sapientia* (wisdom in the sense of a practical understanding of truth, beauty, and the good life), he was indicating the process of *theologia* as we have now characterized it. When the Puritan William Perkins defined theology as "the science of living blessedly for ever"[7] and when his disciple William Ames spoke of it as "the doctrine of living unto God,"[8] they were similarly charting the course from *scientia* to *sapientia.* This is the whole-person, whole-soul track that we all need to get back on. A great deal of what is called theology today is specialist speculation and does not bear at all on the Christian's personal existence. But *theologia*—theology in the best sense—needs, as we can now see, to be a matter of conscientious concern to every Christian who aims at a life that honors God.

So far, so good; but how is the equating of wisdom with *theologia,* thus understood, to be justified? Space forbids more than the outline of an answer, but let us at least glance again at what Scripture says to us and shows us regarding wisdom's scope, structure, source, and sanctifying effect.

First, we recall wisdom's scope. Wisdom begins with the worship of God for his goodness revealed in both the created and covenantal order, coupled with wonder at human folly—all the nuttiness of egoism, self-aggrandizement, idolatry, immorality, and mishandling of relationships (see Proverbs and Ecclesiastes). In this way, discerning doxology is the beginning not only of "the fear of the Lord" but of *theologia* too. Wisdom goes on to ask what direction and style of life make sense in light of what is known of God's presence, preferences, and providential government. Within the reverential frame that "the fear of the Lord" has established, an across-the-board vision of humble, thoughtful, and God-centered living emerges. *Theologia* and "the fear of the Lord" thus raise the same questions and come up with similar answers.

Second, we point out wisdom's structure. Wisdom appears as a habit of contemplating life to see what, if anything, we should do about this or that in light of what in general terms Yahweh has already set forth. Here a sense of human limitation emerges, for wise people know that while God has told us much about what he is doing in his world, much is kept hidden from us, and we must not claim to know more of God's current actions than in fact we do (a point emphasized repeatedly in Ecclesiastes and on the grand scale in the book of Job). Even when in frantic pain, wise persons settle for not knowing, and not even trying to guess, God's unrevealed purposes in their lives. *Theologia* thinks similarly; it works out the application of divine truths to the ups and downs of life with full awareness of the limits of revelation and the greatness of the divine mystery. Calvin's *Institutes,* which in its final form labors reverently to map the boundaries of what is revealed at every point, is perhaps the supreme example of this.

Third, we note wisdom's source. No more need be said about this than that wisdom is a gift of God's free grace, just as *theologia* is. Neither should be seen as the fruit of intellectual acumen as such; both are effects of the divine illumination that comes to those who seek to practise "the fear of the Lord."

Fourth, we highlight wisdom's sanctifying effect. Wisdom literature assumes that while the fool is a bad and irreligious man, his wise counterpart is good and godly. A doctrine of sanctification by grace is thus implicit in Wisdom writing, for while moral badness in our fallen race needs no special explanation, goodness does (and the Wisdom writers are not Pelagians!). That *theologia* is an aspect of God's work of sanctification is a point that we have already made.

V. Conclusion

Here I must close. Starting from the fact that theology today appears as a "rum 'un," I have argued that true *theologia* encases the biblical concept of wisdom and is a *sine qua non* of Christian discipleship. If this argument is sound, it raises questions on the one hand about the study of theology as merely one of a group of separate disciplines and, on the other hand, about any form of spiritual theology that accepts this separateness as an immutable given.[9] Sooner or later these questions must be faced and changes made. I hope that what I have said will stir others to join me in my thinking about the recovery of true *theologia* and true wisdom.

My friend Bruce Waltke, to whom I offer this essay, has always seemed to me to embody the reality of *theologia*—a living, holy faith in the God and Christ of the Bible, profoundly expressed by the exercise of biblical skills and preaching that indicates a deep Spirit-given understanding of God and life. The Eastern Orthodox theologian Sergius Bulgakov proposed that theology *(theologia!)* should be renamed "sophiology": I cannot think of a better word to describe the uniquely flavored contribution with which Bruce enriches so many of us. Thank you, Bruce, for all that you—say? do? yes, and more than that—for all that you are.

Notes

The Scripture quotations in this article are taken from the NIV.

[1] Edward Farley, *Theologia* (Philadelphia: Fortress, 1983), 81–82.

[2] Ellen Charry, *By the Renewing of Your Minds: The Pastoral Function of Christian Doctrine* (New York: Oxford University Press, 1997).

[3] Ibid., 237.

[4] Farley, *Theologia,* 35. For a contemporary statement of this understanding, based on Thomas Aquinas, see "The Habitus of Theology in the Theologian" in Yves M.-J. Congar, *A History of Theology* (Garden City, N.Y.: Doubleday, 1968), 260–68.

[5] So the Lutheran scholastic J. A. Quenstedt, who writes, "The term theology is taken either essentially, absolutely, and as a mental habitude for the knowledge

which the mind holds and to which it clings . . . or accidentally, relatively, systematically, in so far as it is the doctrine . . . which is taught and learned, or contained in books. The former is the primary, the latter the secondary application of the term" (*Theologia Didactico-Polemica* 1.11, 1685; cited in Heinrich Schmidt, *Doctrinal Theology of the Evangelical Lutheran Church* [Minneapolis: Augsburg, 1961], 19). The Reformed scholastic J. Wollebius affirms that "theology consists of both contemplation and action. It is both wisdom and prudence; wisdom in that it apprehends principles through divinely illumined intelligence and reaches conclusions from them through knowledge; and prudence, in that it guides the human soul in its actions" (*Compendium Theologiae Christianae*, Prolegomena 1, 1626; cited in *Reformed Dogmatics* (ed. and trans. John W. Beardslee III; Grand Rapids: Baker, 1977), 30.

[6] Cornelius Plantinga, *Not the Way It's Supposed to Be* (Grand Rapids: Eerdmans, 1995), 118.

[7] William Perkins, *A Golden Chain;* cited in Ian Breward, ed., *William Perkins* (Abingdon, U.K.: Sutton Courtenay, 1969), 177.

[8] William Ames, *The Marrow of Theology* (trans. by J. D. Eusden; Grand Rapids: Baker, 1997), 77.

[9] As Simon Chan does in his otherwise very useful *Spiritual Theology* (Downers Grove, Ill.: InterVarsity Press, 1998), 17.

A Wisdom Composition of the Pentateuch?

John H. Sailhamer

One of the most promising features of recent pentateuchal criticism has been the revival of interest in the final shape *(Endgestalt)* of the Pentateuch. Serious attention is again being given, even by critical scholarship, to the question of how to identify and trace the composition of the Pentateuch's final form. In the classical critical theories, the final shape of the Pentateuch was commonly identified with a "priestly" redactor. Though serious interpretive consequences followed from that assessment, such as the widely held notion that the Pentateuch was intended to promulgate the "priestly laws," little was ever actually said about the overall theology and purpose of the final form of the Pentateuch as such. Attention focused almost solely on the final P-redaction.

Recent literary approaches, which seek to discover the final form of the Pentateuch in an overarching theme, genre, or macrostructure, have also rarely attempted to shed light on the Pentateuch's overall purpose. Such approaches often overlook important theological questions that are tied to specific historical settings. They also fail to see an author at work in putting together the larger text.

I. The Final Shape of the Pentateuch

In my opinion, one of the most promising approaches to the shape and purpose of the Pentateuch has come from the study of the "tradition history" of the Pentateuch, particularly the form that traces its interest and influence back to the work of Gerhard von Rad. Unlike many modern critics, von Rad did not stray far from the basic theological questions that lay behind the Pentateuch in its present shape. Though few today would fully embrace the theoretical starting point of his analysis of the Pentateuch, much still remains to be said about his basic observations on the text—in particular, his working model of the Pentateuch as a whole structure built of large blocks of independent narratives, each ultimately traced to its own unique and independent setting in the life of ancient Israel. Long after the considerable erosion of von Rad's methodological grounds for making this observation, the fact remains that distinct blocks of narrative such as Gen 1–11, the story of the patriarchs (Gen 12–50), the exodus (Exod 1–15), and the wilderness wanderings (Num 10–25) do stand out as literary staging points in the formation of the Pentateuch and seem to be linked by a conscious effort to tie the whole of the work together under a single theological rubric. This is true regardless of one's particular view of the authorship of the Pentateuch. Not the least in importance of von Rad's observations has turned out to be the recognition that his tradition criticism contained the seeds of the ultimate demise of the classical Documentary Hypothesis. If the Pentateuch was, in fact, built from large independent blocks of narrative, where in its history could one posit the existence of documentary sources?

Though one might rightly reject a tradition-historical approach as a whole, its basic observations about the "final shape" of the Pentateuch seem to me to be valid and confront any reader of the Pentateuch with two important, and as yet unanswered, questions. The first is how Gen 1–11, as a compositional unit, can be integrated into the other large pieces of the Pentateuch, such as the patriarchal narratives, the exodus narratives, the wilderness narratives, and the book of Deuteronomy. What compositional "links" tie it to the other large blocks of narrative and to the rest of the Pentateuch? As is well known, hardly a trace of the kind of "cross-referencing" links is easily identifiable between Gen 1–11 and the rest of the Pentateuch: for example, between the patriarchal stories (e.g., Gen 15:13–15) and the exodus story (e.g., Exod 2:24). In view of the rather tight cohesion between the other blocks of narrative, Gen 1–11 gives the impression of being conspicuously detached from the remainder of the Pentateuch. It is only a kind of overture.

The second question raised by the tradition-historical approach to the final shape of the Pentateuch is the need for a clearer distinction between what we might call the *redaction* of the Pentateuch and its *composition.* This distinction is of much more importance than merely the correct use of terminology. It is, rather, a question of properly understanding the notion of the "authorship" of the Pentateuch. Redaction usually means the literary *reworking* of an existing text. Composition, on the other hand, focuses on the final shape of a written work.[1] The process of composition produces a text; that of redaction reworks an existing text. In traditional discussions of the Pentateuch's authorship,[2] the focus has largely—and correctly, I believe—been on composition.[3] Critical scholarship,[4] on the other hand, has often cast the issue as one of the Pentateuch's redaction.

The quest for the final *redaction* of the Pentateuch can, and usually does, take us far beyond the question of the authorship of the Pentateuch itself. Recent *redaction critical* studies of the Pentateuch, for example, have suggested that in Gen 50 there are already redactional levels pointing beyond the Pentateuch to the final chapter of the book of Joshua.[5] In this sense, a redactional approach leads quickly to the question of the final shape of a *Hexateuch,* not the *Pentateuch.* It is in this sense that the idea of a "final redaction" of the Pentateuch may only be an a priori assumption.[6] If we focus on the last stages of redaction in the Pentateuch, we may never arrive at the final form of the Pentateuch—that is, the Pentateuch that begins in Genesis and ends in Deuteronomy.

The quest for the final compositional shape of the Pentateuch, on the other hand, takes us immediately to its conclusion in Deuteronomy. Compositionally, the most important question is, what literary strategies can we uncover that take us from the beginning of the Pentateuch in Genesis to its literary conclusion in Deuteronomy? If our goal is to discover the composition *of* the Pentateuch, we will need to do more than discover the final redaction *in* the Pentateuch.

I believe the answer to the first question stated above, that of the relationship of Gen 1–11 to the rest of the Pentateuch, holds the key to the second question, an overall view of the Pentateuch that enables us to distinguish redaction *in* the Pentateuch from the composition *of* the Pentateuch. In the present essay, I would like to address these two questions from the quite different perspective of a compositional approach.[7] I will look, first, for the most comprehensive literary strategy within the present shape of the Pentateuch.[8] Then I will seek to uncover the central theological idea, the *leitmotif,* that lies behind that strategy.

I will argue that the author of the block of narrative we call Gen 1–11 in its present form was the author of the present shape of the Pentateuch that takes us from Genesis to Deuteronomy.[9] As for the *leitmotif* of this strategy, I will suggest it lies within the thought world of the biblical Wisdom traditions. Hence the larger purpose of the Pentateuch was to portray the events of Israel's formation, early history, and codified laws as Israel's answer to mankind's search for wisdom and well-being. It does so, I will further argue, within the context of a fully developed eschatology grounded in the notion that biblical texts are the primary source of hope for the future and serve at the present time as our only source of divine guidance.[10]

II. The Compositional Strategy of Genesis 1–11

Genesis 1–11 is a loose collection of small, self-contained narratives. The narratives are, of course, held together by the well-known story line of Gen 1–11, but there are also signs of considerable literary composition. Proceeding primarily diachronically and from the smallest units to the larger, Markus Witte has reconstructed a complex web of narration and redaction that spans the whole of Gen 1:1–11:26.[11] Viewed from the top down, however, a much simpler compositional strategy is discernible within and between each of the smaller individual narratives. The strategy consists simply of the attachment of a number of small poetic texts to the conclusion of each block of narration. In attaching these poems to the narratives, they are cast as the final "discourse," or "last words," of the central characters of the narrative. The content of each poem expresses the character's own reflection on the events recounted in the narrative. By means of the poems, the central characters are allowed to make programmatic statements about key events of the narrative. The poems function like the songs in a Hollywood musical: they thematize what the author intends the reader to draw from the narratives. By means of these poems, the reader's own assessment of the narratives is closely monitored by the author and limited to a narrow range of meaning.

Each poem is followed by an appropriate epilogue. The role of the epilogue is to return the narrative to the *status quo in medias res.* In the present shape of the narrative, the creation account in Gen 1–2 concludes with Adam's poem about his newly created wife (2:23); an epilogue follows in 2:24.[12] The account of the fall in Gen 3 concludes with a poem (3:14–19) and an epilogue (3:20–24). The account of Cain in ch. 4 concludes with Lamech's poem (4:23–24) and an epilogue (4:25–26). Even the genealogy of ch. 5 concludes with the poem of Lamech (5:29)[13] and an epilogue (5:30–32). The story of the flood (6:1–9:24) concludes with Noah's poem (9:25–27) and an epilogue (9:28–29).

After Gen 9, the pattern within Gen 1–11 ceases. The Table of Nations, which follows in Gen 10, is not a narrative, and there are no further poetic texts in Gen 1–11. There is, of course, a purpose for ch. 10 after Noah's poem in 9:25–27. Among other things, ch. 10 gives a preview of the historical identity and implications of Noah's statement (9:27) that the sons of Japhet will dwell in the tents of Shem and the Canaanites will serve them.

The Table of Nations in ch. 10 addresses several questions raised by Noah's poem: It identifies the descendants of Japhet who will dwell in the tents of Shem. In addition, it identifies the descendants of Shem and Ham. Finally, it recounts in summary form what will become of these people in light of Noah's poem.

According to Gen 10, the sons of Japhet are Gomar, Magog, Madai (Medes), Yavan (Greece), Tubal, Meshek, and ultimately the Kittim (10:2, 4). Among the sons of Ham who will be subject to Japhet and Shem are Babylon (10:10), Assyria (10:11), the Canaanites (10:6), and the Philistines (10:14). Among the sons of Shem, in whose tents will dwell the sons of Japhet, are Assyria (10:22; Assur = Persia?)[14] and Eber (10:24–25; the Hebrews?).[15] When viewed in light of Noah's poem in 9:27, the Table of Nations informs us that the Medes, the Greeks, and the

Kittim will ultimately "dwell in the tents of" Babylon and Assyria, along with the Canaanites, the Philistines, and both Assyria (or Assur = Persia) and Eber (the Hebrews).[16]

There is a further observation to be made about the compositional shape of Gen 1–11. Spliced into the final lists of the descendants of Shem in Gen 11 is an account of the rise and fall of the city of Babylon (Gen 11:1–9). This is the same Babylon that figures prominently in the narrative additions to the Table of Nations (Gen 10:8–12). The people of the city of Babylon want to make a name (שֵׁם) for themselves; but in Gen 12:1–3, God promises Abram that he will make his name (שֵׁם) great. The end of Gen 1–11 thus links up seamlessly with the patriarchal narratives in Gen 12:1–3.

Viewed as a whole, Gen 1–11 follows a recognizable compositional strategy that links together an otherwise loose collection of independent narratives. The strategy consists of attaching poems to the end of individual segments of narrative. Noah's pronouncement in Gen 9:25–27 is an example of how programmatic such poems prove to be in the overall context. Noah's poem provides the interpretive context for the Table of Nations, the account of the building of the city of Babylon, and, ultimately, the call of Abraham.

III. The Compositional Strategy of Genesis–Deuteronomy

A. The Four Major Poems of the Pentateuch

Are there traces of the same compositional pattern at higher levels within the Pentateuch, specifically, those spanning Genesis to Deuteronomy? To answer that question I must turn to the four major poems in the Pentateuch: Gen 49, Exod 15, Num 23–24, and Deut 32–33. Several features of these poems suggest they are part of the same compositional strategy we have traced in Gen 1–11.

Genesis 49 comes at the conclusion of the large block of narrative representing the patriarchal history, Gen 12–48; Gen 49:29–33 is an epilogue. The poem in Exod 15:1–18 concludes the large block of narrative representing the exodus from Egypt, Exod 1–14; Exod 15:19–21 is an epilogue. The poems in Num 23–24 conclude the narratives dealing with the wilderness wanderings, Num 10–23; Num 24:25 is an epilogue.[17] The poems in Deut 32–33 conclude the narratives of the conquest of the Transjordan of which the book of Deuteronomy is now a part; Deut 34 is an epilogue.[18]

In light of these initial observations I want to draw the following provisional conclusions: The arrangement of the larger poems in the Pentateuch reflects a conscious literary (compositional) strategy that spans the whole of the Pentateuch from Gen 1 to Deut 34.[19] It begins with the narrative of Gen 1 and concludes with the last poem(s) and epilogue in Deut 32–34. Since this strategy is identical with the compositional strategy within Gen 1–11, it is reasonable to conclude, at least provisionally, that it comes from the same hand. There are several further observations that support that initial conclusion.

B. Extensive Evidence of Compositional Activity in the Poems

Firstly, there is a focus on the tribe of Judah. It is well known, for example, that in Gen 49 the sayings attached to Judah and Joseph are considerably expanded. The most notable feature of that expansion is a clear focus upon a future kingship in the tribe of Judah (Gen 49:8–12). Perhaps the most telling comment on the poetic material in Gen 49 is that which comes from within the OT itself. According to 1 Chr 5:2, "Judah prevailed over his brethren, and from him came the chief ruler; but the birthright *was* Joseph's." The Chronicler saw Gen 49 as a programmatic statement regarding the passing of the kingship in Israel to the tribe of Judah.

Secondly, in the process of composition, the juxtaposition of the poetry in Num 23 and that in Num 24 has produced a significant "innertextual" reading of these key poetic passages. An important example of this is the way in which the concept of an individual king in Num 24:8 ("God will bring/has brought *him* out of Egypt," אֵל מוֹצִיאוֹ מִמִּצְרַיִם) has shifted the reader's focus away from the collective "people of Israel" in Num 23:22 ("God has brought *them* out of Egypt," אֵל מוֹצִיאָם מִמִּצְרָיִם) and onto an individual national redeemer. Whereas the poetry in Num 23 is about the people of Israel and the historical exodus from Egypt, the poetry in Num 24 is manifestly about a future individual king of Israel and his kingdom (מַלְכוּת).[20] That this is the author's meaning in these two poems is clear from the fact that in Num 23:24 he explicitly identifies the pronoun *them* (Num 23:22) with "the people" (הֶן־עָם), whereas the antecedent of the pronoun *him* (מוֹצִיאוֹ) in Num 24:8 is the individual "king" (מַלְכּוֹ) in 24:7.

Thirdly, the poetry in Deut 32–33 also shows considerable development of earlier pentateuchal themes. Most notable is the fact that Deut 33 focuses on a future king (מֶלֶךְ) who is to unite the tribes of Israel (Deut 33:4–5, 7).[21]

C. Explanatory Comments within the Poetic Texts

These same three poems (Gen 49, Num 24, and Deut 32–34) also share another important compositional feature: at strategic points in the ancient, and often obscure, poetry, certain poetic features—such as parallelism, meter, and imagery—have been expanded by the addition of concise, explanatory comments. It will be an important part of our purpose to show that this explanatory material was the work of the author of the Pentateuch and not that of a later scribe. Though these comments are frequently dismissed as mere scribal glosses, I suggest they are the work of the author who gave us the Pentateuch as we now have it, since a considerable amount of the material in these comments is linked to the compositional strategy we traced above in the use of poetic texts in Gen 1–11. To illustrate this point, I will look at a few examples in Balaam's last oracle in Num 24:17–24 (see sec. F below).

D. A Focus on "in the Last Days" (בְּאַחֲרִית הַיָּמִים)

A further observation that can be made about these poems is that each one is consciously linked to its preceding narrative by a similar (almost identical) programmatic introduction (Gen 49:1; Num 24:14; Deut 31:29). In the introduction to each poem, for example, the central narrative figure (Jacob, Balaam, and Moses, respectively) calls together an audience (using imperatives) and advises them (cohortatives) of what will happen[22] "in the last days" (בְּאַחֲרִית הַיָּמִים).

The phrase *in the last days* is found only once elsewhere in the Pentateuch—in Deut 4:40. The phrase occurs 14 times in the Hebrew Bible (13 times in Hebrew, once in the Aramaic of Daniel). W. Staerk understood the phrase to have been developed by Ezekiel in 38:16. There it was linked to the fall of Gog and the establishment of the messianic kingdom.[23] Staerk thus viewed each of the phrases in the Pentateuch as late eschatological interpolations. Hermann Gunkel rejected Staerk's view and held that, at least in Gen 49:1, the phrase referred to the time of David.[24] Gunkel suggested the remaining occurrences in the Pentateuch were drawn from the later prophetic literature (e.g., Ezekiel and Daniel).[25] Recent commentaries and recent translations tend to view the phrase as more flexible in meaning. It is generally recognized, however, that by the time of the exile the phrase had assumed an eschatological meaning.

Viewing this phrase from the perspective of the present shape of the Pentateuch, it seems clear that the phrase *in the last days* (בְּאַחֲרִית הַיָּמִים) is a conscious part of the same compositional strategy that has used the poetic texts in Gen 49, Num 24, and Deut 32–33 to connect the various blocks of narrative in the Pentateuch from Gen 1 to Deut 34. It is thus reasonable to assume its meaning is the same throughout the Pentateuch and that it is an integral part of that composition. We are not, of course, excluding the possibility that the content of the poems also plays an important role in determining the sense of the words *last days.* It would be natural to read this phrase in connection with the interest in the future "king" noted in each of these poems. Also of particular importance is the sense of the explanatory material attached to many of these poems (as noted above) and whether that material can also be related to the same level of composition (see below).[26]

E. Cross-Referencing between the Poems

We can also observe that these three poems (Gen 49, Num 24, and Deut 32–34) all have considerable cross-referencing (innertextuality) with each other.

A striking example of the conspicuous cross-referencing between these poems is the remarkable fact that what is said about the king in Num 24:9a[27] is identical to what is said about the king from the tribe of Judah in Gen 49:9b:[28] "He crouches down, he lays down like a lion; and like a lion, who will arouse him?" This is certainly a self-conscious compositional link between the two poems.[29] In addition, the literary parallels between Deut 33 and Gen 49 are well known. Whole phrases from one poem have been inserted into the other.[30] Such cross-referencing and borrowing is indicative of a single hand working at a very broad level of composition.

F. Summary

The above observations on the major poems in the Pentateuch support our initial conclusion that the arrangement of the larger poems reflects a conscious compositional strategy that spans the whole of the Pentateuch from Gen 1 to Deut 34. Moreover, the similarity between that strategy and the compositional strategy of Gen 1–11 noted earlier suggests both strategies reflect the work of the same hand.

Further support for our thesis comes from the close literary relationship between the explanatory comments on the poems in the Pentateuch and the compositional strategy we have already noted in Gen 1–11. Our examples here also come from the poems in Num 24.

In Num 24 there is extensive explanatory material within Balaam's final oracles. The poems are obviously very ancient and potentially obscure, and thus the author must go to some lengths to bring out the sense of the images the poems intend to evoke. A good deal of the explanatory material is found in connection with the use of proper names in Balaam's oracles. Within the poetry of Num 24:17–24, for example, there are two sets of proper names. The first group of names is those of Israel's historical neighbors. Within their present context, these names represent the central characters of the surrounding narratives. This group consists of five proper names: Moab, Edom, Seir, Amalek, and the Kenites. These names occur within the poetic passages themselves and hence are *not* a part of the explanatory material.

That is not the case, however, for the second group of names. In the second group there are also five proper names: Seth (v. 17), Cain (v. 22), Assur (v. 24), Eber (v. 24), and the Kittim (v. 24). What is striking about these names is that they refer to nations that are not part of the immediately surrounding narratives but, rather, appear elsewhere in the Pentateuch, in the genealogical lists in Gen 1–11. Moreover, these names occur only *in* the explanatory material in the poetic sections of Num 24. In other words, if our thesis is correct, they are part of the final composition of the Pentateuch.

It is noteworthy that three of the five names in this explanatory material occur specifically in the Table of Nations (Gen 10): Assur, Eber, and the Kittim. They are, in fact, the names that are part of the explanation of Noah's poem in Gen 9:27 ("Japhet shall dwell in the tents of Shem, and Canaan will be their servants"). As we have noted, these same sections of the early chapters of Genesis are an integral part of the compositional strategy interlinking the whole of Gen 1–11. Within that strategy, the purpose of the Table of Nations is to show that Noah's poem in Gen 9:27 is ultimately about the Medes, the Greeks, and the Kittim who will "dwell in the tents of" Babylon, Assyria, and Eber.[31]

The existence of this second set of names in the explanatory material in the poetry of Num 24, as well as in the Table of Nations, suggests a conscious link between that material and the compositional strategy of Gen 1–11. The explanatory material in the poetic texts appears to be part of the same compositional strategy not only within Gen 1–11, but also within the larger poems in the Pentateuch. We have already noted that the Table of Nations has cast Noah's last words to his sons into the future history of the nations. The explanatory material in the poetry of Num 24 appears to point in the same direction. They deflect Balaam's words away from their immediate narrative-historical context and into the future historical context envisioned in Gen 10.

Another important instance of explanatory material in the poetry of Num 24 is v. 24a. In vv. 23–24, Balaam says, "Woe! Who shall live when God has established him? There will be ships from the side of the Kittim and they will afflict Assur and they will afflict Eber, and also he is destined for destruction."[32] The sense of the explanation in Num 24:24a has long been understood in light of later biblical texts and postbiblical historical events. The general consensus is that this explanatory comment assumes the same historical events as does Dan 11:30.[33] Hence, it relates to events in the Maccabean period and beyond. That interpretation assumes that the names Assur and Eber are code names for Syria and that the Kittim are Rome. According to the latter view, Num 24:24 states that the Romans "shall humble Ashur [i.e., Syria], and shall humble Eber [Abarnaharaim], and he [Antiochus!] shall be [destined for] destruction."[34] August Freiherr von Gall understood v. 24b to be about the ultimate destruction of Rome.[35] There are many similar identifications in the history of interpretation of this text. Common to all of these is the assumption that the explanatory material is the work of a later scribe (a gloss) and thus is not related to the composition of the Pentateuch as such.

What has not been noted before, however, is the innertextual link between the explanatory material in the poetry in Num 24 and the Table of Nations. As we have suggested, not only do the names in Num 24 draw intentionally on the lists of proper names in the Table of Nations (Gen 10), they also assume the compositional link between Noah's poem in Gen 9:27[36] and Gen 10. When Balaam's words are explained in the text of Num 24 as "ships from the side of the Kittim which will afflict Assur and Eber," this is tantamount to saying "the sons of Japhet will dwell in the tents of Shem." The intent of the explanatory material in Num 24:24a, therefore, appears to be a conscious link to Noah's poem. It shows that the future that Balaam foresaw was the same as that forecast by Noah's poem in Gen 9:27. By means of this explanatory material, Balaam's vision in Num 24 extends Noah's prediction in Gen 9 into the far-off future.[37] It is thus significant that in Num 24:24, the coming of the Kittim is also linked to the time of the "last days" (בְּאַחֲרִית הַיָּמִים) mentioned in Num 24:14. This is the same link that is found in the book of Daniel, where the "Kittim ships will come against [the king of the North] in the last days (בְּאַחֲרִית הַיָּמִים)" (Dan 10:14).

Let me summarize the still tentative conclusions I think follow from these observations:

1. The compositional strategy of Gen 1–11 is part of a larger compositional strategy that encompasses the whole of the Pentateuch. The author of Gen 1–11 is the author of the present Pentateuch, Gen 1–Deut 34 (or, at least, Gen 1–Deut 32).

2. The explanatory material in the poetic texts in the Pentateuch focuses the reader's attention on key events in Gen 1–11. This explanatory material is not redactional; that is, it does not consist of isolated comments on particular texts. It is, rather, part of a compositional strategy that extends to the whole of the present Pentateuch.

In light of the possibility of such a composition, which extends from Gen 1 to Deut 34, I want to make a further observation regarding the placement of the phrase *in the last days* (אַחֲרִית הַיָּמִים) within the seams linking the poetic texts to the narratives. There is an intentional link between the phrase *in the last days* and the word רֵאשִׁית in Gen 1:1.[38] As far as I know, Franz Delitzsch was the first to explain the term רֵאשִׁית in Gen 1:1 in terms of its antonym, אַחֲרִית.[39] According to Delitzsch, the "beginning" (in Gen 1:1) implies an "end," an אַחֲרִית. Otto Procksch further suggested the רֵאשִׁית in Gen 1:1 was deliberately chosen to correspond to the אַחֲרִית in the expression *days* (אַחֲרִית הַיָּמִים).[40]

Neither of these scholars, however, went any further in their observations about בְּרֵאשִׁית. They did not note, for example, the occurrence of the phrase אַחֲרִית הַיָּמִים in the compositional seams throughout the Pentateuch. Nor did they note the relationship of the phrase *in the last days* to the content of the various poetic texts it serves to introduce. In my opinion, they have overlooked a crucial piece of the puzzle.

Seen from the broad perspective of the composition of the Pentateuch, אַחֲרִית הַיָּמִים (the last days) in the poetic seams and רֵאשִׁית of Gen 1:1 appear to be part of a single literary or compositional strategy. That strategy has already developed a specific vocabulary of eschatology. There is a primeval period, an *Urzeit,* and a "last days," an *Endzeit.*[41] By the use of the terms רֵאשִׁית and אַחֲרִית, Israel's history is bounded by a beginning (רֵאשִׁית) and an end, a "last days" (אַחֲרִית הַיָּמִים). By opening the Torah[42] with the statement about the "beginning" (בְּאַחֲרִית), the author assigns the early chapters of Genesis to an eschatological (or apocalyptic) schema in which its events are cast as those of the *Urzeit.*

Within that broad schema, there are numerous links between the *Urzeit* of Gen 1–11 and the "last days" described in the later poetic texts. Those parallels are found not only in the poetic texts themselves but also, and probably more importantly, in the explanatory material added to those texts. Such material, as we have attempted to show, is not redactional in nature, but is part of a single compositional strategy that extends from Gen 1 to Deut 34.

IV. Wisdom and the Theological *Leitmotif* of the Pentateuch

We turn now to an assessment of the central themes at work in the compositional strategy outlined above. Our approach will be to identify terms and ideas within our compositional strategy with parallel terms and ideas in the OT texts as a whole. Do the ideas and terminology of the literary strategy of the Pentateuch, for example, reflect the views of "priestly," "deuteronomic," "apocalyptic," or "wisdom" tradents? In the present study we can make only general observations. Moreover, we must be on guard not to introduce diachronic considerations into our analysis. To identify the compositional strategy of the Pentateuch with "priestly" views is not necessarily to date it in the postexilic period or to assume the existence of a P-Document. It is rather to raise the question of whether the composition of the present shape of the Pentateuch is intended to highlight the interest of those texts in the Pentateuch that stress the central role of the priests in Israel's (or humankind's) relationship with God (e.g., Exod 25–31).

In my view, a close examination of the literary strategy of the Pentateuch outlined above suggests that, at least in broad terms, the notion of wisdom is a central theme of the Pentateuch, perhaps even *the* central theme. It seems clear from the preceding discussion that a clearly defined eschatology also played an important part in shaping the present Pentateuch. It is generally acknowledged that Wisdom themes, messianism, and eschatology frequently merge within OT texts. It ought not then surprise us to find these same themes at work in the composition of the Pentateuch.

There is room here only to suggest various lines of evidence that support the claim that the Pentateuch is a part of the biblical Wisdom literature,[43] and the most likely points for the author of a compositional strategy to reveal the central themes and ideas are the beginning and end of his work. This leads to a search for Wisdom terms and themes in Gen 1–11[44] and Deut 33–34.

A. The Beginning of the Pentateuch: Genesis 1–11

Much has been written on the influence of Wisdom themes in Gen 1–11. Witte has concluded that the theological profile of Gen 1–11 is most closely related to "the spirit of late Wisdom."[45] We need only look at the way the story of the fall of humankind is told in Gen 3. The central event of the story is the eating of the forbidden fruit. It was the fruit of "knowing good and evil," and its eating led to the loss of the "tree of life." The expression "good and evil" in a Wisdom text such as Eccl 12:14 means the totality of all knowledge, "including every secret thing" (NRSV). The biblical phrase "knowing good and evil" means having divine wisdom (2 Sam 14:17, 20). The "tree of life" is found frequently in the biblical Wisdom literature (Prov 3:18; 11:30; 13:12; 15:4). The central theme of the fall story is humanity's quest for wisdom. It was when Eve saw that the tree would "make her wise" (לְהַשְׂכִּיל) that she took its fruit and ate (Gen 3:6). The story thus contrasts the view of wisdom as "obedience and trust in God" with that of "disobedience and doubt." The fall is not cast as a rebellious act, but as a foolish act. Wisdom is portrayed as trust and obedience whereas folly is portrayed as our mistrust of God's word and disobedience.

B. The Conclusion of the Pentateuch: Deuteronomy 33–34

In an earlier study of the theological shaping of the OT canon, I drew attention to a number of Wisdom features in the canonical stages of the Hebrew Bible's formation, "the Law, the Prophets, and the Writings" (Tanak).[46] I suggested that a close look at the composition of the Pentateuch from the "top down" made it fairly clear that Deut 33–34, along with Josh 1:1–8, Mal 3:22–24, and Ps 1, was a part of a larger "canonical redaction" of the OT. Central to the shaping of the Hebrew Bible, I suggested, was the attempt to understand the Torah as wisdom and to see it within the context of a futuristic, or eschatological, hope. In such a viewpoint divine revelation was seen to center on the written word as the locus and source of wisdom, or divine guidance. The prophetic words, which were once delivered by angels, were now held in one's hands in the written Torah—the "possession of the assembly of Jacob" (Deut 33:2–4).

This view of the Torah in Deut 33 presents a significantly more Wisdom-oriented perspective than that in Deut 31:24–26. There we find Moses, as an author or scribe, writing out the Torah by hand and giving it to the priests for safe keeping. Such a view seems a far cry from the fiery letters or words hand-carried by angels in Deut 33:1–4. Thus, the canonical edition of the Pentateuch has a much more focused Wisdom concept of the written Torah. In Deut 33 we see much more clearly that the written Torah is divine revelation given by divine inspiration. Moses received the words of the Torah directly from the angels, the messengers of God (33:2b–3a). The Torah is an oracle of God, written in the tongues of angels. This view of the Torah is remarkably similar to the view in Ps 1 (cf. Ps 19 and 119). The written Torah is the locus of divine revelation. Moses is now dead. The written Torah has taken the place of the prophet Moses, who gave it to Israel.

There is also a new perspective given in Deut 33–34 on the role of Joshua as Moses' replacement. In Num 27:18–21, it is recounted that Joshua would replace Moses as God's leader. Moreover, Joshua was commissioned by Moses (Num 27:22–23). But the commissioning of Joshua is recounted a second time in Deut 34:9, an important part of the canonical redaction. Also in Deut 34:9, an important feature is added to the description of Joshua. In Num 27:18, Joshua is described as a Spirit-filled leader, which in that context identifies him as a prophet (cf. Num 11:25). In Deut 34:9 Joshua is described as one who is "filled with the Spirit of wisdom (חָכְמָה)," identifying him with a wise man. Joshua, the prophet, in Num 27, has thus become Joshua, the wise man, in Deut 34:9. The new leadership represented by Joshua at the close of the Pentateuch is thus characterized by wisdom, not prophecy. This is the same view of Joshua found in Josh 1:8, where he is instructed to meditate in the Torah day and night, just as the wise man in Ps 1 is instructed. Then he will have wisdom (וְאָז תַּשְׂכִּיל). The intention of these seemingly isolated shifts in viewpoint appears, at closer look, to be to show that when Joshua replaced Moses, wisdom replaced prophecy as the means whereby God would lead his people. Moses, the inspired prophet who gave Israel the Torah (Deut 33:4), makes way for a new kind of leader: Joshua, the wise scholar, whose task was meditation on the written Torah given by Moses.

In Deut 33–34 the dependence on the written Torah as a source of divine wisdom is also viewed as a temporary measure. A prophet like Moses had not yet come, but since one had been promised (Deut 18:15), the mere reminder was enough to raise the anticipation of a future return of the role of prophecy as a source of divine revelation (Deut 34:10). At the time of the formation of the OT, prophecy had ceased, but there was still the hope that it would be revived in the future. In the meantime, Scripture, which was given by the prophets of old, was to be the only source of divine wisdom. To know the will of God and to become wise, one should meditate day and night on Scripture (Josh 1:8; Ps 1).[47]

Therefore, both at the beginning of the Pentateuch (Gen 1–11) and at its conclusion (Deut 33–34) one finds a deep interest in wisdom and Wisdom themes. The blessing of life, which was lost in the eating of the tree of knowing good and evil, is regained by meditating day and night on the Torah. Wisdom themes are thus found along the seams of the composition we have sketched out in the earlier parts of this article.

C. Torah as Wisdom and "the Last Days" (אַחֲרִית הַיָּמִים) *in Deuteronomy 4*

One important question remains. We have seen that the phrase *the last days* (אַחֲרִית הַיָּמִים) plays an important role in the compositional strategy of the present shape of the Pentateuch—a strategy that we have suggested is related to the theme of Wisdom. We have also noted that within the Pentateuch there is still one use of the phrase *in the last days* that is not a part of the introductions to the major poems in the Pentateuch. We are speaking of the use of the phrase in Deut 4:30. Deuteronomy 4, then, appears to be an important part of the compositional structure of the Pentateuch we have been discussing. For that reason, it is important to raise the question of the relationship of Deut 4 to the theme of Wisdom. Here we must note it is precisely in Deut 4 that we find the explicit identification of the Torah with wisdom. In Deut 4:6, Moses tells Israel to observe the "statutes and ordinances" he has taught them,

> for this is your wisdom (חָכְמַתְכֶם) and discernment (וּבִינַתְכֶם) before the eyes of the nations who will hear all these statutes and will say, "Surely this great nation is a wise (חָכָם) and discerning people (נָבוֹן)."

The words of Moses in Deut 4 thus embody the basic message of the Pentateuch as a whole. Wisdom comes from knowing and obeying the written word of God, the Torah.

V. Conclusion

In our consideration of the Pentateuch's overall composition, we were led to focus on the poetic seams that link the large blocks of narratives within the book. Those seams reveal an intentional compositional strategy spanning the whole of the present Pentateuch. The first block of narrative, Gen 1–11, was written by the same hand that gave the Pentateuch its present shape. The primary interest of that writer was to show that the events of Israel's past are a map of their eschatological future. The "last days" will be like the "beginning." At the center of God's future plans for Israel is a king who will arise from the house of Judah and bring peace to the nations. The Pentateuch appears to have been written in part to give comfort and hope to those awaiting the coming king. It is both eschatological and messianic.

The author of the Pentateuch appears to be quite concerned about the religious and ethical behavior of those who are awaiting the coming king. His book, the Pentateuch, is intended as a sort of guide to the perplexed. The author of the

Pentateuch is convinced that, in the present age, divine guidance can come only through the reading and study of written Scripture. It, and it alone, is the source of divine wisdom. Though Israel is open to a future renewal of the prophetic word, wisdom and success can now come only through the written words of God's ancient prophets.

~ *Notes* ~

The Scripture quotations in this article are my own translation unless otherwise noted.

[1] Rolf Rendtorff, *Das Alte Testament: Eine Einführung* (Neukirchen-Vluyn: Neukirchener Verlag des Erziehungsvereins, 1983), ix–x.

[2] By "traditional discussions" I refer to the generally accepted opinions about the Bible one finds in popular Christian literature.

[3] For an early evangelical example of the approach taken in this article, see Robert Jamieson, A. R. Fausset, and David Brown, *A Commentary Critical, Experimental, and Practical on the Old and New Testaments* (Grand Rapids: Eerdmans, 1945): "Independently of any hypothesis, it may be conceded that, in the composition of those parts of the Pentateuch relating to matters which were not within the sphere of his personal knowledge, Moses would and did avail himself of existing records which were of reliable authority; and while this admission can neither diminish the value nor affect the credibility of his history as an inspired composition, it is evident that, in making use of such literary materials as were generally known in his time, or had been preserved in the repositories of Hebrew families, he interwove them into his narrative conformably with that unity of design which so manifestly pervades the entire Pentateuch" (xxxii).

[4] By "critical scholarship" I mean modern historical-critical approaches to the Bible. I do not use the term in a negative sense.

[5] Erhard Blum, *Studien zur Komposition des Pentateuch* (Berlin: Walter de Gruyter, 1990), 364.

[6] Ibid., 380.

[7] See John H. Sailhamer, *Introduction to Old Testament Theology: A Canonical Approach* (Grand Rapids: Zondervan, 1995), 98.

[8] "So wird man auch beim Pentateuch von den das Gesamtwerk umspan-

nenden Redaktionen ausgehen müssen und erst nach der Klärung der redaktionellen Verhältnisse nach vorgegebenen Quellen und Traditionsblöcken fragen dürfen." (Thus also with the Pentateuch, one must begin with the editorial work that spans the whole of the book, and only after the clarification of the editorial relationships may one inquire about the sources and blocks of tradition lying behind it.) Hans-Christoph Schmitt, "Redaktion des Pentateuch im Geiste der Prophetie: zur Bedeutung der 'Glaubens'—Thematik innerhalb der Theologie des Pentateuches," *VT* 32 (1982): 172.

9 The reader will note that I have used two different sets of terminology to describe the "shape" of the Pentateuch. I refer to both the "final shape" and the "present shape" of the Pentateuch. This is an attempt to remain faithful to the largely diachronic terminology used in pentateuchal studies today, and, at the same time, an attempt to approach the question within the framework of evangelical synchronic views of authorship. In recent pentateuchal studies, the term *final shape (Endgestalt)* means the shape of the pentateuchal text as it was reached through a long process of literary growth and development. I do not intend, nor do I think it is possible, to describe, even provisionally, that aspect of the pentateuchal text. I have, however, used the term *present shape* of the Pentateuch in this paper to describe the actual version of the Pentateuch now in our Hebrew Bibles. (More precisely, it is the Hebrew text that preceded the present Masoretic Text as well as the Hebrew Vorlage of the early versions.) To be sure, this, itself, is not a merely flat text. There are diachronic dimensions to its composition. Earlier versions of this text surely existed and now survive within the present shape. What we have before us, however, is the present shape alone, and it is our primary task to explain it. For a more detailed discussion of the diachronic aspects of the present shape of the Pentateuch, see Sailhamer, *Old Testament Theology*, 239–52.

10 This is a view remarkably similar to the one in 2 Pet 1:19, "And we have the prophetic word made more sure. You will do well to pay attention to this as to a lamp shining in a dark place, until the day dawns and the morning star rises in your hearts" (RSV).

11 Markus Witte, *Die biblische Urgeschichte, Redaktions- und theologiegeschichtliche Beobachtungen zu Genesis 1,1–11,26* (Berlin: Walter de Gruyter, 1998).

12 The somewhat "poetic" statement in Gen 1:27 is not included here because it is the saying of the narrator, not of a central character. Gen 1:28 is not poetic.

13 This poem comprises line a, זֶה יְנַחֲמֵנוּ מִמַּעֲשֵׂנוּ, line b, וּמֵעִצְּבוֹן יָדֵינוּ, and a comment, מִן־הָאֲדָמָה אֲשֶׁר אֵרְרָהּ יְהוָה. For a helpful discussion of the poetic features of Gen 5:29b, see Witte, *Die biblische Urgeschichte*, 213.

[14] In Ezra 6:22, "Assur" is the name given to Persia.

[15] According to Witte, the identification of Eber as the father of the Hebrews was the main purpose of the comment in Gen 10:21. See Witte, *Die biblische Urgeschichte,* 105.

[16] There are, of course, other ways to identify the historical references of these names. The argument of this essay does not depend on the specific identifications noted above.

[17] It may also be that Num 23–24 merely concludes the Balaam pericope, Num 22–24.

[18] It is also possible to see Deut 32:1–43 as the poetic text and Deut 32:44–52 as the epilogue. See Sailhamer, *Old Testament Theology,* 239–52.

[19] Or Deut 32. See previous note.

[20] This is the only use of מַלְכוּת in the Pentateuch.

[21] Unlike these three poems, the other major poem in the Pentateuch, Exod 15:1–17, does not have the same compositional focus. Moreover, its central theme is virtually identical to the poem in Num 23 (cf. Exod 15:18 with Num 23:21b). Both are about the historical circumstances of Israel and the exodus. This suggests that for the author of the Pentateuch the narratives of Exod 1–14 were not to be immediately associated with the kingship ideal, and it raises the question of what role the poem in Exod 15 was to play within the overall strategy of the Pentateuch. We will not, however, attempt to address that question in this article.

[22] אֲשֶׁר־יִקְרָא (Gen 49:1), אֲשֶׁר יַעֲשֶׂה הָעָם הַזֶּה (Num 24:14), וְקָרָאת אֶתְכֶם הָרָעָה (Deut 31:29).

[23] "באחרית הימים läßt sich in den älteren Prophetenschriften wie überhaupt in der vorexilischen Literatur *nirgends* belegen; die Wendung findet sich vielmehr zuerst bei Ezechiel in der Weissagung gegen Gog und bezeichnet daselbst deutlich den *Anbruch des messianischen Reiches.*" (In the older prophetic texts as well as overall in the preexilic literature, באחרית הימים is not found; the expression is found rather for the first time in Ezekiel in the prophecy against Gog and denotes there quite clearly *the dawning of the messianic kingdom.*) W. Staerk, "Der Gebrauch der Wendung באחרית הימים im AT Kanon," *ZAW* 11 (1891): 247–53.

[24] Hermann Gunkel, *Genesis übersetzt und erklärt* (Göttingen: Vandenhoeck & Ruprecht, 1977), 478.

[25] Ibid.

[26] Regarding the rest of the terminology in the seams, it is important to note that Gen 49:1 uses the verb קָרָא, "what will happen (קָרָא) to you [Israel]"; Num 24:14 uses עָשָׂה, "What this people [Israel] will do (עָשָׂה) to your people"; Deut 31:29 uses both קָרָא and עָשָׂה, "The trouble will happen (קָרָא) to you because you did (עָשָׂה) evil." (The inclusion of both קָרָא and עָשָׂה in Deut 31:29 suggests a conscious awareness of the need to merge the terminology of the other seams.) It is also significant that the spelling of קָרָא, with א rather than ה—meaning "to happen"—is found in both Gen 49 and Deut 31. קָרָא, with א, occurs four times in the Pentateuch, apart from the two times in Gen 49:1 and Deut 31:29. The spelling of קרה, with ה, occurs twelve times in the Pentateuch and is the more common spelling. Of the two occurrences of קרא, with א, two are stereotyped with אָסוֹן (Gen 42:4, 38), one with מלחמה (Exod 1:10).

[27] כָּרַע שָׁכַב כַּאֲרִי וּכְלָבִיא מִי יְקִימֶנּוּ

[28] כָּרַע רָבַץ כְּאַרְיֵה וּכְלָבִיא מִי יְקִימֶנּוּ

[29] C. F. Keil, apparently without taking note of the far-reaching consequences of his observation, simply says that these are "words taken from Jacob's blessing in Gen. xlix.9" (K&D 1:190).

[30] Compare Gen 49:25 (תְּהוֹם רֹבֶצֶת תָּחַת) with Deut 33:13 (וּמִתְּהוֹם רֹבֶצֶת תָּחַת). Compare also Gen 49:26 (תִּהְיֶיןָ לְרֹאשׁ יוֹסֵף וּלְקָדְקֹד נְזִיר אֶחָיו) with Deut 33:16 (תָּבוֹאתָה לְרֹאשׁ יוֹסֵף וּלְקָדְקֹד נְזִיר אֶחָיו).

[31] "To dwell in the tents of" means "to conquer" in 1 Chr 5:10. That is apparently also its meaning here.

[32] It is likely that the original oracle can still be seen in Num 24:23b: "Woe! Who can survive when God establishes him?" (Line a, אוֹי מִי יִחְיֶה, and line b, מִשֻּׂמוֹ אֵל). That v. 24a is an explanation of v. 23b appears likely from two considerations: *(a)* v. 24a is not poetic because it has no meter or parallelism, and *(b)* the pronoun shifts from the *singular* in v. 23b ("when God establishes *him*") to the *plural* in 24a ("*they* will subdue Assyria [Assur] and *they* will subdue Eber"). Also, the *singular* "he" in v. 24b is unaware of the *plurals* in v. 24a.

[33] H. Holzinger, *Einleitung in den Hexateuch* (Leipzig: J. C. B. Mohr [Siebeck], 1893), charts, 9.

[34] James A. Montgomery, *The Book of Daniel* (ICC; Edinburgh: T&T Clark, 1927), 455.

[35] August Freiherr von Gall, "Zusammensetzung und Herkunft der Bileam-Perikope in Num. 22–24" in *Festgruss Bernhard Stade zur Feier seiner 25 jährigen Wirksamkeit als Professor* (ed. W. Diehl; Giessen: J. Ricker'sche Verlagsbuchhandlung, 1900), 46.

[36] Witte has recently noted that both Num 24:24a and Gen 9:27 appear to refer to the same contemporary event(s). Witte, *Die biblische Urgeschichte,* 322.

[37] Witte has also recently noted that "Gegenüber den späten prophetischen Belegen teilt Gen 9,27 mit dem Spruch in Num 24,24, der möglicherweise in den Kontext der Endredaktion des Pentateuchs gehört, die Einbettung der Gegenwartserfahrung der makedonischen Eroberungen in eine ur- bzw. frühgeschichtliche Weissagung." (Over against the later prophetic evidence, Gen 9:27, along with the saying in Num 24:24, which in all probability belongs in the context of the final edition of the Pentateuch, is part of the embedding of the contemporary experience of the Macedonian invasion into a primeval, or early, historical prophecy.) Ibid., 322.

[38] The use of the word רֵאשִׁית is unusual in Gen 1:1 because elsewhere in the Pentateuch the adverbial notion of "beginning" is not expressed with רֵאשִׁית but with רִאשֹׁנָה or תְּחִלָּה (see Rashi).

[39] "Denn alle Geschichte ist ein von der Ewigkeit umschlossener Verlauf von רֵאשִׁית bis zu אַחֲרִית; ihre רֵאשִׁית ist der Anfang der Creatur und mit ihr der Zeit, ihre אַחֲרִית die Vollendung der Creatur und damit der Übergang der Zeit in die Ewigkeit." (For all history is an all encompassing course arising out of eternity from רֵאשִׁית to אַחֲרִית; its רֵאשִׁית is that of the beginning of what was created, and with it, time itself; its אַחֲרִית is the completion of what was created, and with that, the passing over of time into eternity.) Franz Delitzsch, *Kommentar über Die Genesis* (Leipzig: Dörffling und Franke, 1860), 91.

[40] Otto Procksch, *Die Genesis übersetzt und erklärt* (Leipzig: A. Deichertsche Verlagsbuchhandlung, 1913), 265. "Der Gegensatz ist nicht שנית, שלשית, sondern אחרית (Dt 11,12. Jes 41,22); auch hier (1,1) schwebt אַחֲרִית הַיָּמִים vor, das absolute Ende der gegenwärtigen Welt. Wahrscheinlich hat P den Ausdruck im Hinblick auf die אַחֲרִית der Dinge geformt." (The antithesis of רֵאשִׁית is not שנית, or שלשית, but אחרית [Deut 11:12; Isa 41:22]; also here [in 1:1] comes to mind the notion of the אַחֲרִית הַיָּמִים, the absolute end of the present world. In all probability, P has deliberately chosen the expression רֵאשִׁית with a view to the אַחֲרִית of all things.) Ibid., 425. In an early edition of his Genesis commentary, Delitzsch had also noted the relationship between רֵאשִׁית and אַחֲרִית in Gen 1; see previous note.

[41] D. Wilhelm Bousset and Hugo Gressmann, *Die Religion des Judentums im späthellenistischen Zeitalter* (Tübingen: J. C. B. Mohr [Siebeck], 1966), 283.

[42] I am using the Hebrew word *Torah* to denote the first five books of the OT, commonly called the *Pentateuch.*

[43] Having said that, I am well aware that the notion of wisdom in the OT is itself in need of further clarification. In the use of the term *wisdom* in relationship to the Pentateuch, I have no other meaning in mind than the use of certain Wisdom terminology within important compositional seams within the Pentateuch. Just what the meaning of those terms is and how they are used by the author of the Pentateuch is not at issue at this point.

[44] I owe this suggestion to an observation shared with me personally by Dr. Daniel Frederickson.

[45] "Die Intention des R^{UG} war es nicht nur, seine Quellen zu bewahren und aus neutraler Perspektive miteinander zu harmonisieren, sondern diese bewußt zu gestalten und zu einer neuen Komposition mit einer eigenständigen Theologie zu verbinden. Diese ist weder als einseitig 'priesterlich' gefärbt noch als entschieden 'prophetisch' zu bezeichnen, sondern besitzt ihren Schwerpunkt in spätweisheitlichem Denken. Als Kennzeichnung des Profils des R^{UG} bietet sich somit die Kategorie *'Redaktion und Komposition im Geist der späten Weisheit'* an." (The intent of R^{UG} was not only to preserve its sources and to harmonize them with each other from a neutral perspective, but also to shape these sources intentionally and to combine them into a new composition with its own distinct theology. This theology is neither one-sidedly "priestly" tinted, nor is it to be described as distinctly "prophetic." It rather finds its center of gravity in late Wisdom thought. As a way of describing the profile of R^{UG}, the category of "redaction [edition] and composition in the spirit of the late Wisdom" commends itself.) Witte, *Die biblische Urgeschichte,* 328–29. Witte has also suggested the so-called "Jahwistic Primeval History" should rather be called the "Wisdom Primeval History" (205); see esp. 200–204. My purpose at this point is not so much to add to what Witte and others have written as it is to point out the significance of the concentration of Wisdom themes just at this point in the Pentateuch. If our analysis of Gen 1–11's role within the composition of the Pentateuch as a whole is correct—namely, if the author of Gen 1–11 is, in fact, the author of the present Pentateuch—then any indication that this section of the Pentateuch is guided by Wisdom themes would also suggest the importance of those themes to the present shape of the entire Pentateuch.

[46] Sailhamer, *Old Testament Theology,* 243–52.

[47] "If we pull back and view the TaNaK in terms of its boundary markers, comparing Deuteronomy 34 with Malachi 3 and Joshua 1 with Psalm 1, we can see a remarkably coherent line of thought. Prophecy, or at least the great prophets of old, have ceased to be the means for gaining divine guidance. For the time being, the wise man has taken the role of the prophet as the ideal leader. Scripture is now the locus of divine revelation. There still lies in the future, however, the hope of a return of prophecy. The Scriptures themselves (e.g., Dt 18) point in that direction. In the meantime, one 'prospers' by meditating on the written Word of God." Ibid., 249.

Noah: Sot or Saint? Genesis 9:20–27

Walter E. Brown

As little Davie Lurie, Chaim Potok's prodigious central character in the novel *In the Beginning*, moves more deeply into the wonderful world of Torah study at the tender age of eleven, he says,

> I don't understand it, and I don't understand how Rashi and Ibn Ezra and the Ramban or any of the others explain it. . . . I can't get a picture in my eyes of what happened, Papa. It bothers me. They all try to give good explanations, but they can't really answer all the questions. . . . I have a picture of Noah. But I don't have a picture of this thing that happened to him and who was cursed.[1]

Potok's depiction, though fictional, reflects a long-standing struggle with the Noah story, as the references to the rabbis reflect.[2] But while Potok's character struggled with what was done to Noah and the identity of the person Noah cursed, my struggle is with an aspect of the passage with which little Davie seemed not to struggle—the character of Noah himself.

Of course, consideration of Noah's character has been an issue through the years. In almost every study, beginning with the most ancient, Noah has been castigated for being a despicable character because of his drunkenness and nakedness.[3] More recently, much of the negative assessment of Noah has come from scholars who analyze the text using traditional source-critical methodology. At this juncture in the text, they see the positive depiction of Noah in Gen 6:9 and the apparently negative assessment in Gen 9:20–27, and they conclude that different sources are reflected here, as at many other places in the narrative. Supposedly, there was a righteous Noah and a sinful Noah, the two traditions being patched together by an editor who did not seem to notice the contradiction he or she had created.[4]

The development of newer literary approaches, which focus on the final form of the text and assume a coherent sense to the whole of narrative texts, has brought hope for a more positive approach to such (so-called) problematic portions of the biblical text. But conservative evangelical scholars embracing these approaches typically have also judged the character of Noah negatively.[5] So alas, Noah still keeps missing the boat. There he lies, a sot, sprawling disgracefully in his sin, his sainthood in shambles.

But such assessments do not adequately take into account the evidence related to a number of important issues in the text of Gen 9:20–27, the most prominent of which are the traditional descriptions of Noah as "drunk" and "naked." The first description reflects the universal translation of the key word שָׁכַר in v. 21 as "to be or become drunk." However, as will be shown, the uses of the verb in the Hebrew Bible demonstrate that the verb often designates a positive action not only in metaphorical uses but also in literal ones. Therefore, since the broader literary context reflects an overwhelmingly positive assessment of the character of Noah, and since the historical and cultural background included the image of drinking wine as a vital part of positive celebration and worship, I propose that שָׁכַר in Gen 9:21 should be translated as "to be fully content" or "to be satiated to sleep." Noah's action was not negative and despicable; rather, it was positive and laudable. In planting the vineyard, he was cultivating the ground that was no longer cursed as before; and in drinking its wine, he was celebrating the blessings of the Lord.[6]

Similarly, since Noah's "nakedness" has usually been considered objectionable because of a prior condemnation of Noah's "drunkenness," a re-evaluation of Noah's "nakedness" is appropriate. The text attributes to Noah only an "uncovering" of himself. The picture reflects very natural and normal developments. Noah drank in celebration, then fell asleep, and—in a wine-warmed sleep—uncovered himself. This "uncovering" was private and inoffensive. The mention of it is incidental to the larger narrative, since it would never have been known without Ham's actions. And only in the depiction of Ham's actions does the word for nakedness actually appear in the narrative.

Therefore, my thesis is that Gen 9:20–27 as a whole, in its literary context, does not detract from the overall positive assessment of Noah's character elsewhere in Gen 6–9. On the contrary, its content complements that positive assessment, and it is specifically related to the broader theme of blessing in the narrative as a whole, so that Noah's actions constitute an enjoyment of the productivity and fruitfulness resulting from that blessing.

The procedure for the study will be to consider Noah's drunkenness, Noah's nakedness, and the characterization of Noah in the broader context and, finally, to offer a summary and conclusions based on the study.

I am happy to dedicate this study to Professor Bruce K. Waltke, whose faith, humility, and generosity reflect indisputable character.

I. Noah's "Drunkenness"

A. Grammatical and Syntactical Considerations

The first verse of this passage has been the object of extended scrutiny because the first verset is ambiguous: the syntax will allow two different interpretations. The phrase אִישׁ הָאֲדָמָה, "man of the land," may be taken as a complement of the verb חָלַל, or it may be understood to stand in apposition to "Noah." The resulting translations would be either "Noah began to be a man of the land and planted [a vineyard]" or "Noah, the man of the land, was the first to plant a vineyard."[7] Although the debate continues, there is a clear consensus that the latter alternative is preferable.

That consensus is built on several factors. First, the verb חָלַל clearly is used at times to indicate a "beginning" in the sense of a first occurrence.[8] Second, reading the phrase אִישׁ הָאֲדָמָה as a verbal complement would be unusual, and some authorities consider it impossible.[9] Third, the natural way to treat the above phrase is to read it as standing in apposition to the noun "Noah."[10] Fourth, since Cain has already been described as the first farmer (Gen 4:2), the literary context calls for the consensus reading as well.[11]

The consensus reading of Gen 9:20 allows the suggestion, therefore, that vines, wine, and drinking were new for Noah, and it implies that his experience with them and his resultant drunkenness would not have been something he could have predicted. Consequently, his drunken state may be judged less harshly or may not be condemned at all.

C. F. Keil's assessment reflects the idea well: "In ignorance of the fiery nature of wine, Noah drank and was drunken, and uncovered himself in his tent."[12] A more modern example is Derek Kidner's observation that "Noah's drunkenness is recounted without moral comment on his part in the scandal: the word *began* (20) could imply that only inexperience was to blame; we cannot be certain."[13] Most commentators seem to be more ambivalent on this viewpoint,[14] while some directly reject the suggestion, emphasizing Noah's culpability.[15]

Because there is some basis for stressing the idea of the newness of Noah's experiences, one can lend some support to the contention that the larger narrative maintains throughout a positive view of Noah's character. However, given the nature of the evidence, it is difficult to see that the narrator intended to exonerate Noah through the statement of v. 20. In addition, if, in light of the narrative as a whole, we do not judge Noah's "drunkenness" itself negatively, then the narrator would have no need to excuse Noah's actions at the beginning of the account.

B. Verbal and Contextual Considerations

I am unaware of any translation of the first part of v. 21 that varies from the following: "And he drank of [some of] the wine and became [or was] drunk."[16] The sentence can certainly be translated legitimately this way, but the Hebrew verb glossed "drinking and becoming drunk" in the ancient context did not always have the negative connotation that it typically does in modern culture. This fact is borne out by a survey of the use of the key verb שָׁכַר in the OT.

Abraham Even-Shoshan lists nineteen occurrences of the verb, nine of which are in the Qal stem, including Gen 9:21. A look at both the non-Qal and Qal occurrences is insightful.[17]

1. Non-Qal Occurrences of שָׁכַר

Habakkuk 2:15–16

This text is of particular interest because it is routinely cited in connection with Gen 9:21. Since the thrust of the Habakkuk text is negative—that is, condemning drinking and nakedness—interpreters have supposed that it supports the condemnation of Noah's drinking and nakedness. John Davis's treatment is representative of this perspective. He notes Noah's drunkenness, along with the fact that no details of the incident appear, and then adds, "Quite evidently his grandson Canaan was involved in the debauchery. Perhaps Habakkuk's observation is appropriate: 'Woe unto him that giveth his neighbor drink, that puttest thy bottle to him, and makest him drunken also, that thou mayest look on their nakedness!' (2:15). Wine is indeed a 'mocker' (Prov. 20:1)."[18] Some have also made the connection in the opposite direction, citing the Genesis passage as significant in interpreting the Habakkuk passage. For example, O. Palmer Robertson suggests the existence of what is "almost a universal principle that the sin of drunkenness is associated with sexual impurity and the degradation of the body." He mentions Lot's daughters' actions with their father and Noah's drunkenness—a state "which led to the exposure of his nakedness before his son." He concludes, "The case of Noah is particularly significant for the present context in Habakkuk."[19]

Determining the legitimacy of any connection of Gen 9 and Hab 2 begins with a translation of the Habakkuk passage, a task that offers some significant challenges, as reflected in the *BHS* critical apparatus, in the variation in modern translations and in commentaries. The Hebrew text of Hab 2:15–16 and a basic translation are as follows:

הוֹי מַשְׁקֵה רֵעֵהוּ מְסַפֵּחַ חֲמָתְךָ וְאַף שַׁכֵּר
לְמַעַן הַבִּיט עַל־מְעוֹרֵיהֶם׃
שָׂבַעְתָּ קָלוֹן מִכָּבוֹד שְׁתֵה גַם־אַתָּה וְהֵעָרֵל
תִּסּוֹב עָלֶיךָ כּוֹס יְמִין יְהוָה וְקִיקָלוֹן עַל־כְּבוֹדֶךָ׃

Woe to the one giving drink to his neighbor,
mixing your wrath and even making drunk,
in order to look upon their nakedness.
You will be satiated with dishonor more than honor;
you yourself also drink and show yourself as uncircumcised.
It will come around upon you,
the cup of the right hand of the Lord
and disgusting dishonor upon your honor.

First, the verb "to drink" is the Hiphil form of שָׁקָה, which is clearly related in usage to the verb "to drink," שָׁתָה, occurring in v. 16 as a Qal imperative.[20] But the Hiphil indicates that the action here is different from that described in Gen 9. Here the woe is pronounced on a person who *causes* another person to drink; Gen 9 describes a person who drinks wine, apparently of his own volition.

Second, the word מָעוֹר, translated "nakedness" in v. 15, is a hapax legomenon. Consensus exists on the rendering, but the ancient versions clearly reflect historical uncertainty regarding its meaning. Although some suggest that other terms for nakedness, including the one used in Gen 9:21, are synonyms for the word used here,[21] the suggestion is somewhat misleading, since no other biblical contexts exist to demonstrate any relationship in usage between the two terms.

Third, the phrase וְהֵעָרֵל, traditionally rendered "and expose . . . nakedness" in v. 16, is obviously from a different word than that of v. 15, as well as that of Gen 9. It too is a hapax legomenon. The MT reading means something like "to show the foreskin,"[22] "to show oneself as uncircumcised," or "to be counted uncircumcised."[23] Some translations follow a variant reading, וְהֵרָעֵל, meaning "to stagger."[24] If this alternative reading were adopted, the image of "nakedness" would be eliminated. In this case, however, the evidence supports the MT so that the metaphor of v. 15 is resumed in a graphic way.[25] Babylon will suffer the same kind of treatment it had given others, except at the hands of God, and the result will be its own experience of shame and degradation.

Fourth, the passage is probably metaphorical. J. J. M. Roberts observes, "The prophet is not concerned here with the evils of alcohol abuse, but merely uses imagery drawn from a particularly shocking abuse of it to illustrate the evils of imperial power, which is Habakkuk's real concern."[26] In light of this fact, the focus in v. 16 is not so much on physical or sexual exposure as it is on religious or spiritual exposure: God's judgment will make clear Babylon's moral depravity, and shame before God will result.

Consequently, little, if anything, in the text of Hab 2:15–16 suggests any legitimate connection with Gen 9:21, as demonstrated above. The traditional suggestion of a connection is based on a negative reading of the Genesis passage and on a leap from key words there to what *appear to be* the same key words in the Habakkuk passage.

Jeremiah 51:57

This text contains an oracle of judgment against Babylon. The Lord will make Babylon's leaders drunk (וְהִשְׁכַּרְתִּי), so they will "sleep a perpetual sleep and not wake up" (NASB; cf. 51:39). The interesting idea here is the implication that the normal result of drunkenness is sleep, although here it is intensified as a part of the image of judgment.

2 Samuel 11:13

This text records David's effort to cover up his adultery with Bathsheba by making Uriah drunk (וַיְשַׁכְּרֵהוּ), so that he would go home and have sex with Bathsheba. What is striking in this context is that although Uriah was drunk ("he made him drunk," according to traditional glossing), he still acted honorably. This account suggests that drunkenness as expressed by the verb שָׁכַר does not necessarily equal disgraceful conduct or character nor a loss of control that involves demeaning conduct.

Summary

This survey of the non-Qal occurrences of שָׁכַר[27] prompts some interesting conclusions. On the one hand, none of the uses has any direct connection to the Genesis text or any significant bearing on the interpretation of that text. On the other hand, at least two of the uses reflect two facts that may be relevant for translating שָׁכַר in other contexts, including the Gen 9 context: Jeremiah 51:57 reflects the common connection between drunkenness and sleep, and 2 Sam 11:13 depicts an individual who is "drunk" but who still is characterized as honorable.

2. Qal Occurrences of שָׁכַר

The verb שָׁכַר also appears eight times in the Qal stem (besides the occurrence in Gen 9:21). Four occurrences are not relevant to an interpretation of the Genesis passage, since the depiction of drunkenness in these texts is obviously symbolic.[28] A fifth occurrence (Lam 4:21) is of the same type as these four, but, nevertheless, it has been routinely linked with Gen 9. The remaining three passages (Gen 43:34; Song 5:1; Hag 1:6) reflect notable verbal similarity to the Gen 9 passage, and the verb שָׁכַר in each of them describes the enjoyment of good, positive experiences.

In addition, in the Haggai passage שָׁכַר describes a good, positive experience clearly understood to be the result of God's blessings.

Lamentations 4:21

Genesis 9 has often been linked with Lam 4:21 because it contains the phrase תִּשְׁכְּרִי וְתִתְעָרִי, which the NASB renders, "You will become drunk and make yourself naked." Examples of this kind of linking, and its negative implications for Noah's actions, can readily be found. Consider Claus Westermann's observation on the Lamentations passage: "The effect of Yahweh's intervention will be 'that you expose yourself while in delirium' (cf. Gen 9:20–27). In other words, to the actual experience of being conquered will be added the shame of defeat."[29] Delbert Hillers's comment on the Lamentations passage is similar: "The association of drunkenness and self-exposure occurs also in Gen 9:21–22; Hab 2:15–16."[30] Granted, the English glossing here is very similar to that of Gen 9:21, but the verb rendered in Lam 4:1 as "make yourself naked" is not גָּלָה of Gen 9:21 but עָרָה.[31] In addition, the description is clearly one of God's judgment on Edom, since the previous phrase reads, "also upon you [the] cup will pass." Therefore, Hillers is correct in linking the Lamentations passage with the Habakkuk passage, but the similarity that establishes that link also sets both passages apart from Gen 9. The substance of the argument above regarding the Habakkuk passage can be applied to this passage as well. In the end, the connections are more apparent than real. More important for this study are the remaining three passages, which all reflect noticeable verbal similarity to Gen 9:21.

Song of Songs 5:1

The speaker first describes his own action. He has gathered myrrh, eaten honeycomb and honey, and drunk wine with milk—all apparently symbolic of his fulfilling experience of sexual love. Then he (or an unknown speaker) offers an invitation to others to embrace the same experience of love: "Eat, friends; drink and be [or get] drunk, O lovers" (שְׁתוּ וְשִׁכְרוּ דּוֹדִים).

This expression is reflective of a common pattern of using terms for eating and drinking to describe sexual fulfillment. For example, Prov 5:15 contains the command, "Drink water from your [own] cistern; [drink] flowing waters from your [own] well." Prov 5:18 makes clear that the point of this metaphor is faithfulness to one's wife, and 5:19 adds, "in her love, may you be intoxicated continually." In the more immediate context of the Song of Songs, the lover describes the overwhelming impact of his bride's love, indicating that it is much better than wine, and the association of the images suggests an intoxicating effect (Song 4:9–10).

For this reason, Michael Fox suggested that the imagery implied such expressions as " 'eat' and 'drink' love [and] 'Get drunk on love' (lit., 'drink and get drunk of love'")," with the sense being "to give oneself over to sexual ecstasy."[32] Othmar Keel expressed a similar view, with an additional observation: "Eating and drinking are metaphors for the lovers' erotic pleasures, but that metaphor does not exhaust the meaning of these terms. Eating and drinking imply appropriation in the fullest sense. . . . The object of a person's love becomes part of that person."[33]

Although the terminology here is obviously symbolic, the point is that שָׁכַר is used in this context to describe a good, positive, and fulfilling activity. If the word only designated a negative, unacceptable activity, it certainly would not have been appropriate to use it in describing the beautiful experience of loving, sexual fulfillment.

Haggai 1:6

This verse reads, "You have sown/planted much, but harvested little; [you have] eaten, but not to being satisfied; [you have] drunk, but not to becoming drunk (שָׁתוֹ וְאֵין־לְשָׁכְרָה); [you have] put on clothes, but not to becoming warm; and he who hires himself out, hires himself out to a bag with holes."[34] In this case, drinking enough to become drunk seems to be a good thing that is not being realized. Certainly, the parallel activity—eating until one is satisfied—is good and expected under normal circumstances. Putting on enough clothing to be warm is also good and expected. The implication seems to be that the same would be said about drinking, so that in good times the expected and normal experience would be having enough so that drinking would bring "drunkenness."

Or perhaps a better way to approach the issue is to note the parallelism of שָׁכַר with שָׂבַע. On that basis, one could render the ideas more positively: "eating until full," "drinking until fully satisfied." Consequently, the function of the verb שָׁכַר is to denote a good and positive experience. As Carol and Eric Meyers noted, the problem for the people of Judah was shortages, not complete deprivation, so the clause under consideration "conveys the idea that one ought to be able to drink enough wine once in a while in order to become cheerful; i.e., 'to become drunk.' . . . Although the word 'drunk' has negative connotations in English, it probably would have been neutral for the biblical mind. Its usage here implies that some wine is available but not as much as would be desirable."[35] Hans Walter Wolff expresses the idea even more directly: "As a parallel to 'satiety,' שָׁכַר does not really have the (usual) meaning of being drunk (after immoderate enjoyment). In this context what is clearly meant is not having enough to drink."[36]

It is interesting to note that in this context the people's lack of wine is due to God's judgment on them because of their sins. This reality is restated in ch. 2, where it is specifically described as resulting from the Lord's "striking" the work of the people (2:17). But the remedy for the problem is also alluded to: the situation can be reversed through the Lord's blessing. When the Lord begins blessing the people again, one of the positive results would be being able to drink enough "to get drunk." Given all the evidence regarding the sense of the verb שָׁכַר here, therefore, not only can the action described by it be seen as a positive one, but it can also be seen as the direct result from and evidence of the blessing of God.

Genesis 43:34

This passage is particularly interesting because it appears in the same canonical section of the OT as the Noah story and reflects almost verbatim grammar. The differences are that the language here is plural whereas in Gen 9:21 it is singular, and in Gen 9:21 the additional phrase מִן־הַיַּיִן, "from the wine," appears between the two verbs. In this context, Joseph's entertaining of his brothers, including his favoring of Benjamin, is followed by the phrase וַיִּשְׁתּוּ וַיִּשְׁכְּרוּ עִמּוֹ.

The translations typically given this clause are noteworthy. They usually are of two varieties: "And they drank and were merry with him"[37] or "So they feasted and drank freely with him."[38] The commentaries usually follow the same patterns. An example is S. R. Driver, who glosses the clause, "And they drank, and were merry with him," and then comments, "The Heb. word is the one which is regularly rendered to *be drunken,* and generally (e.g., ch. ix. 21) is so used as certainly to imply that meaning. In itself, however, it may not have denoted more than *drink largely.* . . . [Compare] the other two passages in which EVV render similarly, Cant. v. 1 ('Drink, yea, *drink abundantly*'), Hag. i. 6 ('Ye drink, but ye are not *filled with drink*')."[39] Keil's observation is similar: "They were perfectly satisfied with what they ate and drank; not, they were intoxicated."[40] Others have rendered the clause differently ("So they ate and drank with Joseph until they were drunk"), but they are in the minority.[41] However, none of these sources offered any indication that their translations implied a negative assessment of the action described in this context.[42]

Summary

While at least one of the non-Qal occurrences of שָׁכַר allows a positive sense for the action or state described, all three of the Qal occurrences that reflect notable verbal similarity to Gen 9:20–27 do so. Consequently, the evidence indicates that the verb שָׁכַר cannot always be glossed appropriately as "to be or become drunk," which is understood as denoting a morally unacceptable action. On the basis of the use of the word in other contexts, the occurrence of שָׁכַר in Gen 9:21 need not be translated in such a way as to imply a negative assessment of Noah's actions. Given the negative connotation in much of Western culture to the phrase "to be or become drunk," perhaps the best option would be to render the verse in a manner such as these: "And he drank from the wine, and he became fully content" or "He drank from the wine, and he was satiated to sleep."

C. Historical and Cultural Considerations

The suggested positive sense of Noah's actions fits well in the broader background of celebration in the life of ancient Israel. The importance of such celebration is well-known, and it characteristically involved the drinking of wine, which was viewed as one of God's many good gifts. The psalmist expressed the conviction well: "[The] one causing the grass to sprout for the cattle and green plants for the labor of human beings, to bring forth bread from the earth, and wine [which] makes the hearts of mortals glad, to make faces shine with oil, and [to bring forth] bread [which] strengthens the hearts of mortals" (Ps 104:14–15). The broader context of the book of Genesis reflects God's promise of such gracious provision not only as rooted in the purposes of creation, but also as basic to God's covenant work.

In Isaac's blessing of Jacob (Gen 27:27–29), the terminology clearly reflects that Isaac was extending the blessing that first came to Abram (Gen 12:1–3). A part of that blessing's content is made more clear here than in ch. 12: Isaac prays for God to give Jacob "from the dew of the heavens and from the fatness of the earth," which he then specifies as "an abundance of grain and new wine."

The same image is clear in the covenant promises aimed at the nation as a whole. As Moses challenged the people to obedience, he reminded them of God's covenant love for them and God's promise to bless them: God will "bless the fruit of your womb and the fruit of your land, your grain and your new wine" (Deut 7:12–13). So dominant was this reality in ancient times that the experience came to be viewed as a paradigm for the expression of joy: "You have made great the joy [of the nation]; they rejoice before you like the rejoicing in the harvest, just like they dance around when they divide the spoil" (Isa 9:2 [EVV 9:3]).[43] The importance of the picture is reflected also in the prophets' depiction of the eschatological future when, beyond judgment and exile, the covenant would be restored. The blessings of that age include return, rebuilding, planting vineyards and drinking of wine, planting gardens and eating of their produce, as well as great joy and celebration (Jer 31:12; Amos 9:14–15).

Apparently, the blessings of God were celebrated most directly and graphically in the prescribed festivals related to harvest. Direct detail regarding the nature of festival celebration, however, is limited. Examples are the commands regarding the Feast of Weeks. The Leviticus (23:15–21) and Numbers (28:26–31) texts simply describe the requirements for the offerings, while the Deuteronomy text (16:9–12) adds encouragement to celebrate with a freewill offering and expressions of joy before the Lord. Certainly, the joyful and celebrative character of these events generally was assumed. In addition, the exuberant, joyful, and sometimes raucous nature of the festivals is strongly implied by the texts already noted above (Isa 9:2 [EVV 9:3]; Jer 31:12; Amos 9:14–15; Hag 1:6; see as well Isa 16:9–10).

Perhaps the best example of a positive command for full celebration of the harvest is found in a Deuteronomy text giving instruction on the tithe (14:22–27). The worshipers are told to eat the tithe of grain, new wine, and oil in the presence of the Lord; but if they cannot carry the substance of the tithe because the distance is too great, they are to sell it, travel to the designated place, buy whatever they want (livestock, wine, and so forth), consume it, and rejoice before the Lord.

The significance of these observations for the subject at hand becomes clear when the text's depiction of Noah as a new Adam is considered.[44] First, in the genealogy announcing the birth of Noah, he is described as one "who will comfort us from our work and from the toiling labor (וּמֵעִצְּבוֹן) caused by the land (הָאֲדָמָה) which the Lord cursed (אֵרֲרָ)" (Gen 5:29). This announcement obviously depicts Noah as an answer to and corrective for the problems precipitated by the sinful action of Adam and Eve, who both were destined to endure "toiling labor" (עִצָּבוֹן)—Eve as a part of childbirth (Gen 3:16) and Adam as he tilled the ground (הָאֲדָמָה), which the Lord had cursed (אָרַר) because of him (Gen 3:17).

Second, in repeated references, Noah's obedience is set in contrast to Adam and Eve's disobedience (Gen 6:22; 7:5, 9, 16). In the narrative the references culminate with Noah's sacrifice to the Lord and the Lord's response, his promise to "not again curse (קָלַל) the ground (הָאֲדָמָה) on account of mankind (הָאָדָם)" (Gen 8:21).

Third, God's command to Noah after the flood contains terminology that clearly links this new beginning with the creation account: "Every living thing with you from all flesh, birds and beasts and every creeping thing which creeps upon the earth, bring [them] out with you, so that they can swarm in the earth and be fruitful and multiply upon the earth" (Gen 8:17; see also 8:19). Compare Gen 1:20–26, which climaxes in the plan to create people who will "rule over the fish of the sea, over the birds of the heavens, over the beasts, and over all the earth, and over every creeping thing that creeps upon the earth." The only noticeable difference is that Gen 8 makes no mention of the fish, a part of the creation that presumably fared well in the watery world upon which Noah and all the rest of the creation remnants floated.

Finally, Noah is blessed along with his sons (Gen 9:1), as were Adam and Eve (Gen 1:28). Noah and his family would be preeminent in creation (Gen 9:2), as were Adam and Eve. The difference here is that Noah is not told to "subdue the earth and rule over it," as Adam and Eve had been instructed (Gen 1:28); Noah is told that "his fear and dread" would be upon all the created beings (Gen 9:2). This leads naturally to the availability of all creation as provision for Noah and his family, with some qualifications concerning eating meat (Gen 9:3–4), just as Adam and Eve had been provided for fully (Gen 1:29–30). The privileged position of Noah and his family as well as his connection with Adam and Eve are highlighted by the statement in Gen 9:7, which forms an inclusio with Gen 9:1 (cf. 1:28): "You yourselves be fruitful and multiply; swarm over the earth and multiply in it."

When Noah then planted a vineyard and drank from the wine of that vineyard, he was benefiting from God's blessing of the ground as well as God's blessing on him personally. The sense is reflected in the following comment: "The curse was set aside, and the earth not only brought forth enough produce for the sustenance of mankind, but also wine that rejoiced their hearts."[45] Noah's celebration then presages, literarily, the experience of all the patriarchs and of the nation as a whole in their joyful response to the covenant blessings of God, blessings rooted in God's creation intentions.

II. Noah's "Nakedness"

A. Drunk and Naked?

What becomes quite clear in a close study of this text is that the condemnation of Noah's "nakedness" is directly related to a condemnation of his "drunkenness." Consequently, if Noah's state of "being drunk" must be assessed more positively, then the evaluation of his nakedness must be reassessed as well. The connection of these ideas is reflected in the fact that almost every commentator cites Hab 2:15 and Lam 4:21 as evidence for condemnation of both Noah's drunkenness and his nakedness. These two passages were discussed above, and it was concluded that no legitimate connection exists between either of them and Gen 9. Numerous other passages—with similar imagery and focus, although without the same apparent verbal parallels—have been cited in the discussion of nakedness, but the same judgment must be made of them: they simply are not relevant.[46]

B. Naked and Exposed?

Several other passages have often been cited in support of a negative assessment of Noah's nakedness, all of which are concerned with the issue of public nakedness and its shamefulness or suspected shamefulness.[47] The seriousness of these realities in ancient times cannot be denied. However, since Noah's nakedness was a private matter (בְּתוֹךְ אָהֳלֹה) until Ham broadcast it (וַיַּגֵּד ... בַּחוּץ), none of the passages cited in this connection have any relevance for assessing the subject at hand.

C. Naked like Adam?

One other biblical passage—Gen 3:7, 10–11, which describes Adam and Eve's nakedness and their fear of God because of that nakedness—is routinely linked to the Noah passage, and the question of its relevance requires a closer look. Warren Gage proposes that "the chronicle of prediluvian history (Genesis 1–7), is composed of five theologically fundamental narratives, each of which finds consecutive, synthetic parallel in the history (and prophecy) of the postdiluvian world." He suggests that understanding the early history would lead to a better understanding of "the relationship between the beginning and ending of biblical history." After demonstrating the connections between Adam and Noah so as to suggest that Noah was depicted as a new Adam,[48] Gage cites Gen 9:20–27 and entitles it "The Fall Renewed":

> The structural and literary correspondence between the story of Noah's sin and the record of Adam's Fall is striking. Noah's transgression begins with a vineyard (Gen 9:20) while Adam's sin is set in a garden (Gen 3:1). Noah drank of the fruit of the vine while Adam ate of the fruit of the tree (Gen 9:20; 3:2), both being acts of deliberate disobedience resulting in the sinner's awareness of shameful nakedness (Gen 9:21; 3:7). While Noah's nakedness was covered by his eldest sons (Gen 9:23), Adam's nakedness was covered by God (Gen 3:32), and both the sin of Noah and the sin of Adam issued into a fearful curse and enduring division in their respective seed (Gen 9:25; 3:15). In both accounts the narrative moves from the sin of the father to the resulting blessing and cursing of the seed and finally to the genealogical development (Genesis 10 and 5). The authorial intention to relate the story of Noah's sin to Adam's Fall is literarily evident in the wordplay in Gen 9:20 (cf. אִישׁ הָאֲדָמָה with אָדָם in Gen 2:7) and in the parallel of Gen 9:24 ("Noah awoke," i.e., by metonymy, his "eyes were opened," cf. Gen 3:7a).[49]

John Sailhamer takes a similar view. He sees the author's purpose in placing this pericope here as a working out of the plan "of casting the Flood narrative as a recursion of the Creation account."

> The author's intent is to point to the similarities of Noah and Adam. He wants to show even here, too, after the salvation from the Flood, that human enjoyment of God's good gifts could not be sustained. Like Adam, Noah sinned, and the effects of that sin were to be felt in the generations of sons and daughters to follow. As in chapter 3, the effect of Noah's sin is seen in his "nakedness" (cf. 2:25; 3:7). When read in the context of the events of the Garden of Eden (chap. 3), the allusive details of Noah's drunkenness become quite transparent. In a subtle parody of humanity's original state ("They were both naked and not ashamed," 2:25), Noah in his drunkenness "uncovered himself in his tent."[50]

The author of Genesis clearly intended to link Noah to Adam, and Gage's summary, under the heading of "The New Adam," is clear and cogent; and compelling evidence for the connection is reflected in the verbatim repetition to Noah in Gen 9 of the commission and blessing given to Adam in Gen 1.[51]

However, the idea that Noah is like Adam in a second fall is forced. This fact is evident in that Gage can offer, in contrast to the dramatic verbatim repetition noted above, only one weak wordplay in Gen 9:20, a comparison of הָאֲדָמָה with אָדָם in Gen 2:7.[52] Sailhamer's evidence is quite sparse as well: the notation of the phrase "God planted" (וַיִּטַּע in 2:8) and Noah "planted" (וַיִּטַּע in 9:20) and the "subtle parody" of the description "They were both naked and not ashamed" (2:25) in the "drunk" Noah's "uncovering himself in his tent" (9:21).

The weakness of the connection between Adam and Noah, at this point, is further demonstrated when two verses that are often linked are juxtaposed:

וַתִּפָּקַחְנָה עֵינֵי שְׁנֵיהֶם וַיֵּדְעוּ כִּי עֵירֻמִּם הֵם (Gen 3:7)
וַיִּיקֶץ נֹחַ מִיֵּינוֹ וַיֵּדַע אֵת אֲשֶׁר־עָשָׂה־לוֹ בְּנוֹ הַקָּטָן (Gen 9:24)

And they were opened, the eyes of the two of them,
and *they knew* that they were naked. (Gen 3:7)
And he awoke, Noah, from his wine,
and *he knew* what his youngest son had done to him. (Gen 9:24)

The only similarity at all is in the repetition of one verb "to know." While the issue of nakedness is the connection most often suggested here, Noah's realization (יָדַע) had nothing to do with discovering his own nakedness; rather it had to do with his realizing what his son had done to him. In fact, the term עֶרְוַת does not even appear here, and even if it had, it would not have paralleled the term for nakedness in Gen 3 (עֵירֻמִּם).

D. Uncovered and Naked?

The text as a whole seems to quite deliberately disassociate nakedness in any negative sense from Noah in that the term עֶרְוַת is only used to refer to him in an indirect way. Verse 21 reads simply, "He uncovered himself." The word for "nakedness" does not appear.[53] Nakedness is an issue for the sons, not for Noah.[54] It only becomes an issue for them because of Ham's act. Ham is the one who sees the nakedness of his father (וַיַּרְא ... אֵת עֶרְוַת אָבִיו); Noah does not see his own nakedness. Shem and Japheth put clothing on their shoulders, walked backwards, covered the nakedness of their father (אֵת עֶרְוַת אֲבִיהֶם), and turned their faces backward so they did not see the nakedness of their father (וְעֶרְוַת אֲבִיהֶם לֹא רָאוּ).

E. To Uncover Nakedness?

One other issue related to the subject of nakedness in this passage should be noted. In the broader discussion, the prominent use of more common forms of the verb גָּלָה with the term for nakedness, עֶרְוַת, comes into consideration. These uses consistently describe the action of one person toward, or against, another, and the clause serves as an idiom for sexual intercourse.[55] However, since the verb and substantive do not appear in any direct syntactical relationship in this context and since Noah's actions here are solitary (reflected in the use of a reflexive verb), the focus of the discussion really is on Ham and his act of "seeing" Noah's nakedness (וַיַּרְא ... אֵת עֶרְוַת אָבִיו).[56] In this discussion, the character of Noah is not really at issue.

F. Summary

The evidence suggests that nothing in the immediate pericope, in the literary context of the book of Genesis, or in the broader canonical context indicates that Noah's nakedness should be assessed negatively. It is becoming more clear that any negative assessment grows out of a prior assumption that Noah's "drunkenness" was the first sin, which then produced the second sin, "nakedness." Therefore, if the first assumption cannot stand, the weakness of the second surely lies exposed.

If the negative assessments of Noah's nakedness are to be rejected, what can be said, finally, about the matter? The best answer is, apparently, very little, since this reflects the emphasis of the text itself. Noah's state can legitimately be seen as a natural and harmless result of his drinking of wine to "full satisfaction." He simply went to sleep inside his own tent and uncovered himself as he slept. The suggestion is validated at least partially by v. 24: "and Noah woke up."[57] The description is an example of typical economy in Hebrew narrative; the uncovered state of Noah is mentioned only because it becomes important as a result of Ham's actions.

III. The Characterization of Noah

A. Character Analysis

This study aims to address the issue of how one evaluates Noah's character. The renewed interest in studying the Bible as literature in recent years provides more basis for treating the subject at hand—the formal analysis of characterization in narrative. In applying this methodology to the study, the models of Shimon Bar-Efrat and Robert Alter, scholars who have led the way in popularizing an appreciation of the literary art of the Bible, are adopted.[58]

B. Principles of Characterization

Bar-Efrat suggests that the techniques of characterization may be either direct or indirect. He depicts the direct shaping of characters as occurring either by a description of their outward appearance or by statements about their inner personality, with the latter being more important than the former. In addition, those direct statements that refer to character traits are more important than are those that refer to mental states. One reason such direct statements are important in biblical narrative is that they are relatively rare, so that "the trait noted by the narrator is always extremely important in the development of the plot." In addition, if that direct characterization is attributed to God, it should be considered to have "absolute validity."[59]

Alter cast his description of characterization in terms of a "scale of means, in ascending order of explicitness and certainty, for conveying information about the motives, the attitudes, [and] the moral nature of characters." That scale ranges, on the lower end, from reported actions and appearances, to direct speech of the main character or of other characters about him or her, to reports of inner speech ("conscious intentions"), to a narrator's "explicit statement" about a character, at the top end. What one can know about the character in question then also ranges from inference, on the low end of the scale, to "the weighing of claims" in the middle, to "relative certainty" with inner speech, to the narrator's "explicit statement" at the top end, which is to be "accorded certainty."[60] The importance for Alter of this latter aspect of characterization is that the omniscient biblical narrator usually "displays his omniscience with a drastic selectivity" and only on occasion chooses "to privilege us with the knowledge of what God thinks of a particular character or action."[61]

C. Direct Characterization of Noah

The biblical description of Noah contains striking examples of direct statements of characterization. In Gen 6:8 the narrator indicates that, in contrast to the sorry state of the people in general, "Noah found favor in the eyes of the Lord." Although that statement might be ambiguous,[62] the narrator leaves no doubt about what is meant by adding in 6:9 a clear and comprehensive statement, bounded by a subtle inclusio of "Noah": "Noah was a righteous man, blameless in his generation; with God he walked, Noah." This description reverberates with other biblical portrayals of people of extraordinary character, linking Noah with Abraham, the righteous one (Gen 15:6); with Job, the blameless one (Job 1:1, 8; 2:3; Ezek 14:14, 20); and with Enoch, the one who walked with God (Gen 5:22). These associations clearly constitute "unimpeachable accolades in biblical language."[63]

While the above statements are the narrator's observations about Noah, they are to be understood as equated with the Lord's assessment of Noah (not simply insights based on the narrator's omniscience) because the content of v. 9 explains the content of v. 8. Moreover, what is strongly implied here is clearly stated in Gen 7:1, when the Lord says, "You I have seen righteous before me in this generation."

At least one statement about Noah fits into the middle range of Alter's scale. In Gen 5:29, Lamech says of Noah, "This one will comfort us from our work and from the toiling labor of our hands, because of the ground which the Lord cursed." Although the implication is positive for the character of Noah, its significance only becomes clearer when considered with characterization from the lower range, namely, the report of actions (Gen 8:20–22).

D. Indirect Characterization of Noah

As is to be expected, indirect techniques of characterization occur more commonly than the direct techniques. Bar-Efrat writes, "Whereas the importance of the direct ways of shaping the characters lies in their quality (the fact that they are clear and unequivocal), that of the indirect ways lies in their quantity."[64] The indirect technique that abounds in the characterization of Noah is reported actions; and those reported actions that are most prominent—due to the setting of wickedness, corruption, and violence—are reports of Noah's obedience to the Lord's commands. The first occurrence, bounded by another inclusio, occurs in Gen 6:22. In response to the Lord's command to build an ark, the narrator indicates, "And he did, Noah, according to all which God commanded him, thus he did." Similar descriptions occur in Gen 7:5, 7–9, 13–16, along with a less direct statement in Gen 8:15–19.

Noah is next described at worship (Gen 8:20). After leaving the ark, Noah built an altar to the Lord and offered burnt offerings on it. As is typical, the narrator does not offer direct evaluation of the action, but the description of the Lord's response indicates that Noah's actions were desired and approved. In fact, the positive nature of Noah's action is made clear in that the Lord's response apparently mitigated the curse that had been placed on the ground because of Adam and Eve's sin (see Gen 3:17). In addition, it fulfilled the prediction Lamech had made about Noah's destiny when he named him (Gen 5:29).

What follows in Gen 9 can be seen as directly linked to the content of the latter part of Gen 8 and is also reflective of the Lord's approval of Noah and his actions. The Lord will not again curse; on the contrary, the Lord will bless.[65] In addition, a part of that blessing is a covenant established with Noah and his family (9:8–17). The importance of this covenant, in light of the current subject, is obvious in some of the literary qualities of the passage describing its establishment. First, the event is characterized by the Lord's direct speech to Noah (cf. 6:13; 7:1; 8:15). The account of that direct speech constitutes an inclusio, marking off the pericope. In addition, the body of the section is peppered with first-person statements of the Lord to Noah (cf. 9:9, 11–12, 15).

With the exception of the passage that is the focus of the study, two other reported actions occur. The first is Noah's cursing of Canaan and his blessing of Shem and Japheth. With the earlier depiction of the Lord (who did not curse but then blessed), the logical assumption is that Noah functions in a positive role—indeed, in a role like that of God—as he himself now curses and blesses. The last reported action for Noah is that he died (9:29). Although the narrator offers no evaluative comment, the fact that Noah lived 350 years after the flood (9:28) apparently excludes the idea that any of his actions precipitated a judgment of God that would have shortened a normally expected life span.[66]

E. The Character of Noah

In summary, Noah is described positively in the strongest possible fashion—in direct statements by the narrator and by God (statements "accorded certainty")[67]—and these statements are never contradicted or rejected by any other direct statements. Since these statements carry the most weight in determining character, it is expected that all other information about the person in question will be consistent with these direct assertions. In this case, all the reported action, besides that of the text in question, reflects or implies a positive assessment of Noah. When the evidence from the substance of the study, which supports a positive assessment of Noah's actions in Gen 9:20–27, is brought into consideration, the conclusion is clear. From the perspective of character analysis, the positive reading of Gen 9:20–27 is expected, and it confirms the overall positive assessment of the character of Noah in the larger narrative.

IV. Summary and Conclusions

The assessment of the person and character of Noah in the larger narrative is overwhelmingly positive. Noah is the one righteous exception in an extremely wicked generation. God chose him to be the instrument through which the creation is saved from total destruction. After the flood, he appears as a new Adam, blessed of God and charged to "be fruitful and multiply, fill the earth" (9:1). God affirmed to Noah that he would not curse the ground again. Moreover, he made a covenant with him and promised no future similar destruction of the world.

When Noah planted a vineyard that produced grapes for wine, he demonstrated that indeed the curse, which had made getting food from the soil difficult, was no longer in effect as before. When he drank the wine, he was realizing and enjoying God's blessings; when he "drank to full contentment," he was celebrating God's good gift.

When Noah uncovered himself, he was not in public, and thus his "nakedness" was not "folly." We might even ask, "If a man cannot get naked in the privacy of his own tent, where, pray tell, could he get naked?" His uncovered state would never have been revealed had it not been for Ham's actions, which exposed no shameful state of Noah; rather, they exposed the shameful state of Ham's own character.

Noah eventually is the one who pronounces both the blessing of God on two of his sons and the curse of God on the other. His actions indicate not a diminished stature and role due to failure but an enhanced stature and role, emulating the pattern of God in the earlier narrative. He then dies at a ripe old age. Consequently, the positive assessment of the character of Noah remains unbroken.

Notes

I am grateful to two colleagues, Harold Mosley and David M. Howard Jr., who took the time to review this essay. The latter actually did a close reading of two different drafts. Also, my secretary Julie Hager did an excellent job proofreading. The resulting work has been enriched because of their observations and suggestions, although any deficiencies remain my own.

The Scripture quotations in this article are my own translation unless otherwise noted.

[1] Chaim Potok, *In the Beginning* (New York: Fawcett Crest, 1975), 283–84.

[2] For example, Rashi, *Commentaries on the Pentateuch* (trans. Chaim Pearl; New York: W. W. Norton, 1970), 34–37; *Ibn Ezra's Commentary on the Pentateuch: Genesis (Bereshit)* (trans. and anno. H. Norman Strickman and Arthur M. Silver; New York: Menorah, 1988), 124–31; *b. Sanh.* 70a, 108a.

[3] See *b. Sanh.* 70a (ca. A.D. 400–600), which reflects the rabbis' view that Noah should have known better, since Adam's sin was caused by wine; and *b. Sanh.* 108a, which reflects both negative and positive assessments. Rashi, *Commentaries,* 34, reflects the negative idea of the Talmud.

[4] Examples of these are John Skinner, *A Critical and Exegetical Commentary on Genesis* (ICC, 2d ed.; Edinburgh: T&T Clark, 1930), 181–82; W. Malcom Clark, "The Righteousness of Noah," *VT* 21 (1971): 261–80; Gerhard von Rad, *Genesis: A Commentary* (OTL, rev. ed.; trans. J. H. Marks; Philadelphia: Westminster, 1972), 116–39; and Claus Westermann, *Genesis 1–11: A Commentary* (trans. John J. Scullion; Minneapolis: Augsburg, 1984), 395–96, 482. The latter two lack any stress on a supposed contradiction in the character of Noah in the sources.

[5] See, e.g., Gordon J. Wenham, *Genesis 1–15* (WBC 1; Waco: Word, 1987), 198–99. Wenham, who is somewhat ambivalent on the matter as he dialogues with Westermann's position, still stresses the negative possibilities more than the positive. He uses terminology such as the "dangers of wine," the deprecation of "self-exposure," "publicly demeaning," and so forth. See also Kenneth A. Mathews, *Genesis 1–11:26* (NAC 1A; Nashville: Broadman & Holman, 1996), 412, who does the same, but more forcefully, with more graphic terminology. He uses phrases such as "the deflating debacle of Noah's drunkenness," "that sordid incident," and "Noah's drunken affair." John H. Sailhamer, *The Pentateuch as Narrative: A Biblical Theological Commentary* (Grand Rapids: Zondervan, 1992), 129, promotes a similar view but does so on the basis of narrative similarity to the Adam and Eve incident. He captions the section "Noah's Drunkenness" and indicates that Noah "ate of the fruit of his orchard and became naked." In doing so, he followed the sinful pattern of Adam and Eve who ate the fruit and became aware of their nakedness.

[6] I am convinced that traditional translations and interpretations have been influenced by modern cultural concerns about alcohol abuse, the specter of public drunkenness, and the damage caused by habitual addiction to alcohol. I myself share those concerns, but reading those modern concerns back into the ancient setting is a mistake. Struggling with this text reminds us that we must properly handle the cultural aspects of any biblical text. Considering this fact should help readers to understand that, by my treatment of this text, I am not making a case for the recreational use of wine or any other alcoholic beverage.

[7] See Wenham, *Genesis,* 155, 151, for the translations; then see Mathews, *Genesis,* 416–17, for a summary of the issues.

[8] Westermann, *Genesis,* 487; Mathews, *Genesis,* 61; Paul P. Saydon, "The Inceptive Imperfect in Hebrew and the Verb הֵחֵל, 'To Begin,' " *Bib* 35 (1954): 43–50; Victor P. Hamilton, *The Book of Genesis: Chapters 1–17* (NICOT; Grand Rapids: Eerdmans, 1990), 320.

[9] C. F. Keil and F. Delitzsch, *The Pentateuch* (vol. 1 of *Biblical Commentary on the Old Testament;* trans. James Martin; Grand Rapids: Eerdmans, 1949), 155; U. Cassuto, *From Noah to Abraham* (pt. 2 of *A Commentary on the Book of Genesis;* trans. Israel Abrahams; Jerusalem: Magnes, 1964), 158–59; Skinner, *Commentary,* 182; Gesenius read the phrase as predicate but only after omitting the article (GKC 120b).

[10] Keil and Delitzsch, *Pentetuch,* 155; Cassuto, *Noah to Abraham,* 159;

Skinner, *Commentary,* 182; E. A. Speiser, *Genesis* (AB 1; Garden City, N.Y.: Doubleday, 1964), 61.

[11] Speiser, *Genesis,* 182.

[12] Keil and Delitzsch, *Pentetuch,* 155; cf. also von Rad, *Genesis,* 136.

[13] Derek Kidner, *Genesis: An Introduction and Commentary* (TOTC 1; London: Tyndale, 1967; repr., Downers Grove, Ill.: InterVarsity Press, 1967), 103.

[14] See, e.g., Wenham, *Genesis,* 198–99, and Mathews, *Genesis,* 416–17.

[15] See, e.g., Hermann Gunkel, *Genesis* (trans. Mark E. Biddle; Macon: Mercer University Press, 1997), 79–80; and Westermann, *Genesis,* 487–88.

[16] See the KJV, NASB (1995), RSV, NRSV, NKJV, NAB, NLT.

[17] Abraham Even-Shoshan, ed., *A New Concordance of the Bible* (Jerusalem: Kiryat Sefer, 1989), 1145.

[18] John J. Davis, *Paradise to Prison: Studies in Genesis* (Salem, Wis.: Sheffield, 1998), 128.

[19] O. Palmer Robertson, *The Books of Nahum, Habakkuk, and Zephaniah* (NICOT; Grand Rapids: Eerdmans, 1990), 201.

[20] The Hiphil of שָׁתָה is related to the form שָׁקָה by suppletion. For the terminology, see *IBHS* 23.2.1b. For this verb, see Robert H. O'Connell, "שׁתה," *NIDOTTE* 4:260.

[21] See, e.g., J. J. M. Roberts, *Nahum, Habakkuk, and Zephaniah* (OTL; Louisville: Westminster John Knox, 1991), 124.

[22] "ערל," *HALOT* 2:885–86.

[23] "עָרֵל," BDB 790c.

[24] See, e.g., NRSV, NEB, GNB, NIV (mg.); cf. LXX, Qumran, Aquila, Syriac, Vulgate.

[25] See Roberts, *Nahum,* 125.

[26] Ibid., 124.

[27] Two other occurrences are found in Jer 48:26 and 1 Sam 1:14. The Jeremiah verse contains part of an oracle in which the judgment of Moab is depicted as drunkenness that will cause Moab to be degraded and become a laughingstock: the Lord will make the Moabites drunk (הַשְׁכִּירֻהוּ); they will

wallow in vomit and become an object of ridicule. The 1 Samuel verse records Eli's response to Hannah when he thought she was drunk: "How long will you make yourself drunk (תִּשְׁתַּכָּרִין)? Put away your wine." Obviously, Eli's action was based on the fact that Hannah was at Shiloh, a holy place. Perhaps the context—his sons were committing a grave sin against the holy place and against God—also contributed to his concern. Neither of these texts has any direct relevance to the study.

[28] Isa 29:9; 49:26; Jer 25:27; and Nah 3:11 describe images in which Jerusalem, her leaders, and/or enemies of Jerusalem, of Israel, or of the Lord will "become drunk" as a result of judgment falling on them.

[29] Claus Westermann, *Lamentations: Issues and Interpretation* (trans. Charles Muenchow; Minneapolis: Fortress, 1994), 206

[30] Delbert R. Hillers, *Lamentations* (AB 7A; Garden City, N.Y.: Doubleday, 1972), 93.

[31] The verb גָּלָה does appear in v. 22, which suggests a synonymous relationship with the verb עָרָה.

[32] Michael V. Fox, *The Song of Songs and the Ancient Egyptian Love Songs* (Madison: University of Wisconsin Press, 1985), 139.

[33] Othmar Keel, *The Song of Songs* (CC; trans. Frederick J. Gaiser; Minneapolis: Fortress, 1994), 183–84.

[34] The infinitive absolutes are translated on the pattern of the perfect form, which opens the verse. See Paul Joüon, *A Grammar of Biblical Hebrew* (trans. and rev. T. Muraoka; 2 vols.; Rome: Pontifical Biblical Institute, 1991), 2:430–31; and *IBHS* 35.5.2.

[35] Carol L. Meyers and Eric M. Meyers, *Haggai, Zechariah 1–8: A New Translation with Introduction and Commentary* (AB 25B; Garden City, N.Y.: Doubleday, 1987), 26.

[36] Hans Walter Wolff, *Haggai: A Commentary* (trans. Margaret Kohl; Minneapolis: Augsburg, 1988), 30.

[37] KJV, RSV, NRSV, NEB.

[38] NIV, NASB, NLT.

[39] S. R. Driver, *The Book of Genesis* (WC; London: Methuen & Co., 1913), 357; see also Keil and Delitzsch, *Pentateuch*, 362; Wenham, *Genesis*, 414, 424.

[40] Keil and Delitzsch, *Pentetuch,* 362.

[41] GNB; cf. Everett Fox, *The Five Books of Moses: A New Translation with Introductions, Commentary, and Notes* (vol. 1 of *The Schocken Bible;* New York: Schocken, 1995), 208: "Then they drank and became drunk with him"; and Robert Alter, *Genesis: Translation and Commentary* (New York: W. W. Norton, 1996), 258: "and they drank, and they got drunk with him."

[42] Alter's comment (*Genesis,* 258) could be seen as possibly implying an ominous quality to the event: "The meeting . . . appears to end on a note of conviviality, which will quickly be reversed in the next scene of the drama Joseph has carefully devised for his brothers."

[43] The psalmist used the same imagery, but he depicted the joy he had received from the Lord as *greater* than that which comes to others when their grain and new wine increase (Ps 4:7 [EVV 4:8]).

[44] The links between Adam and Noah have been noted through the centuries. For modern examples, see the next section and Cassuto, *Noah to Abraham,* 124–26, who seems to have been a major source for Gage. See also Robert W. E. Forrest, "Paradise Lost Again: Violence and Obedience in the Flood Narrative," *JSOT* 62 (1994): 3–18.

[45] Cassuto, *Noah to Abraham,* 160; see also Dwight Young, "Noah," *EncJud* 12:1193, who, against the ancient background, describes Noah's actions as not to be condemned. He says that the text "seems to reflect an ancient attitude that grape culture and the making of wine were essential to civilization. The account also takes for granted that grapes were properly utilized by turning the juice into a fermented drink. Furthermore, Noah's drunkenness is presented in a matter-of-fact manner and not as reprehensible behavior. It is clear that intoxication is not at issue here."

[46] See Isa 3:17; 20:4; 47:3; Hos 2:11–12 [EVV 2:9–10]; Mic 1:11.

[47] *Exod 32:25.* Mathews, *Genesis,* 420, cites this passage with the comment that "nakedness was commonly associated with public misconduct." The Hebrew makes no reference at all to nakedness, notwithstanding the KJV rendering of the verse; cf. NASB, NRSV, NIV.

Exod 20:26. This passage records the Lord's instructions to the people to not go up on the altar by steps, so as not to expose their nakedness. Other passages reflect similar concerns. Exodus 28:42 indicates that the sons of Aaron were to wear linen pants so as to cover their nakedness; and Deut 23:12–14 [EVV 23:13–15] indicates that the people are to take proper precautions because the

Lord walks in their midst and must not see the nakedness of anything. All these passages deal with the particular issue of coming into, or being in, the presence of the Lord or of serving in the presence of the Lord. Not exposing one's nakedness in this situation was only one part of sensible and expected deference before a holy and awesome God. These passages then are not relevant to Noah's situation.

2 Sam 6:16, 20. These verses describe David's exuberant worship before the Lord as the ark was being brought into Jerusalem. It is not clear what those who cite these passages as evidence for condemning Noah's nakedness have in mind, since David rejects Michal's critique, implying that his "naked" state is not wrong. Perhaps they are alluding to Michal's reference to the רֵקִים, "worthless men," to whom she compares David.

2 Sam 10:4–5. This passage records what Hanun the Ammonite did to the representatives David had sent to mourn the loss of Hanun's father. Hanun considered them spies, shaved half their beards, cut off their clothes at the middle, and sent them away. His intent was to humiliate them publicly.

[48] Warren Austin Gage, *The Gospel of Genesis: Studies in Protology and Eschatology* (Winona Lake, Ind.: Carpenter, 1984), 9–11. To be fair, Gage did note that certain correspondences of his might be challenged.

[49] Ibid., 12.

[50] Sailhamer, *Pentateuch as Narrative,* 129.

[51] Gage, *Gospel of Genesis,* 11.

[52] Ibid., 12.

[53] Some modern translations are misleading at this point. For example, both the NAB and the NLT gloss the phrase, "and lay naked."

[54] See Marc Vervenne, "What Shall We Do with the Drunken Sailor? A Critical Re-examination of Genesis 9.20–27," *JSOT* 68 (1995): 45–46, for the suggestion that the LXX translator's word choice reflected an effort to downplay any negative sexual connotations to Noah's nakedness.

[55] Ludwig Koehler and Walter Baumgartner, גלה, *HALOT* 1:192. The Piel stem is most often used. The classic examples of the use of this phrase are the Lev 18 and 20 texts where all the verbs are Piel. The authors rendered the idiom with the modern euphemism "to sleep with."

[56] This phrase is interpreted by many to be equivalent to גִּלָּה עֶרְוַת, "uncovering [the] nakedness [of X]." This equation is problematic. The only time the phrase רָאָה עֶרְוָה appears in the Hebrew Bible with this sense is in Lev 20:17,

and in this verse the phrase is used twice: once in reference to the man in question and once in reference to the woman in question. The sense of the phrases is qualified by the inclusion of the parallel phrase גִּלָּה עֶרְוָה. None of the other occurrences have such emphasis or connotation. See Frederick W. Bassett "Noah's Nakedness and the Curse of Canaan: A Case of Incest?" *VT* 21 (1971): 232–35, and Gene Rice, "The Curse that Never Was (Genesis 9:18–27)," *JRT* 29, no. 1 (1972): 11–12.

[57] Cassuto, *Noah to Abraham,* 161, explains that Noah's nakedness resulted from the sleep that came from the "drunkenness"; Rice offers a similar but more specific explanation: "The heat from the wine would have caused Noah to uncover himself" ("Curse," 23 n. 95).

[58] Shimon Bar-Efrat, *Narrative Art in the Bible* (trans. Dorothea Shefer-Vanson; JSOTSup 70; Sheffield: Almond, 1989; repr., Sheffield: Sheffield Academic Press, 1997); Robert Alter, *The Art of Biblical Narrative* (New York: Basic, 1981).

[59] Bar-Efrat, *Narrative Art,* 48–54.

[60] Alter, *Art of Biblical Narrative,* 116–17.

[61] Ibid., 126.

[62] See A. N. Barnard, "Was Noah a Righteous Man?" *Theology* 74 (1971): 311–12.

[63] Forrest, "Paradise Lost Again," 10.

[64] Bar-Efrat, *Narrative Art,* 64. Two further observations from Bar-Efrat are helpful. First, he suggested that "the quality denoted through direct characterization almost always emerges indirectly, . . . through either the actions or speech of the character involved or through both of them" (53). Second, he noted, "It is in the nature of the indirect method that characters are not defined comprehensively, but that their personalities emerge gradually from the totality of their appearances and actions during the course of the narrative" (89).

[65] The Lord's blessing of Noah was discussed above.

[66] Contra Sailhamer, *Pentateuch as Narrative,* 119–20, who saw in the simple statement "and he died" evidence that the narrator was, in Gen 9:18–27, depicting Noah as not living in a way pleasing to God.

[67] Alter, *Art of Biblical Narrative,* 117.

Judah's Argument for Life as Wise Speech

David A. Diewert

The book of Proverbs often describes the wise in relation to their speech, whether it be in terms of listening to the admonition of others (1:5; 9:8–9; 10:8; 12:15; 15:31; 18:15; 21:11) or in offering words of their own (12:18; 13:14; 14:3; 15:2, 7; 16:21, 23; 22:17; 24:23). A person marked by wisdom speaks judiciously and persuasively (16:23), while the utterances of the wise bring healing and life to those who receive them (13:14). Proverbs itself, of course, contains many wise sayings—practical insight into general life situations and prudent advice on matters of social and personal relationships. Yet the speech described in Proverbs is detached from the immediacy and particularity of historical existence. What this collection of proverbial wisdom does not offer is an instance of wise speech expressed as a sustained argumentation embedded in a specific, dramatic moment. It asserts that the speech of the wise is persuasive and life-giving, but it does not allow us to hear such speech in an actual historical setting. Consequently, in order to observe wise speech in action, one must turn to the narrative portions of the Old Testament.

There are a handful of characters in the Old Testament narratives who are designated "wise" *(ḥāḵām)* either by the narrator or by some other person in the story. Often the characters' wisdom is demonstrated within the story through the speeches they make; specifically, this wisdom is evident both in the speech's artful design as well as in its persuasive effect upon the audience. In most of these cases, the wise person's speech is marked by a keen discernment of the various facets of a situation, and it is rhetorically powerful enough to alter the speaker's circumstances in some way, usually by moving it away from impending disaster and toward life. So, for example, Pharaoh calls Joseph "discerning and wise" *(nāḇôn wĕḥākām)* not only because Joseph can interpret the dreams, but also because of his proposal for avoiding the coming famine (Gen 41:33, 39). The speech of the wise woman of Tekoa is rhetorically persuasive and moves David to bring Absalom back to Jerusalem (2 Sam 14:1–20), while the wise woman of Abel convinces Joab to spare the innocent inhabitants of her city by offering him the head of Sheba (2 Sam 20:14–22). Solomon expresses his newly gained wisdom in the case of the two women who each claim a single living son as her own: using the threat of death, he ends up saving the child and revealing the true mother (1 Kgs 3:16–27). In all of these instances, wise people use persuasive speech to change a situation from the threat of death or danger to the preservation of life.[1]

In this light I would like to consider Judah's climactic speech before the vizier of Egypt, Joseph himself, as an instance of wise discourse (Gen 44:18–34). His speech reflects a vivid awareness of the potentially destructive circumstance in which the sons of Jacob are enmeshed; but by his persuasive argument, he is able to move the dire situation to a place of life and provision for the family. The task of this article is to trace the contours of Judah's speech and show how it effectively dispels the threat of death for the patriarchal family. In so doing, I hope to demonstrate how his intervention illustrates the principles of wise speech found in Proverbs.

I. Setting the Stage

To appreciate the rhetorical thrust of Judah's speech, we must review the events leading up to it. Twenty years earlier, Joseph's brothers—because of their hatred of Joseph and their desire to sabotage his dreams (37:1–37)—sold him to merchants bound for Egypt. Now the brothers are forced by a severe famine to journey to Egypt to purchase grain (42:1–5). Joseph has since risen to heights of power within the Egyptian administration and, at the time of his encounter with Judah, has been given the task of overseeing the distribution of the grain. When Joseph's brothers appear before him, he immediately recognizes them, but they do not recognize him; he conceals his identity from them and makes sure that this advantage is maintained (42:7–8). This discrepancy constitutes a major element in the relational dynamics between Joseph and his brothers throughout the central section of the Joseph story (42:1–44:34). As a result, the encounters between the brothers and Joseph in Egypt are always reverberating on a number of levels at once. So while Judah delivers his lengthy speech, believing he is addressing an Egyptian official, Joseph (and the readers) know the familial relationship that exists between himself and the brothers.

Initially Joseph accuses his brothers of being spies who have come to scout out the weakness of the land. He throws all of them into prison, threatening to keep them there and to send only one brother back to fetch Benjamin, the youngest son of the family. Benjamin's presence will somehow verify their story of kinship and so disprove the charge of spying (42:9–17). Three days later, Joseph changes his mind and sends them all back with a full supply of grain, keeping only Simeon with him. He tells them that they can return for their brother Simeon and for more grain only if Benjamin comes with them (42:18–20).[2] Then, unknown to them, Joseph hides the silver with which they purchased the grain in their sacks. They return home to Jacob, discovering the silver along the way (42:27–28). When they recount their experiences to their father, he is greatly distressed, primarily because he fears losing Benjamin as he had lost Joseph, these two being the only sons of Rachel, his favorite, but now deceased, wife (42:36, 38).

Eventually the grain runs out, and Jacob orders his sons to return to Egypt to buy more. They remind him that if Benjamin does not accompany them, their journey will be entirely unsuccessful (43:1–5). Judah then steps forward and pledges himself as Benjamin's guardian, promising to bring him back to his father (43:8–10). The pressure of the famine weighs heavily on the patriarch, and he consents. In order to appease "the man" in Egypt (i.e., Joseph), Jacob sends his sons off with double the amount of silver (half of which was intended to cover what they brought back after their first visit), plus a gift of spices and, of course, Benjamin (43:11–14). Upon the brothers' arrival in Egypt, they explain the previous episode with the silver to Joseph's chief steward in an attempt to clear themselves of any guilt, and they bring forward the gifts. Joseph receives the brothers warmly and sets out a meal for them; moreover, he is moved deeply by the sight of Benjamin (43:27–34).

The morning after the meal he sends the brothers off but orders his steward to put his special silver cup into Benjamin's sack (44:1–2). They depart but are soon overtaken by the steward, who accuses them of theft. They are shocked by the charge and declare that, should the cup be found in their possession, the one who is guilty should be put to death and the others should be taken as slaves (44:6–9). The steward determines instead that the one who is guilty will be enslaved, not killed, and that the rest will be free to return home. Their sacks are searched, and the cup is found in Benjamin's (44:10–12). They are thoroughly dismayed, but rather than going home to their father, the brothers return with Benjamin and the steward to Joseph, who, it seems, is awaiting their arrival (44:13–15). In this scene, Judah speaks for all the brothers. He first accepts their inescapable guilt and then offers himself and his brothers as slaves to the Egyptian lord. Joseph, however, states firmly that this is not necessary; only Benjamin must remain in Egypt as his servant; the rest are free to return to their father in Canaan (44:16–17).[3]

II. Judah's Speech

At this point Judah delivers his crucial speech. The situation he faces is extremely desperate. If the brothers choose to stay in Egypt with Benjamin, as they suggest in their initial declaration of innocence (44:9), the family remaining in Canaan will die of starvation. If they leave Benjamin in Egypt and return home, as the Egyptian official demands (44:17), Jacob will be overcome with grief, hastening his death. Both options will bring death to the family. Judah's speech, therefore, attempts to avoid these fatal options by opening up a new possibility—namely, that the Egyptian official release Benjamin to them and allow them all to return to their father. In order to persuade the official to adopt this plan, Judah must (1) highlight the disaster that looms over the family, (2) subtly convince the Egyptian official of his responsibility in this life-and-death situation, and (3) encourage the official to change his course of action by proposing that he, Judah, stay in Egypt as a slave in Benjamin's place.

The genius of Judah's speech lies in the way he implements his argument. In order to convince the Egyptian of his father's or his family's certain death and to show the significance of the Egyptian's decision, Judah—without overstepping the bounds of his perceived relational subservience[4]—takes up the role of narrator and re-presents the past in a manner that suitably reinforces his central points.[5] In this way he remains inconspicuous in the argument; the past, as he tells it, bears on the present situation in a clear and unmistakable way, yet as narrator his own shaping of the past is covert and subtle, in keeping with biblical narratorial style in general. Furthermore, he leaves his own suggested solution to this deadly conundrum until the very end of his speech, that is, when his addressee would feel most keenly the desperation of the situation. Of course the impact of his argument on his interlocutor is even more powerful than Judah might have imagined, given the familial tie between them.

A. Judah Recounts the Past

Judah's narrative construal of the past encounter between the brothers and the Egyptian official is especially intriguing because it can be compared with the biblical narrator's own presentation of these events (chs. 42–44).[6] Such a comparison clarifies Judah's intention: his version of the past highlights the close bond between Jacob and Benjamin in order to support the contention that permanent separation of father and youngest son would result in the father's certain death. It is this bond that he foregrounds in his retelling; in effect, the "bond" becomes the central focus of his interest point of view.[7] In addition, Judah's construal of the past subtly lays the blame for the threat looming over the father's life on the Egyptian.

Judah's presentation of the past can be divided into two parts. In part one, he describes the brothers' first encounter with the Egyptian official (44:19–23); in part two, he speaks of the subsequent conversation between the brothers and their father, Jacob, back in Canaan (44:24–29). Judah's version of their initial meeting with the Egyptian official consists of a dialogue in which Joseph has three short speeches (44:19, 21, 23), and the brothers speak twice in response to his words (44:20, 22).

Judah's Presentation of the Past	**The Narrator's Presentation of the Past**
"My lord asked his servants, saying, 'Have you a father or a brother?'" (44:19)	When Joseph saw his brothers, he recognized them, but he treated them like strangers and spoke harshly to them. "Where do you come from?" he said. They said, "From the land of Canaan, to buy food." Although Joseph had recognized his brothers, they did not recognize him. Joseph also remembered the dreams that he had dreamed about them. He said to them, "You are spies; you have come to see the nakedness of the land!" (42:7–9)

According to Judah, the Egyptian official initiated the conversation by asking the brothers, "Have you a father or a brother?" In the narrator's own account, Joseph had posed no such question to the brothers. He began rather by asking them where they were from (42:7) and continued by accusing them of being spies come to survey the weakness of the land (42:9). It is the brothers who, of their own accord, volunteer information concerning their family ("We, your servants, are twelve brothers, the sons of a certain man in the land of Canaan; the youngest, however, is now with our father, and one is no more," 42:13), in order to stress their innocence. When the brothers later recount their experiences in Egypt to their father, they do not attribute to the Egyptian lord an inquiry concerning their family situation (42:30–34). It is only when Jacob laments their disclosure of the younger brother's existence that they declare, "The man questioned us carefully about ourselves and our kindred saying, 'Is your father still alive? Have you another brother?'" (43:7). Here, for the first time in the story, this interrogative is attributed to the Egyptian; and it is introduced when the brothers attempt to avoid blame for freely offering information. In Judah's narration, however, this inquiry, placed on the lips of the Egyptian official, serves as the essential focus of his speech: the relationship between father and youngest son.

Judah's Presentation of the Past	The Narrator's Presentation of the Past
"And we said to my lord, 'We have a father, an old man, and a young brother, the child of his old age. His brother is dead; he alone is left of his mother's children, and his father loves him.'" (44:20)	They said to him, "No, my lord; your servants have come to buy food. We are all sons of one man; we are honest men; your servants have never been spies." But he said to them, "No, you have come to see the nakedness of the land!" They said, "We, your servants, are twelve brothers, the sons of a certain man in the land of Canaan; the youngest, however, is now with our father, and one is no more." . . . "But we said to him, 'We are honest men, we are not spies. We are twelve brothers, sons of our father; one is no more, and the youngest is now with our father in the land of Canaan.'" (42:10–13, 31–32)

The brothers' original response to Joseph, as Judah presents it here, is even more interesting. They reply, "We have a father, an old man, and a young child, born in old age. His brother is dead; he alone is left of his mother's children, and his father loves him" (44:20).[8] According to the narrator's previous account, the brothers disclosed without solicitation that they were all brothers, sons of one man in the land of Canaan; that they had a younger brother at home with their father; and that one brother was no more (42:10–11, 13, 31–32). What is noteworthy about Judah's retelling of the past is his portrayal of Jacob as elderly—and therefore as fragile and deserving of respect—as well as his emphasis on the close bond between the patriarch and the young Benjamin. In particular, the brothers had not previously informed the Egyptian official that Benjamin was a child born to their father in his old age, that he was the only remaining son of his mother, and that their father loved him. The addition of these elements serve to heighten the special attachment Jacob has for this particular son. Moreover, although the brothers had been vague about Joseph's disappearance ("the one is no more"),

Judah now states outright, "His brother is dead." With this brother definitively removed, the father's affection rests solely and completely on the one remaining son of his favorite wife. It is also particularly striking that much of the language Judah uses to depict the bond between Benjamin and Jacob (44:20) recalls the earlier description of the bond between Joseph and Jacob (cf. 37:3—*ben/yeleḏ zĕqūnîm,* "son/child of old age"; *ʾāhaḇ,* "he loves"). In this way, one understands that Benjamin, taking the place of the absent Joseph, is the object of his father's special attention. The use of such language, while rhetorically significant within Judah's effort to persuade the Egyptian official, is profoundly moving because it is, unknowingly, addressed to Joseph himself.

Judah's Presentation of the Past	**The Narrator's Presentation of the Past**
"Then you said to your servants, 'Bring him down to me, so that I may set my eyes on him.' We said to my lord, 'The boy cannot leave his father, for if he should leave his father, his father would die.' Then you said to your servants, 'Unless your youngest brother comes down with you, you shall see my face no more.'" (44:21–23)	But Joseph said to them, "It is just as I have said to you; you are spies! Here is how you shall be tested: as Pharaoh lives, you shall not leave this place unless your youngest brother comes here! . . . And bring your youngest brother to me. Thus your words will be verified, and you shall not die." . . . "'Bring your youngest brother to me, and I shall know that you are not spies but honest men. Then I will release your brother to you, and you may trade in the land.'" (42:14–15, 20, 34)

The Egyptian's response, as Judah tells it, was to demand that the brothers bring Benjamin to Egypt so that he might set his eyes on him. In the narrator's original account, however, they were to bring Benjamin to Egypt to prove that they were not spies, as the official had accused (42:15, 20, 34). Note that Judah does not refer to the official's accusation of spying, since this would detract from the positive rhetorical intention of his speech. Again it becomes clear that Judah is not addressing the brothers' role but rather the tie between father and son and the strain put on it by the Egyptian's demand. The brothers' reaction to the official's order (an order that now, without the motivation of determining innocence, seems quite capricious) was to make its consequences explicit: the youngest son is not able to leave his father, for this would result in the father's death (44:22).

Jacob's love for Benjamin and Benjamin's presence with him are life itself: if father and son are separated, the father will die.

It is clear that the Egyptian's insistence on Benjamin's being brought to him threatens the very life of the father. Yet in spite of this warning, according to Judah, the official reiterated his demand to see Benjamin, declaring that the brothers will not gain an audience with him again, and thus not have access to the food supply, unless they return with their young brother (44:23). It is noteworthy that the official is not just asking to see Benjamin (cf. 43:3–5) but is making the latter's presence obligatory for the survival of the family. In Judah's version of the past, then, the Egyptian's intense determination to see the youngest brother and the resulting threat of death that hangs over the family is brought clearly into focus. Against the deep love of father for son, the Egyptian's seemingly groundless request appears fatally cruel.

Judah's Presentation of the Past

"When we went back to your servant my father we told him the words of my lord. And when our father said, 'Go again, buy us a little food,' we said, 'We cannot go down. Only if our youngest brother goes with us, will we go down; for we cannot see the man's face unless our youngest brother is with us.' " (44:24–26)

The Narrator's Presentation of the Past

And when they had eaten up the grain that they had brought from Egypt, their father said to them, "Go again, buy us a little more food." But Judah said to him, "The man solemnly warned us, saying, 'You shall not see my face unless your brother is with you.' If you will send our brother with us, we will go down and buy you food; but if you will not send him, we will not go down, for the man said to us, 'You shall not see my face, unless your brother is with you.' " Israel said, "Why did you treat me so badly as to tell the man that you had another brother?" They replied, "The man questioned us carefully about ourselves and our kindred, saying, Is your father still alive? Have you another brother?' What we told him was in answer to these questions. Could we in any way know that he would say, 'Bring your brother down'?" (43:2–7)

Judah's Argument for Life as Wise Speech

Judah continues his rhetorical mission in the second phase of his narrative. After making a quick transitional statement locating the scene back in Canaan ("When we went back to your servant my father we told him the words of my lord," 44:24), Judah abbreviates the narrator's story considerably. There is no reference to the discovery of the money in the sacks, the anxiety of the brothers, Reuben's rejected offer to look after Benjamin, or Jacob's intense grief. Instead, Judah focuses his report on the discussion between Jacob and the brothers at the outset of their second trip to Egypt. Jacob instructs his sons to return to Egypt to purchase grain (44:25 par. 43:2), and they respond by reiterating the Egyptian lord's demands. This part of Judah's version is very close to what the narrator presented earlier (43:4–5).[9] The one word that appears uniquely in Judah's presentation of the brothers' response to Jacob is the verb *yāḵōl,* "be able" (cf. 44:22), with the negative, which stresses the impossibility of their going down to Egypt without Benjamin. The balanced structure of the brothers' speech as told by Judah captures unmistakably the crisis Jacob faces: the starvation of the family on the one hand or the separation and potential loss of the son he loves on the other.[10]

Judah's Presentation of the Past	**The Narrator's Presentation of the Past**
"Then your servant my father said to us, 'You know that my wife bore me two sons; one left me, and I said, Surely he has been torn to pieces; and I have never seen him since. If you take this one also from me, and harm comes to him, you will bring down my gray hairs in sorrow to Sheol.'" (44:27–29)	Then their father Israel said to them, "If it must be so, then do this: take some of the choice fruits of the land in your bags, and carry them down as a present to the man—a little balm and a little honey, gum, resin, pistachio nuts, and almonds. Take double the money with you. Carry back with you the money that was returned in the top of your sacks; perhaps it was an oversight. Take your brother also, and be on your way again to the man; may God Almighty grant you mercy before the man, so that he may send back your other brother and Benjamin. As for me, if I am bereaved of my children, I am bereaved." (43:11–14)

Judah now formulates Jacob's response to the present dilemma in a way that differs significantly from Jacob's speeches reported earlier (see 43:1–14). According to the narrator, Jacob first laments the fact that his sons divulged so much family information (v. 6); and then, after being persuaded by Judah to send Benjamin with them, he consents to let them go, devising a plan to placate "the man" with the return of the silver and a gift of spices (vv. 11–14). He even concludes his speech with a wish for the mercy of El Shaddai, resigning himself to the possibility of losing yet another son (vv. 3–14).

In Judah's account, however, Jacob delivers a speech that reinforces the bond between himself and Benjamin, expressing to his sons what was for them common knowledge: "You know that my wife bore me two sons; one left me, and I said, 'Surely' he has been torn to pieces; and I have never seen him since. If you take this one also from me, and harm comes to him, you will bring down my gray hairs in sorrow to Sheol'" (44:27–29). It does not make much sense for Jacob to remind his sons of this family history. It is understandable, however, for this information to be intended for the ears of the Egyptian official now before Judah. Through the voice of the father himself, Judah stresses the bond that exists between father and youngest son, validating the brothers' earlier argument (44:22) that separation without return would mean their father's death. Furthermore, the previous points voiced by the brothers in Judah's rendition of the past (i.e., the importance of Benjamin for his father derives from the identity of Benjamin's mother and the loss of Benjamin's older brother) are emphasized again, though in the mouth of Jacob there is some elaboration in the details (e.g., "surely he has been torn to pieces," 37:33). The father fears he will lose Benjamin as well, and such misfortune would send him to the grave.

Judah ends the narrative portion of his speech by speaking of the father's certain death should Benjamin fail to return. Given this re-presentation of the past, the Egyptian lord is the one on whom Jacob's life depends. Both his demand for Benjamin's presence and his intention to keep him in Egypt threaten to bring death to their father. The irony of the situation, of course, is that Jacob is the Egyptian official's father as well! In addition, while Joseph knows more than Judah thinks he does regarding his father and his family, Joseph now hears for the first time elements of the story of the family back in Canaan. Jacob's final words—which among other things capture his grief over the disappearance of his favored son, Joseph ("one left me, and I said, Surely he has been torn to pieces; and I have never seen him since")—certainly make an impression on Judah's addressee.

B. Judah's Rhetorical Climax

As Judah moves toward the climax of his speech, Joseph is reminded of his father's love for him, expressed as deep grief over his disappearance—grief that has been redirected as an affection for his younger brother, Benjamin. He is also faced with the knowledge that his current demands will precipitate his father's death. Judah drives this latter point home, summing up the thrust of his speech thus far: "Now therefore, when I come to your servant my father and the boy is not with us, then, as his life is bound up in the boy's life, when he sees that the boy is not with us, he will die; and your servants will bring down the gray hairs of your servant our father with sorrow to Sheol" (44:30–31). That the life of the father is intimately bound up with the life of Benjamin is voiced repeatedly in Judah's selective retelling of the past. Although the weight of the decision remains fully in Joseph's hands, Judah here shies away from directly placing responsibility on him ("*your servants* will bring down the gray hairs of your servant our father with sorrow to Sheol"). As a narrator, Judah can implicitly accuse the Egyptian of bringing about the father's downfall by the way he presents the official's groundless demands to see Benjamin (44:23); but in a deft move as he directly addresses "the man" himself, he puts the blame for their father's destruction upon the sons themselves, perhaps in an effort to respect the status difference between speaker and addressee while arousing pity for their precarious though undeserved predicament. The essential point of Judah's speech is the inevitability of Jacob's death should Benjamin not return to him. The way Judah re-presents the past makes this conclusion inescapable; any other outcome than Jacob's demise is unthinkable.

With the relational lines clearly drawn in these ways, and given the mood of death that hovers over the scene, Judah is now ready to offer a solution (44:32–34). His proposal is that he remain as the Egyptian's slave in Benjamin's place so that the boy can return to his father. This proposal is neatly sandwiched between two segments that serve to ground it both in the past (v. 32) and the future (v. 34).[11] The suggestion makes good sense in light of Judah's past pledge to his father that he would bring the boy back to him (see 43:8–10) and in light of the future misfortune that he would witness should he return without his younger brother. Judah had omitted any reference to his past pledge in his recounting of the story because it was not rhetorically useful at that point. Now he brings this piece of information forward as a way of substantiating his proposal. His past obligation to return the boy makes him the most likely candidate for voluntary slavery. The entire speech, then, ends with a reference once again to Jacob's ominous future and the disaster about to engulf him. This leaves the Egyptian official in the position of determining whether the family patriarch lives or dies. The speech has a powerful effect because Judah has made this the only imaginable outcome; and now the Egyptian, Joseph, is faced with the decision of bringing life or death to this—his own—family.

Overcome with emotion, Joseph reveals himself to his brothers and immediately asks about the state of his father: "I am Joseph. Is my father still alive?" (45:3) This is not a real question requiring an actual answer. He had asked it previously—"He inquired about their welfare, and said, 'Is your father well, the old man of whom you spoke? Is he still alive?' They said, 'Your servant our father is well; he is still alive.' And they bowed their heads and did obeisance" (43:27–28). Now the brothers do not answer. Joseph's question is an emotional outburst, for he clearly realizes, as a result of Judah's speech, that his manner of wielding power has threatened his family's sustenance and that his actions have threatened the life of his own father. When he understands the precariousness of his father's life, he is broken. Judah's speech moved Joseph from the point of bringing about the family's demise through the enforcement of his demands to the point of disclosing himself and of promoting the life of his family.

III. Narrative Art and Wise Discourse

On this basis, we can find in Judah's speech the distinctive marks of wise discourse. As the family spokesperson, Judah is keenly aware of the situation's various dimensions, and through his speech transforms the situation from death to life. The speech itself exemplifies the words of the sage, "The teaching of the wise is a fountain of life, so that one may avoid the snares of death" (Prov 13:14). Judah's perceptive and persuasive words bring about a measure of healing ("the tongue of the wise brings healing," Prov 12:18) to the patriarchal family, whose history had been characterized by much internal fragmentation and self-destruction.

It is clear, therefore, that speech marked by wisdom is not only expressed in proverbial maxims distilled from experience in the world, but can also take the form of a rhetorically persuasive argument uttered in a moment of dramatic tension. That such wise speech can be found embedded in narrative is not surprising given that speech pervades this literary genre. Moreover, even when the adjective *wise (ḥāḵām)* is not applied explicitly to characters or to their speech, the features of their speech and the outcome generated by it may cause us to designate it as such. The challenge is for us to be attentive to such instances of wise speech within those genres traditionally located outside the Wisdom corpus. For who knows where wisdom might be found?

Notes

The Scripture quotations in this article are taken from the NRSV.

[1] Jonadab is also designated "wise" (2 Sam 13:3), and his wisdom can be seen in the effective advice he offers Amnon for dealing with his personal despair.

Yet Jonadab's "wise" counsel is unusual in that it precipitates abuse, treachery, and death rather than life and health.

[2] Joseph's speech to his brothers after their three days in prison has a much less aggressive or hostile tone. He begins with "Do this and you will live" (42:18) and ends with "and you shall not die" (42:20). The revised plan is clearly advantageous to the well-being of the family, since more food will be transported to the starving family if nine, rather than one, are sent back.

[3] Joseph's words to the brothers at this point are full of irony. He says, "the one in whose possession the cup has been found shall be my slave; but as for you, go up in peace *(šālôm)* to your father." As Judah will now argue, returning to Jacob without Benjamin would instead bring disaster, the antithesis of *šālôm.*

[4] Judah frequently employs the term *ʿeḇeḏ* to refer to himself, his siblings, and his father; but he uses *ʾāḏôn* when referring to Joseph. This deferential posture is rhetorically advantageous since it reinforces Joseph's superiority while insinuating his responsibility for the current, precarious situation. Note also the flattery contained in his opening words: "O my lord, let your servant please speak a word in my lord's ears, and do not be angry with your servant; for you are like Pharaoh himself" (44:18). Of course Judah does not realize that his addressee is, within a kinship scheme, equal or even inferior to him. On the social significance of the designations employed, see E. J. Revell, *The Designation of the Individual: Expressive Usage in Biblical Narrative* (CBET 14; Kampen: Kok Pharos, 1996), 34–39.

[5] The narrative mode of discourse is evident in the series of nine *wayyiqtol* clauses (44:20–29) that form the backbone of this section of the speech. This includes one instance of the *wayhî* + temporal phrase construction, which is a particularly marked feature of Hebrew narrative discourse. For a sound presentation of discourse analysis applied to the Joseph story, see R. E. Longacre, *Joseph: A Story of Divine Providence* (Winona Lake, Ind.: Eisenbrauns, 1989). For more recent discussions of biblical Hebrew narrative syntax, see the collected essays in B. Bergen, ed., *Biblical Hebrew and Discourse Linguistics* (Winona Lake, Ind.: Eisenbrauns, 1994), and W. R. Bodine, ed., *Discourse Analysis of Biblical Literature: What It Is and What It Offers* (Winona Lake, Ind.: Eisenbrauns, 1995).

[6] For other examples of the same phenomenon, see George W. Savran, *Telling and Retelling: Quotation in Biblical Narrative* (Bloomington: Indiana University Press, 1988), 58–59.

[7] On the various types of point of view, see Adele Berlin, *Poetics and*

Interpretation of Biblical Narrative (Winona Lake, Ind.: Eisenbrauns, 1994), 43–82; see esp. 47–48.

[8] Although Benjamin is a key figure in the argument of the speech, he does not emerge as a full character, since no action or speech is attributed to him. He functions as a prop in the story. Note as well that Judah's preferred designation for Benjamin is *hannaʿar,* "the boy" (6*x* in 44:30–34), rather than *ʾāḥ,* "brother," (2*x* in 44:26). Even in response to the direct question about the existence of a brother, Judah answers with the term *yeleḏ,* "child." While the latter designation signals Benjamin's link to the family, *naʿar* presents him primarily as one who is dependent on and subordinate to others (Revell, *Designation of the Individual,* 31–33). In short, Judah's primary concern is Jacob, not Benjamin.

[9] They have similar vocabulary: *yāraḏ,* "go down"; *rāʾāh pānîm,* "see the face"; the existential particles *yēš* and *ʾên;* reference to Joseph as "the man," *hāʾîš;* and the noun *ʾāḥ,* "brother." They also share syntactic formulations: conditional *ʾim* and causal *kî.*

[10] The initial statement "We cannot go down" (44:26) is followed by a balanced protasis-apodosis/apodosis-protasis pattern, laying out clearly the different projected results conditioned by the presence or absence of Benjamin.

[11] The proposal itself is marked by *wĕʿattâ,* "and now; so then" (44:33), whereas the supporting reasons are introduced with the conjunction *kî,* "for, since" (44:32, 34). Understanding the *kî* clause of v. 32 as connected to what follows rather than as connected to what precedes makes more sense here; the offer and its surrounding rationale could be paraphrased as follows: "*since (kî)* I made the promise, *so then (wĕʿattâ)* let me stay in his place, *for (kî)* witnessing the impending disaster would be overwhelming."

The Way of Wisdom:
Conflict Resolution in Biblical Narrative

Elmer A. Martens

Wisdom, biblically defined, is skill in living. The pithy proverb, the arresting aphorism, and the summarizing sentence—all these offer guidelines for living well. One such proverb about Wisdom reads, "Her ways are ways of pleasantness, and all her paths are peace" (Prov 3:17). In the Bible it is not essays but stories that exposit this text. Two quite disparate narratives—the story of Isaac in conflict with Abimelech over wells (Gen 26:1–33) and the story of David about to come to blows over Nabal's refusal to supply food (1 Sam 25:2–42)—each offer pointed commentary on this Wisdom utterance.

In both stories, potentially volatile situations are defused through wise action. In the former, Isaac diplomatically defers to feisty Philistines, who eventually come begging for a covenant of peace. In the latter, Abigail risks interfering, and because she does, David, who was ready to annihilate Nabal, is restrained and negotiates for peace. In each instance, a situation that might have escalated into physical conflict and violence is settled peacefully.

This essay examines the two stories in light of the Wisdom saying from Prov 3:17 cited above, using insights from narrative criticism.[1] An exposition of these two narratives under the rubric of a Wisdom text does more than enrich all three passages: it charts God's path of peace for persons living in explosively violent circumstances. The violence increasingly characteristic of our time screams at us relentlessly, while wisdom urges us to consider an alternative way of dealing with volatile circumstances. Wisdom's call, not shrill but pleading, may still be heard in the streets for any who will listen.

I. The Path of Wisdom: Switch Rather than Fight

Caught in a famine, Isaac makes his way into the Philistines' territory, where his stay (which may have been as long as fifteen years) is punctuated by two major events. The first event is domestic: Isaac misrepresents his wife Rebekah as his sister before King Abimelech (Gen 26:6–11). The second, which is of an economic and political nature, consists of a series of exchanges over water rights between Isaac and King Abimelech (Gen 26:12–33). Helpful exegetical details and penetrating discussions can be found in recent commentaries and in specialized studies.[2] In this essay the exposition focuses rather on the literary dynamics of the narrative and its intended message.

A. Narrative Dynamics

We observe first the narrator's use of stylistic features: the echoes of narrative traditions, the role of speeches, the creation of suspense and resolution, and transformations.

1. Echoes of Narrative Traditions

Robert Alter has counseled Bible readers to be sensitive to narrative analogy.[3] Although the story in Gen 26 is about Isaac, echoes of Abraham's story abound. The name Abraham is mentioned eight times: once in the note about the setting (26:1), three times in connection with excavating wells (26:15, 18 [2*x*]), and four times in the two Yahweh speeches (26:3, 5, 24 [2*x*]). Such references, especially in the context of the divine speeches, are examples of continuity in the narrative. In fact, the promise of blessing, progeny, and land extended to Isaac is essentially the same as the one given to Abraham (cf. 12:1–3). Abraham's name is also linked with the earthy work of digging wells.

The frequent references to Abraham are a clear invitation to the reader to interpret Isaac's story against the background of Abraham's story. Abraham, like Isaac, deceived a foreigner by misidentifying his wife (Gen 12:10–20; 20:1–18). Abraham also sojourned in the land of the Philistines many days (21:34) and made a covenant with Abimelech (21:22–32).[4] Both stories give an etiology of the name Beersheba. Following a theophany, Abraham, like Isaac, builds an altar (12:8). Isaac's deference to Abimelech's herdsmen recalls the time when Abraham yielded to Lot's herdsmen (13:2–13). Isaac's willingness, then, to give up his rights in order to avoid the escalation of a potentially volatile situation is clearly patterned after his father's example and resonates with the Abrahamic tradition of peacemaking.

2. The Role of Speeches

Although Isaac does not remain silent in the drama, the quotations of his speeches are few and brief (26:12–33). In contrast, the long quotations by Yahweh and

Abimelech dominate the story. The two theophanic speeches (vv. 2–5, 24) differ only slightly in content. Both invoke the name of Abraham, and both emphasize the promise of God's presence as well as the promise of blessing and fertility.

Each theophanic speech is strategically placed. The first precedes the story of Isaac's domestic entanglements with Abimelech. In the theophany Yahweh tells of Isaac's being a blessing that will extend to all the nations of the earth; yet in the very next incident Isaac fudges with the truth and endangers Abimelech. In the words of Abimelech, "What is this you have done to us? One of the people might easily have lain with your wife, and you would have brought guilt upon us" (v. 10). Initially, therefore, Isaac mediates guilt, not blessing.

But he will yet be a blessing to the Gentile nation. The second theophany (v. 24) precedes Abimelech's visit to Isaac. Earlier Abimelech had ordered Isaac to leave his region (v. 16); now he visits Isaac, seeking an alliance. Why the change? It is Abimelech's realization that God is the source of the blessing that brings him to a change of heart. The Philistines, who were envious earlier (v. 14), are now eager to come under the aegis of divine blessing. Keen to be on good terms with such a bringer of blessing, Abimelech says, "We see plainly that the LORD has been with you. . . . You are now the blessed of the LORD" (vv. 28–29). This Gentile's verbal witness portrays the outworking of the divine promise that Isaac will be a blessing to the nations. A covenant is concluded; Abimelech departs in peace (v. 31).

The significance of these theophanic reports is that they show how the divine promises were jeopardized but then consummated.[5] But beyond that, the significance of the divine speeches is that they give a distinctly theological cast to the interactions between these two major figures, Isaac and Abimelech. The well-digging incidents are not presented merely as transactions and complications that arise in the ordinary course of events; rather, they are theologically distinguished by God's promise of blessing. The section that reports the first theophany (vv. 3–5) concludes with success in well excavation (v. 22); so also, the section that reports the second theophany (v. 24) concludes with the discovery of a well (v. 32).[6]

Moreover, the significance of Abimelech's speech (vv. 28–29), though it is not as extensive as Yahweh's speeches, should not be missed. Abimelech would hardly have approached Isaac had Isaac responded with force to the Philistines' claim to ownership of the wells. Had Isaac insisted on his rights and resisted Abimelech's efforts to expel him from their land (v. 16), the sequel of covenant making would have been most unlikely. The approach that Abimelech takes can be credited to Isaac's peaceable response to Abimelech's earlier provocation (v. 17). Even more must be said: Isaac's nonretaliatory behavior is part of the outworking of the divine promise that Isaac will be a blessing to the nations. As a result of Isaac's nondefensive posture, Abimelech is eventually drawn to ally himself with this man of blessing. The blessing promised in the theophany is realized, therefore, in Isaac's wise response to potentially volatile situations.

3. Creation of Suspense and Resolution

Genesis 26 consists of two cycles, namely vv. 1–11 and vv. 12–33. During the first cycle, in which Abimelech discovers that Isaac has deceived him concerning Rebekah, the stage is set for a nasty story of revenge. The tension, however, is resolved: Abimelech settles for a warning to his people (v. 11), and Isaac goes his own way. In the second cycle, a complication arises on account of Isaac's prosperity. The Philistines envy him because of his large herds, which tax their grazing and water resources. Limited natural resources, then as now, prompt takeovers. The problem escalates when the Philistines defiantly stop up the wells (v. 15) and, even worse, when they deny Isaac use of wells that his herdsmen had dug themselves (vv. 19–21). Such behavior, already provocative because of water scarcity, is the more vexing because one of Isaac's wells is an artesian spring (lit. "living water"), a water supply much preferred over a cistern. The strife over the wells is memorialized in the names given them: Esek, felicitously rendered by Everett Fox as "Bickering," and Sitnah, a word meaning "adversary" and translated by Fox as "Animosity."[7] With the defiant stance of the Philistines and their repeated and devious maneuvers, the tension mounts.

A moment of temporary relief in the story comes when another well, named Rehoboth—rendered by Alter as "Open spaces"[8] —is uncontested. But the tension between Isaac and Abimelech heightens once more with the visit made to Isaac by the Philistine troika: Abimelech, the king; Ahuzzath, his adviser; and Phicol, the army captain. Relations are strained. Isaac demands, "Why have you come to me, seeing that you hate me and have sent me away from you?" (v. 27). The suspense is finally resolved with Abimelech's request for a covenant and Isaac's reciprocity with the offer of a covenant meal (vv. 28–30). Peace has been restored, for Isaac's servants are now able to celebrate the discovery of yet another major well without incident (v. 32).

How are the tensions about the wells resolved? The answer is bound up with Isaac's actions. He resists making an issue over ownership claims; he yields his rights. The basis for the Philistines' claims may have been that the wells were within Philistine-owned territory and hence belonged to them. The counterclaim by Isaac (and certainly a reasonable one) was that those who expend the energy to dig the well are entitled to the water rights. But Isaac does not choose this tack. Instead, he, as the stronger who could have enforced his claim (v. 16), yields in the interest of keeping the peace. This action is all the more remarkable because earlier the Philistines had ordered him to leave Gerar, which he did, settling in the valley of Gerar (v. 17; cf. v. 6). Already snubbed once, he might have been expected to resist further humiliation through retaliation. Instead he chooses the path of self-effacing, nonretaliatory action.

4. Transformations

The story relates several significant changes and plot reversals. At the outset Isaac is in a famine-stricken land; at the conclusion Isaac is in Beersheba, next to an uncontested well of water. Even before the end of the story he is a man of large material substance. He is at first dependent on the good will of Abimelech, who allows Isaac to settle in his region. By the end of the chapter the roles are reversed: now Abimelech is dependent on Isaac's favor. Abimelech is initially the stronger of the two, but by the end of the story, he, the weaker, comes to Isaac to request a nonaggression pact. Earlier, Abimelech had ordered Isaac to leave his region; later, Abimelech asks Isaac for peaceful coexistence. One hardly needs to read between the lines to realize that Abimelech would not have approached Isaac were it not for his experience with Isaac as a peace-loving man who, although severely provoked, had walked away rather than fuel his grievances. The change in circumstances, Isaac's rags-to-riches story, came because of Yahweh's blessing, which in turn was not apart from Isaac's peaceful resolution of the conflict.

B. Toward the Meaning of the Story

The issue of deriving meaning from a narrative is a complex one. Some wish to go behind the text to ascertain authorial intention; others go in front of the text stressing reader response. The issue is complex. As George Nicol has noted, care must be exercised in drawing theology from narrative.[9] Still, the fact that passages such as Gen 26 are part of the canon suggests that they are intended to inform the believing community on matters of faith and life. As R. W. L. Moberly states, "The primary interest of Israel in the patriarchs was therefore in them as people who could in one way or other exemplify the dynamics of life under God and so would inform and instruct successive generations of Israelites."[10] Stories within the Bible have value beyond their being history, art, or entertainment.[11] Narrative theology, as Tamara Eskenazi explains, "focuses on the specific theological consequence of stories and on the ways this prescriptive literature functions.... Biblical stories, especially the Torah, seek to compel moral and practical assent."[12] One can therefore heartily agree with Walter Brueggemann's assertion about Gen 26: "The text appears ... to be a theological statement."[13]

Without entering into all the complexities of how we determine meaning, it is assumed here that the organization of a text and the dynamics of a narrative can function as clues to the theological message. As for organization, the first theophany, with its promise of Yahweh's blessing, is followed by Isaac's failure to mediate the blessing. Then comes the episode about wells, which highlights

Isaac's peaceable behavior. A second theophany takes place, followed by the making of a covenant, an event that illustrates the way in which Isaac has now become a bringer of blessing. The chapter itself, with its resolution of strife, precedes the story of the Jacob-Esau confrontation over birthright, and it leads Gordon Wenham to pose the question, "If Isaac could achieve so much without manipulating people, why do Jacob and Rebekah have to resort to the tactics about to be described?"[14]

As for the dynamics of the narrative, these have to do with the relationship between Isaac and Abimelech (especially noted in the second cycle). Thanks to Isaac's nonretaliatory response to Abimelech, the outworking of the divine promise is realized in a positive way.

Not all scholars assess Isaac's pacifistic actions in this way. To some, Isaac seems like a man without backbone. His pacifistic action appears to them to be a sign of weakness. Wenham describes Isaac as an "ineffectual man" who made an "ignominious retreat" and who is portrayed as a "rather timid character whom the Gerarites push around." His assessment is that "this narrative thus demonstrates that the power of God can work even through those who by human standards are most unlikely material."[15] I would maintain, however, that in this section Isaac's actions are to be viewed positively, a claim supported by noting that (1) God's appearance to Isaac follows the series of well-digging incidents (cf. Abraham's model behavior given as the reason for promises, vv. 4–5) and (2) such peaceable action psychologically accounts for Abimelech's requesting a covenant with Isaac.

Brueggemann's comments emphasize the fact that the first message of the chapter is about blessing. Given the strategic location of Yaweh's blessing speeches, one can agree that "the entire chapter is preoccupied with the theme of blessing." As he sees it, there are two sides to the blessing theme: "*the theological claim* of blessing from Yahweh" and "blessing as *prosperity judged by worldly standards.*"[16] Brueggemann's extensive comment on blessing quite rightly stresses that God initiates blessing. But if the structure of the narrative and its dynamics are taken into account, must not Isaac's peaceable behavior be more directly incorporated into the message of the chapter? To be sure, much in the chapter revolves around the theological theme of blessing, but the message is also about morality, ethics, and the way in which the person who carries the blessing responds to volatile conflictual situations. According to this interpretation, Isaac is both a hero and a model. The claim here is that the message of peaceable living must at the very least be set alongside the substantive message about blessing.

This kind of practical, theological reading of the story—one that urges conciliatory action for the effective resolution of conflict—can be sustained from the text. More hangs on the episodes of digging wells than a clever narrator's concern for making the report of a desert journey interesting. Oswald Chambers's devotional treatment of the passage may be an overstatement, but he is surely moving in the right direction when he says, "The only right a Christian has is the right to give up his rights."[17]

Such a peaceable response is precisely what is encouraged in the book of Proverbs as well as in the Wisdom psalms. In Ps 37, for example, the meek, those who seek peace, are linked with possessing the land:[18]

> The meek will inherit the land
> and enjoy great peace.
> Wait for the Lord and keep his way.
> He will exalt you to possess the land.
> There is a future for the man of peace. (vv. 11, 34, 37b NIV)

Living skillfully entails living in ways that de-escalate conflictual relationships, by speaking and acting in ways that result in peace. Isaac's willingness to yield his rights did not hurt him in the end. As the Wisdom writers knew, such action was not a matter of losing but of gaining.

II. The Path of Wisdom: Be a Peacemaker

Like the story of Isaac and Abimelech, the story of David, Nabal, and Abigail is also about defusing a potentially volatile situation.[19] Nabal, a wilderness chieftain, insults David (at that time also a wilderness chieftain), whose hot-tempered response nearly leads to violence and massacre. Abigail, Nabal's prudent wife, defuses the conflictual situation through mediation (1 Sam 25:2–42).

A. Narrative Dynamics

Again we focus not on exegetical details that can be found elsewhere,[20] but on the several storytelling dynamics present in this narrative. For our purposes the narrative dynamics to be highlighted in this story are the following: characterization, repetition, the role of speeches, and the echoes of traditions and texts.

1. Characterization

M. H. Abrams distinguishes two types of characterization: showing and telling. In showing, the author "presents his characters talking and acting and leaves the reader to infer what motives and dispositions lie behind what they say and do. In telling, the author himself intervenes authoritatively in order to describe, and often to evaluate, the motives and dispositional qualities of his characters."[21] In 1–2 Samuel, the predominant mode, as V. Philips Long has observed, is that of showing.[22] In this story (1 Sam 25:2–44), however, the narrator intrudes at the very outset by characterizing both Nabal and Abigail. Nabal, the wealthy sheep owner, is described as "surly *(qāšeh)* and mean *(raʿ maʿălālîm)*" (v. 3). This "churlish and ill-behaved" man (v. 3 RSV) will soon show his sullenness by refusing David's request for festival food, insulting David (asking the disdainful question, "Who is David?" v. 10), and humiliating David's young men *(naʿărîm)* by calling them slaves (*ʿăbādîm,* v. 10; cf. *naʿărîm,* v. 9). By their own remarks, Abigail and Nabal's servant reinforce the narrator's characterization. Abigail explains that her husband's name Nabal (*nbl* means fool) fits him perfectly (v. 25). Both Nabal's servant and Abigail refer to him as "good-for-nothing" (lit. "son [or man] of belial," i.e., "ill-natured," vv. 17, 25).[23]

The stark contrast between husband and wife is likewise *told* before it is *shown.* Abigail, Nabal's wife, is said to be intelligent and beautiful (v. 3)—in the words of Alice Bach, "the good-sense wife."[24] Subsequently the story will show by her resolute action that she was in fact a woman of keen mind and good sense (v. 27), as David himself acknowledges: "Blessed be your good sense *[taʿam]*" (v. 33).

2. Repetition

Alter has highlighted the importance of repetition in Hebrew narrative.[25] Within Abigail's speech her vow in v. 26 is programmatic.[26] In the oath she mentions blood, vengeance, enemies, and those seeking to take life. All four of these elements, each apropos to retaliation, are repeated either within her speech (vv. 29, 31) or in David's speech (v. 33). Vengeance is a critical component of the story, as is reinforced by the repetition of David's oath to kill Nabal and his whole tribe (vv. 21–22, 34). Thus, by repeatedly putting the subject of revenge in the speeches, the narrator leaves no doubt that vengeance and restraint from vengeance are key elements of the story.

3. Abigail's Speech

R. P. Gordon comments, "Most are agreed that the center of gravity in the Nabal story lies in Abigail's speech."[27] Her self-imposed assignment is difficult: "She must bring David to the point where he will revoke the irrevocable [an oath!]."[28] The way in which she persuades David and so defuses a potentially volatile situation is noteworthy. She defers humbly to David by speaking of herself as "your servant" and of David as "my lord" and by prostrating herself at his feet. By greeting David with a food convoy (v. 18), she raises David's curiosity. Might Nabal have changed his mind?

Her speech makes the following points:

1. She accepts blame for Nabal's action, refusing to make excuses for him. "Upon me alone, my lord, be the guilt" (v. 24).
2. By distancing herself from her husband, whom she characterizes as mean-spirited (v. 25), she clarifies that her sympathies are with David.

3. Astutely she envisions David's taking a course of nonretaliation, indirectly hinting that persons like Nabal will receive their just due (v. 26).
4. She offers a gift and so reinforces her words with deeds (v. 27).
5. She addresses David's identity and calling. She lifts his eyes, as it were, to see that the agenda he should give his attention to is the Lord's battle (v. 28). Implicit in her remarks is the suggestion that to take on Nabal is to deviate from the divinely appointed task, which is for David eventually to be prince over Israel.
6. She reminds David that God's care for him (which she describes elegantly, saying, "the life of my lord [David] shall be bound in the bundle of the living under the care of the LORD your God," v. 29) can be counted on when anyone rises up to pursue him, but (so she insinuates) this care is not ensured if he takes matters into his own hands.
7. She warns him about "catching a blot on his escutcheon."[29] If he refrains now from taking vengeance into his own hands, then when he becomes king he will not have reason to regret a precipitous action (v. 31).

The speech is intelligible, compelling, and most conciliatory in tone. It is true that others have seen it differently.[30] Here Bruce Birch is perceptive: "Abigail is pictured with bold qualities of character: intelligence, direct and persuasive speech, decisiveness, good sense, and vision."[31] Because of her decisive intervention, David reverses his plans and decides not to carry out his intended vengeance.

4. Echoes of Narrative Traditions and Texts

Drawing on the technique of narrative analogy, scholars enlarge the options of interpretation and meaning. Gordon has defined narrative analogy as a "device whereby the narrator can provide an internal commentary on the action which he is describing, usually by means of cross reference to an earlier action or speech. Thus narratives are made to interact in ways which may not be immediately apparent; ironic parallelism abounds wherever this technique is applied."[32] Thus, for example, Jon Levenson sets the story of David, Abigail, and Nabal alongside the story of David, Bathsheba, and Uriah with its tragic consequences, in which David is *not* deterred from violent action. In that analogy, the stories' common denominator is that in each instance "David moves to kill a man and to marry his wife."[33]

For our purpose, we identify three elements echoed in other stories. First, Abigail's approach to David (1 Sam 25:18–35) is similar to Jacob's approach to Esau (Gen 32:1–33:18). News is brought to Jacob that Esau is approaching him with four hundred men (Gen 32:6; 33:1), just as Abigail is told that David is mobilizing four hundred men (1 Sam 25:13–14). Jacob fears that Esau will retaliate for the loss of his birthright, just as Abigail fears that David will retaliate for Nabal's rudeness. So Jacob, like Abigail, sends presents to appease the offended party (Gen 32:13–21; cf. 1 Sam 25:18–19). In both stories the persons with the presents travel ahead of the giver (Gen 32:16–21; cf. 1 Sam 25:19), and the "hostile" figure is entreated to accept the gift (Gen 33:8–11; cf. 1 Sam 25:27). In each story a conciliatory speech and gifts assuage a perceived or real threat of retaliation.

Second, and more pertinent, since the story falls within the so-called Deuteronomist strand, is the Gideon-cycle narrative of double retaliation involving Abimelech and the Shechemites. Gaal asks, "Who is Abimelech?" (Judg 9:28, 38; cf. Nabal's question, "Who is David?" 1 Sam 25:10). Abimelech takes matters into his own hands in order to redress the insult, but he eventually comes to grief because of a millstone thrown from a tower by an unnamed woman (one who is very different from Abigail). The narrator concludes with a double statement about God's taking vengeance on Abimelech and on the people of Shechem: "Thus God *(Ĕlohîm)* requited (Hiphil of *šwb*) the crime (*raʿ*, "evil") of Abimelech" (Judg 9:56 RSV). David's comment is similar: "The LORD *(Yhwh)* has returned (Hiphil of *šwb*) the evil-doing *(raʿ)* of Nabal upon his own head" (1 Sam 25:39 RSV; cf. "And God also made all the wickedness *(raʿ)* of the men of Shechem fall back (Hiphil of *šwb*) upon their heads," Judg 9:57 RSV). Both stories illustrate that in the end, vengeance belongs to God. That David's words are so close to those of the narrator in Judges may be taken to underscore the difference that mediation makes and, more pointedly, to emphasize the fact that people need not rise to their own defense. The matter can be safely left to God.

Third, Abigail's expressed wish/prayer that David's enemies be slung out (*qlʿ* Piel) as from the hollow of a sling (*qelaʿ*, 1 Sam 25:29) echoes the earlier account of David and Goliath. There, David took a stone from his bag and hurled (*qlʿ* Piel) it at Goliath (1 Sam 17:49). Even more pronounced by way of narrative analogy is Abigail's reminder that David is "fighting the battles of the LORD" (*milḥămôṯ Yhwh,* 1 Sam 25:28). David had approached Goliath declaring that "the battle is the LORD's" (*laYhwh hammilḥāmâ,* 1 Sam 17:47). The significance of this echo is that it redirects David's attention from brushing off his damaged ego to the larger agenda of doing God's work.

B. Toward the Meaning of the Story

Scholars have variously articulated the point of the David, Abigail, and Nabal story. Is its purpose to explain how David secured a wife or how he came to be positioned in Hebron as king? Is its theological message tweaked by the Deuteronomistic editors, as James D. Newsome suggests, to show that "even in the wilderness of the Negev the Lord was guiding the affairs of David"?[34] Is the message one of David's showing restraint—a point reinforced when comparing 1 Sam 25 with its contiguous chapters (1 Sam 24 and 26), in each of which David refrains from putting Saul to death?[35] Enlarging the circumference of interpretation in this way certainly makes for provocative and insightful proposals as to meaning.

But if for the moment we focus on the chapter itself, we can identify the following factors, which are helpful in specifying its primary message: (1) the structure of the narrative, (2) narrative dynamics, and (3) narrative analogy. The structure is by scenes: David and Nabal (vv. 2–13), Abigail and David (vv. 14–35), Abigail and Nabal (vv. 36–38), and David and Abigail (vv. 39–42).[36] The complications of the plot are disclosed in the first scene, where a hostile confrontation seems inevitable. The resolution, in which the confrontation is averted, is detailed in the second scene. The last two scenes present the outcome. Working from the plotline, one can agree with Brueggemann: "The main focus of the narrative is on Yahweh's oversight of vengeance."[37]

Analyzing narrative dynamics is also helpful in discerning the intention of the story. Abigail's conciliatory speech takes center stage. As a peacemaker she functions as the fulcrum of the story. In working to resolve the conflict, she puts herself in harm's way. She accepts blame even though, as she explains, she did not know David's servants had come to visit Nabal. She refocuses the agenda: David has larger matters—the Lord's battles—that should occupy him. She offers theological grounding for his desisting from revenge: God will deal with David's enemies. She outlines possible consequences, such as the besmirching of his reputation, and she takes on the role of the mediator. In short, "Abigail is an important model of moral courage and peacemaking."[38] Persons of intelligence *(śeḵel)* work at reconciliation.[39]

Furthermore, her speech reveals the *theological* argument for desisting from revenge. J. P. Fokkelman rightly points to 1 Sam 25:29 as the "rhetorical pearl of the whole,"[40] in which the argument is essentially this: God's help really does make force superfluous. In effect, Abigail appeals to God's care for David, for God will pitch out the lives of David's enemies as from a sling. She is essentially invoking God's principle, illustrated in the analogical Abimelech story (Judg 9), that "Vengeance is mine" (Deut 32:35). Upon hearing the news of Nabal's death, David says as much: "Blessed be the LORD who has avenged the insult I received at the hand of Nabal" (1 Sam 25:39 RSV).

The whole story, then, is about conflict resolution through mediation. The story is about the experience of restraint, based on persuasive considerations, including theological ones (for example, the conviction that vengeance belongs to God). The report that Nabal dies within days is vindication of that principle. It is the God-fearers who trust in God, the wise who engage in peacemaking.

III. Wisdom's Way: Conflict Resolution through Peaceable Approaches

Each of the two stories discussed here—that of Isaac and Abimelech and that of David, Abigail, and Nabal—deals with conflict and the resolution of strife. In both instances volatile circumstances are defused through nondefensive action. Isaac essentially walks away from the strife, giving his opponent the benefit of the claim. In the Abigail narrative, resolution comes through mediation.

Both stories beg to be related to Wisdom literature. The Abigail story speaks both of wisdom *(śeḵel)* and foolishness *(nāḇāl)*. The contrast between wisdom and folly is made repeatedly in Wisdom literature. Bach is correct when she writes, "The connection [of the Abigail story] to the book of Proverbs where the use of the word *śeḵel* is the most extensive in the Bible is immediate."[41] The noun *śeḵel* is parallel to *ḥoḵmâ* ("wisdom," Ps 111:10). Wisdom is related to existential situations rather than to salvation history. Both these stories deal with common human experiences: shortages of resources, strife between persons of power, insults over such ordinary matters as food. Both stories illustrate what is claimed in Wisdom literature: "[Wisdom's] ways are ways of pleasantness, and all her paths are peace" (Prov 3:17). One may readily assent to the rightness of this proverb, but it is through narrative that such Wisdom sayings take on persuasive energy. The Isaac story illustrates the wise counsel, "You can afford not to insist on your rights." The Abigail story highlights the message, "The wise are peacemakers; vengeance is God's business."

Both stories also illustrate the Wisdom claims made in the New Testament. Jesus says, "Blessed are the meek, for they will inherit the earth" (Matt 5:5). The protagonists in our stories literally did inherit the earth: by covenant Isaac received title to a large region, and through marriage David became lord over a territory around Hebron, a place from which he later ruled. James, who often draws on Wisdom materials, asserts, "But the wisdom from above is first pure, then peaceable.... And a harvest of righteousness is sown in peace for those who make peace" (Jas 3:17–18). Isaac and Abigail show the way. They give evidence that the way of peace works.

Modern societies are marked by violence that repeatedly shatters the hope for *šālôm*, well-being. Clearly, among the many proposed solutions to this state of affairs is the appeal to hear and appropriate the biblical message of nondefensive, even self-effacing action (Isaac) and intentional peacemaking (Abigail). Both stories can be heard in our times in the context of Wisdom literature, and for Christians, in the context of Christ, Wisdom personified, who is the peacebringer and peacemaker par excellence.

Notes

The Scripture quotations in this article are taken from the NRSV unless otherwise noted.

[1] It is with delight as well as deep respect that I salute a valued friend and scholar, Dr. Bruce Waltke. This essay incorporates two of his interests, wisdom and narrative, as well as a third—Isaac! His printed sermon "Reflections on Retirement from the Life of Isaac" (*Crux* 32, no. 4 [1996]: 4–14) is accompanied by a sidebar that reads, "an example of the use of narrative criticism in expository preaching."

[2] For commentaries see, e.g., Victor Hamilton, *The Book of Genesis: Chapters 18–50* (Grand Rapids: Eerdmans, 1994); Gordon Wenham, *Genesis 16–50* (WBC 2; Dallas: Word, 1994). See also George G. Nicol, "Studies in the Interpretation of Genesis 26:1–33" (D.Phil. diss., University of Oxford, 1987); for a published portion see now George G. Nicol, "The Chronology of Genesis: Genesis XXVI 1–33 as Flashback," *VT* 46 (1996): 330–38, and "The Narrative Structure and Interpretation of Genesis XXVI 1–33," *VT* 46 (1996): 339–60.

[3] Robert Alter, *The Art of Biblical Narrative* (New York: Basic, 1981), ix–x, 3–22.

[4] That the names of Abimelech and Phicol appear in that narrative, as they do in Isaac's story, has created difficulties since the interval between the two covenants is more than seventy years. G. Charles Aalders reasons that Abimelech and Phicol in the two stories are the same persons; alternatively, these "names" were possibly titles (Aalders, *Genesis* [Grand Rapids: Zondervan, 1981], 2:84–85).

[5] George G. Nicol presents a helpful chart depicting how each element of the promise—progeny, land, and blessing—is jeopardized by the events of this chapter and how the tension regarding each was (partially) relieved. See Nicol, "Narrative Structure," 340.

[6] Noted by Nicol, "Interpretation of Genesis 26," 58.

[7] Everett Fox, *In the Beginning: A New English Rendition of the Book of Genesis* (New York: Schocken, 1983), 103.

[8] Robert Alter, *Genesis: Translation and Commentary* (New York: W. W. Norton, 1996), 135.

[9] "The possibility that the narrator's purpose was not theological should at least be considered." Nicol, "Interpretation of Genesis 26," 16.

[10] R. W. L. Moberly, *Genesis 12–50* (1992; repr., Sheffield: JSOT, 1995), 37.

[11] Certainly more needs to be said by way of application than this comment from Todd William: "Though to us these disputes seem remote, they serve to remind us of the importance water has in lands subject to prolonged drought, today as in antiquity." (William, *New Light on Genesis* [London: Furnival, 1978], 124). Hermann Gunkel is hardly more helpful when he locates the significance of the story in its being an etiological saga that is spun from the names of the wells (Gunkel, *Genesis* [6th ed.; Göttingen: Vandenhoeck & Ruprecht, 1964], 302). Cf. G. W. Coats, *Genesis* (FOTL; Grand Rapids: Eerdmans, 1983), 193.

[12] Tamara Eskenazi, "Torah as Narrative and Narrative as Torah" in *Old Testament Interpretation: Past, Present and Future* (ed. J. L. Mays, D. L. Petersen, and K. H. Richards; Nashville: Abingdon, 1995), 25–26. Bibliography on the topic includes the following: Shimon Bar-Efrat, *Narrative Art in the Bible* (trans. Dorothea Shefer-Vanson; JSOTSup 70; Sheffield: Almond, 1989); Jan P. Fokkelman, *Narrative Art in Genesis: Specimens of Stylistic and Structural Analysis* (Assen: Van Gorcum, 1975); and Meir Sternberg, *The Poetics of Biblical Narrative: Ideological Literature and the Drama of Reading* (Bloomington: Indiana University Press, 1985).

[13] Walter Brueggemann, *Genesis* (Atlanta: John Knox, 1982), 222.

[14] Wenham, *Genesis*, 188.

[15] Ibid., 192, 194.

[16] Brueggemann, *Genesis*, 221 (italics his).

[17] Oswald Chambers, *Our Portrait in Genesis* (London: Oswald Chambers Publications Association/Marshal, Morgan & Scott, 1957), 29.

[18] Brueggemann helpfully points to this psalm in *Genesis*, 223.

[19] Similarities between the two stories include the following: (1) rural settings related to sheep and cattle raising; (2) involvement of both rich protagonists and servants; (3) provocative behavior that is contrary to common decency; (4) celebration of feasts; (5) evil being returned for good; and (6) actions that pacify rather than inflame.

[20] An extensive literary analysis is offered by Jan P. Fokkelman, *Narrative Art and Poetry in the Books of Samuel: A Full Interpretation based on Stylistic and Structural Analyses* (Assen: Van Gorcum, 1986), 2:474–528; cf. Bruce Birch, "The First and Second Books of Samuel" (*NIB* 2; Nashville: Abingdon, 1998); R. W. Klein, *1 Samuel* (WBC 10; Waco: Word, 1983).

[21] M. H. Abrams, *A Glossary of Literary Terms* (4th ed.; New York: Holt,

Rinehart & Winston, 1981), 21; quoted in V. Philips Long, *The Reign and Rejection of King Saul: A Case for Literary and Theological Coherence* (Atlanta: Scholars Press, 1989), 31.

[22] Long, *Reign and Rejection*, 33.

[23] R. P. Gordon conjectures that there is further word play on the word *Nabal*, since the same consonants with different vowels mean "wineskin." Only after "the wine had gone out of Nabal" did Abigail tell Nabal about her actions (25:37). Gordon, "David's Rise and Saul's Demise: Narrative Analogy in 1 Sam 24–26," *TynBul* 31 (1980): 37–64, esp. 51.

[24] Alice Bach, "The Pleasure of Her Text" in *The Pleasure of Her Text: Feminist Readings of Biblical and Historical Texts* (ed. Alice Bach; Philadelphia: Trinity Press International, 1990), 30.

[25] Alter, *Art of Biblical Narrative*, 88–113.

[26] The oath points to "the main purpose of the entire intervention: preventing a blood bath." Fokkelman, *Narrative Art and Poetry*, 501.

[27] Gordon, "David's Rise," 52.

[28] Fokkelman, *Narrative Art and Poetry*, 494.

[29] Gordon, "David's Rise," 46.

[30] "Abigail's awfully long chatter (vv. 24–31) is supposed to be genuine female calculating. What she says is thoroughly disordered, unlogical, sheer flattery. But she intentionally overwhelms David with her gushing torrent of words, leaving him no time to consider." Alfons Schulz, "Narrative Art in the Books of Samuel" in *Narrative and Novella in Samuel: Studies by Hugo Gressmann and Other Scholars, 1906–1923* (ed. David M. Gunn; Sheffield: Almond, 1991), 137.

[31] Birch, "First and Second Books of Samuel," 1171.

[32] Gordon, "David's Rise," 42–43.

[33] Jon D. Levenson, "1 Samuel 25 as Literature and as History," *CBQ* 40 (1978): 22, 24. Levenson also thinks that Nabal's reply, "Who is this David? Who is this son of Jesse?" (v. 10 NIV) anticipates the disparaging estimate of this David, this son of Jesse, in the outburst by Sheba ben Bichri, described as a "scoundrel" (2 Sam 20:1). The same "narrative echo" is elaborated by George G. Nicol, "David, Abigail and Bathseba, Nabal and Uriah," *SJOT* 12 (1998): 130–45.

[34] James D. Newsome Jr., *1 Samuel / 2 Samuel* (Atlanta: John Knox, 1982), 80; similarly Robert Polzin, *Samuel and the Deuteronomist: A Literary Study of the Deuteronomic History* (San Francisco: Harper & Row, 1989), 208.

[35] Levenson comments on the three chapters, saying, "In each case, David perceives a powerful advantage in killing, but is restrained by a theological consideration." Levenson, "1 Samuel 25," 23. The insight is elaborated by Gordon ("David's Rise," 47) and by Polzin (*Samuel and the Deuteronomist,* 211–12), who makes connections between Nabal and Saul.

[36] Compare Fokkelman's division of three levels: exposition (vv. 1–13), Abigail's intervention (vv. 14–38), and consequence (vv. 39–44); see his *Narrative Art and Poetry,* 477.

[37] Walter Brueggemann, *Power, Providence, and Personality* (Louisville: Westminster John Knox, 1990), 62.

[38] Birch, "First and Second Books of Samuel," 1171.

[39] Kenneth L. Chafin helpfully gives 1 Sam 25:12–35 the headline "When Wisdom Interrupts Anger" in *1–2 Samuel,* The Communicator's Commentary (Dallas: Word, 1989), 196.

[40] Fokkelman, *Narrative Art and Poetry,* 506.

[41] Bach, "The Pleasure of Her Text," 30. Compare the remark by T. Fretheim: "The word *(śeḵel)* is commonly used in literature associated with wisdom" ("שׂכל," *NIDOTTE* 3:1243).

The Purpose of the Book of Job

William J. Dumbrell

It is almost universally agreed that the significance of the book of Job is to be found in the divine speeches (chs. 38–41). Yet no consensus on their interpretation has been reached, underscoring the book's intriguing, enigmatic, and baffling character. As the drama unfolds, the three friends who have claimed to speak for God are discredited, and their doctrine of retribution is proven inadequate. And Elihu, the abrasive young champion of orthodoxy, adds nothing to their arguments. As for Job—beset by physical, social, emotional, and economic problems and suffering from a strong sense of moral injustice—he has insistently challenged God to intervene (13:22–24; 16:19–21; 19:27; 31:35–37). Instinctively, therefore, we feel that a divine solution to the problems raised in the dialogues must be forthcoming. For if God does not intervene, it will mean Job's accusation that God is unfeeling, remote, and capricious will go unanswered. Yet God does intervene: the divine speeches are his response to Job's accusations. However, the question remains, Do the divine speeches also convey the *purpose* of the book? It is often maintained that the main problem addressed in Job is the problem of suffering. Yet we note that the divine speeches contain no allusion to suffering, making it clear that suffering is not the central problem of the book. This conclusion is reinforced by the observation that the fundamental issue with which the book deals (to be explored in sec. III below) is raised before Job's suffering begins (1:6–12) and that his problem is resolved immediately prior to his restoration (42:10–16).

To explore these issues, we will first examine the divine speeches and Job's replies (chs. 38–42), then give a brief overview of the preceding dialogues in the light of our findings (chs. 3–37), and finally assess how the prologue (chs. 1–2) helps us understand the purpose of this enigmatic book.

I. The Divine Speeches and Job's Responses: Job 38–42

The storm theophany of chs. 38–41 brings the divine intervention that Job had requested, suggesting that just as Job's problems were brought by "storms" (1:13–19; 2:7; cf. 9:17; 30:22; 36:33), so they would be resolved by a storm. The length of the divine speeches, however, makes it clear that Job's relief will come not through the theophany alone but primarily through the substantial content of the speeches. These speeches are not intended to provide the solution to the problem that the book of Job poses; rather they give a corrective of the world-view implicit in the major dialogues of Job and his friends (chs. 3–37). In these speeches, God makes two accusations: that Job had "darkened counsel" (38:2) and that, in his attempt to justify himself, Job had accused God of being in the wrong (40:8).

A. The First Divine Speech: Job 38–39

The first divine speech of chs. 38–39 has actually been anticipated by ch. 28, a chapter that proclaims man's dominion over nature by virtue of his almost divine wisdom, snatched at in his attempt to be like God in Gen 3. But search as they will, humans cannot gain divine wisdom and thus cannot unlock the mysteries of the universe or of life itself. Only "God understands the way [to wisdom] and he alone knows where it dwells" (28:23). With this pronouncement, the chapter functions as a kind of closure to the dialogues, exposing the inadequacy and illusory character of the presuppositions common to Job and his friends while, at the same time, creating the expectation and need for a divine word.

When it comes, the divine word confronts Job's charges of divine mismanagement with the rhetorical question, "Who is this that darkens my counsel with words without knowledge?" (38:2). By focusing on the word *counsel (ʿēṣāh),* which refers to God's eternal and immutable purpose as expressed through history, the speech raises immediately the issue of divine wisdom as reflected in the created order. Job had fully agreed that God has a plan; he had merely questioned the justice of it (as can be clearly seen from a passage such as 12:13–25). God's reply is to make creation speak for him. Job's darkening of God's counsel was his failure to accept that God's plan lay behind all that happens.

Chapter 38 presents God's general superintendence of creation. In vv. 3–18 the rhetorical questions relate to God's creation and rule of the four parts of the cosmos: earth, sea, heavens (dawn), and underworld. The rhetorical questions have obvious answers: only God has the knowledge and the power to rule the cosmos, and only God can hold in tension both the positive and the destructive forces in the world: "Have the gates of death been shown to you? Have you seen the gates of the shadow of death? Have you comprehended the vast expanses of the earth? Tell me, if you know all this" (38:17–18). Job, of course, knows nothing of these things.

The second portion of the speech (38:19–38) comprises six hymnic strophes of questions and descriptions of meteorological phenomena. We learn that, contrary to Job's claim that God had manipulated these forces to accomplish his own purposes, beneficent divine ordinances govern the operation of the heavenly manifestations. This implies that a corresponding order of governance exists on earth, one beyond the reach of Job. The point of the next section (38:39–39:30) is to exhibit the providential care for hostile and untamed animals, of which Job again is ignorant. Moreover, God's design for the cosmos is a meticulously controlled network of structures and processes, the depth of which is marked by its inclusion of the world's extremities.[1]

Unlike Elihu, God does not challenge Job's protestations of innocence, his accusation that the innocent suffer unjustly, or his complaint against the hardships of mortal existence. God's speech avoids the problem of innocent suffering in general and Job's case in particular. Thus God rejects the simplistic replies of the friends, who adhere to a mechanical application of the law of rewards and retribution; instead he challenges Job to change his orientation and view his case in the light of the total cosmic design of his Creator. Clearly, in such a world of intricate tensions, we find no simple answers to problems such as the suffering of the innocent, no mechanical law of reward and retribution. Who, but God, could keep such a complex world in balance? Yet Job dared to revolt against this God!

In effect, the first speech makes it clear that Job cannot judge supernatural things by his own experience. The world is not answerable to Job but to the Creator who has established its order. It is acceptable for Job to question the apparent meaninglessness of the cosmos but not to demand that life fit his own world-plan. Job's friends insisted that Job had put God in the wrong so as to maintain his own integrity in the face of life's absurdity. The divine reply demonstrates to Job that his experience was not the ultimate point of reference, since the divine plan cannot be interpreted solely in human terms. Faith means trust, no matter how irrational life appears. Job must learn that a human being cannot judge the purpose for the whole of which he or she is only a part. In short, Job must find the meaning for life outside of himself by taking into account divine purposes that go beyond his own experience. By the end of the speech, therefore, Job has learned that God's ways have a wider purpose than what has been reflected in his previous anthropocentric discussions.

B. Job's First Response: Job 40:1–5

The pivot verse at the close of the first speech repeats the divine challenge: "Will the one who contends with the Almighty correct him? Let him who accuses God answer him!" (40:2). Job's response, when he is invited to speak, is subdued and evasive: "I am unworthy—how can I reply to you? I put my hand over my mouth. I spoke once, but I have no answer—twice, but I will say no more" (40:4–5). The general tendency has been to understand these verses as Job's first step to repentance, that is, a tacit admission of his ignorance and impotence along with a recognition of the wrongfulness of his attack on God. The NIV translation, "I am unworthy," is a typical rendering of the Hebrew *qallōtî*. But the translation "I am held in contempt [by God]" better reflects the Hebrew, indicating that Job's mood may still be that of complaint. On this interpretation of the verse, Job admits that he can provide no satisfactory answers, but he does not admit to having sinned. Job's own experience of chaos is still too powerfully real for him to acknowledge fault, which robs him of the power to praise. He cannot yet speak the language of a new faith.

C. The Second Divine Speech: Job 40:6–41:34

The issue in the second speech is God's just governance (Heb. *mišpāṭ*)—that is, his sovereign control—of the world (40:8), an issue that had also been the major concern of Job and his friends (cf. 12:13–24; 13:15–16; 16:11–17; 19:7–9; 24:12). The passage in 40:7–14 begins with God's challenging Job to take over the rule of the cosmos. But in doing so, Job—like God—must exercise the power that subdues evil. In effect, God is asking Job whether the latter's destructive assault in the dialogues is the first necessary step in reordering a new reality. The parallel questions of 40:9 ("Do you have an arm like God's and can your voice thunder like his?") contrast the power of God with the implied weakness of Job. God is not boasting arrogantly or taunting Job cruelly; rather, God is simply referring to the power necessary to conquer the enemy. If the divine King is to abdicate, then the replacement—in this case, Job—must wield the same power. In v. 10 the language changes from question to imperative, and God challenges Job to dress in the royal vestments of greatness, exaltation, majesty, and splendor—terms describing the sovereignty expressed in creation and history (cf. Pss 21:5; 45:4; 104:1; 111:3).[2] Divine enthronement follows the defeat of chaos. Job must perform the task of a king in order to establish justice; he must conquer the proud, the wicked, and those who arrogantly oppose the ruler's sovereignty. If Job can pour out his wrath (40:11) and bring the wicked into the dust (40:12–13), then God will praise him and only then acknowledge that Job's right hand can save him. God, unlike Job, would not stand by, inarticulate, in the face of such marvelous deeds (40:14).

Behemoth and Leviathan, whose exploits are next referred to (40:15–24 and 42:1–34, respectively), may be interpreted as the symbolic forces of chaos that threaten human existence. If Job wishes to sit on the cosmic throne, he must defeat these enemies. The name *Behemoth* signifies a great beast, perhaps a hippopotamus or water buffalo. But no matter how strong and fearsome he may be (40:15–18), he remains a creature. Still, it is he, not humans, who holds the proud position of the first of God's works (v. 19), a position denoting temporal primacy and chief status. The powers of darkness, which Behemoth signifies, are mighty and fierce and must be confronted to keep the world in harmony.

Leviathan, the chaos monster whom Job must also defeat, receives even more attention in the speech (41:1–34 [MT 40:25–41:26]). Job's inability to defeat the monster is underscored by the rhetorical questions of the first strophe (41:1–7 [MT 40:25–31]), yet for Yahweh this dreaded monster is a mere "pet" (41:5 [MT 40:29]). The absolute impotence of Job is shown by the line, "If you lay a hand on him, you will remember the struggle and never do it again!" (41:8 [MT 40:32]). Only the Divine Warrior dare encounter him. But if mortals are terrified by the thought of arousing Leviathan, how much more should they be afraid to confront the dragon slayer himself (41:10–11 [MT 41:2–3])!

The second divine speech, therefore, presents a scenario in which only God is strong enough to oppose evil—an evil which must be kept under constant control. The denizens of chaos, though defeated, are only restrained, for they continue to inhabit the regions of wilderness and the sea, biding their time until they rise up to challenge the Creator again. In short, there continues to be chaos in the world, albeit always under divine superintendence. Justice thus has a dynamic character to it and must constantly be reestablished by means of victory over evil. This is God's work, but Job is hardly up to the task.

D. Job's Second Response: Job 42:1–6

Job's reply at this point sounds like contrite repentance in which he regrets having attacked the justice of God:

> I know that you can do all things;
> no plan of yours can be thwarted.
> You asked, "Who is this that darkens my counsel without knowledge?"
> Surely I spoke of things I did not understand,
> things too wonderful for me to know.
> You said, "Listen now, and I will speak;
> I will question you,
> and you shall answer me."
> My ears had heard of you
> but now my eyes have seen you.
> Therefore I despise myself
> and repent in dust and ashes. (42:2–6)

Yet the language of repentance *(niḥamtî)* in v. 6 is ambiguous. It could signify the language of the lament ritual, in which dust on the head is indicative of mortality, death, and the grave; by the same token, it could refer to the ash heap itself or even to personal worthlessness. Depending upon the specific nuance of *nḥm* intended, it may mean either that Job is moving away from mourning or that he merely considers himself dust and ashes. But everything considered, including the divine assessment that follows Job's speech (42:7b–8), it is probable that Job is not repenting as such.

Nonetheless, one cannot deny that Job undergoes a significant change of mind. He now knows God can do everything and can be restrained from nothing (v. 2). He relates how he discovered through God's speech that "man in fact tries to subject everything to his own narrow view and reduce it to proportions capable of human comprehension."[3] The order of the universe is now admittedly beyond his comprehension. He realizes that the time for accusation, as well as for mourning and lamentation, is over. Therefore, he now attempts to utter the praise that his previous ambivalence would not permit him.

We see, therefore, that the answers Job gives in 40:3–5 and 42:1–6 might not express heartfelt repentance. Nonetheless, he relinquishes his stance as plaintiff, admits his ignorance, and declares his willingness to drop his suit. Job's answers are thus equivalent to a legal retraction that sets aside his demand for formal vindication as the injured party. But if the book were to end at this point, it would leave the basic questions raised by the prologue (of which Job is unaware) unresolved; the book would then be calling for blind trust in God in all the circumstances of life. But to say that God calls for blind trust in spite of the circumstances experienced makes the character of God himself inscrutable. The book of Job is a theodicy, and as such, it demands that God must say more, despite Job's acquiescence and present contentment. Job's changed attitude now makes it possible for God to render a more complete verdict upon Job's whole situation.

E. God's Response: Job 42:7–9

God now sums up the issues in an address to Eliphaz the Temanite:

> I am angry with you and your two friends, because you have not spoken of me what is right, as my servant Job has. So now take seven bulls and seven rams and go to my servant Job and sacrifice a burnt offering for yourselves. My servant Job will pray for you, and I will accept his prayer and not deal with you according to your folly. You have not spoken of me what is right, as my servant Job has. (42:7b–8)

What Job had said about God was right. God had wronged Job, and Job's complaints were correct (v. 7). In response to Satan's unfounded suspicions, God stripped Job of all his honor, killed his children, and afflicted him with great physical suffering. Was God's sentencing of Job to this fate grossly unjust? Is the verdict of 42:7–9—that Job is in the right and the friends are not—not only an affirmation of Job's integrity but also a divine pronouncement to rescue the tarnished righteousness of God? In this case, it is God's integrity, not Job's, that is rescued by the final judgment. Has Job, like Abraham, rightly questioned divine justice, deconstructed the inadequate naïve language of faith formulated by the friends, and moved to reestablish a discourse that makes faith articulate? If so, then Job indeed has been fully vindicated.

The divine verdict of 42:7b ("You [the friends] have not spoken of me what is right, as my servant Job has") has been rightly assessed to be a guide to our understanding of the purpose of the book of Job.[4] The verdict is emphasized by its repetition in v. 8. But to which section of the book do the words refer—to the divine speeches, the dialogues, or both? Interpreters of these puzzling verses have suggested that the language of v. 7b is comparative: that is, Job did not speak as unwisely as the friends did. Others have proposed that the statement refers to the prologue's presentation of Job as a pious and patient man who had to contend with a wife and friends who advised him to blaspheme God and to die. But such solutions ignore the sophisticated literary characterization of Job and the interdependence of the different parts of the book. Moreover, they do not adequately account for the place of the dialogues in the book and the presentation of Job as belligerent and audacious, a presentation that has always troubled expositors. If solutions such as the above are credible, then no theophany would have been required—indeed nothing beyond ch. 27.[5] And if 42:7–9 is to be regarded as a response to the divine speeches, then, as R. D. Moore points out, in 42:1–6 Job is speaking only about what is true concerning himself and not about what was right concerning God.[6]

The contrast drawn in vv. 7b–8 between Job's words and those of his friends seems to imply, therefore, that the point of reference is the dialogues. The friends are absolutely condemned, and Job is commended; this is a divine assessment of the total course of the dialogues, not just particular aspects of them. Whether the friends are forgiven depends upon Job's prayer of intercession. This is a measure of the divine confidence in Job, echoing God's verdict in 1:8 ("Have you considered my servant Job? There is no one on earth like him; he is blameless and upright, a man who fears God and shuns evil"). Job seems not to require forgiveness; and we are led, therefore, to conclude that Job's contribution to the dialogues has been consistent with his character as presented by God in the prologue. This, of course, is what we would most naturally expect—that such a divine assessment once uttered in chs. 1–2 would be sustained throughout the whole book. The theophany has not altered that assessment; it has simply pointed to the general human problem of the limited horizons of human knowledge. The theophany was revelatory, not in itself corrective, since the issues of dispute in the dialogues were not broached as such in the divine speeches. After the divine speeches, Job's basic problem remained; moreover, his fortunes were not restored until after the issue between Job and the friends had been resolved in Job's favor.

According to 42:7b–8, therefore, it seems that Job was right to question God in the dialogues, that he was acting correctly in raising the question of divine justice. Job knows that his suffering is undeserved, but he does not know how it is possible for undeserved suffering to exist. In his second speech, God allows that suffering exists in a universe over which he is sovereign, and Job now understands this, solving for him the problem of suffering but probably not his theological questions. Of course, the fact that God's commendation of Job relates to the dialogues does not make the divine speeches unnecessary. Job must also learn that no neat human investigation can unfold the character of the inhabited world. Job, after the divine speeches, admits his limited understanding (42:3b). This changed attitude as reflected in 42:2–6 made it possible for God to utter a more complete assessment of Job's whole affair.

F. Review of the Divine Speeches

Job, we know, is suffering because God has given Satan permission to destroy everything that belongs to Job (1:12). Throughout the dialogues, Job and his friends have been united in assuming a direct link between sin and suffering, that is, in accepting a rigid doctrine of retributive justice. The book, however, raises problems for such a view by exposing in ch. 28 the narrow limits of human wisdom. As for Elihu's speeches, they have simply delayed the final denouement and denounced Job for his frontal attacks on God in the dialogues. But the theophany that follows assures Job that his complaints have been heard and makes it clear that the cause-and-effect notion of retribution held in common by Job and his friends does not rigorously operate in human experience. More than that, the theophany reveals the existence of a world beyond human experience, which is held in tension with our world by the wisdom of God, underscoring the sovereignty and omnipotence of God. But the theophany has *not* provided an explanation of Job's particular suffering, rightly understood by him as resulting from divine intervention. For a resolution of the problem raised by the book, therefore, something more than the divine speeches is necessary. This brings us to a consideration of the dialogues themselves.

II. The Dialogues between Job and His Friends: Job 3–37

We now turn to an overview of the major arguments of the dialogues in order to ascertain what in fact was affirmed by God in 42:7–9.

A. First Cycle: Job 3–14

Job's opening reply in ch. 6 addresses God, who has turned against him, fired arrows at him, and terrorized him (6:4). Israel's Divine Warrior has turned his armory upon him. God has become his enemy, spying on him rather than protecting him, preying on him rather than healing him, destroying his creation rather than sustaining it. This attack makes the God of Job's present experience irreconcilable with the God he knew (cf. 6:2–13).

In ch. 7 Job blatantly charges God with having tormented him. Human beings are in the pitiless hands of a ruthless heavenly taskmaster. Job complains that God appears to find him as dangerous as the sea monster (7:12) and that God scares him with terrifying visions (7:13–14). Wishing to be free from divine persecution, he asks, "What is man that you make so much of him, that you give him so much attention, that you examine him every morning and test him every moment?" (7:17–18). Job describes himself as blameless (9:21) in word (6:10, 30) and in deed (10:6–7), but he notes that God destroys the blameless with the wicked (9:22).

In chs. 9–10 Job launches a prolonged argument against God's moral government of the world. Job addresses the doctrine of retribution, touching also on the problem of whether a thing is right because God declares it so or whether God declares a thing right because it is right in itself. Job does not claim to be blameless but recognizes that no person is fully just before God (cf. 9:15, "Though I were innocent, I could not answer him; I could only plead with my Judge for mercy"). Nevertheless, he needs an answer that will explain his present experience. Job's problem is that God appears to act capriciously and arbitrarily in the world, often reversing human fortunes. The lament-like complaint in 10:1–17 sees God as the potter who skillfully fashions men and women in the womb not for the purpose of providentially caring for them but in order to destroy them. God is like a lion, seeking out Job to slay him (10:16). God fashions mortals only to ascertain their weaknesses and to harass them until they die (10:8–17). Far from seeking to promote trust in the deity as the giver and sustainer of life, Job in effect offers a dire warning about the God who readily delights in destroying what has been created.

In Job's second speech (chs. 12–14), he invokes the image of God as the one who provides not providential care but terror (note also this theme in 1:11; 2:5; 6:4; 10:3, 7–8; 13:21). Job 12:1–16 recognizes God's wisdom, knowledge, and skill to make and sustain the structures of creation. Through the gift of divine wisdom, humans are able to shape and maintain social systems that reproduce and reflect the cosmic order; but the chapter concludes (12:17–25) with God as the destroyer of the social order. Job denies that God has any plan for the nations or any goal toward which he guides history. By contrast, the very gift of wisdom by which rulers successfully direct nations to experience life and well-being is withheld. Moreover, without the light of understanding, leaders wander lost in the chaos (12:23–24; cf. Heb. *tōhû*). Job agrees that the friends have tradition on their side but asserts that he has the understanding to test the traditional arguments (12:3, 11–12; cf. 13:2). So the righteous, of which Job is a prime example, suffer the same or worse fates than the unrighteous, yet he (Job) is just and blameless (12:4). He then points to the prosperity of the wicked, who, contrary to orthodox canons, are not punished in this life, a truism that even the beasts of the field recognize (12:5–9). God mocks the good in humankind and makes fun of their attempts to serve him (12:13–25), so the rise and fall of nations does not appear to be governed by any moral principle, providing another example of God's arbitrary use of power (12:23).

B. Second Cycle: Job 15–21

In the second cycle, Job emphasizes the unexpected and violent nature of God's onslaught (cf. 16:12, "All was well with me, but he shattered me; he seized me by the neck and crushed me"). Nevertheless, Job is determined to maintain his rights before God (16:18–17:9) and begs that these may be sustained. He is sure that God has wronged him by dealing with him as a hunter deals with trapped animals, stripping him of the honor and position he once held (16:9). Job asks how often the godless suffer, how often the lamp of the wicked is snuffed out, challenging Bildad's assertion (18:5) that the wicked are so dealt with. Job's skepticism in this second cycle is clearly not a detached theorizing but rather a direct confrontation with an anguished personal experience that calls his old untroubled faith into question. But while Job is skeptical of God's ways and the possibility of a relationship with him, he clings to the hope that, after all, God is just and will listen to humankind. Occasionally skepticism disappears and hope resurfaces, but Job is convinced that the only way out of his predicament is to come face-to-face with God.

C. Third Cycle: Job 22–27

In the third cycle, Job again expresses his desire to find God (23:3–7). He wants to understand why he suffers. Accordingly, he thinks that God should answer him and lay countercharges against him. God should give him a fair hearing and not simply overwhelm him by his power, for then Job could be forever acquitted (v. 7). But in fact, God does what he likes, treating Job as he does for his own reasons. God's inscrutability frightens him: "That is why I am terrified before him; when I think of all this, I fear him. God has made my heart faint; the Almighty has terrified me" (23:15–16). In ch. 24 Job argues that God is inactive in the face of human oppression and injustice. The weak are not protected (24:2–12), and fragile humanity stands on the edge of oblivion, subject to the whim and caprice of a malevolent power. In ch. 26 Job becomes once more critical of the friends, suggesting that false wisdom is plentiful (26:1–4). In 27:2–6 Job repeats that God has taken away his right and made his soul bitter; that as long as he possesses breath, he will speak the truth; and that he will hold onto his integrity and his righteousness. He is proud of what he has been, and his conscience does not reproach him.

D. Final Discourse and Elihu Section: Job 28–37

In his last great discharge of responsibility (chs. 29–31), Job affirms that he was eyes to the blind, feet to the lame, and a father to the poor (29:15–16). But now God has cast him into the mire (30:19), acting cruelly toward him. For when Job looked for good, evil came; and when he waited for light, darkness came (30:26). In the next section (chs. 32–37), Elihu virtually continues the friends' line of argument, summarizing Job's position in 34:5–6. According to Elihu, Job's mind is confused, flexible, and experimental, hence his argument is constantly in flux. Elihu's charge is summed up in 35:16: "So Job opens his mouth with empty talk; without knowledge he multiplies words."

E. Review of the Dialogue Section

We see no development in the friends' theology over the three cycles of speeches. Their minds are set in familiar patterns and static styles of argumentation. But the friends, the resolute defenders of orthodoxy, are wrong about Job. Job insists that he has not denied the words of the Holy One (6:10) and that he is just and blameless. So why is he suffering? While at times he appears to admit having committed minor sins (cf. 7:20; 13:26), he denies having committed sins that would merit the present punishment, for instance, sins such as violent wrongdoing or straying from God. God, who makes him appeal for mercy (9:15), knows that he is innocent. Job is willing to accept punishment for proven sins, but he is convinced of his integrity and innocence; he is also convinced that if there were a trial with a heavenly witness, a redeemer for him, he would be acquitted (9:32–35; 16:19–21). In anguish of soul, Job complains, "Though I cry, 'I've been wronged!' I get no response; though I call for help, there is no justice" (19:7).

The purpose of the dialogues, it may be said, is to demonstrate the bankruptcy of the participants' theological presuppositions. Job's words have been audacious, accusatory, and defamatory, but he is right! Although he shared his friends' assumptions, he found it hard to settle for a facile view of God based on the doctrine of retribution. This lies at the heart of his agonizing dilemma. How now is all of this to be resolved?

III. The Purpose of the Book

If Job's forthright denunciations of a view of God as someone responsible for his suffering are later commended by God, as they seem to be in Job 42:7–9, the problem in the book shifts back to the prologue (chs 1–2). It was God's assent to Satan's progressive moves against Job, after all, that brought about the conflict at the heart of the dialogues. Satan's assertion (that Job's conduct depended upon and followed from divine blessing) led God to grant Satan permission to progressively attack Job. But in suggesting that Job was righteous because he was blessed—not blessed because he was righteous—Satan raised a question of paramount importance that tied God, humans, and action into a tight structure and that, in turn, reflected upon the divine freedom of action. The testing of Job proceeded, seemingly in the interest of demonstrating divine freedom of action and also to refute a theory of strict retributive justice. Job's reaction in the dialogues was to denounce the God of his experience as he continued to hold, along with the friends, to a theory of retribution as prompting divine reaction to human action—all the while clinging to his confessional view of God. The disputants' common appeal to a theory of retribution vanished with the divine theophany of chs. 38–41. The bifurcation between experience and faith similarly vanishes with the divine evaluation of the dialogues in the epilogue (42:7–9). The book concludes with God's restoration of Job materially and personally as an act of grace, not as an illustration of a retribution that has been rejected.

However, by pushing the issue of the book back into the prologue as we must, we have not solved our problems. The doctrine of evil espoused by Job and the friends suggests that God should punish the wicked, reward the righteous, and protect the weak and that people with power should see to this. In this scheme of things, wickedness never profits, righteousness is always rewarded, and innocence is always protected. We as readers, however, know that this is not true of the totality of human experience, though righteousness may at times bring its rewards and wickedness embitter the soul. That God will uphold his moral standards to the end is a firm article of Christian belief. Yet because of the divine decision to let Satan have a free hand, Job is lumped with an experience that he finds theologically unacceptable. The problem is not his suffering or even his undeserved suffering, for we know that such suffering is part of life. Job's problem is that, having been taught that blessing follows righteous behavior, he is at a loss to explain his experience. His problem is corrected in the theophany. Our problem, however, is occasioned by the divine permissive will exercised by Satan in the prologue, unknown to Job. To the argument of most modern theorists—that if God is considered to be the ruler of the whole cosmos, then suffering generally (including animal suffering) is an evil calling into question the goodness of

God—the book itself has virtually nothing to say.[7] Christian apologetics will, however, provide other biblical answers to such criticisms.

The problem is that the prologue appears to have made God the author, albeit permissively, of a particular evil. In general, the doctrine of God as the author of permissive evil seems biblically correct. Since dualism must be avoided, the Bible asserts the responsibility of God for evil. God is often presented as the architect of national misfortunes, and we understand that this is part of his providential control. But here is the rub: the book of Job has made God the ultimate author of specific personal problems. Job became the pawn in a heavenly power struggle, losing his possessions, his family, and his standing. The prologue presents us with a doctrine of God that seems difficult to us and against which Job rightly protests. His laments, his calls for justice, his demands to see God in personal encounter all have been right, we would judge.

Much then depends upon our assessment of the purpose of the book of Job and upon its character as we understand it from the prologue. One approach is to see that the prologue has all the elements of a folktale. If this is so, the prologue is erecting a doctrine of God against which the book will argue and on which God himself will finally pronounce (in 42:7b–8). While God may be accepted as the general author of evil and creation itself will be seen as moving to a final order from an initial provisional and contingent beginning, God reveals himself biblically as one who may test but not tempt by imposing specific evils. We understand that if particular incidents, such as those Job undergoes, do not express the divine intention, the nature of such particular incidents are known to God. In the face of this presentation, the dialogues of Job present the language of protest. The book of Job then becomes a progressive undoing of the presentation of the prologue even to the entire replacement and more, at the end, of Job's losses. In short, the doctrine of God in the prologue flies in the face of the revelation of God to Israel and to us all.

The alternative is to regard the prologue as detailing the exceptional, perhaps as a necessary corrective to a cause-and-effect understanding of divine operations in the world. On such a view the conceivable resolution of the book would have been the divine speeches, without the need of Job 42:7–9. The dialogues then become the indication of what God expects from us all under the baffling mystery of human experience, fortified as we are—and as Job was not—by our informed knowledge of the divine plan (chs. 38–41). The book of Job in turn becomes an illustration of the language of Rom 8:28, that all things work together for the final good of those who love God. But *our* problem would still be the divine endorsement of Job 42:7, which appears to legitimate Job's verbal assault on God in the dialogues. How can it be, in the face of this extreme language of protest, that Job was declared to be in the right? Such a declaration does not merely seem to excuse Job's words as an understandable reaction under extreme provocation, but rather suggests that the actual content of Job's posture is to be commended.

The book of Job remains, therefore, one of the great puzzles of revelation. It is clear that in itself it is not merely a correction of a misplaced doctrine of retribution carried too far, for it is Satan who holds the view that God runs the world in this tit-for-tat way. We know that this is not so, and we look for its denial within the book. That comes in the divine speeches, which are an answer only to this question but not to the essential question raised by the prologue. We are led to the conclusion, therefore, that the puzzling presentation of God in the prologue is the essential problem of the book. It seems that to the problem of divine consistency raised by the prologue and aired fully by the dialogues, only the forthright divine statement of 42:7–9 is the solution.

Perhaps the purpose of the book of Job will continue to elude us, and certainly much further thought needs to be expended beyond the present contribution. But from all the information available to us within the book itself, we must attempt to construct a viable biblical hypothesis. This essay, with all its reservations and tentativeness, is offered to Bruce Waltke as a friend, former colleague, and above all a charming and commanding classroom presence.

Notes

The Scripture quotations in this article are taken from the NIV unless otherwise noted.

[1] Leo G. Perdue, *Wisdom in Revolt: Metaphorical Theology in the Book of Job* (Sheffield: Sheffield Academic Press, 1991), 212–14.

[2] Leo G. Perdue, *Wisdom and Creation: The Theology of the Wisdom Literature* (Nashville: Abingdon, 1994), 176.

[3] E. J. van Wolde, "Job 42, 1–6: The Reversal of Job" in *The Book of Job* (ed. W. A. M. Beuken; BETL 114; Leuven: Leuven University Press, 1994), 248.

[4] S. E. Porter, "The Message of the Book of Job: Job 42:7b as Key to Interpretation," *EvQ* 63 (1991): 291–304.

[5] Gleason Archer has suggested that Job's admission of guilt in 42:6 was so thorough and complete that God could cancel out his guilt entirely; but such a position must hold that previously Job had been in serious error, and this would hardly warrant commendation by God. Porter reviews Archer's and other proposals made in "The Message of the Book of Job," 291, 296–97.

[6] R. D. Moore, "The Integrity of Job," *CBQ* 45 (1983): 21.

[7] John T. Wilcox, *The Bitterness of Job: A Philosophical Reading* (Ann Arbor: University of Michigan Press, 1994), 10. This issue is usually answered by the Christian doctrine of immortality. This present essay is not the place to take this issue further, except to remark that a biblical doctrine of evil demands an evil personal will. A doctrine of "natural evil" seems totally incompatible with the biblical insistence upon human responsibility for evil, so a biblical concept of divine justice is construed totally in terms of what fate awaits individuals.

True Marital Love in Proverbs 5:15–23 and the Interpretation of Song of Songs

Walter C. Kaiser Jr.

One of the most delightful sections of Wisdom literature found in the book of Proverbs is the advice given in Prov 5:15–23. In contrast to the warning given in 5:1–14 against companionship with an adulteress, the instruction in 5:15–23 celebrates the comforts and joys of true marital love. While warning against the "utter ruin" (v. 14) found in sexual liaisons outside of marriage, Proverbs invites the reader by means of a beautiful allegory to contemplate the pure joy of divinely intended marital love.

It is a special joy to honor my good friend Bruce Waltke on his seventieth birthday with this article on the subject of biblical Wisdom literature—an area of study to which Bruce has contributed so much, to our great benefit. In this article I aim to show how the interpretation of Prov 5:15–23 opens up the interpretation of that otherwise mysterious book of the Bible, Song of Songs. Our task is as follows. First, we will make a few observations on the unity and form of the passage.[1] Following this, we will offer an exegesis of the three main sections of the primary text (vv. 15–17, 18–20, 21–23). Third, and in light of the exegesis, we will consider the role of the water metaphors in the passage and the way in which they indicate the text is an allegory. The purpose of the allegory, as we will show, is located in Prov 5:18 ("may you rejoice in the wife of your youth"), which in turn provides us with a positive link to the Song of Songs. Once the common metaphors—between Proverbs 5 and the Song—have been identified, we then will suggest an historical setting for Song of Songs, the main plot of which embodies the principle concerns of Prov 5:15–23. But more than simply recognizing a parallel of themes, we will argue that the contents of Prov 5:15–23 offer us a possible interpretive key to the entire Song.

I. The Unity and Form of Proverbs 5:1–23

Proverbs 5 fits quite well within the category of instruction literature that is so characteristic of Wisdom materials. Similar to much writing within the instruction genre, the chapter opens with the familiar address, "my son" (v. 1). He is warned to "pay attention" and to "listen well" (Heb. imperatives), for the aim of this instruction will be to "maintain discretion" and "preserve knowledge" (Heb. infinitives, vv. 1–2). Introduced by a *kî* clause, vv. 3–6 then supply the reason for this instruction—that though the way of adultery appears sweet and smooth, in the end it is "bitter as gall" and deadly in every way (vv. 4–6).

The warning is then repeated and enlarged in vv. 7–8, this time introduced by *wĕʿattâ* ("Now then") and followed by a second sequence of imperatives (e.g., "Keep to a path far from her, do not go near the door of her house," v. 8). The longer motivational section (vv. 9–14), preceded by *pen* ("lest"), enumerates the negative outcomes of failing to heed this advice (e.g., "lest you give . . . your years to one who is cruel," v. 9).

Over against the two warnings of vv. 1–14, vv. 15–23 set forth a positive example. The structure of these latter verses also has parallels with that which precedes it. It begins with a series of imperatives (vv. 15, 18b), continues with a rhetorical question (v. 16) and Heb. jussives (vv. 17a, 18a, 19a), and is followed by a question (v. 20) and additional motivational pleas (vv. 21–23).

Yet despite the rather straightforward plan of the chapter and the continuity of its argument, some have doubted its unity. For example, R. B. Y. Scott, in his Anchor Bible commentary, questions the unity of the entire passage; others, such as R. N. Whybray and John E. Goldingay, suspect that vv. 15–19 are merely secondary additions.[2] However, as this paper will attempt to illustrate, and as Paul Kruger has previously argued, there is very little reason to doubt the unity of the passage, for reasons that will become clear in the following exegesis.

II. Overview of Proverbs 5:15–23

A. Our Source of Enjoyment (Proverbs 5:15–17)

The Wisdom teacher is not content with merely presenting the negative effects of sexual immorality in Prov 5:1–14; instead, he seeks to set forth a positive picture of what true love is. By means of poetic parallelism, he (who, along with his audience, lives in a land characteristically hot) compares a drink of cool, refreshing water to the thirst-quenching delight that comes from enjoying one's own spouse.

The repetition of the phrases "your own cistern," "your own well," and "your springs" (vv. 15–16) suggests that satisfaction can come only from one's *own* spouse. The "drinking of water" is thus a figure of speech for the satisfaction that comes from conjugal love in a marriage. The wife, who according to Prov 2:17 is in a covenant relationship with her husband, here in 5:15 is likened to a "cistern" *(bôr)* and a "well" *(bĕʾēr)*. While it is true, as Ibn-Ezra has observed, that water is caught in a cistern whereas in a well it rises from within, no such special distinctions must be attached to their use here. To argue, however, as Ibn-Ezra does, that a cistern offers only "stagnant waters" *(mayîm)* while a well offers "running waters" *(nōzĕlîm)* strains the metaphor and presses it beyond the point made by the writer.[3] Here the point is simply that both cisterns and wells are valuable possessions when they are one's *own*. From them one seeks and finds satisfaction, as one should from his *own* wife.

Two more synonyms are added in v. 16: "springs" and "streams of water." This double figure replicates what has just been affirmed in the preceding verse. Some scholars have seen in v. 16 that there is a shift in subject, which may suggest that this reference is to the generative power of the male sperm or that this is a warning to the man to not waste his generative power in wasteful lust.[4] But to make these metaphors speak of male fluids or of progeny just because there is a shift from the singular to the plural (from "water" to "springs") is to miss the sequential and parallel nature of the metaphors.[5] They are not in contrast to one another but rather support the understanding of the wife as the source of personal delight, blessing, and fecundity. What settles the question is that in v. 17 the water sources of vv. 15–16 and 18 are to be "yours alone"; the plural nouns of v. 16 thus still represent the wife of v. 15. The singular ("water") is now plural ("springs") because the latter image would be of a woman who had pursued extramarital relationships: she would be as unrestrained as overflowing springs or streams of water that flood the streets.

B. Our Delight in Our Spouse (Proverbs 5:18–20)

In v. 18a the "fountain" (of sexual intimacy) is "blessed" when we enjoy it as God intended it to be enjoyed: within the boundaries of marriage.[6] In v. 18b the young man is commanded to "rejoice in *(śāmaḥ min)* the wife of his youth"; and with this phrase, we come to the central thrust of the passage, for this programmatic exhortation ("rejoice in") captures the purpose of the entire proverb.[7]

In v. 19a the young man's wife is compared to "a loving doe, a graceful deer," the symbol of agility, grace, form, and beauty. In v. 19b the author connects this symbol with a reference to the satisfaction of enjoying his wife's breasts. Interestingly, there is a deliberate wordplay in the phrase "may her breasts satisfy you always." The Hebrew word for "breasts" *(daḏ)* sounds like one of the Hebrew words for "love" (*dôd;* cf. 7:18). Even the Hebrew word for "satisfy" *(rāwâ)* has the connotation of "drinking to one's fill," a possible reference to the five water metaphors of vv. 15–16 and 18a.

The hope is that the husband may "ever be captivated by her love" ("be exhilarated always" v. 19c; NASB). The word for "captivated" *(šāgâ)* in this context is best rendered "be intoxicated"; hence the man is to be infatuated with his wife, to love her with enthusiasm! Significantly, it is this verb that links vv. 19–20 and 23, for it appears in all three verses. Raymond C. Van Leeuwen notes that this verb "conveys the unfettered passion of love. Through repetition, however, it creates a contrast between marital and extra-marital love (vv. 19–20) and reinforces the parallel between love out of bounds and folly (v. 23)."[8] Thus the husband may choose to be intoxicated and stagger in the pleasure that his wife gives (v. 19) or choose to embrace the bosom of another woman and stagger into the arms of death (v. 23a).

C. Our Exposure to the Gaze of God (Proverbs 5:21–23)

To the previous arguments for marital fidelity are now added two more reasons to be faithful to one's mate. First, God can see everything, so no secret rendezvous escapes divine notice (v. 21a). God examines all our ways, pondering and weighing them carefully so that he might judge fairly but surely (v. 21b). Thus, the rhetorical question of v. 20 ("Why be captivated, my son, by an adulteress?") expects the "son" to draw the only logical conclusion that one can reasonably make—that is, the God who has given the gift of human sexuality is the One who has the right to expect righteous living in that same area. The second reason for being faithful to one's spouse is located in vv. 22–23. The husband who chooses to live promiscuously eventually will find himself bound, or trapped, by the cords of his own sin. Not only will his lack of discipline result in slavery to his corrupt self, it will also wreck his marriage and bring about his own death. This, according to the writer of the proverb, is the height of folly (v. 23).

With this brief exegesis as background, we may now comment on the very prominent water metaphors that appear beginning in v. 15.

III. The Water Metaphors

Within the context of the images of dripping honey and smooth oil (v. 3)—both being metaphors for the speech of the adulteress—lie five Hebrew words, each used of differing yet related water sources. These water sources (cistern, well, springs, streams, and fountain) serve as metaphors of connubial love. And while these figures are not common in this kind of instructional Wisdom material, they serve on this occasion as useful metaphors to depict the complexity and vitality of such a significant topic as marriage.

The images of a cistern, well, fountain, spring, and stream are used because one's spouse, like water, satisfies desire. It is not, as some have said, that the wife gives forth offspring like a fountain issues water. Instead, the metaphors speak of her satisfying her husband's desire (and surely vice versa).

In studying these five words, however, the interpreter must not press for five individual (and specific) meanings nor specifically attempt to seek their equivalent in human anatomical referents. The phenomenon of Hebrew parallelism—the pairing of related words and ideas in Hebrew poetry to enrich and deepen the meaning of content and structure—helps explains the use of these five different yet synonymous terms for rhetorical impact and variety.

Finally, while this poem extols joy-enhancing water, it also highlights water's life-giving qualities. In a land where water is extremely scarce and valuable, water spilled out in the streets is a tragedy; it is as if life itself had been lost. Thus, both of these qualities—life and joy—are celebrated and illustrated with these water metaphors. The cumulation and extension of these metaphors, moreover, suggests to the reader that the passage is meant to be read as an allegory.

IV. The Purpose of the Allegory in Proverbs 5:15–23

Most interpreters, in fact, describe vv. 15–20 as an allegory.[9] An allegory in this case is a poetic device that makes extensive use of words or concepts from one realm of thought (such as nature) in order to describe concepts from another often quite different sphere (such as human relationships). To achieve this, an allegory will often use a story or a unified narrative, employing figurative language to bridge the two thought worlds. It is a form that allows the speaker or writer to indirectly and powerfully discuss a host of concerns.

But how shall we interpret *this* allegory? The first line of inquiry for interpreters of this type of literature should be to determine the allegory's main purpose. The key to discovering the purpose of our passage, as I noted above, is found in v. 18: "May you rejoice in the wife of your youth." Accordingly, if we had nothing else to aid our search for the meaning of the allegory in vv. 15–23, v. 18 would seem to be enough. Yet not everyone has come to the same conclusion regarding the main purpose of this allegory. Jerome and Rashi, for instance, saw the "well" as the word of God given in his law. Others have seen it as true wisdom (C. B. Michaelis) or the goods and possessions of one's estate (Junius, Cornelius à Lapide).[10] In the light of these various opinions, therefore, this single reference in v. 18 is insufficient, so we must look elsewhere for the support of our thesis.

Initial support is found in the preceding context (vv. 1–14): the warning against the waywardness of adultery and the seductiveness of the "strange woman" (v. 3 KJV). Seen in this context, the allegory of vv. 15–23 is part of a preventative statement about the evils and entrapment that result when one abuses the gift of human sexual intercourse. Do not go to a mistress or adulteress, the author writes, for the breaking of covenant results in judgment from God (v. 21; cf. vv. 12–13) as well as in both bitterness (v. 4) and death (vv. 5, 14, 23). Instead, delight yourself in the pleasure of faithful, covenant union with your spouse.

In addition, within the ancient Near East, it was not at all uncommon to describe a wife with metaphors from nature (e.g., a cistern, well, or fountain). In Song 4:15, for instance, the woman is described as a "fountain" *(maʿyān)* in the garden and as a "well" *(bĕʾēr)* of living water "streaming down" *(nōzĕlîm)* from Lebanon.[11]

In the Egyptian writing "The Instruction of Ptah-hotep," the writer declares of the wife, "She is a profitable *field* for her lord"; and in the Amarna Tablets we read, "My *field* is likened to a woman without a husband, because she is not ploughed." Looking specifically within ancient love songs, Kruger notes a line from one Egyptian maiden, in which she notes, "I belong to you like a *field.*" Important as well are the multiple descriptions in Song of Songs of the beloved as a "vineyard" and a "garden" (Song 1:6; 2:15; 4:12–16; 6:2–3; 8:11–12). Finally, the language of v. 19 makes the interpretation above—that the allegory is one of marital fidelity—even more evident. Here, the figure changes, likening the youthful wife to "a loving doe, a graceful deer"; it is "her breasts" that should satisfy her husband "always."

Lastly, in this particular context, drinking water from one's own cistern and streams of water from one's own well can only refer to sexual intercourse solely with one's own wife and the joy that results from this commitment. And with this last statement the dominant concerns of vv. 15–23 thus become manifest: the exclusivity of marriage (so "wife of *your* youth") and the joy in marriage (so "may you *rejoice*"). It is for all these reasons, then, that the majority of ancient and modern interpreters believe that Prov 5:15–23, as an allegory, speaks of the joys of marital fidelity and connubial love.

V. The Connection with Song of Songs

Goldingay comments on our passage, saying, "It is in fact with the Song of Solomon that this section [Prov 5:15–23] has its parallels."[12] We would, however, go even further than that: Proverbs 5:15–23 may well provide an interpretive key to the entire book of Song of Songs. The reason for this conviction follows from two assumptions: (1) both texts, according to ancient tradition, come from the same author, and (2) the metaphors used are so similar in some key places in Song of Songs that the presumption for similar concepts must be the first line of interpretive thought.[13]

In Prov 5:15–18 the cistern, well, and fountain function as metaphors to depict the wife. The same metaphors appear again in the Song of Songs, where the bride is described in the following manner: "You are a garden *(maʿyān)*, a well *(bĕʾēr)* of flowing water streaming *(nōzĕlîm)* down from Lebanon" (Song 4:15). A similar concept is announced in Song 4:12: "You are a garden *(gān)* locked up, my sister, my bride; you are a spring *(gāl)* enclosed, a sealed fountain *(maʿyān)*."[14] In the same way that the writer of Prov 5:15–18 emphasizes the exclusiveness of marriage in the phrase "your own" and "yours alone," so the maiden in Song 2:16 declares, "My lover is mine and I am his" (Song 2:16; 6:3; 7:10). Finally, the comparison in Proverbs between the wife and "a loving doe, a graceful deer" (5:19) finds a counterpart in Song of Songs, though here it is the male who is compared to "a gazelle or a young stag" (Song 2:9, 17). And as Song 4:5 portrays the woman's breasts as twin fawns, so Prov 5:19b connects the image of a deer with a reference to the satisfaction that can come from his wife's breasts.

Significantly, the dominant habit of older Jewish and Christian interpreters was to read Song of Songs as an allegory, *sans* any historical or literal component. Usually the allegorists made Solomon and the Shulammite maiden represent the Lord and his people. When it came to agreeing on the details, however, there was little if any uniformity among scholars. This then became the Achilles heel of the traditional view. Having taken the text outside of its historical context, hardly any two interpreters could agree about the details of the exposition.[15] Not only was the lack of agreement fatal to the allegorists' view, but so too was their denial that the Song had any literal basis. The text was free-floating above history, and the persons and objects in the book were regarded as mere figures of God, Christ, the church, or any other figure of theological fancy. The most telling point, however, against an allegorical or mystical view is that there are no clues within the Song itself that it is an allegory.

This interpretive preference has been so strong, though, that it makes one wary of rejecting it. But reject it we must, and this for two reasons. Firstly, the text of Prov 5:15–23, as we have shown above, provides us with an interpretive anchor for the reading of Song of Songs, thereby precluding a drifting hermeneutic; and secondly, it is important that we affirm the historical background of the Song, for it is with actual, literal marriage that the Song, as well as the passage from Proverbs, concerns itself.

VI. An Alternative Approach to Song of Songs

As stated above, it is the thesis of this article that a convenient entry point into the interpretation of Song of Songs (the "greatest" of songs[16]) is the sequence of metaphors found in Prov 5:15–18, which, as we have noted, are strikingly similar to those found in the Song. And if the purpose of Prov 5:15–23 is to teach the importance of the exclusiveness of marriage and the joys and benefits of marital fidelity, there is every confidence that this is the best way to understand the Song. This suggestion is strengthened by the statements at the book's conclusion, where the writer comes away smitten with the knowledge that

> love is as strong as death,
> its jealousy unyielding as the grave.
> It burns like blazing fire,
> like a mighty flame.
> Many waters cannot quench love;
> rivers cannot wash it away.
> If one were to give
> all the wealth of his house for love,
> it would be utterly scorned. (Song 8:6b–7)

Therein, we contend, lies the purpose of the whole book; and truly it appears to have been written by someone who loved and lost. But in so losing, he discovered that the object of one's desire cannot be intimidated, bought, or bullied into a loving relationship.

Were someone to ask what the setting for this story was, it would seem best to answer that there were three important characters, not just two: King Solomon, the Shulammite maiden (6:13 [MT 7:1]), and the shepherd man to whom this maiden had been pledged prior to Solomon's intrusive courting. Each plays a key role in the story of Song of Songs.[17]

The first question, then, is who is this Shulammite woman? Abishag, "the Shunammite" (1 Kgs 1:3, 15), who had been brought in to warm King David's aging and dying body, is a likely candidate. The girl had been sought out during David's last days to act as his nurse, though it is quite clear from the text that she had no relations with David (1 Kgs 1:4), nor was she a member of his harem. Abishag was noted for her exceptional beauty (1 Kgs 1:3), and as such may well be the same woman as the Shulammite maiden of Song of Songs who is regarded as the "fairest among women" (Song 1:8; 5:9; 6:1).

Assuming this identity, the passage in Song 6:8–13 [MT 6:8–7:1] may be interpreted along the following historical lines. The "daughters of Jerusalem" (possibly Solomon's harem) found the Shulammite maiden one day as the king's retinue passed by the Valley of Jezreel, near the village of Shunem, where this maiden had gone out into the nut orchard and vineyard to work (vv. 9–10). Before this maiden knew it, she had wandered over to see Solomon's caravan of princely people with the king himself being born along on his palanquin, supported by the shoulders of sixty strong warriors. Her first impulse was to run away, sensing she had attracted undue attention from the retinue. But they begged her to "return" (v. 13 [MT 7:1]). In the event, this swarthy, northern girl was taken by the royal party to Jerusalem and lived there for a time as the king tried to buy her affections and love.

The maiden refused to be influenced by any of Solomon's promises of wealth, fame or jewels. Instead, she longed for her true love, the shepherd who remained back home tending the flocks. Hence, the oft-repeated theme of "My lover is mine and I am his" (2:16; 6:3; 7:10) climaxed as the shepherd and the maiden were reunited in 8:4–14. Captured in this poignant phrase, moreover, are the two emphases of Prov 5:15–23: the exclusivity of marriage and the delight of marital fidelity. On the one hand, the exclusiveness of connubial love is likened in Song of Songs to a "locked garden." The word *garden* in the Song is always used of the woman (4:15–16; 5:1; 6:2; 8:13). The fact that the garden is locked denotes the woman's virginity, for in Arabic the term for a deflowered virgin is *opened.* But the maiden in the Song was also a "sealed fountain" in the sense of being blocked from view and access. Even the Targum relates the sealed garden and fountain to the need for propriety in sexual relations. Into this intimacy, Solomon was to have no entry. On the other hand, the delight in the love relationship between the Shulammite and her shepherd lover is encapsulated in texts such as these:

> How beautiful you are and how pleasing,
> O love, with your delights! (7:6)
>
> Thus I have become in his eyes
> like one bringing contentment. (8:10)
>
> Come away, my lover,
> and be like a gazelle
> or like a young stag
> on the spice-laden mountains. (8:14)

VII. Conclusion

In conclusion, while much work yet remains, the point of entry for solving the interpretive key to Song of Songs seems to be the metaphors and the teaching found in the allegory of Prov 5:15–23. Rather than viewing Song of Songs as an unhistorical allegory that is not concerned with an actual marriage relationship, it is best to interpret it as a book celebrating that marriage, as intended by God, was meant to be private or exclusive and yet also full of joy and delight, filling the couples with refreshing harmony and vigorous love, fully intimate, fully physical. When the marital covenant is maintained faithfully to the glory of God, the kind of satisfaction described in Prov 5:15–23 and throughout Song of Songs must surely be seen as the God-given, and life-giving, result of and blessing over marriage.

~ *Notes* ~

All Scripture quotations are taken from the NIV unless otherwise noted.

[1] I am indebted to Paul A. Kruger of Stellenbosch for the general overview of Proverbs 5 in "Promiscuity or Marriage Fidelity? A Note on Prov 5:15–18," *JNSL* 13 (1987): 61–68.

[2] R. B. Y. Scott, *Proverbs and Ecclesiastes* (AB 18; Garden City, N.Y.: Doubleday, 1965), 55; R. N. Whybray, *Wisdom in Proverbs: The Concept of Wisdom in Proverbs 1–9* (SBT 45; London: SCM Press, 1965), 47–48; and John E. Goldingay, "Proverbs V and IX," *RB* 84 (1977): 80–83. Compare, e.g., Patrick W. Skehan, "Proverbs 5:15–19 and 6:20–24," *CBQ* 8 (1946): 290–92.

[3] Admittedly, that distinction is made in Song 4:15 in another connection, but it does not seem to be made here in Prov 5:15.

[4] See, e.g., the argument of G. Boström, *Proverbia Studien: Die Weisheit und das fremde Weib in Spr. 1–9* (Lund Universitets Årsskrift: Gleerup, 1935), 142; cf. William McKane, *Proverbs: A New Approach* (OTL; Philadelphia: Westminster, 1970), 319; L. A. Snijders, "The Meaning of *zār* in the Old Testament: An Exegetical Study," *OtSt* 10 (1954): 93.

[5] Compare Kruger, "Promiscuity or Marriage Fidelity?" 66. Even more damaging to this view (which reads the waters in v. 16 as referring to the "male generative power") is that such an interpretation is contradicted by v. 17, which warns that dissemination of the springs in the streets is to be avoided.

[6] At this point the LXX reads, "Let your fountain be for yourself alone."

[7] See sec. IV. "Rejoice from" (the literal rendering) means almost the same thing as "rejoice in" (cf. Eccl 2:20; 2 Chr 20:27), with the only nuance being that the rejoicing is coming from some place rather than being found in something. Compare Franz Delitzsch, *Biblical Commentary on the Proverbs of Solomon* (trans. M. G. Easton; Grand Rapids: Eerdmans, 1970), 1:130.

[8] Raymond C. Van Leeuwen, "The Book of Proverbs: Introduction, Commentary, and Reflections" (*NIB* 5; Nashville: Abingdon, 1997), 69.

[9] Compare Arndt Meinhold, *Die Sprüche* (ZBK 16; Zürich: Theologischer Verlag, 1991), 1:99–106.

[10] These references are found in Milton S. Terry, *Biblical Hermeneutics: A Treatise on the Interpretation of the Old and New Testaments* (Grand Rapids: Zondervan, 1974), 304.

[11] Kruger, "Promiscuity or Marriage Fidelity?" includes other nature images that highlight the erotica in the husband-wife relationship.

[12] Goldingay, "Proverbs," 81. He cites as further confirmation of his assertion H. Ringgren, *Sprüche* (ATD 16; Göttingen: Vandenhoeck & Ruprecht, 1962, 1967), 29.

[13] Compare Roland E. Murphy, *Proverbs* (WBC 22; Nashville: Thomas Nelson, 1998), 31–33.

[14] Notice that along with the water metaphors in the Song is the "garden" motif that appears in Song 5:1, "I have come to my garden *(gān),* my sister, my bride," and 6:2–3, "My lover has gone down to his garden *(gān),* to the bed of spices, to browse in the gardens *(gān)* and to gather lilies. I am my lover's and my lover is mine; he browses among the lilies."

[15] To say that all the details carried a mystical sense that could be unlocked and applied to later believers seemed too high a claim. Thus, for example, the eighty concubines in Song 6:8 were said to prefigure the eighty heresies of Christendom, according to Epiphanius; the winter in 2:11 denoted the sufferings of Christ; and the voice of the turtledove in 2:12 was the preaching of the Apostle Paul!

[16] The title, "Song of Songs," is an example of the Hebrew idiom for expressing the superlative (*IBHS* 9.5.3j).

[17] For an older evangelical discussion of the three-person view, though presented as a three-act drama, see Fredrick Godet, "The Interpretation of the Song of Songs," in *Studies in the Old Testament* (9th ed.; New York: Hodder & Stoughton, 1894), 241–90; repr. in *Classical Evangelical Essays in Old Testament Interpretation* (ed. Walter C. Kaiser Jr.; Grand Rapids: Baker, 1972), 151–75.

Divine Hospitality and Wisdom's Banquet in Proverbs 9:1–6

Robert C. Stallman

Proverbs 13:14 aptly characterizes Bruce Waltke: "The instruction of the wise is a fountain of life." His ministry blends discerning scholarship and tender spirituality in a way that not only refreshes, but leaves one thirsty to know the Scriptures even better. It is therefore a delight to present this study of divine hospitality in honor of Bruce with the hope that careful readers of Scripture may experience more of God's bountiful and loving provision.

This essay will first survey the meaning and operation of a metaphorical perspective in biblical hermeneutics and introduce a sampling of ways in which Scripture portrays God in the role of a host. It will then focus on the banquet of Wisdom in Prov 9:1–6 and present some concluding reflections.

I. Metaphor and Biblical Hermeneutics

If it is a truism that the God of Scripture is beyond comparison (cf. the prophet's rhetorical question, "To whom will you compare God and to what image will you compare him?" [Isa 40:18]), it is also true that even a casual reading of the Bible reveals that God is seldom spoken of in literal terms. Rather, God appears in a surprisingly diverse array of verbal images that range, for example, from Rock (Deut 32:4) to King (Ps 5:2). These metaphorical depictions of God are rooted in the world of human experience, yet they point at the same time to the nature of God, usually highlighting some aspect of God's relationship and dealings with people.

Up until about the middle of the twentieth century, literary theorists and philosophers based their reflections on metaphorical language on the conviction that metaphor is essentially a rhetorical device whose chief value consists in adding polish and appeal to statements that can otherwise be phrased in purely literal terms.[1] Hence, since the time of Aristotle the cognitive value of metaphor has been almost entirely overshadowed by its stylistic utility. Mark Johnson summarizes this view of metaphor as follows: "Metaphor is a *deviant* use of a *word* to point up *similarities*."[2]

More recently, in addition to noting metaphor's ornamental function, several have recognized its cognitive value. Seminal studies by literary critic I. A. Richards[3] and philosopher Max Black[4] argue cogently for a view of metaphor as a distinct mental accomplishment. In metaphor, two subjects are brought into a dynamic relation that resists simple reduction to literal restatement. Black's classic case in point is the metaphor "man is a wolf." Depending on the context of the statement, certain features of what people commonly associate with the word *wolf* are applied to the other subject, man/humankind. Black labeled this view of metaphor "interactive" because neither subject remains unchanged: "If to call a man a wolf is to put him in a special light, we must not forget that the metaphor makes the wolf seem more human than he otherwise would."[5] G. B. Caird affirms this "two-way traffic in ideas" with special reference to biblical metaphors for God, showing their ability to shape not only our understanding of God's nature, but the effect of that understanding on those who accept these metaphors.

> The metaphors derived from human relationships have a special interest and importance, because they lend themselves to a two-way traffic in ideas. When the Bible calls God judge, king, father or husband it is, in the first instance, using the human known to throw light on the divine unknown, and particularly on God's attitude to his worshipers. But no sooner has the metaphor traveled from earth to heaven than it begins the return journey to earth, bearing with it an ideal standard by which the conduct of human judges, kings, fathers and husbands is to be assessed.[6]

Far from viewing metaphor as a dispensable literary device or even an occasionally insightful way of stating truth, some have gone so far as to claim that metaphor is fundamental to thought itself.[7] Substantiation of this claim lies beyond the boundaries of this essay,[8] but George Lakoff and Mark Turner are not wide of the mark in stating that "because metaphor is a primary tool for understanding our world and ourselves, entering into an engagement with powerful poetic metaphors is grappling in an important way with what it means to have a human life."[9]

When faced with a biblical metaphor such as "Yahweh is a warrior" (Exod 15:3), readers who seek to comprehend the value of such a statement must ask questions about both similarity and difference: How is God like a warrior? How is God unlike a warrior? But even more than this level of analysis is involved. Metaphor brings these two "subjects" into juxtaposition, and the lines of correlation between them do not always fall into simple positive and negative categories. Often there is a more neutral and undetermined sort of relationship that encourages the reader to consider other potential connections. In the words of Ian Barbour,

> a metaphor proposes analogies between the familiar context of a word and a new context into which it is introduced. There is a tension between affirmation and denial; in other words, both positive and negative analogy are present. For metaphors, as for models, it is the *neutral analogy* which invites exploration, and which prevents reduction to a set of equivalent literal statements.[10]

The divine metaphors of Scripture, like the parables of Jesus, draw on existing similarities but do not come with directions for precise application. Instead, they present a comparison and invite the reader to discover fresh insights.[11] Through their own imagination readers can observe what is present in a metaphor; yet the power of metaphor is not so easily captured, for metaphors often have the power to call readers into active participation. Relying somewhat on Michael Polanyi's notion of "participant knowing," Peter Macky notes that the potent metaphors of the Bible have more to do with participation than observation.

> Participating in an author's metaphorical thinking is an imaginative process, one that cannot be fully represented verbally. However, verbal guidance for that journey can be offered.... In the end, however, it all depends on the reader. Those who have eyes to see, will begin to see.[12]

The ubiquitous presence of metaphor in Scripture is a powerful argument for a hermeneutic of personal involvement. To remain at an objective distance from the text is to fail to grasp its intent. Erich Auerbach makes the point that in contrast to the stories of Homer, which offer the reader temporary relief from reality, the literature of the Bible seeks to displace our reality. Its invitation to discovery is pointedly serious.

> The world of the Scripture stories is not satisfied with claiming to be a historically true reality—it insists that it is the only real world, [and] is destined for autocracy.... The Scripture stories do not, like Homer's, court our favor, they do not flatter us that they may please us and enchant us—they seek to subject us, and if we refuse to be subjected we are rebels.[13]

The metaphorical statements about God in Scripture encourage us to subjectively consider our relationship to God. They seldom present God in the abstract, as within himself, but they present him as he stands in association with humanity as Monarch, Judge, Father, Husband, Rabbi, and Servant.[14] According to Leland Ryken, biblical metaphor "is a prime weapon in combatting a built-in tendency of religious subject matter, namely, its tendency toward moral and spiritual abstraction."[15] Hence, through studied attention to the poetic language of Scripture, readers move from being spectators to participants, from mere students to disciples.

II. God as Host in Scripture

Scripture often presents God's actions as those of a host providing food for guests. As Creator, God satisfies the desires of the earth's animals who look to his hand for food (Ps 104:27–28; Job 38:39–41). But the objects of God's benevolence are usually his covenant people, those who know him as their redeemer. The divine-host motif is clearly present in the OT and refers to God's historic care for Israel as well as to future blessings as foreseen by the prophets. The most extensive use of the motif in the NT appears in Jesus' life and teaching, particularly as presented in the gospels of Luke and John, but it is also picked up in the prophetic ideal of future blessings in the final chapters of Revelation.

A. The Old Testament

The image of God as a divine host pervades the Bible from first creation to new creation and appears with striking clarity at each pole of redemptive history. Scripture closes with an invitation for the thirsty to freely drink the water of life (Rev 22:17) and opens with the invitation to eat "from every tree of the garden" except from "the tree of the knowledge of good and evil" (Gen 2:16–17). This initial invitation, together with its accompanying prohibition, sets the stage for Adam and Eve's fall through unlawful eating, which is followed by God's curse on the ground so that only through physical labor would Adam be able to provide food for himself and his family (Gen 3:1–7, 17–19). After depicting the couple's banishment from the life-giving garden, Scripture continues to show God as a host, albeit more selectively; but it also anticipates a promising future when people will again be invited to feast on God's generous provision.

Before the exodus, God sustained Israel's patriarchs through times of famine. Israel's dependence on God as a host reached a critical point in the wilderness wanderings immediately after the exodus, when the community asked skeptically, "Is God able to prepare a table in the desert?" (Ps 78:19). God provided abundant water from the rock (Exod 17:1–7; see 1 Cor 10:3–4), plus so much manna and quail that the people could eat no more (Exod 16; Ps 105:40–41). To underscore the point that divine provision should be greeted with human obedience, God supplied extra manna before the Sabbath (Exod 16:23–30) as well as a superabundant harvest before the Sabbatical and Jubilee Years in which the land was to rest (Lev 25:2–12; see also 26:3–5).

This experience of God's special provision in the wilderness, however, served to prepare the Israelites for life in the promised land, which is typically described as a land "flowing with milk and honey" (20*x*). Hardly limited to the abundance of cows, goats, and bees, the phrase pictures the whole experience of living in the promised land as eating a rich banquet from God's own table (Deut 6:3). These images were a source of great encouragement to David, who praised the Lord as the one who took superb care of him when his life was being threatened: "You prepare a table before me in front of my enemies; you anoint my head with oil; my cup is overflowing" (Ps 23:5; see 2 Sam 17:27–29).

Part of what made Israel distinct among its neighbors was its diet, which had to be "clean" (Lev 11). As the one who provided all food, God reserved the right to specify what was permissible and what was not. In addition to not being allowed to eat certain animals, Israel was also prohibited by God from participating in sacred meals to other gods (Exod 34:15), especially those on mountain shrines (Ezek 18:6, 11; 22:9).

The prophets use the image of God as a host both negatively and positively. In contrast to the image of the land as a banquet table spread for the obedient is the image of God's cup of wrath, which the prophets employ to communicate the idea of judgment, judgment not only upon Israel but upon the unbelieving world as a whole (Isa 51:17–23; Jer 25:15–17; Rev 14:10; 16:19). Not only would the land fail to offer food and satisfaction, but its produce would be taken by invaders and its inhabitants would be reduced to the point of cannibalism (Deut 28:16–57). In a gruesome reversal, the people themselves essentially become food for consumption by beasts and birds (Ezek 32:4–6; 39:17–20), dogs (1 Kgs 21:23–24), and—metaphorically—wicked leaders (Mic 3:1–3).

Positively, however, Isaiah invites the people to participate in God's redemption as in a feast: "All who thirst—come to the waters! And those who have no silver—come, buy, and eat! Come, buy wine and milk without silver and without price! . . . Listen, listen to me, and eat what is good, and your soul will take delight in fatness" (Isa 55:1–2). He describes the eschatological future in terms of a rich banquet of meat and wine (Isa 25:6); even the mountains will drip with wine (Joel 3:18; Amos 9:13). The composite picture evokes a sense of abundance, satisfaction, and joyful celebration all made possible by the lavish generosity of God.

B. The New Testament

Jesus' teaching developed the negative and positive aspects of the divine-host motif as seen in the Prophets. To emphasize the connection between sin and judgment, he spoke of his future vicarious sufferings as a cup given by the Father (John 18:11; Matt 26:39, 42). Also, he compared the kingdom of God to a banquet by telling a parable with a jarring twist: those who had received invitations refused to attend (Luke 14:15–24). Israel's patriarchs would be there, but so would Gentiles from the four compass points of the earth; thus the "last" will be "first" (Matt 8:11–12; Luke 13:29; see also Luke 14:7–14). In another parable, a prodigal son who has had enough of feasting with the pigs returns to a banquet prepared by his father (Luke 15:23). Jesus illustrated the new situation brought about in the coming of the kingdom of God by teaching that new wine belongs in new wineskins (Matt 9:16–17).

Jesus also taught by demonstration, thus further developing the motif by becoming a host himself. In his first miracle he gave concrete expression to the present reality of the kingdom of God by turning water into wine (John 2:1–10). He told the Samaritan woman at the well he could provide water that would bring eternal life (John 4:13–14), and he invited the thirsty to come and drink from him, indicating the new presence of the Spirit (John 7:37–39; 1 Cor 12:13). Twice he miraculously fed thousands of people (Matt 14:15–21; 15:32–38) and taught that he himself was the bread of life, the true manna sent from heaven (John 6:30–51). After his resurrection he served bread to disciples from Emmaus (Luke 24:30) and prepared a breakfast of bread and fish for Peter and the other disciples (John 21:9–14).

By far, Jesus' most powerful and dramatic use of the divine-host motif was at the Last Supper when, having served his disciples bread and wine, he taught them that he was not simply the host but the meal itself (Matt 26:26–29; 1 Cor 11:23–26). The bread is his body; the cup is his blood of the covenant, poured out for the forgiveness of sins. This meal became a way for Christians to demonstrate the Lord's death as well as to anticipate the heavenly banquet of the kingdom.

The book of Revelation is replete with motifs from the NT and picks up two in particular: an eschatological banquet and the garden of Eden. The message to the church of Laodicea hints at this future meal in Jesus' invitation: "If anyone hears my voice and opens the door, I will go in and eat with him, and he with me" (3:20 NIV). The banquet is the "wedding supper of the Lamb," and those invited to it are blessed (19:9). This meal should be clearly distinguished from the grisly "great supper of God," at which the birds come to feast on the flesh of those who have rebelled against God (19:17–19).

The close of the book marks the consummation of redemptive history, signaled by a reprise of Edenic images. The New Jerusalem has a life-giving river, and the thirsty are invited to freely drink from it (22:1, 17). Beside this river is the tree of life, which yields an abundant monthly harvest and provides leaves for healing (22:2). With the enemy defeated and the curse removed, God brings his people back into a life of unbroken harmony with himself, as these images illustrate.

III. Wisdom's Banquet

In Proverbs, the banquet of Wisdom (9:1–6) appears in counterpoint to the invitation of Folly (9:13–18). The parallels between them are clear but not strict, and together they form a fitting conclusion to the Wisdom poems that introduce the book of Proverbs.[16] Both of the hosts issue urgent summons to a meal, but otherwise the situations presented in these two passages are very different. Wisdom has taken great care to prepare for her guests by building her house. She prepares her table and menu, and she dispatches servants to relay her invitation far and wide.

In contrast, Folly is without discipline. She sits at her doorway and yells to those who happen to come within earshot. At first, the invitations of these two are identical (9:4, 16), but only Wisdom calls for the simple actually to partake of her meal. Folly simply characterizes her illicit fare: "Stolen water is sweet; food eaten secretly is pleasant" (9:17). Instead of offering meat and wine, Folly offers only water and bread. Wisdom shows concern for her guests, calling them to embark on a new life. Folly is no teacher; she conceals a dark and selfish motive. It is left to the author to drive home the lesson in Prov 9:6. Those who respond to Folly's proposal embark on a one-way trip terminating at a party composed entirely of the dead.

My discussion of Wisdom's banquet will begin with a translation of Prov 9:1–6 and include a brief exegetical analysis.[17] I will then adopt a metaphorical perspective to further explore the message of this text.

A. Translation and Analysis

Wisdom[18] has built her house,
  She has set up[19] her seven pillars.
She has butchered her meat, she has mixed her wine.
  She has also arranged her table.
She has sent out her maidservants. She calls
  from the top of[20] the heights of the city,
"Whoever is simple—let him turn in here!"
  To the one who lacks sense[21] she says,
"Come! Eat my bread!
  And drink the wine which I have mixed.
Abandon simple people[22] and live!
  And walk in the way of insight." (Prov 9:1–6)

The figure of Wisdom is enigmatic, and many have sought to identify her based on her appearances here as well as in Prov 1:20–33 and 8:1–36.[23] She has been regarded as a hypostasis, a goddess, and a purely literary figure.[24] The literature on this topic is extensive, and no simple catalogue of conclusions about the figure of Wisdom in biblical theology can do justice to the complexity of the carefully reasoned and worded arguments set forth. In addition, much hinges on the precise definition of key terms such as *hypostasis* and *personification*.[25] Roland Murphy judiciously states that much of this discussion has been highly speculative and that it tends to deal with the potential extent of outside influences on Israel's theology. In short, the efforts to discover the origin and development of the concept of Wisdom deal more with her pedigree than with her identity in the canonical text.[26] Murphy concluded that "the point is that the biblical presentation [of Wisdom] itself is independent enough to be heard largely on its own as something new and unique."[27] The portrait of Wisdom as personified in Proverbs is diverse, and models for her identity may include a teacher, a prophet, a herald, an angel, a wise wife, a lover, a provider, and a scorned lover.[28] In Prov 9:1–6, however, the image is unambiguous: she is a host.

The passage also does not exactly identify Wisdom's house and its seven pillars. The wide variety of suggestions fall into three categories: cultic, cosmological, and literary.[29] The last option, which makes the best sense within the framework of the book of Proverbs, treats the house as an example of poetic imagery. In order to invite guests to a banquet that she has prepared, Wisdom must first have a home. The high quality of the house's design and construction testifies to her credentials as a host and teacher. The number seven need indicate nothing more than perfection. Richard Clifford interprets the seven pillars as a "metonymy for a grand house, befitting the exalted status of Wisdom."[30]

Following the account of her house, the text proceeds to describe Wisdom's banquet of meat and wine (9:2). The association of building and banqueting is well-known in the literature of the ancient Near East[31] and the Bible.[32] Nothing in the text of Prov 9, however, indicates that her dinner actually celebrates the completion of her house. Neither does her meal appear to be the result of cultic activity (in contrast to the meal that the wayward wife offers the simpleton in Prov 7:14–20). Rather, Wisdom's dinner is likely just a generous banquet offered freely to those with enough sense to recognize its virtue and worth.

Finally, Wisdom's invitation in Prov 9:3–6 resounds from the prominent places of the city (as in 1:20–21 and 8:1–2) and is aimed at those in need of instruction (as in 1:22 and 8:5). Here she is kindhearted to the simple, unlike in 1:23–31, where she says that those who rejected her when she called will "eat the fruit of their ways and be filled with the fruit of their schemes." Her invitation is as urgent and generous as the one in Isa 55:1–2, which also holds out the promise of life.

B. A Metaphorical Approach to Interpreting Wisdom's Banquet

The banquet of Wisdom in Prov 9:1–6 is an extended metaphor that uses the model of a host and her feast to characterize the eminence of Israel's Wisdom tradition and commend it to untutored youth. The poetic features of the passage certainly contribute to its appeal, but the value of the text's metaphorical foundation is more than just ornamental. The personification of Wisdom as a host is, more importantly, a significant cognitive achievement. Consequently, a competent reading of the pericope must press beyond clarification of the imagery in terms of literal restatement. It must encourage the reader to consider the interaction of the two main subjects: an inviting host and the biblical concept of wisdom. Speaking of the metaphorical process in Wisdom theology, Leo Perdue says that the metaphors of creation are more than poetic enhancement of unencumbered, declarative speech. They are cognitive, linguistic construals of God, human nature, and the world. He writes,

> They helped to present the most cherished beliefs and values of Israel's sages. Metaphors provoked the imagination to conceive of and experience reality in compelling ways that required commitment and devotion. Indeed, they became the organizing centers for ethical life and moral discourse.[33]

In order to understand the content of Scripture's message, interpreters must accept and account for their cultural and linguistic distance from the world of the text. Yet at the same time, believing readers claim to share in the same spirituality as those whom God used to produce the text. Objectivity and subjectivity are both present, and it simply will not do to relegate one to the realm of interpretation and the other to that of application. As James Houston has taught, "One must stand under an object to understand it."[34] Proverbs 2:6 rightly states, "The Lord gives wisdom" (NIV). Exegetical learning and submission to God belong together. Using the metaphorical language of eating, Waltke affirms, "A right spirit is necessary for the interpretation of Scripture, and Scripture so read *nourishes* the spirit."[35]

A metaphorical perspective values the fruit of traditional exegesis but then calls upon readers to engage their imagination by exploring various analogies suggested by the metaphor. In this case, how is the message of wisdom in the book of Proverbs both like and unlike the call of a woman who invites the needy into her house for a sumptuous home-cooked dinner? Furthermore, what other connections might exist that do not fit the categories of similarity and difference? For example, how and where do people "hear" an invitation to learn wisdom? What actual behaviors are suggested by the words *come, eat,* and *drink?* A metaphorically sensitive interpretation can suggest answers to these questions, but the undetermined nature of the text's governing metaphor prohibits a definitive literal restatement. But this inability is hardly a loss, for one of the virtues of metaphor is its power to invite the reader to participate actively.

The following analysis is one such response. It will deal with the two parts of the passage: a third-person description of Wisdom's feast and its preparation (9:1–3) plus a second-person account of her invitation (9:4–6).

1. Wisdom's Feast (9:1–3)

The sage has fashioned Wisdom in the style of a wealthy host who is highly skilled in construction and the culinary arts. Her house is elegant and her larder well stocked. Although she has servants to relay her invitation while she stays at home (presumably to receive her guests), she takes a decidedly "hands-on" approach to preparing her banquet. She is capable, deliberate, and confident. Because she is distinct from the fine meal she offers, Wisdom does not represent the content of the sage's wisdom but rather its source: God.[36] Just as Wisdom promises life (9:6), the fear of the Lord "adds length to life," "leads to life," and brings life (10:27; 19:23; 22:4). In essence, it is "a fountain of life" (14:27). Divine hospitality offers the substance of wisdom for those who seek God: "Wisdom will enter your heart, and knowledge will be pleasant to your soul" (2:10 NIV). But this wisdom also brings material benefit: physical health (3:8; 4:22) and abundance of food (13:25; 15:15; 27:23–27). Always the thoughtful host, "the Lord does not let the righteous go hungry, but he thwarts the craving of the wicked" (10:3 NIV).

Wisdom's meal is well prepared and presented. Her intent is to gladden her guests, who will enjoy her hospitality and be pleased enough to return to her table for the rest of their lives. What she offers is what God gives in Proverbs: words of insight, knowledge, learning, and guidance (1:2–5). As Prov 16:24 metaphorically states, "Pleasant words are a honeycomb, sweet to the soul and healing to the bones" (NIV). But is not something more than just words meant? After all, Wisdom asks for her guests to leave "simple ways," and she promises that they will "walk" in the way of understanding (9:6). According to the prologue to chs. 1–9, the purpose of the book is "for acquiring a disciplined and prudent life, doing what is right and just and fair" (1:3 NIV). This is life lived to the full, life in harmony with God and the entire created order. Clifford has observed that, despite the name *Proverbs,* the instructions do not primarily impart information. Rather, they encourage the reader to be open toward wisdom and defensive against deception: "A central metaphor is trustful relationship, variously, to Wisdom herself, to a teacher, to a father, to both parents, to a wife."[37]

Thus, the menu of Wisdom's banquet consists of more than just teaching. She offers the benefits of a spiritual relationship with God inherent in the phrase "the fear of the Lord." For the guest as an individual, these include peace of mind

(1:33; 3:23–26), victory (2:7), protection (2:11), a home in the land (2:21), a long and prosperous life (3:2), a good reputation (3:4), and indeed much more. For the guest in association with others, these encompass the gift of parenthood and the pride of belonging to a good family (17:6) as well as the bond of kinship and devoted friendship (17:17). These blessings include a happy and virtuous marriage full of delight (5:18–19; 18:22; 19:14; 31:10), and they engender the favor and friendship of even the king himself (14:35; 22:11). As Raymond Van Leeuwen expresses, "The food and drink prepared by Lady Wisdom are metaphors for the life-giving gifts of creation (9:6).... In Wisdom's house all the goods of creation are to be found, for God made them all 'by wisdom.'"[38]

The preparation of Wisdom's banquet includes arrangements for publicity. She multiplies her offer through the voices of her maids, who advertise with volume and visibility (9:3). She does not furtively whisper an invitation to the elite of society, nor does she attempt to limit the size of her guest list, for she has none. In her high status, she is neither arrogant nor aloof. Her words are as open as they are honest, and she expects to be both heard and heeded. In real terms, the teaching of the book of Proverbs is public, understandable, and available. The sage does not offer secret wisdom to those who must first qualify through superior intellect or birth. Rather, the book is aimed at the "son" (1:8), and, by virtue of its placement in the canon, it speaks directly to every member of the covenant community and indirectly to all who are in the "public squares" (1:20).

2. Wisdom's Invitation (9:4–6)

Wisdom's voice is heard in 9:4–6, where she calls out to the simple and those who lack good sense. Initially, she expects nothing from them except willingness to attend. There is no mention of appropriate attire or ability to pay. But before she is finished speaking, it is clear that her hearers must make a choice. Just as a man must "leave" his former family and "stick" to his wife (Gen 2:24), so must the simple leave their simple ways if they would have a lasting seat at Wisdom's table.

But Wisdom is offering more than provision, for she does not set up shop or offer food for free in the marketplace. She opens her home and, with it, her heart (1:23). Unlike her petulant demeanor in 1:20–33, or her majestic serenity in 8:1–36, Wisdom's disposition in 9:1–6 is energetic and liberal. Without guests there can be no banquet; there can be only a silent and somber banquet hall. As Michael Fox observes, "Wisdom realizes her potential only through human activity. Her desire for love shows that human minds—from the callow juvenile's to the educated sage's—fill a role in the intellectual economy of the universe."[39] In life, the best disciple is not one who prizes correct information above relationship with God. The wise know that through hungering for insight and understanding, one will find the knowledge of God, for the Lord gives it (2:3, 5–6). Ultimately, knowledge and understanding do not come from a book but from the mouth of the Lord (2:6). Tremper Longman issues this needed reminder: "No matter how much we love the pages of Scripture, we must keep in mind that it is the Christ of Scripture who claims our deepest affection."[40]

IV. Concluding Reflections

The account of Wisdom's banquet in Prov 9:1–6 invites hermeneutical analysis, but according to the theology of the book, it would be simplistic to truncate our involvement at the level of reading instead of responding personally. In the context of the book of Proverbs, this response should be made to Yahweh. In the context of the Christian canon, however, disciples answer the call of Jesus Christ, the divine Host. Just as Prov 1–9 closes with two contrasting houses, Jesus' great sermon closes with a teaching based on two houses, one built by a wise person and the other by a fool (Matt 7:24–27; Luke 6:46–49). Wisdom invites the simple; Jesus says, "Come to me, all you who are weary and burdened, and I will give you rest. Take my yoke upon you and learn of me, for I am gentle and humble in heart, and you will find rest for your souls. For my yoke is easy and my burden is light" (Matt 11:28–30 NIV).[41] Wisdom offers meat and wine; Jesus offers living water (John 4:13–14; 7:37–38) and himself as manna from heaven, the bread of everlasting life (John 6:32–58). Wisdom instructs her listeners to leave their old, simple life; Jesus says that those who would find life in him must first lose their own life (Matt 10:37–39; Luke 14:25–27). Wisdom's banquet, however, is situated in the context of normal human life. With eschatological interest, Jesus tells a parable of a great banquet and teaches, "Blessed is the man who will eat at the feast in the kingdom of God" (Luke 14:15 NIV).

The image of God as Host provides one avenue of insight into the nature and ways of God. It does not stand alone but complements other scriptural depictions of God as King, Warrior, Father, Shepherd, and so forth. In addition to the knowledge of God that can be found in these metaphors, the personal and relational elements that unite them stand as an open invitation to experience God on a personal level where commitment, learning, and imagination combine in a lifestyle of joyful discipleship.

In the poem titled "Love (III)," George Herbert artfully uses personification and the image of a shared meal to express the tender character of a humble yet trusting response to God's offer of grace.

> Love bade me welcome: yet my soul drew back,
>   Guiltie of dust and sinne.
> But quick-ey'd Love, observing me grow slack
>   From my first entrance in,

Drew nearer to me, sweetly questioning,
 If I lack'd any thing.

A guest, I answer'd, worthy to be here:
 Love said, You shall be he.
I the unkinde, ungratefull? Ah my deare,
 I cannot look on thee.
Love took my hand, and smiling did reply,
 Who made the eyes but I?

Truth Lord, but I have marr'd them: let my shame
 Go where it doth deserve.
And know you not, sayes Love, who bore the blame?
 My deare, then I will serve.
You must sit down, sayes Love, and taste my meat:
 So I did sit and eat.[42]

If in Herbert's poem we substitute "Wisdom" for "Love," we are not far from the message of Prov 9:1–6.

Notes

The Scripture quotations in this article are my own translation unless otherwise noted.

[1] Among several excellent discussions of the history of intellectual reflection on metaphor are the following: Mark Johnson, "Introduction: Metaphor in the Philosophical Tradition," in *Philosophical Perspectives on Metaphor* (ed. Mark Johnson; Minneapolis: University of Minnesota Press, 1981), 3–47; Paul Ricoeur, *The Rule of Metaphor: Multi-disciplinary Studies of the Creation of Meaning in Language* (trans. Robert Czerny with Kathleen McLaughlin and John Costello, S.J.; Toronto: University of Toronto Press, 1977); and Janet Martin Soskice, *Metaphor and Religious Language* (Oxford: Clarendon, 1985).

[2] Johnson, "Introduction," 11 (italics original).

[3] I. A. Richards, "Metaphor," in *The Philosophy of Rhetoric* (Oxford: Oxford University Press, 1964; Galaxy, 1965), 87–112.

[4] Max Black, "Metaphor," in *Models and Metaphors: Studies in Language and Philosophy* (Ithaca: Cornell University Press, 1962), 25–47; repr. from *Proceedings of the Aristotelian Society*, n.s., 55 (1954–1955): 273–94.

[5] Black, "Metaphor," 44.

[6] G. B. Caird, *The Language and Imagery of the Bible* (Philadelphia: Westminster, 1980), 19.

[7] George Lakoff and Mark Johnson, *Metaphors We Live By* (Chicago: University of Chicago Press, 1980), 6.

[8] I discuss this claim at length in chs. 2–3 of my dissertation, "Divine Hospitality in the Pentateuch: A Metaphorical Perspective on God as Host" (Ph.D. diss., Westminster Theological Seminary, 1999), 7–101.

[9] George Lakoff and Mark Turner, *More than Cool Reason: A Field Guide to Poetic Metaphor* (Chicago: University of Chicago Press, 1989), xii.

[10] Ian Barbour, *Myths, Models, and Paradigms: A Comparative Study in Science and Religion* (New York: Harper & Row, 1974), 42 (italics original).

[11] Ibid., 17.

[12] Peter W. Macky, *The Centrality of Metaphors to Biblical Thought: A Method for Interpreting the Bible* (Studies in the Bible and Early Christianity 19; Lewiston, N.Y.: Edwin Mellen, 1990), 297. See Michael Polanyi, *Personal Knowledge: Towards a Post-Critical Philosophy* (Chicago: University of Chicago Press, 1958).

[13] Erich Auerbach, *Mimesis: The Representation of Reality in Western Literature* (trans. Willard R. Trask; Princeton: Princeton University Press, 1953), 14–15.

[14] Paul Ricoeur, "Naming God" (trans. David Pellauer), *USQR* 34 (1979): 226; first published as "Nommer Dieu," *ETR* 52 (1977): 489–508.

[15] Leland Ryken, "Metaphor in the Psalms," *ChrLit* 31, no. 3 (1982): 26.

[16] Scholars typically regard the intervening vv. 7–12 as intrusive. For an interpretation that stresses the integration of the chapter's three parts, see Rick W. Byargeon, "The Structure and Significance of Prov 9:7–12," *JETS* 40 (1997): 367–75.

[17] The scope of this present essay prohibits extensive discussion of grammatical details. In addition to the time-honored commentaries on the book of Proverbs, see the following excellent recent treatments: Richard J. Clifford, *Proverbs: A Commentary* (OTL; Louisville: Westminster John Knox, 1999); Roland E. Murphy, *Proverbs* (WBC 22; Waco: Word, 1998); and Raymond C. Van Leeuwen, "The Book of Proverbs: Introduction, Commentary, and Reflections" *NIB* 5 (Nashville: Abingdon, 1997). Forthcoming commentaries include Michael

V. Fox, *Proverbs* (AB; Garden City, N.Y.: Doubleday) and Bruce K. Waltke, *Proverbs* (NICOT; Grand Rapids: Eerdmans).

[18] The feminine gender of the noun correlates with the personification of Wisdom as a mediatrix (Prov 1:20–33), sister (7:4), and host (9:1–6); see *IBHS* 6.3.1e. The noun's plural marking may be honorific and thus indicate a close association with God (ibid., 7.4.3), or it may simply indicate an abstract noun (ibid., 7.4.2). That the word is used with a singular verb (as in 1:20–21) indicates that the personified figure should be understood as singular.

[19] The MT reads *ḥaṣĕḇâ*, a Qal form of the verb *ḥṣb,* meaning "to hew out." Although the verb is used with reference to stone (1 Kgs 5:29; 2 Chr 2:2, 18; Isa 5:2), it is probably best to assume that the reading in the MT resulted from a very understandable orthographic confusion between the letters *ḥ* and *h.* The LXX, Syriac Peshitta, and the Aramaic Targum suggest the original reading was *hiṣṣiḇâ,* a Hiphil form of *nṣb,* meaning "to set up." The verb commonly appears in relation to stone objects, including pillars (Gen 33:20; 35:14, 20; Josh 6:26; 2 Sam 18:17–18; 1 Kgs 16:24; 2 Kgs 17:10).

[20] The Heb. *ʿal-gappê* appears only here in the OT. Its meaning is not clear.

[21] The word translated here as "sense" is literally "heart" *(lēḇ).*

[22] The noun is plural and may be understood in an abstract sense as "foolishness" (cf. LXX *aphrosynē*). However, Derek Kidner wisely notes, "There is no need to emend 'fools' to 'folly' (cf. RSV), for the feast represents more than a new outlook: it is a changed pattern of life in new company" (Kidner, *Proverbs: An Introduction and Commentary* [TOTC; Downers Grove, Ill.: InterVarsity Press, 1964], 82).

[23] See also Job 28:23–27; Wis 7:1–9:18; Sir 24:19–22; and Bar 3:9–4:4.

[24] For a summary of options, see Bernhard Lang, *Wisdom and the Book of Proverbs: An Israelite Goddess Redefined* (New York: Pilgrim, 1986), 126–46; Roland E. Murphy, "The Personification of Wisdom," in *Wisdom in Ancient Israel* (ed. John Day, Robert P. Gordon, and H. G. M. Williamson; Cambridge: Cambridge University Press, 1995), 222–33; as well as Michael V. Fox, "Ideas of Wisdom in Proverbs 1–9," *JBL* 116 (1997): 624–29.

[25] Roland E. Murphy, *The Tree of Life: An Exploration of Biblical Wisdom Literature* (2d ed.; Grand Rapids: Eerdmans, 1990), 133.

[26] Ibid., 134.

[27] Murphy, *Proverbs,* 279. This statement rests on a presupposition that I

share: those who produced the material in the book of Proverbs worked within the intellectual framework of a Yahwistic worldview. That is to say, the God of wisdom was Israel's God, Yahweh (Van Leeuwen, "Book of Proverbs," 27). This position stands in contrast to the one advanced by James L. Crenshaw, that Israel's earliest sages were humanistic and cosmopolitan. According to this view, the essence of wisdom is the belief that all people, regardless of nationality or religious orientation, have the means to secure their own well-being without divine assistance. In Israel, the wedding of wisdom and Yahwism must therefore have been a secondary development (Crenshaw, *Old Testament Wisdom: An Introduction* [rev. and enl. ed.; Louisville: Westminster John Knox, 1998], 15).

[28] See Fox, "Ideas of Wisdom," 625, for documentation of each persona.

[29] For further discussion and documentation, see R. N. Whybray, *Proverbs* (NCB; Grand Rapids: Eerdmans, 1994), 142–44. To these should be added the view of G. Baumann, that Wisdom's "house" is the book of Proverbs itself (*Die Weisheitsgestalt in Proverbien 1–9: Traditionsgeschichtliche und theologische Studien* [FAT; Tübingen: J. C. B. Mohr (Siebeck), 1966]). This is also the view of Patrick Skehan ("Wisdom's House," in *Studies in Israelite Poetry and Wisdom* [CBQMS; Washington: Catholic Biblical Association, 1971], 27–45).

[30] Clifford, *Proverbs,* 106.

[31] See the Sumerian text "Hymn to the Temple of Enki and Eridu" and "The Installation of Ningirsu of Lagash" in A. J. Ferrara and S. B. Parker, "Seating Arrangements at Divine Banquets," *UF* 4 (1972): 38–39. In the creation epic "Enuma Elish" (tablet VI), Marduk throws a banquet in celebration of the building of Babylon and his palace, Esagila (trans. E. A. Speiser [*ANET,* 69]). In the human world, the Assyrian king Ashurnasirpal II preserved a detailed description of a banquet ceremony that followed an account of military conquest and subsequent construction of a temple and royal palace in Calah that opened in 879 B.C.E. (D. J. Wiseman, "A New Stela of Aššur-naṣir-pal II," *Iraq* 14 [1952]: 24–44).

[32] Solomon held a feast following the completion of the temple (1 Kgs 8:62–66).

[33] Leo Perdue, *Wisdom and Creation: The Theology of Wisdom Literature* (Nashville: Abingdon, 1994), 339.

[34] As reported by Bruce K. Waltke, "Hermeneutics and the Spiritual Life," *Crux* 23, no. 1 (1987): 6.

[35] Bruce K. Waltke, "Exegesis and the Spiritual Life," *Crux* 30, no. 3 (1994): 35 (emphasis mine).

[36] Against Gerhard von Rad, who identified wisdom not as an attribute of God but as an attribute of the world, namely, the mysterious created order. In his view, Israelite sages believed that man did not experience the primeval order as a static organism but as a bestower of gifts, something that actively assailed him (*Wisdom in Israel* [Nashville: Abingdon, 1972], 174).

[37] Richard J. Clifford, *The Wisdom Literature* (Interpreting Biblical Texts; ed. Gene M. Tucker; Nashville: Abingdon, 1998), 51.

[38] Van Leeuwen, "Book of Proverbs," 103–4.

[39] Fox, "Ideas of Wisdom," 630–31.

[40] Tremper Longman III, *Reading the Bible with Heart and Mind* (Colorado Springs: NavPress, 1997), 45.

[41] The yoke of which Jesus speaks not only concerns the continuing validity of the Torah as fulfilled by him but his additional instruction as well. These together are the treasury of Wisdom (Ben Witherington III, *Jesus the Sage: The Pilgrimage of Wisdom* [Minneapolis: Fortress, 1994], 360).

[42] George Herbert, "Love (III)," *The Works of George Herbert* (ed. F. E. Hutchinson; Oxford: Clarendon, 1941), 188–89.

"A Bribe Is a Charm": A Study of Proverbs 17:8

David J. Montgomery

A bribe is a charm to the one who gives it; wherever he turns, he succeeds.
~ *Prov 17:8*

In 1994 Dr. Bruce Waltke assigned his Hebrew class several proverbs for exegesis and analysis. One of the proverbs given to me was Prov 17:8, which awakened my interest in the subject of bribery, particularly since I had previously heard this verse quoted as biblical justification for bribery in situations where no other option seemed possible. It is therefore with gratitude and respect that I contribute to this publication and offer my exegesis of this verse along with some reflections on its practical application. It is largely due to the influence and encouragement of Dr. Waltke that I am a pastor-preacher of the Scriptures, with a special love for the OT.

When I first began researching the wider issue of bribery in 1995, I was astounded by the paucity of material written on the subject. Out of the thousands of entries in the ATLA CD-ROM catalogue, only a very few were found to relate to this topic.[1] Moreover, several key reference works, including *The Tyndale Bible Dictionary, Baker's Dictionary of Christian Ethics, The Concise Dictionary of Christian Ethics,* and, unbelievably, the six-volume *Anchor Bible Dictionary,* contained no entries on bribery or extortion.[2] However, I did discover two major works on the subject, one by missionary Richard L. Langston[3] and the other by legal scholar and professor John T. Noonan Jr.[4]

Why is the literature on this subject so scarce? In the following sections, I will deal with the paradox of an activity that is almost universally recognized as wrong yet is often excused or ignored because the participants say they have "no other option." One of the passages often used to support such a position is Prov 17:8. Many see this as an "old wisdom" proverb that accepts bribery as a way of life. For instance, Michael L. Goldberg claims that Prov 17:8 is one of the passages in which a bribe is "a perfectly valid and respectable practice"[5] and that the book of Proverbs "praises" such action. In a similar vein, Noonan regards the Wisdom literature, and Proverbs in particular, as "a mixed bag of secular and spiritual advice" that is hostile to some forms of bribery (e.g., "A greedy man brings trouble to his family, but he who hates bribes will live," 15:27) while more positively disposed to others (e.g., "A gift opens the way for the giver and ushers him into the presence of the great," 18:16).[6] But one has to ask, Is this really the sort of advice given by the Wisdom writers, bearing in mind that the purpose of Proverbs is to do "what is right and just and fair" and that the key to wisdom is "the fear of the LORD" (1:3, 7)? It is my contention that if we are careful with the lexical data, significant distinctions can be made between the various words for bribery, which in the end will lead to a rather different assessment of the biblical perspective on this important yet infrequently analyzed subject.

I. Exegetical Considerations

A. Exegesis of Proverbs 17:8

Our key text reads as follows:

אֶֽבֶן־חֵ֣ן הַ֭שֹּׁחַד בְּעֵינֵ֣י בְעָלָ֑יו
אֶל־כָּל־אֲשֶׁ֖ר יִפְנֶ֣ה יַשְׂכִּֽיל

A bribe is a charm to the one who gives it;
wherever he turns, he succeeds. (Prov 17:8)

This verse is set within the context of sayings that have a particularly domestic theme (vv. 1–2, 6), emphasizing the necessity of good speech (vv. 4–5) and decrying the foolishness of reliance on outward impressions (vv. 1, 3, 5).

There are at least six main questions—lexical, grammatical, and theological—in relation to this problematic proverb that must be answered in order to understand its significance for the broader topic of bribery. The lexical questions are "Does שֹׁחַד necessarily refer to a 'bribe,' or can it mean something more neutral, such as a 'gift'?"[7] "What is the precise definition of שָׂכַל?" and "What is the exact nature of an אֶבֶן־חֵן?" The grammatical concerns are "Who is the בַּעַל—is it the one who gives the שֹׁחַד or the one who receives it?"[8] and "What is the subject of פָּנָה and שָׂכַל—is it the בַּעַל or the שֹׁחַד?"[9] Finally, we pose the theological question, "What is the ethical teaching of this proverb?"

1. שֹׁחַד—bribe or gift?

The reference literature does not shed much light on the question of whether שֹׁחַד should be regarded as a negative or as a morally neutral quality. Both BDB and *HALOT* acknowledge "bribe" as a possible definition in addition to noting the less negative gloss "present" and "gift," respectively.[10] It is interesting to observe that although שֹׁחַד occurs only twenty-one times,[11] it is found in all major genres of the OT. Sixteen of these occurrences are clearly negative.[12] For instance, the law pronounces a curse on those indulging in giving a שֹׁחַד (Deut 27:25); Jehoshaphat demands a fair judiciary based on the theological premise that "with the Lord our God there is no שֹׁחַד" (2 Chr 19:7); Ezekiel lists שֹׁחַד alongside bloodshed and usury as a sin of the people (Ezek 22:12); while the psalmist regards שֹׁחַד as a characteristic of the sinner and its rejection as a mark of the righteous (Pss 15:5; 26:10 [where it is in parallel with זִמָּה, "wicked schemes"]). Elsewhere, specifically in Proverbs, שֹׁחַד is seen as the last resort of the adulterer (6:35) and the wicked man (17:23).

While it could be argued that another four of the twenty-one occurrences of שֹׁחַד are neutral, upon closer examination even these yield negative connotations. Three of these occur in the context of international politics. The reference to Cyrus's being raised in righteousness and his rebuilding Jerusalem without recourse to שֹׁחַד is simply a recognition that, although material incentives were often used in international diplomacy, they would have no part in the Lord's purposes to reestablish his people in their land (Isa 45:13). In 2 Kgs 16:8 Ahaz sends a שֹׁחַד to Tiglath-Pileser; however this "gift" consisted of the temple treasures and cemented an unholy alliance. In context this must be seen as one of the many wicked acts of a detestable and idolatrous king (cf. 2 Kgs 16:2–4). The third use of שֹׁחַד is more problematic because according to 1 Kgs 15:19, honorable King Asa—whose heart "was fully committed to the LORD all his life" (1 Kgs 15:14b)—sent a שֹׁחַד to Ben-Hadad of Aram to seal a treaty. It is worth remembering, however, that in spite of his general moral rectitude, Asa was far from perfect: the OT records that he did not remove the high places (1 Kgs 15:14a; cf. 2 Chr 16:1–14), and in 2 Chr 16 he is specifically criticized (and judged) for the treaty with Ben-Hadad.

The only other use of שֹׁחַד that may not immediately appear to be negative is found in Prov 21:14: "A gift [מַתָּן] given in secret [בַסֵּתֶר] soothes anger, and a bribe concealed in the cloak [שֹׁחַד בַּחֵק] pacifies great wrath." Secrecy, however, is not regarded as a virtue in Proverbs, and its gains are only of short-term value.[13] Specifically, 21:14 needs to be read in the light of 17:23, where it is clear that it is the wicked person who receives a bribe "from the cloak" (בַסֵּתֶר; "in secret," NIV) and thus perverts the ways of justice. No matter the temporary pleasures, its way leads to corruption and moral death.

There is very little, if anything, therefore, in the usage of שֹׁחַד that suggests it can be regarded neutrally, much less positively. As Derek Kidner rightly observes, שֹׁחַד is "never used of a disinterested gift."[14] It is condemned because it perverts justice and shows partiality,[15] is akin to robbery,[16] is used by the rich to further the exploitation of the poor,[17] and puts those who practice it under God's judgment.[18] The parallels in Mic 3:11—where bribe-taking judges are compared to mercenary priests and prophets—show quite clearly the rationale behind such condemnation: bribery prospers a few elite while it denies the rest of the community their basic benefits of justice, worship, and revelation.

In light of the above, what are we to make of the only other occurrence of שֹׁחַד, namely the one in 17:8? If שֹׁחַד cannot mean "gift" or "present" and the verse is not a direct contradiction of the Torah, the clue to its interpretation must lie elsewhere.

2. שָׂכַל—wisdom or success?

The usual rendering of שָׂכַל is to be prudent, to act wisely, or to be intelligent.[19] However, the lexicons also record "to prosper" or "to succeed."[20] This latter gloss fits the present context well; nevertheless, it is worth keeping the primary meaning of the word ("to be wise") in mind, for even when it is glossed "success," it is a success based upon the subject's insight, wisdom, and shrewdness reflected in obedience (cf. Deut 29:8 [EVV 29:9]; Josh 1:7–8; 1 Sam 18:5; 2 Kgs 18:7). In Proverbs, שָׂכַל is always closely related to knowing how to act wisely (1:3; 10:5; 16:23). Arndt Meinhold makes the point well that in Prov 17:8 שָׂכַל deals with success, though it could be success based on insight.[21]

3. אֶבֶן־חֵן—gem or talisman?

The two possible renderings of the unique construction אֶבֶן־חֵן[22] (lit. "stone of grace/favor") are "precious stone"[23] or "lucky stone," that is, "charm" or "talisman."[24] Although חֵן in Proverbs can denote something that adorns[25] or makes beautiful (1:9), the underlying connotation is that of acceptability—whether it be on account of the character (3:4; 11:16), speech (22:11), or appearance (5:19) of a person. Yet חֵן is ultimately not to be trusted, for it can deceive and, to some degree, can even be found in the immoral (Nah 3:4). True חֵן is more than surface deep.[26] With this wider semantic field in mind, אֶבֶן־חֵן could refer to a stone of acceptability (a charm or talisman) rather than to one that is merely outwardly beautiful (a gem).[27]

Furthermore, "talisman" best fits the preferred interpretation of שֹׁחַד as "bribe" and שָׂכַל as "prospering through insight." Rather than possessing a passive beauty, the אֶבֶן־חֵן is actively involved in achieving the desired success; it is a stone by which one "finds favor," thus achieving one's desires. In this respect—

and regardless whether the subject of שָׂכַל is the bribe or the briber (see point 5 below)—the traditional causative dimension of the Hiphil (here יַשְׂכִּיל) may have some significance in this context.[28]

4. בַּעַל—donor or recipient of the שֹׁחַד

The use of the form בְּעָלָיו[29] is somewhat problematic. Is the בַּעַל of the bribe the donor or the recipient? The שֹׁחַד may be demanded and therefore originate with the person in authority, or it may be offered and thus originate with the person who is trying to corrupt the one in authority.[30] Jacob Finkelstein sheds interesting light on this subject by showing that in Assyrian law bribery was often accepted, and legal action could actually be taken against a judge who took a bribe but did not act on it. In all of this, the ones who suffered most were the poor. As Finkelstein writes, "It is not that the judges rule against the poor as a result of bribery. It is rather that the poor could not have their cases heard at all—an effective way of thwarting justice without resort to flagrant illegality."[31] The Torah of Israel however was radically different; such action was unacceptable because it was opposed to the character of Yahweh, who shows no partiality and accepts no bribe (Deut 10:17). While the OT most often speaks against those in authority who demand bribes from the poor (Ps 15:5; Isa 1:23; Ezek 22:12; Mic 3:11), it also prohibits the practice of offering bribes. In short, this proverb (17:8), as well as the one in 21:14 (see point 1 above), depicts a person who voluntarily resorts to bribery and imagines he can buy success or favor by means of his material assets.

5. פָּנָה and שָׂכַל—what is the subject?

Since Scripture does not judge guilt or innocence on the basis of the origin of the bribe but rather condemns the overall corruption that emanates from a culture of bribery, the use of the Hebrew word בַּעַל is felicitous and enables a wider application of the moral issues than would be possible through simplistic categorization. Put simply, the בַּעַל is the instigator of the bribe, the one who, either by offering it or by demanding it, profits himself at the expense of others. Either way, he is the one in control, the master.[32] The subject of the verbs in question, therefore, is this instigator, not the bribe.[33]

6. Proverbs 17:8—ethical or not?

This leaves us with the question of the proverb's meaning. Commentators seem to be split between those who regard this as an "old wisdom" proverb—advocating a shrewd or wise use of bribery in order to achieve the desired goal of prosperity[34]—and others who regard this proverb as simply stating "a fact of experience."[35] Meinhold, however, more helpfully raises the possibility of an ironic interpretation of the proverb: the proverb accurately describes the way things are in life; yet ironically, things are often not what they appear to be.

The key to this ironic interpretation of the verse lies in the lexical evidence, specifically the construct phrase בְּעֵינֵי. Here, the preposition used is a ב of estimation,[36] and it implies something that is true only with regard to the subject and may in fact have no foundation in reality. This is a common OT construct appearing 149 times. In addition, it appears fifty-one times with the third masculine singular pronominal suffix, the book of Proverbs accounting for nearly a quarter of these occurrences.[37]

On at least eight occasions in Proverbs the phrase בְּעֵינֵי(ו) reflects a state of self-delusion. There are those who are right (12:15; 21:2), pure (16:2; 30:12), and wise (26:5, 12, 16; 28:11) "in their own eyes." Interestingly, the subjects of these verses cover a wide range of "villains": the fool (אֱוִיל, 1:7; 12:15; 15:5; כְּסִיל, 1:22; 18:2; 26:5), the sluggard (עָצֵל, 6:6, 9; 26:16), the filthy ones (צוֹאָה, 30:12), and the rich man (עָשִׁיר, 18:23; 28:6, 11).

If one looks at the parallels and contrasts within the proverbs listed above, the negative force of the construction בְּעֵינֵי(ו) becomes even more apparent. Five of these proverbs reflect antithetical parallelism. Thus, in contrast to those people who exist in a state of self-delusion, there are those who answer discreetly (26:16), the wise who listen to advice (12:15), the poor man who truly has discernment (28:11), and the Lord who weighs the motives of the heart (16:2; 21:2). Furthermore, in the other proverbs it is clear that self-delusion leads simply to greater folly (26:5), hopelessness (26:12), and corruption (30:12).

Therefore, in Prov 17:8, the sage—far from being accepting of or ambivalent toward bribery—highlights the dangerous irony of regarding a bribe as a lucky charm. As far as the giver of the bribe is concerned, he has been successful; his actions have achieved their purpose. He imagines that he has acted cleverly, that he is prosperous; but in reality, he is only wise in his own eyes. This is surely not true wisdom. On the contrary, the careful reader will immediately pick up the implicit condemnation. This is underscored by Scripture's unequivocal opposition to bribery and Proverbs' consistent testimony concerning the fate awaiting one who is חָכָם בְּעֵינָיו. In context, the reader is meant to understand the futility of the actions of the self-deluded who imagine that everything can be bought.

B. Other Bribery-Related Words

1. מַתָּן (mattān)

While I have shown that שֹׁחַד is consistently regarded negatively in the OT (including the Wisdom literature), מַתָּן is more ambiguous in its usage and, in certain contexts, should be understood positively. In some of these, מַתָּן is clearly used for gifts where there is no thought of reciprocation;[38] for example, מַתָּן can be used of offerings to God and even of God himself, and it is thus a more general term than שֹׁחַד. Furthermore, the fact that it can be used of both good and bad gifts argues for its moral neutrality. God gives gifts to us (Ps 68:19; cf. Eph 4:8); we in turn can give acceptable gifts to God (Exod 28:38; Lev 23:38; Num 18:11) as well as unacceptable ones (Ezek 20:26, 31, 39). Thus, only according to context can one determine the moral value or the motivation behind the מַתָּן.

In Wisdom literature, however, the use of מַתָּן is more specific and is usually linked with the idea of self-interest. While a מַתָּן averts anger (Prov 21:14), in the end it will bring trouble upon the giver of the "gift" (Prov 15:27). As well, in Ecclesiastes, it is synonymous with a bribe, for it corrupts the heart (7:7). However, what about Prov 18:16 and 19:6, two passages in which some scholars consider מַתָּן to be understood as neutral?

Langston, in his research on bribery, differentiates between transactional bribes, which are given to facilitate a process that is deemed both just and within the law (e.g., processing of immigration documents), and variance bribes,[39] which are given with the expressed intention of perverting the course of justice (e.g., processing of invalid immigration documents).[40] A clear example of a "transactional bribe" is Prov 18:16 ("A gift [מַתָּן] opens the way for the giver and ushers him into the presence of the great"), but the case is quite different with 19:6.

This problematic verse comes in the midst of a series of proverbs about friendship. It reads, "Many curry favor with a ruler, and everyone is the friend of a man who gives gifts." This verse could be interpreted as positive—commending gift giving to gain friendship—but such an interpretation does not fit the broader literary context, which deals with the nature of true friendship. Proverbs 18:24 affirms that a true friend "sticks closer than a brother," while 19:4, 6–7 makes the point that false friendship is based solely upon selfish interests. According to context, therefore, Prov 19:6 can only be understood as ironic, and מַתָּן, as negative (much as שֹׁחַד in 17:8).

2. כֹּפֶר

Another term related to this topic is the noun כֹּפֶר, derived from the root כפר, meaning "to cover over" and used of a "life-price."[41] Even though this "life-price" was allowed under the law—perhaps as an act of grace—the כֹּפֶר sometimes was used to pervert justice or to cover-up an offense (Job 36:18; Prov 6:35; Amos 5:12).[42] In Prov 13:8 we see that כֹּפֶר probably has a negative connotation, referring to the ability of the rich to pay off the authorities.[43] More often than not, in human interactions the כֹּפֶר was part of a deceitful practice aimed at avoiding the full measure of justice.

3. נָשָׂא פָּנִים

Ethically, the concept of נָשָׂא פָּנִים (lifting up the face) is central to this whole discussion. The phrase is a Semitic colloquialism for going surety (2 Sam 2:22) or showing partiality (Deut 10:17).[44] It may also signify the granting of a request by looking favorably toward someone.[45] As for "showing partiality," this is universally condemned; the contexts in which this phrase is found generally imply that it is a clear injustice, usually as a result of undue influence or bribery. This condemnation within Scripture is based on the character of God, who is totally impartial (Deut 10:17; Job 34:19), in contrast to the gods of the nations (Ps 82:2). Therefore, in human interactions, showing partiality is outrightly forbidden (Lev 19:15) and implicitly discouraged (Mal 2:9); it warrants a divine rebuke (Job 13:8, 10) and the godly shun it (Job 32:21).[46]

4. בֶּצַע and עֹשֶׁק

The point at which bribery evolves into extortion, or the question of whether any bribe solicited by a person in power is in fact a subtle form of extortion, is open to debate. The lines are certainly blurred, but two Hebrew words, בֶּצַע and עֹשֶׁק, come close to the modern concept of extortion.[47] While עֹשֶׁק may be a more general term for oppression (which often involves extorting money), בֶּצַע has connotations of violence and unrighteous gain. That bribery is included in the universal condemnation which covers extortion and oppression[48] can be seen from the instances where שֹׁחַד and מַתָּנָה/מַתָּן appear in parallel to, or in close proximity to, בֶּצַע or עֹשֶׁק.[49]

C. The New Testament

Since the OT has several references to bribery, the virtual absence of this subject from the NT is somewhat surprising. The theme is limited to a couple of cases of actual bribery (in the Gospels) and one celebrated case of attempted bribery (in Acts). No exhortations on this topic are found in the Epistles. However, it should not be assumed that this silence implies approval of bribe payment as a fact of life; it is just as likely that the subject is not addressed because the ethic was clear and the early church knew it had to resist the practice.

The two NT incidents in which bribe money was paid are those of Jesus' betrayal by Judas and of the lie by the chief priests (via the soldiers) that Jesus' body had been stolen. Langston is right to point out that this latter incident "illustrates the progressive escalation that often occurs when people resort to bribery":[50] Judas is bribed to betray Jesus to death; as a result of this death and subsequent resurrection, the soldiers need to be bribed; and having bribed others twice in this situation, the chief priests would have had no problem bribing Pilate if necessary (cf. Matt 28:12–15).

The only other NT incident immediately relevant is found in Acts 24:26,[51] where it would appear that Paul not only refused to pay the sought-after bribe anticipated by Felix, but chose instead to highlight the message of "justice" and "judgment" in order to arouse shame in the governor for expecting payment of such a bribe.[52] In short, the NT gives us no indication that a different ethic from the OT was now in operation with respect to bribery. All three test cases are overwhelmingly negative.

D. Summary of Biblical Data

First, there is an element of lexical ambiguity in the Hebrew words surveyed. Just as the English word *bribe* is morally loaded and the term *gift* is neutral, so in Hebrew שֹׁחַד always has a negative connotation whereas מַתָּן is neutral. However, in Wisdom literature the מַתָּן is often denounced since it occurs in contexts that presuppose partiality toward those with the resources to pay.

Second, the concept of a payoff is present in the term כֹּפֶר. Although the word is used as a redemption metaphor to describe God's gracious activity toward us, in ad hoc interactions between people the term is negative and the כֹּפֶר is condemned.

Third, the OT stance against bribery is inextricably linked to the character of God; he hates bribery (שֹׁחַד) and does not "lift his face" (נָשָׂא פָּנִים, i.e., show partiality) on the basis of a person's gift or status within society.

Fourth, the NT upholds the impartiality of God and presupposes a negative stance toward bribery.

Fifth, in general, the weight of condemnation lies with the person receiving the bribe; however, bribers are also condemned (1 Kgs 15:19; 2 Kgs 16:8; Prov 6:35). No moral condemnation is directed against the victims of extortion.

Sixth, and finally, other secondary reasons for Scripture's denunciation of bribery include such considerations as the perversion of justice in individual cases (Prov 17:23), the wider effect on a culture,[53] the bias toward those with resources, and the counterproductivity of the bribe (Prov 15:27).

III. Ethical Considerations

A. Definitions

In closing, I wish to draw out some of the practical implications of this study for Christian discipleship. But first I need to distinguish between certain related terms on the topic.

1. Bribery and extortion

The real difference between bribery and extortion resides not so much in the person who takes the initiative as it does in the presence or absence of force, real or threatened, physical or emotional. The delay of a computer at customs poses a different dilemma from the threat of kidnapping and "protection money." It is only right that they be discussed separately.

2. Bribery and gifts

The necessity and indistinguishability of various kinds of reciprocities in human society are often given as a reason to tolerate—or at least to not vocally condemn—bribery. One of the arguments used in support of this position is the Hebrew linguistic ambiguity documented above. But even if the Hebrews had several words for a bribe, they were in no doubt as to what constituted justice and what was a clear breach of trust. The validity of moral concepts does not lie in linguistics alone. As we have seen, other factors were much more powerful, notably the character of God. In contrast to the character of the gods who were the subject of Finkelstein's study, Yahweh's character is different.[54] Reciprocity is a perfectly legitimate part of social interaction, but, like any other custom, it can be abused. Noonan summarizes this, saying, "A bribe expresses self interest, a gift conveys love; a bribe subordinates the recipient to the donor, a gift identifies the donor with the recipient. A gift brings no shame, a bribe must be secret. A gift may be disclosed, a bribe must be concealed. The size of a gift is irrelevant; the size of a bribe, decisive. A gift does not oblige, a bribe coerces."[55]

3. Bribery and access payments

The question arises whether access payments (e.g., whereby individuals or companies gain entry into a country) should be treated as bribes or simply as "entrance fees." Our position is that unless these "fees" are uniform and freely applied to all, they constitute bribery because of their tendency to show partiality and to favor the rich. Admittedly, gray areas do exist in other areas of life, particularly with regard to non-cash transactions: for example, government appointments, company promotions, and even the beginning of a romantic relationship. In such cases it is sometimes difficult to tell whether one is dealing with genuine acts of honor and affection or with subtle attempts to gain loyalty and control.

B. Community and Personal Implications: A Call for Radical Repentance

Unquestionably bribery is a problem. It can be found worldwide; and where it has its roots most deeply in society, the citizens are often reduced to a fatalistic tolerance caused by distrust and the desire for quick results with minimum confrontation. It is often justified by emphasizing the low pay of officials and the lack of viable alternatives, though Langston has demonstrated how bribery is common even among higher-paid civil servants.[56] Certainly Western corporations are not immune from the practice, even if political scientist Syed Alatas has argued that bribery is one of the foremost problems in the developing nations.[57] Distrust of government discourages ordinary citizens from going through official channels to report bribery, preferring instead to walk the path of least resistance, especially if it succeeds in speeding things up. This in turn leads to a collective feeling of powerlessness which simply perpetuates the climate of corruption.

As Christians, how are we to respond to this culture of corruption? Marvin R. Wilson puts the question this way: "If the Bible were being written today, . . . would [Paul] not deal with such vices as hush money, black-market food operations, kick-backs from contractors to politicians, the fixing of speeding tickets, money on the side to building inspectors or welfare workers?"[58] Wilson believes that the NT's silence on the matter is due to the fact that the first-century Christians—who were learning at increasing cost what it meant to be disciples of Jesus and what it meant to have no Lord but Christ—would not have considered collaborating with corruption in any way. Like Paul, they would have resisted and used the occasion to proclaim justice. It is hard to believe that people who were willing to face execution rather than say "Caesar is Lord" would have resorted to bribery in order to make economic gain or "speed things up." We need to look for ways in which Christians dealing with bribery can model the values of the kingdom with creativity and integrity.

Some may say that a negative absolutist stance on bribery, such as the one advocated here, is tantamount to legalism. On the contrary, we believe that the thoroughgoing and consistent application of biblical principles to this problem is actually liberating. We must remember that Scripture has nothing good to say about bribery. Its statements are either explicitly or implicitly negative. Bribery offends God, and by participating in it or giving tacit approval to it, we misrepresent the character of God. By perpetuating the practice, those who bribe may be guilty of unwittingly oppressing the poor and weak.

Extortion is a particularly odious form of bribery. Often victims will have no option but to submit. Recurring extortion and racketeering needs to be opposed vehemently by the church. Individuals cannot tackle this evil on their own. The church must become the community of creative alternatives. We need to create a countercultural environment in which Christian businesspeople, bureaucrats, politicians, professionals, blue-collar workers, and others in the service industries can use and develop their gifts within a framework of honesty and integrity. Such idealism may be criticized as impractical and naïve, but the alternatives are worse: continued corruption, hopelessness, crime, economic underdevelopment, oppression, unequal distribution of resources, and privatized (hence, socially impotent) faith.

In our personal relationships, we can be generous without bribing; we can consistently refuse to stand up for our own rights and property while protecting the rights and property of others. In all of this the aim is not to enforce a "new ethic" or extend the law code, but to combat evil and reflect life in the kingdom of God. Christians should not refrain from paying bribes because they want to keep the money for themselves but because they hate corruption. Resisting bribery, therefore, is only the beginning. To avoid self-righteousness we must then turn our attention to reflecting God's character in what we say "yes" to. The most obvious answer in this context is that we are to be a people characterized by the generosity of our generous God. We give freely because God, the Great Donor, has freely given to us out of his abundance (Matt 10:8).

Notes

The Scripture quotations in this work are from the NIV.

This is an abridged and updated version of an unpublished ethics paper presented to Dr. Tim Dearborn. I am grateful to Dr. Dearborn for his encouragement and thoughts on this subject. The earlier, longer paper was posted on the "Scruples for Marketplace Christians" Web site (www.scruples.org/_articles/00000013.html).

[1] See, e.g., Jacob J. Finkelstein, "Middle Assyrian *Sulmānu* Texts," *JAOS* 72 (1952): 77–80; Marvin R. Wilson, "Prophets and Green Palms: Bribery in Biblical Perspective," *CT* 18, no. 8 (January 1974): 13–14, 19; Michael L. Goldberg, "The Story of the Moral: Gifts or Bribes in Deuteronomy?" *Int* 38 (1984): 15–25; Rodney R. Reeves, "To Be or Not to Be? That Is Not the Question: Paul's Choice in Philippians 1:22," *PRSt* 19 (1992): 273–89.

[2] The omission of any entries concerning the various words related to bribery, which occur numerous times in the OT, is all the more surprising when one notices some of the minor and almost trivial subjects treated in these volumes. *ISBE* gives twelve lines to bribery; *IDB* and *The Zondervan Pictorial Bible Dictionary* do slightly better with 23 lines and 25 lines, respectively, which consist mostly of a listing of the biblical verses.

[3] Richard L. Langston, "A Biblical Perspective on Bribery and Extortion and Its Implications in the Philippine Context From a Missionary Viewpoint" (D.Miss. diss., Trinity Evangelical Divinity School, 1989).

[4] John T. Noonan Jr., *Bribes* (New York: Macmillan, 1984).

[5] Goldberg, "The Story of the Moral," 18.

[6] Noonan, *Bribes*, 19, 26.

[7] For "bribe" see NIV, RSV, NASB, NEB, BERKELEY; for "gift" see KJV, RV, NJB, The Message.

[8] For the former (the one who gives it), see most English translations, e.g., NIV, NRSV; for the latter (the one who receives it), see Tg.; BERKELEY; The Message; BDB, 127.

[9] For בַּעַל, see most English translations; for שֹׁחַד, see KJV, RV, LXX. (The Greek seems to have read שֹׁחַד as מוּסָר [discipline], probably to avoid the apparent condoning of bribery.)

[10] For "present," see BDB, 1005; for "gift," see *HALOT* 4:1457.

[11] This excludes the two occurrences of the verb in Job 6:22 and Ezek 16:33.

[12] Exod 23:8; Deut 10:17; 16:19; 27:25; 1 Sam 8:3; 2 Chr 19:7; Job 15:34; Pss 15:5; 26:10; Prov 6:35; 17:23; Isa 1:23; 5:23; 33:15; Ezek 22:12; Mic 3:11.

[13] See the "food eaten in secret" (לֶחֶם סְתָרִים; Prov 9:17) and the secretive or "backbiting" tongue (לְשׁוֹן סָתֶר; Prov 25:23 NRSV).

[14] Derek Kidner, *Proverbs: An Introduction and Commentary* (TOTC; Downers Grove, Ill.: InterVarsity Press, 1964).

[15] Exod 23:8; Deut 16:19; Prov 17:23; Isa 5:23.

[16] 1 Sam 8:3; Isa 33:15.

[17] Ps 15:5; Isa 1:23, where the contrast is with those who defend the fatherless and widows.

[18] Job 15:34; Ps 26:9–10.

[19] So the Tg. and Vulg.

[20] BDB's first definition is "look at" (968) which, if possible, would add support to the possibility of translating אֶבֶן־חֵן as "precious stone," but this definition seems unsustainable. As BDB's secondary sources and the progressive parallelism of the immediate context indicate, in the only verse relevant for our discussion (Gen 3:6), שָׂכַל is best translated "gaining wisdom."

[21] Arndt Meinhold, *Die Sprüche* (2 vols.; ZBK 16; Zürich: Theologischer Verlag, 1991), 2:287.

[22] Attributive genitive, see *IBHS*, 9.5.3b.

[23] So BDB, 6d, 336b; also GKC, Syr., Vulg., KJV, RV, ASV, BERKELEY, The Message.

[24] So *HALOT* 1:8, 332; also RSV, NASB, NIV, NEB, JB, GNB, LB. Compare William McKane, *Proverbs: A New Approach* (OTL; Philadelphia: Westminster, 1970), 502: "the stone with magical properties . . . the amulet."

[25] Edwin Yamauchi describes חֵן as having "an aesthetic significance of charm or beauty" ("חָנַן," *TWOT* 1:302–4).

[26] Compare "a man's charm is his truthfulness" ("Words of Ahiqar" [trans. H. L. Ginsberg; *ANET*, 429]).

[27] Moreover, more common constructions for "precious stone" exist in Scripture. The most common of these is אֶבֶן יְקָרָה, which occurs fourteen times (see 2 Sam 12:30; 1 Chr 29:2). There is also אַבְנֵי־מִלֻּאִים, "set or mounted stones" (Exod 25:7; 35:9, 27) as well as constructions that seem to indicate specific gems such as onyx (אֶבֶן הַשֹּׁהַם; Gen 2:12; Exod 25:7; 28:9; 35:9, 27; 39:6) and sapphire (אֶבֶן־סַפִּיר; Ezek 1:26; 10:1). See also אַבְנֵי־חֵפֶשׁ אַבְנֵי־אֶקְדָּה, sparkling stones, precious or delightful stones (Isa 54:12); אַבְנֵי־פוּךְ וְרִקְמָה, variegated stones (1 Chr 29:2); and also אַבְנֵי־אֵשׁ, stones of fire (Ezek 28:14, 16—although these could refer to thunderbolts).

[28] Since שָׂכַל only appears once in the Qal (1 Sam 18:30) this should not be pressed too much.

[29] Honorific plural, see *IBHS*, 7.4.3c.

[30] For the former (it originates with the one in authority), see 2 Kgs 16:8; Ps 26:10; Prov 21:14; for the latter (it originates with the other), see Prov 17:23; Isa 1:23; 5:23; Mic 3:11. Some of the שֹׁחַד passages are simply general denunciations of the concept of bribery, and in others it is impossible to tell where the bribe originates.

[31] Finkelstein, "Middle Assyrian *Sulmānu* Texts," 79.

[32] Compare the use of בַּעַל in Eccl 7:12: "wisdom preserves the life of its *possessor*."

[33] The transition from plural noun (בְּעָלָיו) to singular verbs (יַשְׂכִּיל and יִפְנֶה) is not problematic. See *IBHS*, 7.4.3b.

[34] So McKane, *Proverbs*, 502.

[35] Bruce Waltke, "Notes to the New American Standard Study Bible" (unpublished), lines 1982–83; cf. Kathleen A. Farmer, *Who Knows What Is Good? A Commentary on the Books of Proverbs and Ecclesiastes* (ITC; Grand Rapids: Eerdmans, 1991), 88.

[36] See *IBHS*, 11.2.5e.

[37] Prov 6:13; 12:15; 16:2; 20:8; 21:2, 10; 24:18; 26:5, 12, 16; 28:11; 30:12. All statistics in this section are taken from Evan-Shoshan, 854–56.

[38] For example, the aged Abraham's and Jehoshaphat's gifts to their sons (Gen 25:6; 2 Chr 21:3), gifts to servants (Ezek 46:16–17), and most notably the spontaneous generous gifts of the celebrating Jews to the poor (Esth 9:22). Compare, however, the reciprocation expected in the surplus gift of Shechem (Gen 34:12).

[39] This is what Goldberg defines as "rendering a verdict *solely with the intention of and on the condition of* his receiving some specific reward in return for his issuing this or that particular decision" ("The Story of the Moral," 24 [italics mine]).

[40] Here Langston follows W. Michael Reisman, *Folded Lies: Bribery, Crusades, and Reforms* (New York: Free Press, 1979), 69.

[41] The price for a life was permitted in some circumstances under the law (Exod 21:30) but not in more serious ones (Num 35:31–32)—although the unscrupulous sometimes let the guilty go free in exchange for a life-price (1 Sam 12:3). At the census it acted as a kind of poll tax and symbolized the value of a person's life (Exod 30:12), but essentially no cash value could be attached to human life (Ps 49:8).

[42] The ransom terminology of Prov 21:18 and Isa 43:3 further establishes the basic semantic idea of a payoff.

[43] However, this verse could possibly be understood more neutrally as their ability to pay the designated sum according to the law.

[44] BDB, 669–72.

[45] Examples of this are as follows: God toward us (Mal 1:8–9; cf. Job 42:8–9), the angels toward Abram (Gen 19:21), Esau toward Jacob (Gen 32:20), David toward Abigail (1 Sam 25:35), or the general respect for the aged (Deut 28:50; Lam 4:16).

[46] The phrase is specifically paralleled with שֹׁחַד in Prov 6:35 (where כֹּפֶר also appears) and the subversion of justice in Prov 18:5.

[47] בֶּצַע is used throughout the OT for profit or advantage (Gen 37:26; Job 22:3; Ps 30:9; Mal 3:14), and the dominant sense is of gain achieved at the expense of others, usually by violence, extortion, or oppression. Violence is implicit in the references to kings carrying off plunder (Judg 5:19), the shedding of innocent blood (Ezek 22:13, 27), and the ultimate destruction and self-ruination of the perpetrator (Prov 1:19) and his family (Prov 15:27).

[48] בֶּצַע is essentially something that one can set one's heart on, and this selfish idolatry gains the clear disapproval of God, who is angered by it (Isa 57:17; Jer 22:17; Hab 2:9). In contrast, the Lord blesses those who turn away from such pursuits (Isa 33:15), and it is to this end that the godly should pray (Ps 119:36).

[49] For בֶּצַע with שֹׁחַד see 1 Sam 8:3; for עֹשֶׁק with שֹׁחַד, Ezek 22:12; for בֶּצַע with מַתָּנָה, Prov 15:27; for עֹשֶׁק with מַתָּנָה, Eccl 7:7; for בֶּצַע with עֹשֶׁק, Isa 33:15 (where שֹׁחַד also appears) and Jer 22:17.

[50] Langston, "A Biblical Perspective," 70.

[51] Both Noonan and Langston discuss the case of Simon the sorcerer in Acts 8 and view it as a case of attempted bribery. This is far from clear. It is more likely that Simon, in his spiritual blindness, was simply attempting to buy something that was not for sale. Either way, the example is yet again negative.

[52] The subject of Paul's preaching in Acts 24 is interesting. As well as preaching about "Jesus Christ," his dominant motif, he preached about "righteousness, self-control and judgment to come" (v. 25). The first and third are significant in relation to expectations of bribes; the second is relevant considering Drusilla's status as an adulteress under Jewish law.

[53] For an example of the effect the contrasting morals of leaders can have on a culture, compare Samuel, who never took a bribe (1 Sam 12:3), with his sons, who were leaders in the corruption of their day (1 Sam 8:3).

[54] A point well made by Goldberg ("The Story of the Moral," 19, 23). Since the judge was a representative of the divine, he would have been repudiating God's character to accept a bribe. Given Paul's statements in Rom 13, there is no reason to believe this is any different today.

[55] Noonan, *Bribes,* 697.

[56] Langston, "A Biblical Perspective," 111.

[57] Syed H. Alatas, *The Problem of Corruption* (Singapore: Times Books, 1986), 102, referenced by Langston, "A Biblical Perspective," 5.

[58] Wilson, "Prophets and Green Palms," 13.

The Terrors of the Night: Love, Sex, and Power in Song of Songs 3

Iain W. Provan

In the last twenty-five years, biblical scholarship has gone from having a fixed (and often obsessive) interest in the *parts* that make up our biblical texts to having a gradual, but inexorable, renewed and widespread interest in the way the parts contribute to the *whole.* Although rigorous inquiry into the nature of even the smallest part of a text is important for gaining a full understanding of it, it has been more clearly seen that our comprehension of the part itself is intrinsically bound up with our understanding of the whole to which it contributes. The common idea that one can arrive at an entirely objective account of what various sections of text once meant in isolation from each other and what they mean independent of the interpreter's preunderstanding has been largely discredited. One consequence of this shift in perspective has been that biblical scholars are now prepared to revisit many texts previously characterized (and often caricatured) as having little internal coherence. Where scholars once assumed incoherence, they are now open to finding coherence.

This article is offered as such a second look at the two parts of Song of Songs 3:1–11 and also as an evaluation of the way in which this two-part passage contributes to our understanding of the whole "way of wisdom" that Scripture reveals regarding male-female relationships. For although this biblical book is described in its heading as *the Song,* modern commentators commonly identify it as an anthology of love lyrics more or less loosely associated with each other.[1] Scholarship has allowed for little true coherence between the parts, beyond the most general thematic and linguistic links. Certainly the widespread perception of ch. 3 in particular is that only the loosest, if any, connection exists between its two sections, vv. 1–5 and vv. 6–11. Roland Murphy presents the common view in writing thus of vv. 6–11: "These verses describe a procession of 'Solomon,' which has nothing to do with the episode of the woman's search in vv 1–5."[2]

The juxtaposition of the two sections, or "poems," in ch. 3 is thus understood to be merely fortuitous. The interpreter is to make nothing of it.[3] Yet here I will contend that as we grasp the connection between the two parts, we will both understand Song of Songs as a whole more clearly and comprehend more precisely what it says about being truly human. Indeed, as we see the relationship among the parts of the chapter, the whole Song, and the Scriptures in their entirety, we shall begin more fully to understand our need to move, with God's help, beyond the fragmentation of our humanness and toward a restoration to wholeness. But before we can draw out the far-reaching implications of such a reading (sections II and III below), we will need to engage in some detailed exegetical analysis of the language and syntax of Song 3 (sec. I).

I. The Chapter as a Whole

We begin our reconsideration of Song 3 with an exegetical review of its opening five verses.[4] Here we read of a bed *(miškāḇ)* upon which a woman lies and upon which she seeks "the one [her] heart loves" (v. 1). This phrase is repeated in vv. 2, 3, and 4, and in its repetition it communicates the intensity of the longing. This woman is most naturally understood as the one who has already spoken in the opening chapters (1:2–7, 12–14, 16; 2:1, 3–13, 15–17), not least because the warning she offers to the daughters of Jerusalem in 3:5 is also found in 2:7. The man she seeks is also most naturally understood as the lover who is addressed or spoken of in these earlier passages and who speaks himself in 1:8–11, 15, 17; 2:2, 14.

The wording of the opening verses of ch. 3 implies, however, that what is described is a dream rather than an everyday reality (as we are also in a dream in 5:2–8; cf. Dan 2:28–29) and that 3:2 is intended not to tell us what happened *next* (as the NIV's "I will get up now" implies) but rather to describe what this woman said to herself and did during the dream; that is, she does not look first for the man while in the bed and then later while in the city. She looks for the man *only* while in the bed, saying to herself in her dream, "let me arise ... [and] search" (v. 2). Verses 1–2 have identical reports of failure that refer to the same, dreamt search; the first part of v. 2 simply expands upon the first part of v. 1. The city in which she searches is not identified, and given that we are in dreamland, we should probably not seek to identify it. But if one does seek a "location," then Jerusalem is the obvious candidate, given the mention of that city in v. 5. In the midst of her own frantic "rounds" of the city (*sbb,* v. 2; "go about the city," NIV) and of her failure to "find" her beloved (*mṣ*ʾ, vv. 1–2), the woman is "found" (*mṣ*ʾ, v. 3) by watchmen as they "make their rounds" of the city (*sbb,* v. 3)—watchmen who are likewise the shadowy figures of dreams. They neither challenge the woman about her unusual presence in the city at nighttime (cf. 5:7) nor answer her question. The shadows of the night simply flit past as the desperate woman moves through the streets; and then suddenly (no details are provided), she finds her man (v. 4).

Her anxiety is communicated in what happens next. She grasps hold of him (*ʾḥz),* refusing to let him go (*rph* in the Hiphil; "to leave alone, forsake"), and escorts him to her mother's house and then to her mother's bedroom (*ḥeder,* as in 1:4). Now they are reunited in intimacy once again. Whether the dream bed is the same as the real bed of 3:1 is not made clear, but it is unlikely given the previous reference to the woman's presence in the king's chambers (1:4). Perhaps in the dreamworld the maternal home is symbolic of the security and safety for which the woman yearns—the security and safety of younger days.[5] And so the mother, we may imagine, embraces both her daughter and her daughter's lover and hides them away in her inner chamber, with all its associations with the womb ("the room of the one who conceived me," v. 4). A frightening separation has been overcome, and the lovers lie together under parental protection and blessing.

The alarming power of love, which is also displayed in the opening chapters (e.g., 2:5–7), has once again been demonstrated. This is a love that can invade even the realm of the unconscious, and it brings with it unsettling thoughts. It is no surprise, therefore, that the warning that follows the embrace in 2:6–7 should also follow the embrace in 3:4–5. The daughters of Jerusalem, we are told, should be wary of stirring up love until the time is right.[6] The power of love is far beyond their control, and it drives one to dream crazy dreams, if not to enact them.

It is with these opening five verses that vv. 6–11 and their "procession of Solomon" allegedly have nothing to do. Yet even a cursory reading of the chapter reveals that there are connections between the two parts, connections that invite further reflection. Both parts tell us of things that happen during the night (note the unusual plural *ballêlôṯ* in vv. 1, 8) and things involving a bed (*miškāḇ,* v. 1; *miṭṭâ,* v. 7, NIV's "carriage"), and both place a mother in a prominent position (*ʾēm,* vv. 4, 11). Further reflection in turns reveals (I shall argue), that it is far from clear whether any real Solomonic procession (usually thought of as a wedding procession) can be found in the passage at all. Once the idea of the wedding procession is banished from the mind—and once we resist all the questionable interpretations of individual verses that follow from this false premise—the two parts of ch. 3 appear to have more in common than one might at first think. For the text does not concern, as some commentators believe, the pilgrimage of a princess across the desert from Egypt (or some other distant land) in a heavily defended and very expensive sedan chair.[7] It concerns instead the heavily defended bed of the wealthy Solomon, who has all things at his disposal (including women) and possesses no neurotic fear of losing a unique beloved (in contrast to 3:1–4). Yet despite all he has, he knows nothing of intimacy and fulfillment.

We begin with the ʾ*appiryôn* that Solomon made (v. 9), which, in spite of the highly misleading definite article in NIV ("the carriage"), is not to be presumed to be identical with the carriage (representing a different word, *miṭṭâ*) about which the NIV tells us in v. 7. The word ʾ*appiryôn* is unique in the OT, and its precise derivation is problematic;[8] but the description of it in vv. 9–10 clearly suggests a stationary structure (or part of one) rather than a portable structure. First, its interior or middle *(tôkô)* is said to be "paved with love" (v. 10; "lovingly inlaid," NIV). The verb *rsp* does not otherwise appear in the OT, but the noun *riṣpâ* does, and it always refers to the paved floor of a temple or palace (2 Chr 7:3; Esth 1:6; Ezek 40:17–18). The associated noun *marṣepeṯ* appears in 2 Kgs 16:17 of a stone pavement in the temple in Jerusalem (cf. *riṣpâ,* "glowing stone," in 1 Kgs 19:6 and Isa 6:6). These words never appear in the context of the inlaid interiors of movable objects, which would not actually move very far if encumbered by many stones. Therefore, even if (as I shall argue below) the "paving" is metaphorical rather than literal, the word is clearly associated with large, permanent structures rather than smaller, movable ones.

Second, the word ʿ*ammûḏ* (NIV translates the plural form as "posts," v. 10) always refers to large pillars of a size and strength sufficient to support a building, except where it refers to a column of smoke. It is used, for example, of the pillars in Solomon's palace (1 Kgs 7:2–6) and in Ezekiel's temple (Ezek 42:6) as well as of the prominent bronze pillars, Jakin and Boaz, that stood before the Jerusalem temple (1 Kgs 7:15–22). It is also used of the movable tabernacle's pillars (e.g., Exod 27:10–11); but this structure was also a large one that could not be simply be lifted up *in toto* and carried across the wilderness. The point is that the word ʿ*ammûḏ* never refers to the kind of smaller "post" that might be found on an allegedly movable ʾ*appiryôn.* If such hypothetical posts were indeed fashioned out of silver, they would also add considerable weight to such a structure. The same is true of the gold mentioned in v. 10, whatever the unique noun *rěp̄îḏâ* ("base," NIV) refers to. The verb *rpd* has already appeared in Song 2:5 in reference to the refreshment or support that fruit gives. It seems natural, therefore, to understand the *rěp̄îḏâ* as something that supports the pillars (cf. Job 17:13; 41:30 [MT 41:22], where the verb refers to something spread out on the ground), and thus as the floor or as the foundation or base of the structure.

As we add all this detail together, we begin to see that the overall impression is not of a carriage at all, but of a large, fixed structure constructed (at least to a significant extent) of wood with silver supporting pillars and a gold base or floor. The associations are above all with Solomon's major building works as described in 1 Kgs 5–10. The two main building materials mentioned in 1–2 Kings are indeed wood from Lebanon (1 Kgs 5:6–10; 7:1–12) and gold (1 Kgs 6:19–22, 30–35; 10:16–21), which can even be used for flooring (1 Kgs 6:30).

It is not surprising, then, that some commentators have understood this passage as alluding to Solomon's throne hall (1 Kgs 7:7; cf. 10:18–20 for the impressive throne),[9] taking the seat of Song 3:10, which is upholstered with expensive purple cloth, as the throne. Certainly one can interpret the description of vv. 9–10 as a visual movement from a vast hall dominated by wood, presumably including a wooden ceiling, down past the great silver pillars to a golden floor, and at last arriving at the centerpiece of the whole scene—the throne that sits on a specially paved area (a mosaic of other precious stones, perhaps?) in the middle of the hall (cf. 2 Kgs 16:17, the analogous setting of the great Sea in the temple on a paved area). At least one of the suggested derivations for *ʾappiryôn* (from the Egyptian for "house" or "great house") would fit this scenario.

I agree that *ʾappiryôn* most likely refers to a room within Solomon's palace, which was known as the Palace of the Forest of Lebanon because of the abundant use of wood from Lebanon in its construction. It is important to note, however, the highly metaphorical language used in the second part of v. 10. The centerpiece is not a regular throne (*kissēʾ*, as in 1 Kgs 7:7; 10:18–20) but literally "a chariot" (*merkāḇ*, Lev 15:9; 1 Kgs 4:26); and the "middle" is not paved in the normal way with stone but with love. In the context of the Song, this last reference to love (*ʾahăḇâ*, as in Song 2:4–5, 7)—a troubling reference for those commentators who approach ch. 3 too literally—is much more likely a reference to acts of physical love than to the loving construction of a pavement or mosaic. The chariot is therefore, in my view, best thought of as a bed and not as a throne. It is the finely upholstered "vehicle" upon which the king travels, as it were, on his journey of sexual delight. The daughters of Jerusalem (the king's many wives and concubines as well as other women; cf. 1 Kgs 11:3; Song 6:8) pave his way, as it were, by lying with the king in the center of his *ʾappiryôn*, his bedchamber. These are the people who provide the "stones" that enable the ongoing royal journey. There is, therefore, "movement" in vv. 9–10 of our section: it is the movement, however, not of a sedan chair or carriage but of the "chariot" upon which the king rides to meet the dawn.

It is now clear that this "chariot" within the *ʾappiryôn*—and not the *ʾappiryôn* itself—is the *miṭṭâ* of v. 7. *Miṭṭâ* is a regular word for bed or couch, a common item of furniture in the OT that is found in, among other places, a bedroom.[10] Beds can sometimes be lifted up and moved, of course (e.g., 1 Sam 19:13–16), depending upon their mode of construction; and *miṭṭâ* is therefore used also of a funeral bier (2 Sam 3:31). There is no justification elsewhere in the OT, however, for understanding the word as referring to a carriage or sedan chair. It is a bed; and it only "moves" in Song 3 because it is, metaphorically, a chariot.

It is not inappropriate, given the context of such fictive movement, to refer to the sixty warriors associated with the bed as "escorting" it (NIV), so long as it is remembered that they are said simply to be *sāḇîḇ lāh,* "around it" (v. 7; cf. *sbb* in vv. 2–3). The soldiers are the most striking feature of the scene, and thus they attract detailed comment from our observer. They are "warriors from the warriors of Israel" (*gibbōrîm . . . miggibbōrê yiśrāʾēl,* v. 7; "warriors, the noblest of Israel," NIV)—an elite guard, similar to David's bodyguards (e.g., 2 Sam 23:8–39) but twice as many in number.[11] They are all men who are "held fast by the sword" (*ʾăḥuzê ḥereḇ,* v. 8; "wearing the sword," NIV), devoted to and possessed by their profession (cf. *ʾḥz* in v. 4, "I held him"). They are battle-hardened and ready for action (note the repetition of *sword* in v. 8, emphasizing military readiness). It is a heavily guarded bed, this "chariot" of Solomon. He goes into "battle" with good men around him to protect him from the "terrors of the night" (v. 8)—if it is indeed Solomon's protection that they are concerned with.

This raises the question, however, of what this section of ch. 3 is really about. It is very difficult to read it in the Hebrew, stripped of all the interpretative translation that has confused fictive with real motion, without thinking that we are dealing with satire. Here is the great Solomon, driving around in his pretentious chariot-bed. He is the mighty Solomon, yet he needs sixty elite warriors to stand around his "chariot" and help get him safely through the night. In truth he cuts a rather pathetic figure, inhabiting a lonely world of materialism and sexual conquest—for conquest is implied by the military overtones of vv. 7–8. The charioteer Solomon rides roughshod over the daughters of Jerusalem, on a road paved with sexual acts. Perhaps their terror, rather than his, is alluded to in v. 8: the guards are stationed both to keep the women in and to keep intruders out.

In this light, it is intriguing that the language of v. 6—which seems partly designed to evoke the picture of clouds of myrrh and incense rising up from the bed—is at the same time very much the language of temple and sacrifice. The NIV's "perfumed" is *qṭr* in the Pual, a verb that regularly means in the Piel "to make sacrifices smoke." Myrrh can be an ingredient of sacred oil (e.g., Exod 30:23), and frankincense *(lĕḇônâ)* is heavily associated with sacrifice (e.g., Lev 2:1–2; 5:11). The Hebrew feminine noun *ʾăḇāqâ,* "spices," is unique, but a masculine noun from the same root refers figuratively on one occasion to the clouds (or dust) under God's feet (Nah 1:3). Smoke *(ʿāšān)* is itself associated with the divine presence in verses like Exod 19:18 and Isa 6:4 and also Joel 2:30 [MT 3:3], which gives us the only other occurrence of *tîmărôṯ ʿāšān,* "billows of smoke." The related *tîmōrôṯ* actually designates ornamental palm figures in the Solomonic temple.[12] Finally, the feminine participle *ʿōlâ,* "coming up," is identical in form to the feminine noun *ʿōlâ,* "burnt offering," and the verb *ʿlh* is often used of offering up a sacrifice.

A good case can thus be made for taking Song 3:6 as an allusion to the sacrificial female victim who lies upon the "altar," which is Solomon's bed. This is the force of the question, "Who is this coming up from the desert?" with its feminine pronoun *zōʾt*, "this." It is a woman who "comes up"; but she is not moving laterally across a (real) desert in the direction of Jerusalem, as has sometimes been argued. She is, rather, rising up from the royal bed in the way that smoke rises up into the sky when sacrifices are burnt. We might translate v. 6 this way: "Who is this, ascending from the wilderness like a column of smoke, burned with myrrh and frankincense made from the dust of the merchant?" There is, again, movement, but on this occasion it is the movement of the sacrificial victim upward and not (at least in the first instance) of the royal "chariot" forward. It is in fact this initial "movement" in v. 6 that first draws the attention of the observer to the chariot-bed in v. 7. Perhaps we are meant to imagine a watchman standing on a city wall, looking out intently into the wilderness and perceiving in the distance what looks like a column of smoke. As he watches the smoke clears and he sees, for the first time (*hinnêh*, "look!"—emphasizing the dramatic discovery), the detail of the "chariot." The situation is analogous to that in 2 Kgs 9:14–29, where a watchman sees troops approaching in the distance and is gradually able to make out Jehu, son of Nimshi, driving his chariot. So it is possible that, in the end, the "column of smoke" has a double function, suggesting both sacrifice and the dust cloud stirred up by the royal entourage as (in the mind's eye) it approaches the one observing it.[13]

The characterization of the royal bed as a "wilderness" is, of course, a clever touch, for the wilderness, or "steppe," in the OT is uncultivated and unsettled land; it is an uncivilized place often described as harsh and infertile, and it is regarded as a place of danger, evil, and death.[14] It is the antithesis of the garden of Eden (Isa 51:3).[15] To name the royal bed a wilderness is to offer an understanding of it that, we presume, is very different from Solomon's understanding, given all his wealth and cultured sophistication. It is also to contrast most forcibly the love making that happens there with the love making that happens elsewhere in the Song, which is so routinely associated with fertility and abundant vegetation (e.g., Song 1:13–17; 2:1–13).

If Song 3:6–11 is thus a dark and bitter satire concerning Solomon and his string of sacrificial female victims, then the point of the juxtaposition of vv. 1–5 and vv. 6–11, already suggested in the contrast just mentioned between the royal bed and other beds, becomes clearer. The first part of our chapter concerns an individual woman who is in love with an individual man and who initiates an anxious search for him. She is certainly not an unwilling sacrificial victim in this relationship—although Song 1:4, 12, which set her in intimate proximity to the king, have previously implied that she has indeed been one of *his* victims, as a member of the royal harem. She is not, in this relationship, simply a stepping stone on the man's road toward sexual utopia. She is an initiator; she knows no terrors of the night but instead steps out bravely into the darkness to find her man. Her fear is not that she will be required to spend time with him; her fear is that she will not be able to spend such time. Hers is a vulnerable bed, unguarded by any military force; and her lover can leave it when he wishes. It is not surrounded *(sbb)* by warriors who are "grasped" *(ʾḥz)* by their swords. She herself must therefore "go around" *(sbb)* looking for her lover, risking the encounter with the guards who make their rounds of the city *(sbb)*, and she herself must "grasp" him *(ʾḥz)*. Yet in the midst of the vulnerability there is intimacy and joy, offered and overseen by the woman's mother, who provides her ordinary bedchamber (with all its associations with fertility) for the lovers. There is, on the other hand, no true intimacy experienced in the wilderness, the extraordinary royal bedchamber. It is not even clear that there is Solomonic joy. We do read that Solomon rejoiced on his wedding day, when his mother, too, was involved in the proceedings (v. 11); but that wedding day, for all we know, may be far in the past. The "crown" of v. 11 may be only a sad reminder of better days—once symbolic of joy but now symbolic only of the royal power to command and of the unequal terms upon which Solomon meets women in his bed.[16] There is certainly no clear evidence elsewhere in vv. 6–11 that a wedding is currently being celebrated and no overall emphasis throughout the passage on joy.

The juxtaposition of the two sections of Song 3 thus seems far from fortuitous; on the contrary, the two parts fit well together as aspects of one whole whose purpose is to present, for the reader's consideration, two contrasting types of male-female relationship. The two kinds of relationship are already in view in Song 1–2, although their precise nature is less clear in these chapters. We do hear, however, of the relationship between the woman and her lover, who address each other and enter freely into love and sexual intimacy in joyful abandonment, without reservation or shame; and we do hear also of the relationship between the woman and the king, a third party to the loving couple who has power over the woman because she is a member of the royal harem. In Song of Songs generally, in fact, Solomon explicitly appears only in this third-person mode, whether it be in Song 1:4, 12; 3:6–11; or 8:10–12. This last passage is part of another entire chapter of the Song that is also best read as contrasting two male-female relationships: the relationship between the woman and her lover versus the kind of relationship more commonly experienced by women in the ancient world, one in which the male had dominance and power over the female. In this situation, the woman did not necessarily enter the relationship by choice; she was often only a pawn in a man's game that had to do with legal contracts, money, and the collection of objects of pleasure. In Song 8, the woman proclaims her resistance to Solomon, the famous collector of women (vv. 11–12), and to the brothers who claim rights of disposal of her in marriage (vv. 8–9).[17]

There are thus clear indications that we have in Song of Songs three main characters (the woman, her lover, and the king) rather than merely two (the woman and her lover, who is the king)—an insight derived ultimately from the medieval Spanish exegete Abraham ibn Ezra, who first distinguished the "king" in the Song from the "shepherd" of the opening chapter. When one understands this, it is a relatively easy matter to go on to articulate a coherent reading of the whole Song. Different versions of such a reading have been proposed, but I understand the movement of the Song in the following way: The woman, already a member of the king's harem, expresses her continuing love for her lover (and, implicitly, her disdain for the king), and her lover reciprocates (chs. 1–2). The contrast between king and lover is forcibly underlined in ch. 3, where both the woman's determination to overcome threats to her relationship with her lover and her negative view of the royal bed and its owner are clear.[18] The threats to and the depths of the relationship are evidenced in chs. 4–5, where both the language and the imagery speak of a committed, marital-like relationship between the man and the woman;[19] chs. 6–7 portray in further detail the nature of this relationship. Chapter 8 provides a strong closing statement of the woman's passion for her lover and her resistance to those other males who claim possession of her, whether they be her brothers or the king. The Song thus reveals itself to be a stirring tale of fidelity to first love in the face of power and of all the temptations of the royal court. It is a poetic account of one ancient couple's insistence that sexual intimacy should be bound up with freedom and love rather than with coercion and domination.

II. The Song and the Biblical Whole

Just as Song 3 (when read as a whole) both illuminates and is illuminated by the broader context of the whole Song of which it is a part, so also it illuminates and is illuminated by the still broader context that is, for the Christian reader who seeks to walk in "the way of wisdom," provided by the Bible as a whole. First we think of the other biblical materials concerning King Solomon, which make for interesting reading; for the memory of him that was kept alive in Israel after his death was not always flattering. He was remembered as a wise king, yet he was also portrayed as one whose wisdom was not always used for honorable ends (cf. 1 Kgs 2:13–46, where he snatches every opportunity to remove threats to his sovereignty over Israel). Toward the end of his reign, his wisdom had degenerated considerably into a self-indulgent game of words (1 Kgs 10:1–13).[20] He was known as a king who was committed to worshiping and obeying God, yet questions about his integrity have persisted. During his reign, he defied in increasing measure the Mosaic law concerning kingship (Deut 17:14–20), as he accumulated first horses (1 Kgs 4:26, 28), then large amounts of gold (1 Kgs 9:10–28), and finally large numbers of women (1 Kgs 11:1–3). Eventually his accumulated individual indiscretions turned to outright apostasy (1 Kgs 11:4–8).

He was in many ways an ideal king ruling over an ideal kingdom, but the ideal and the reality were always in some degree of tension, and eventually the reality was much less than ideal. This was true to such an extent that some rabbis of a much later time spoke of Solomon in the same breath as such notorious kings of Israel as Manasseh (2 Kgs 21). Already in the book of Ecclesiastes, the negative memory of Solomon provides the necessary backdrop against which Qohelet can enact his "Solomonic" quest for gain (Eccl 1:12–2:26).[21] Here "Solomon" is presented as one who initially finds, as he strives for profit from his labor, that wisdom's achievements are limited; he then discovers that pleasure is also a cul-de-sac. He was one who set out in a godlike way to transform his environment and, thereby, to facilitate his enjoyment of life by building houses, gardens, vineyards, and "parks" (*pardēs* in Eccl 2:5, as in Song 4:13) and by filling this earthly paradise with slaves, herds and flocks, hoards of treasure, and women. All of this did not, however, bring him any advantage. He was not able to burst through the limitations of mortality and frailty and somehow get ahead in the game of life.

It is in the context of 1 Kgs 1–11 and Eccl 1:12–2:26 (which themselves direct us back, in particular, to the story of creation and fall in Gen 1–3 and the following chapters) that we must first of all understand ch. 3 of Song of Songs. From the biblical story we are to learn that at the heart of the human problem lies a refusal to live life within the confines God has ordained for mortal beings, even though this may involve living in a paradise where joy abounds. From the beginning, human beings have chosen to transgress these God-given boundaries in search of something more, turning the life that comes as a gift to be enjoyed into capital that might fund imperial plans for exploitation and expansion. The more power we have, the more we become intent on creating our own paradise to supplant the kingdom of God—which is why kings like Solomon, more than any other sort of human being in the OT, are portrayed as grasping after godlikeness and seeking to fashion reality after their own liking. They have at their disposal the resources to make a credible attempt at equivalence with the gods. Yet their lives are blatant representations of what the Bible presents as the characteristic set of human choices; and these choices have enormous repercussions for other people as well as for the aspirants to godhood. For if I, as a human being, grasp after divinity and regard myself (rather than God) as the center of the universe, it is inevitable that I will no longer view my fellow human beings as my equals, made in the image of God, toward whom I have a duty of love and respect. Instead I will see them as those whose interests must be repressed in favor of my own and whose value can be measured only in terms of their value to me.

The narrative of Gen 1–6 shows us all too clearly how the progression works. Rebellion against God leads to alienation between the man and the woman. They were created to be one flesh, naked but not ashamed (2:24–25); but now they are divided, at odds with each other, and concealed from one another (3:7). These humans, at least, stay together and build community; but in Gen 4:1–16 we read of the alienation of brother from brother, which has serious consequences (death for one and exile for the other). Here we have the complete breakdown of community, and the alienation progresses even further, outward from the center of the family circle: neighbor and neighbor are divided and alienated (4:23–24), and the community slides into complete chaos and anarchy (6:11–13). Even humankind's many achievements of culture (cities, music, etc.; 4:17–22) cannot disguise this slow but remorseless breakdown of community; sophistication, we are shown, is quite compatible with barbarism. Some people are valued only when they serve the interests of the others, as is suggested in 5:28–31, where a father welcomes a new son into the world (Noah) not so much as a son but more so as a worker who will release his father from the toil imposed upon Adam's descendants (5:29).

When we first hear of a man being married to more than one wife (4:19–24), it is in this context of broken-down communities. This man, Lamech, is not a man of character (he boasts to his two wives of the elevenfold and entirely disproportionate retribution visited on another man; note 4:23–24), which makes the readers question the rightness of his polygamy. His taking two wives is a striking departure from the creation ideal articulated in 2:23–24, where it is clear that the marriage relationship should involve one man and one woman. That polygamy became accepted by many Israelites does not, of course, mean it was ever intended by God (any more than was the case with divorce; cf. Mal 2:16; Mark 10:2–9).

In this broader context, the juxtaposition of Song 3:1–4 and 3:6–11, separated by the warning about love's dangers in 3:5, may be more fully appreciated. The first passage focuses our attention on a woman's desires, hopes, and fears; and it reminds us that she is not an object to be possessed, nor a number to be called, but a person to be encountered. In the world of her dreams, at least, she is able to pursue the man of her choice, grasp hold of him, and enjoy the deepest intimacy with him. We, as readers, are exhorted to respect that dream and not to hinder its achievement (just as the watchmen do not, on this occasion, prevent its consummation). The world of love is a dangerous one, however, and in 3:6–11 we see its dark side. Here a king who has sought to build paradise sits in a chariot-bed that is, ironically, a desert. He is the polygamist par excellence, adding ludicrous numbers of women to his collection of objects, and the damage both to these women and to himself is plain. The women are victims sacrificed on his altar; he himself cuts a pathetic figure, surrounded by his elite troops and his luxurious furnishings as he waits for his next "offering." The mutuality of the garden of Eden, so desperately sought by the woman in 3:1–4, is entirely lacking here. There remains only power and objectification.

So it has often been for women throughout history, whether in biblical times or later. The male lust for divinity has had terrible consequences for women as the enormous social costs of idolatry have been passed on, especially to those who have lacked independence and power. Women have typically been the property of men, traded between them without the slightest consideration for the women's desires and with the shared assumption that the matter was somewhat akin to horse trading—the money earned, the status gained, and the breeding potential being the main concerns. Outside the realm of law, including marriage law, women have been vulnerable before a deeply rooted male compulsion toward sexual conquest and domination, and they have frequently been the victims of the abuse of power. Song of Songs gives us a glimpse of life through the perspective of one of these victims: one of many women collected by Solomon (and men of his kind) for his pleasure, who were to him (and men like him) merely "a breast or two," to use the casual and offensive words of Eccl 2:8.[22]

III. Conclusion: The Bible and Human Wholeness

By putting a description of a woman's dream alongside a description of the typical female life, Song of Songs—in concert with those other voices that make up the chorus that is Scripture—calls us beyond merely acknowledging the all-too-common reality of our distorted male-female relationships and onward in pursuit of a different vision. For the Song rejects common reality as either inevitable or normative and looks beyond it to a different way of being, one in which persons are taken seriously first of all as persons, whether men or women, and in which joyous mutuality of relationship is the norm. Although the Song reminds us not to be romantic about a world in which coercion and violence often mark human affairs, it nevertheless lauds romance. While it reminds us that sexual activity is not itself intimacy and can even express estrangement, it nevertheless praises sexual intimacy. And in its presentation of ideal love, which we constantly fail to achieve both individually and societally, Song of Songs summons us to repent and to determine to live differently before God and our fellow human beings. It exhorts us to place the erotic in the context of all that is wholesome and most deeply human and to resolve not to allow our sexuality to wreak havoc on human life by escaping its proper time and place.

The Song calls us beyond repentance, however, to healing: to face the darkness within us, to understand it, and to have dispelled it by God's light in due time. When we read of the woman's dream in Song 3, we are reminded that God did not make the world the way it is and that he does not ask us to pretend that he did (nor does he commend us when we do so). Even if the false gods of the cosmos, whether human or not, are apt to regard women only as somewhat anonymous means to their own ends, we know this is certainly not how the living God regards women (or any of his creatures). On the contrary, the Bible teaches us that God made us creatures who possess freedom of will. Each of us is precious to God as an individual, and God desires to have each of us in a right and good relationship with him. God is not interested in relating to human beings coercively (although in the end all mortal beings must reckon with his power if they will not embrace his love), and his relationship with each of us is highly personal, not anonymous. None of us is merely a means to his ends. We are ends in ourselves.

So it is that in the book of Hosea, for example, God speaks of wooing his bride, Israel, back from her sinful ways and restoring that one-to-one relationship that she had previously had with him (Hos 2:14–23). In the Gospels, we find that when Jesus comes among his people he likewise invites, rather than forces, those to whom he speaks to pursue a relationship with him. Above all, it is clear that those who yearn for the divine Lover and pursue him will indeed find him, just as the woman finds the man in Song 3:1–4 (cf. Matt 7:7–11). It is striking to note how often throughout the Gospels Jesus is found relating to women in ways that would have been offensive to many first-century Jewish men but that testify to God's equal love and esteem for women and men.[23] Since God's relating to us should always be the largest context within which we work out our relationships to each other, it should be especially clear to those who know the Gospels which of the two kinds of male-female relationship described in Song 3 we should pursue. Only as we pursue relationships of joyful mutuality, rather than those of oppression and coercion, shall we testify truly about who God is.

Notes

I am delighted to be able to offer this paper in the context of a volume honoring Bruce Waltke, my predecessor in the Marshall Sheppard Chair of Biblical Studies at Regent College. I am grateful to my teaching assistant, Sungmin Min Chun, for his help in preparing this paper for publication.

The Scripture quotations in this article are my own translation unless otherwise noted.

[1] See, e.g., Robert Gordis, *The Song of Songs and Lamentations* (rev. and aug. ed.; New York: Ktav, 1974), 16–18; Marcia Falk, *Love Lyrics from the Bible* (*BL* 4;

Sheffield: Almond, 1982), 62–70; John G. Snaith, *The Song of Songs* (NCB; London: Marshall Pickering, 1993), 6–8.

[2] Roland E. Murphy, *The Song of Songs* (Hermeneia; Minneapolis: Fortress, 1990), 151.

[3] Nothing is in fact generally made of it in modern writing on the Song: cf. Snaith, *Song*, 45–57; Tom Gledhill, *The Message of the Song of Songs: The Lyrics of Love* (The Bible Speaks Today; Leicester: Inter-Varsity Press, 1994), 143–52; Othmar Keel, *The Song of Songs* (CC; trans. F. J. Gaiser; Minneapolis: Fortress, 1994), 119–37. George A. F. Knight and Friedemann W. Golka, *Revelation of God: A Commentary on the Books of the Song of Songs and Jonah* (ITC; Grand Rapids: Eerdmans, 1988), 20–22, at least hints at the kind of reading of 3:6–11 for which I shall be arguing, when Knight suggests that the "editor has assumed it wise to contrast at this point the pomp and worldliness of a royal wedding with the simplicity and holiness of the union of two lovers from a village situation" (21); but the point is not made in pursuit of a link with 3:1–5.

[4] For the sake of convenience and accessibility to the nonspecialist in Hebrew, I shall refer to the NIV as the base English text in the following exegesis, although as we progress I shall offer various alternative translations.

[5] The mother's house is the natural home of the woman who is not married (cf. Gen 24:28; Ruth 1:8).

[6] If the word *love* in the charge is taken to refer to one of the lovers themselves, the charge could in principle be understood as a less ominous request to not disturb the beloved as he sleeps but to leave him in peace until he is eager to arise. Yet the focus of Song 8:6–7 is the terrible power of love, which follows closely on a similar aside to the daughters of Jerusalem in 8:4, so this suggests that we are to understand the charge as a warning. Because love can be devastating and overpowering, these young women should ensure that it is awakened only when the timing and circumstances are right. There is, in effect, "a time to embrace and a time to refrain" (Eccl 3:5). To awaken love when it does not desire to be woken is as dangerous as rousing the sleeping animal of modern proverbial tradition. The oath laid upon the Jerusalem women refers, appropriately, to gazelles *(ṣĕḇāʾôṯ)* and does *(ʾayyālôṯ)*; see also Song 2:7. The man himself is portrayed as a gazelle *(ṣĕḇî)* or young stag *(ʾayyāl)* in Song 2:8–9, 17 and 8:14, whereas 4:5 and 7:3 compare the woman's breasts to two fawns of a gazelle *(ṣĕḇiyyâ)*; cf. Prov 5:19, where the woman is "a loving doe, a graceful deer." The emphasis of the imagery falls upon, among others things, grace and beauty (underlined by the fact that *ṣĕḇî* also means "beauty," as in Ezek 7:20). In shifting the focus from the singular

"gazelle" and "doe" to the plural, the oath appears to set the particular relationship that is described in Song 3:1–4 (and in 2:3–6) in the context of all other similar relationships. The daughters of Jerusalem are to think of the "gazelles and does" generally (i.e., all lovers) as they consider whether to arouse or awaken love. The verse thus has a "love your neighbor as yourself" aspect to it, for these daughters of Jerusalem are themselves some of the "does" who might in the future be found embracing their "gazelles." They swear as those who have common cause with our speaker and his or her beloved.

[7] See also Gordis, *Song,* 18–23.

[8] See Marvin H. Pope, *Song of Songs* (AB 7C; Garden City, N.Y: Doubleday, 1977), 441–42, for a discussion.

[9] See, e.g., Gillis Gerleman, *Ruth: Das Hohelied* (BKAT 18; 2d ed.; Neukirchen-Vluyn: Neukirchener Verlag, 1965). The Targum already thinks of it as a fixed structure, namely the temple.

[10] Thus, e.g., Exod 8:3 [MT 7:28], where the *miṭṭâ* is in Pharaoh's *hădar miškāḇ;* cf. Song 3:1, 4 above.

[11] That is, "sixty" to David's "thirty"—itself a round number, cf. 2 Sam 23:24, 39.

[12] 1 Kgs 6:29–35; cf. also Ezekiel's temple in Ezek 40–42.

[13] The "bed" of v. 7, being a feminine noun, could itself in principle be connected with the pronoun *zōʾt,* and v. 7 could be the answer to the question in v. 6: "Who is this? . . . The bed!" We might then understand *mî* (normally "who?") as meaning "what?" following Akkadian usage; or we might simply think of the bed itself as personified. It is by far the most natural reading of v. 6, however—when both normal Hebrew grammar and syntax and the similar question in 8:5 are considered—to understand the question as referring to a woman *on* the bed rather than to the bed itself. See further P. B. Dirksen, "Song of Songs 3:6–7," *VT* 39 (1989): 219–24.

[14] For example, Ps 107:33–38; Isa 32:15; Jer 4:26.

[15] See Leland Ryken, James C. Wilhoit, and Tremper Longman III, eds., *Dictionary of Biblical Imagery* (Downers Grove, Ill.: InterVarsity Press, 1998), 315–17, 948–51.

[16] It should be noted that the women in v. 11 are invited to view only the crown, not a wedding. The word *ʿăṭārâ* is itself ambiguous and could refer to a

royal crown or a wedding garland (cf. Isa 61:10). Given the passage's satirical edge, it is possible that the intended picture is of Solomon reposing on his ridiculously overstated bed wearing nothing *but* his crown (cf. Amos 6:1–7 and Ezek 23:40–41, with its interesting association of illicit sexual conduct and misuse of sacrificial incense and oil). The invitation is, in essence, to view a pathetic spectacle.

[17] The speakers in Song 8:8–9 are not explicitly identified, but the mention of "little sister," the role of brothers in overseeing the arrangements for the marriages of sisters elsewhere in the OT (e.g., Gen 24:29–60; Judg 21:22), and the earlier reference to brothers in Song 1:6 lead us to think of the woman's brothers as the contributors at this point. It is not their precise identity that is the focus here, however, but their attitude toward their sister. They regard her as their possession ("*we have* a young sister") as well as their responsibility ("what shall we do for our sister for the day she is spoken for?"—that is, the day when her hand is requested in marriage, 1 Sam 25:39). They see their task, in other words, both as ensuring that men stay away from their sister until the proper time and as making sure that she is a prize catch when that time comes. They themselves are, evidently, the arbiters of what the proper time might be. Possession is also the focus of 8:11, 12b. Here Solomon himself owns something: a "vineyard" in Baal Hamon, which is entrusted to others so that they may "tend" its fruit *(nṭr)*. The verbal root also appears twice in 1:6, where the woman tells the daughters of Jerusalem that her brothers made her "take care" of the vineyards, although she did not "take care" of her own. This particular Solomonic vineyard is extraordinarily valuable: "a man would bring for its fruit one thousand silver pieces" (8:11). The fantastic price alerts us to the fact that we are not dealing with a literal vineyard. The "vineyard" is, characteristically, simply a metaphor for a woman, one of the most valuable of Solomon's possessions in "Baal Hamon." The place name is interesting: not only does it mean "husband of a multitude" (alluding to Solomon's harem, as the phrase "one thousand" possibly also does; cf. 1 Kgs 11:3), but it also evokes through its use of Baal (the Canaanite deity so often mentioned in 1–2 Kings and elsewhere in the OT) the story in 1 Kgs 11, where Solomon's many wives lead him into idolatry. Here is one prized possession among the many possessions of the idolater king (cf. Song 6:8).

[18] The most natural assumption is that the woman speaks throughout ch. 3, being the one who refers to the king in the third person also in 1:4, 12. It may even be that we are to think of 3:6–10 as a continuation of the dream in 3:1–4, as she invites the group of females around her ("daughters of Jerusalem," in v. 5; "daughters of Zion" in v. 11, probably in order to avoid the immediate repetition of "daughters of Jerusalem" from v. 10) to consider the nature of these relationships

in which she is alternately eager participant and reluctant victim (like the woman she observes in v. 6). The dream of vv. 1–4 bespeaks her fear of loss and even her longing to return to the safety and security of her youth. The vision of vv. 6–10 bespeaks her resentment of royal possession and her longing for release from royal coercion.

[19] A second dream, possessing obvious points of contact with ch. 3 (although on this occasion the lover is lost and *not* found), is recounted in 5:2–7. Between the two dream sequences we find the intriguing verses in 4:1–5:1, the appropriateness of whose location in the book has not been sufficiently discussed. Responsive to the unsettling dream and distasteful vision of ch. 3, the beloved man now showers the woman with intimate affirmations, placing the "events" of ch. 3 in the context of their special relationship. He commends her for her beauty while respecting her as one who has her own boundaries and who must be wooed so that their physical acts of love will be truly mutual. The imagery is once again gentle and pastoral, in contrast to the imagery of the frightening dream and the fortified palace of ch. 3. What is striking about 4:3–4 in particular is the way in which the verses echo 3:6–11 not only in the reference to the warriors (*gibbôrîm,* 3:7, 4:4), but also in their use of the unique *miḏbār* in 4:3 (where presumably it means "mouth" in parallel to "lips"), which reminds us of the common *miḏbār,* "wilderness," in 3:6. It is as if the lover is recontextualizing his beloved's traumatic experience, placing it once again in a larger and more familiar framework (4:1, 5–6; referring back to 1:13, 15; 2:16–17). The fearsome warriors who guard the king's bed are now stripped of their weapons, which hang like trophies around the beloved's neck. The thought of the barren wilderness, which is the same royal bed, is replaced now by the thought of the beloved's mouth, described as "lovely" *(nāʾweh)* but also evoking the image of the pastures *(neʾôṯ;* sing. *nāwâ)* in which sheep and goats graze. Here is a "wilderness" (the beloved's mouth) that is fertile and inviting to one who is a "gazelle" (cf. 2:8–17). The idea of fertility may also be hinted at in the use of *śep̄āṯayim,* "lips," which is often used of riverbanks (e.g., Gen 41:3, 17), and in the use of *rimmôn,* "pomegranate," a well-known symbol of fertility. The connections between the chapters serve to emphasize the contrast of the two relationships described therein. The woman is to Solomon only one among many daughters of Jerusalem—readily available and coerced to join him in his desert prison—but to her lover she is an expansive and fertile landscape, magnificent, flawless (v. 7), and self-possessed. She is to be affirmed and enjoyed rather than controlled. See further my forthcoming commentary on Ecclesiastes and Song of Songs in the NIV Application series (Grand Rapids: Zondervan, 2000).

[20] On this and other aspects of the ambiguous presentation of Solomon's

reign in 1–2 Kings, see Iain W. Provan, *1 and 2 Kings* (NIBCOT 7; Peabody, Mass.: Hendrickson, 1995), 23–102.

[21] For further details here, see again my forthcoming commentary on Ecclesiastes and Song of Songs in the NIV Application series.

[22] The Hebrew phrase is *šiddâ wĕšiddôṯ* (NIV's "and a harem as well"), the correct interpretation of which is arrived at, in my view, via Judg 5:30a, *raḥam raḥămāṯayim lĕrō᾿š geḇer:* "a womb or two for each man." A phrase like this is often explained in terms of synecdoche, whereby part of something can stand for the whole; thus the NIV translation of Judg 5:30a: "a girl or two for each man." It is not always clear, however, that the intention is to refer to the whole female person rather than to the part in which the men, whose perspective dominates the text, are interested (whether "womb," because of child-bearing potential, or "breast," where it is perhaps the potential for sexual fulfillment that is in mind). In the context of Eccl 2:4–8, which is focused resolutely on possessions, we are thus led to the following translation of the second part of Eccl 2:8: "I acquired for myself male and female singers and the delights of the male—a breast or two." Even if translated "a girl or two," of course, the line would be no less offensive.

[23] Rikk E. Watts, "Women in the Gospels and Acts," *Crux* 35, no. 2 (1999): 22–33.

The Fall of Lucifer (in More Ways Than One)

Ronald Youngblood

As far as I can recall, I was first exposed to the word *lucifer* when I was a small child. My grandfather was warning me about the dangers of what I later came to know as "farmer matches," long wooden sticks that were tipped with antimony sulphide and potassium chlorate. He called them "lucifers." Needless to say, at that time I had no idea that *lucifer* was a word of Latin derivation meaning "light-bearer."

When I was in my early teen years I began reading the Bible with some degree of seriousness. It was only then that I learned that *Lucifer*—capitalized this time—referred to something (or someone) much more sinister than a wooden match. I saw his name in Isa 14:12, and when I asked about him I was told that he was none other than the devil himself: Lucifer was one of Satan's many names.

At that time I had no reason to doubt the equation of Lucifer with Satan. Accepting at face value the unimpeachable authority of the notes in my copy of the *Scofield Reference Bible,* I learned a number of things about Lucifer from the note on Isa 14:12:

> Verses 12–14 evidently refer to Satan, who, as prince of this world-system, . . . is the real though unseen ruler of the successive world-powers, Tyre, Babylon, Medo-Persia, Greece, Rome, etc. . . . Lucifer, "day-star," can be none other than Satan. This tremendous passage marks the beginning of sin in the universe. When Lucifer said, "I will," sin began.[1]

I tried to make sense of that paragraph in light of my admittedly rudimentary understanding of Gen 3, which describes the temptation of Eve and Adam by the serpent (whose craftiness betrays his evil nature and who is equated with Satan in Rev 12:9; 20:2). I eventually concluded that Satan/Lucifer must have rebelled against God and been thrown out of heaven before the events recorded in Gen 3. His fall from divine grace must have preceded the fall of humankind. And, if C. I. Scofield was right, the details of Satan's fall are vividly described in Isa 14:12–15.

I. Historical Usage of the Term *Lucifer*

As it turns out, the identification of Lucifer with Satan has a long history. The early church father Tertullian (ca. A.D. 160–230) twice implies such a connection in his polemic treatise *Against Marcion* when he speaks of the devil's boast that he would establish his throne in the clouds of heaven and be "like the Most High" (citing Isa 14:14).[2] Origen (ca. A.D. 185–254) is even more specific:

> We are taught as follows by the prophet Isaiah, . . . "How is Lucifer, who used to arise in the morning, fallen from heaven!" . . . Most evidently by these words is he shown to have fallen from heaven, who formerly was Lucifer, and who used to arise in the morning. . . . Nay, even the Saviour Himself teaches us, saying of the devil, "Behold, I see Satan fallen from heaven like lightning."[3]

With this last phrase, Origen adds another piece to the developing picture of Lucifer's fall by connecting it with Jesus' statement to his disciples (Luke 10:18) and thus giving it dominical sanction.

The formidable Augustine (A.D. 354–430) soon lends his considerable intellectual and scholarly weight to the discussion. He interprets 1 John 3:8, "The devil sins from the beginning," to mean that "from the time he was created he refused righteousness." He understands Jesus' words concerning the devil in John 8:44, "He was a murderer from the beginning, and abode not in the truth," to imply that "he had fallen from the truth, in which, if he had abode, he would have become a partaker of it, and have remained in blessedness along with the holy angels." He then continues his discussion by affirming that in Isa 14:12 "Isaiah . . . represents the devil under the person of the king of Babylon, 'How art thou fallen, O Lucifer, son of the morning!' "[4]

So the emerging picture of the devil's forced descent from heaven may be summarized as follows: In the hoary mists of eternity's past eons, before God created the first human beings, Lucifer (who is Satan, the devil) was an angel of light, a respected member of the inner circle of celestial counselors. But at an undisclosed point in time, and for reasons that can no longer be discerned, he fell prey to vaunting ambition and resolved to ascend to a level above the other members of the heavenly host. Indeed, he proposed to ensconce himself on a divine throne at the very top of the sacred mountain where the Lord was reputed to live. In effect, he decided that he was at least as good as, if not better than, the Most High God himself. As a result of that supreme act of rebellion, the Lord inflicted judgment on him by casting him out of heaven and relegating him to the deepest part of the netherworld. And all of this is clearly documented in the soaring poetry of Isa 14:12–15:

How you have fallen from heaven,
  O Lucifer, son of the dawn!
You have been cast down to the earth,
  you who lie helpless on your back!
You said in your heart,
  "I will ascend to heaven;
I will raise my throne
  above the stars of God;
I will sit enthroned on the mount of assembly,
  on the utmost heights of the sacred mountain.
I will ascend above the tops of the clouds;
  I will make myself like the Most High."
But you are brought down to Sheol,
  to the depths of the pit.[5]

Given the inherent attractiveness of the interpretive scenario summarized above, it is not hard to understand why so many Bible readers from the days of the church fathers down to the present time have chosen to read Isa 14 in that way.[6] After all, in *The Canterbury Tales,* Geoffrey Chaucer canonized it near the beginning of the Monk's tale:

With Lucifer, though he was angel fair
And not a man, with him will I begin;
For though Fortune may not an angel dare,
From high degree yet fell he for his sin
Down into Hell, and he lies yet therein.
O Lucifer, brightest of angels all,
Now art thou Satan, and thou may'st not win
From misery wherein thou far did'st fall! (lines 1999–2006)[7]

And in *Paradise Lost,* John Milton mentions Lucifer several times, referring to his fall as well as to his identity with Satan. Typical are the following:

Know then, that after Lucifer from heaven
(So call him, brighter once amidst the host
Of angels, than that star the stars among)
Fell with his flaming legions through the deep

Into his place, and the great Son returned
Victorious with his saints, the omnipotent
Eternal father from his throne beheld
Their multitude, and to his Son thus spake.... (7.131–38)

Through the gate,
Wide open and unguarded, Satan passed,
And all about found desolate; for those
Appointed to sit there had left their charge,
Flown to the upper world; the rest were all
Far to the inland retired, about the walls
Of Pandemonium, city and proud seat
Of Lucifer, so by allusion called,
Of that bright star to Satan paragoned. (10.418–26)[8]

II. Contextual Interpretation of the Isaiah Passage

But having given such an impressive list of theological and literary luminaries their rightful due,[9] are we to assume that they have understood Isaiah correctly?

In a word, no. In this case, the devil is not in the details.

Just as in buying real estate the three most important elements to consider are location, location, and location, so also in arriving at the proper interpretation of a text the three most important elements are context, context, and context. The passage quoted earlier, Isa 14:12–15, is nestled at the center of a longer section (14:3–23) that in its turn constitutes the last half of a prophecy concerning Babylon (chs. 13–14), itself the first in a series of oracles against (foreign) nations (chs. 13–23).[10] Nor is the book of Isaiah unique in this regard: similar series appear in Amos 1–2, Jer 46–51, Ezek 25–32, and Zeph 2:4–15.

In Isaiah's case, 14:3–23 is clearly labeled a "taunt against the king of Babylon" (vv. 3–4). It is a poem that heaps scorn and ridicule upon him. The nations he has oppressed burst forth into singing (vv. 4–7). Nature itself rejoices at his fall (v. 8). The spirits of deceased kings are symbolically pictured as greeting him when he arrives in the netherworld (v. 9). They point out to him that he is just as weak (v. 10)—indeed, just as dead (v. 11)—as they themselves are. They ponder his fate as they stare at him (vv. 16–17). All of them lie peacefully in their own tombs (v. 18), but ultimately his corpse is unceremoniously thrown out of his tomb and trampled underfoot (vv. 19–20). For all intents and purposes his dynasty has come to an end (v. 21)—and all of this has come about as the result of divine judgment (vv. 22–23).

If the above paragraph is a reasonably accurate summary of Isa 14:3–11, 16–23 (and few would deny that it is), what likelihood is there that Isa 14:12–15—

with no advance warning or contextual warrant—suddenly speaks of the fall of Satan? Very little, it seems to me. The unnamed[11] king of Babylon has "subdued nations" (v. 6), has "become like" other kings (v. 10), is in the grave where "worms cover" him (v. 11), and is referred to as a "man" (vv. 16–17). And vv. 12–15 are totally consistent with this overall characterization, as I will now attempt to show.

Hebrew scholars are generally agreed that the original text of this stanza, which appears to be free of scribal error,[12] "is one of the most magnificent pieces of poetry" in the Hebrew Bible.[13] "You have been cast down to the earth" (v. 12c) not only parallels "you have fallen from heaven" (v. 12a; the merism "from heaven ... to the earth" emphasizes how very far the king has fallen) but also is recapitulated in "you are brought down to Sheol" (v. 15a). Thus the first and last verses of the stanza form a frame around the two verses in the center. In addition, Sheol, the most common metaphor in the Old Testament for the realm of the dead (whether conceived of as the netherworld or, more prosaically, the grave), is frequently referred to as "the earth" in ancient Semitic texts (including the Hebrew Bible). So there may be a deliberate ambiguity in the way the word *earth* is used in v. 12. Moreover, the very fact that the stanza is composed of seven couplets (vv. 12a–b, 12c–d, 13a–b, 13c–d, 13e–f, 14a–b, 15a–b) helps to underscore its completeness and delimit its boundaries.

Its first word, the exclamatory *How* (v. 12), echoes the *How* that begins the entire lament (14:4) and serves to connect the stanza to its wider context. *How* often appears at the beginning of other biblical laments as well (cf. Lam 1:1; 2:1; 4:1).[14] "How you have fallen" (v. 12) is strongly reminiscent of one of the most poignant elegies in the Bible—David's lament for Saul and Jonathan: "How the mighty have fallen!" (2 Sam 1:19, 25, 27).

The king's fivefold *I will* in vv. 13–14 ties together the middle section of the stanza, which is the heart and center of the entire poem.[15] His language displays both bombast and pride as he claims to be divine. In his mind's eye he pictures himself ascending "to heaven" (v. 13)—indeed, "above the tops of the clouds" (v. 14). He envisions himself as raising his throne "above the stars of God" (v. 13d, probably a reference to the angels; cf. Job 38:7; Rev 9:1–2) and sitting enthroned "on the utmost heights of the sacred mountain" (v. 13f).[16] Then comes the ultimate blasphemy: "I will make myself like the Most High" (v. 14). Babylon's king is guilty of the detestable sin of self-deification. This was by no means entirely out of character for him, however, since the kings of Babylon and Assyria often presumed themselves to be gods worthy of worship.[17]

The pronoun *you* links vv. 12–15 with the other verses of Isaiah's taunt song. Beginning in v. 8 and continuing almost without interruption through v. 20, it refers throughout to the king of Babylon. The phrase "brought down to Sheol" is shared by stanzas C and D' (vv. 11, 15; see n. 15). The king's fall is cataclysmic:

thinking himself to be securely enthroned on "the utmost heights of the sacred mountain" (*yarkĕṯê ṣāp̱ôn,* v. 13), he is in fact brought down to "the depths of the pit" (*yarkĕṯê-ḇôr,* v. 15).

But whence the term *Lucifer*? It comes to us through the Greek and Latin translations of the Bible, the Septuagint and the Vulgate, respectively. The Hebrew word *hêlēl* in v. 12, meaning "morning star," was translated in the Septuagint by the term *heōsphoros* (dawn-bringer) and in the Vulgate by *lucifer,* a common noun meaning "light-bearer," not a proper name. Both translations clearly understood the Hebrew *hêlēl* to refer to the morning star, usually identified with Venus.[18] Thus *lucifer,* far from being another name for Satan, is used by Isaiah as a metaphor for the king of Babylon. While heralding the approach of dawn, the light of the morning star is much too faint to overwhelm it. Likewise Babylon's king, bright shining though he be, fades into obscurity when compared to God Most High. If he aspires to ultimacy, he cannot but fail. His doom is sealed.

III. Derivation of the Term *Morning Star*

But why did Isaiah call the king of Babylon "morning star, sun of the dawn"? Although the jury is still out on this question, it is likely that Isaiah drew on one or more Near Eastern mythological sources (as he did, for example, when discussing Leviathan's future in Isa 27:1). One promising possibility is that he drew from Canaanite myths, some of which were written on clay tablets unearthed at Ugarit since 1929. They refer to *hll,* who in Canaanite religion was the god of the crescent moon and therefore is not necessarily to be equated with Isaiah's *hêlēl.*[19] They also speak of Shahar, the deified dawn, the equivalent of Isaiah's *šaḥar*. In addition they tell the humorous story of the minor god Athtar's proposed elevation to kingship in replacement of the deceased Baal:

> And Lady Athiratu of the Sea answered:
> "Shouldn't we make king ʿAthtaru the Rich?
> Let ʿAthtaru the Rich be made king!"
> Then ʿAthtaru the Rich
> went up into the highlands of Sapanu *(ṣāp̱ôn),*
> he sat down on the throne of Baʿlu the Almighty.
> His feet did not touch the foot-stool,
> his head did not touch the top of the back.
> And ʿAthtaru the Rich said:
> "I cannot be king in the highlands of Sapanu!"
> ʿAthtaru the Rich descended,
> he descended from the throne of Baʿlu the Almighty
> and became king on all the divine earth.[20]

If we substitute *hêlēl* for Athtar and God Most High for Baal, the comparisons between this section of the Canaanite Baal epic and Isa 14:12–15 are striking indeed.

Another myth that Isaiah might have drawn from is the Babylonian epic of Gilgamesh. The relevant stanza is found on tablet 11, lines 1–7:

> Gilgamesh said to him, to Utnapishtim the Faraway:
> "As I look upon thee, Utnapishtim,
> Thy features are not strange; even as I art thou.
> Thou art not strange at all; even as I art thou.
> My heart had regarded thee as resolved to do battle,
> [Yet] thou liest indolent upon thy back!
> [Tell me,] how joinedst thou the Assembly of the gods,
> In thy quest of life?"[21]

The parallels between these seven lines and Isa 14 are numerous and impressive. "Those who see you stare at you" (Isa 14:16) is reminiscent of "As I look upon thee." "You have become like us" (v. 10) is almost an echo of "even as I art thou." And "I will sit enthroned on the mount of assembly" (v. 13) presents a picture similar to that in Gilgamesh 11.7: "How joinedst thou the Assembly of the gods . . . ?"

Recently, still another parallel has been suggested. It hinges on the translation "You who lie helpless on your back!" for *ḥôlēš ʿal–gwym* in v. 12. If that rendering is defensible, the echo of "thou liest indolent upon thy back" (Gilgamesh 11.6) is obvious. Although the Masoretes understandably vocalized *gwym* here as the common word *gôyim* (people), Raymond Van Leeuwen has proposed that, since the verbal root *ḥlš* always implies weakness in the Hebrew Bible, *gwym* should be read *gĕwî(m)* here and translated "back."[22] If he is right, another ironic feature of these verses would be that Isaiah made use of a Babylonian epic to ridicule a Babylonian king. It is perhaps best, however, to conclude that no one myth explains all of the allusions in this taunt song.[23] As Robert O'Connell has written, "Even without a precise identification of the culture of origin for the mythic language in Isa. xiv 12–14 it is clear that its function is to portray the Mesopotamian tyrant as a mythic usurper who arrogantly attempts to exceed his proper status and to take the place of the most high god."[24]

In short, the "morning star, son of the dawn," is a vivid metaphor symbolizing a Babylonian king who, like Venus, was outshone by a still brighter star. As Brevard Childs says,

> The mythical mind saw a cosmic battle . . . in the brilliant rise of the morning star in the heavens with its sudden dimming before the increasing rays of the sun. . . . The prophetic writer . . . compares the mighty king of Babylon to the upstart, Helal. He also had a brilliant

start, but then Yahweh hurled him down to become the laughing stock of the nations.[25]

This is similar to what Isaiah himself would later say: "Babylon has fallen, has fallen!" (21:9; cf. Rev 18:2).

IV. Final Reflections

As for *lucifer,* which appears in (some versions of) the Bible only here, we can no longer insist that the word is a proper noun or that it primarily refers to Satan.[26] But it is also true that since the days of the tower of Babel (Gen 11:1–9) the name of Babylon has been applied to political and religious systems opposed to the living God. Babylon's king in Isa 14 embodied satanic power, and he may well be a prefiguration of the "beast" that will be followed by many (Rev 13:1–3) and will be associated with the "Babylon" of the last days (Rev 17:3–8). Jesus' vision of Satan's fall (Luke 10:18) was not that of an alleged primordial fall from pristine innocence. On the contrary, it resulted from the successful venture of seventy-two of his followers, who reported that "even the demons" submitted to commands uttered in the name of Christ (Luke 10:17). It is striking indeed that the ruins of the latter-day "Babylon" are pictured as a "home for demons and a haunt for every unclean spirit" (Rev 18:2). The devil fell, falls, and will fall again. The sovereign might of God Most High can always be counted on to overwhelm the demonic powers of every Babylon, whether earthly or heavenly.[27] Indeed, the true Morning Star (*phōsphoros,* "light-bearer"), who guarantees the ultimate doom of Satan and his minions, is Jesus Christ himself (2 Pet 1:19; cf. Rev 22:16).

But as for *Lucifer,* he is fallen, in more ways than one.

Notes

A shorter version of this article appeared under the title "Fallen Star: The Evolution of Lucifer" in *BR* 14 (1998): 22–31, 47.

[1] *Scofield Reference Bible* (New York: Oxford University Press, 1909), 726.

[2] Tertullian, *Against Marcion* 5.11, 17 (*ANF* 3:454, 466).

[3] Origen, *First Principles* 1.5 (*ANF* 4:259).

[4] Augustine, *City of God* 11.13–15; cf. Saint Augustine, *The City of God* (trans. Marcus Dods; New York: Modern Library, 1950), 358–59.

[5] The translation is that of the NIV, except that "Lucifer" has been substituted for "morning star" (v. 12) and "Sheol" for "the grave" (v. 15). In addition, I am

reading "you who lie helpless on your back" instead of the traditional "you who once laid low the nations" (v. 12) or the like. The reason for the latter change will be explained below.

[6] Although the number of serious scholars who still equate Lucifer and Satan has dwindled considerably, that viewpoint continues to attract its advocates (cf. Merrill F. Unger, *Biblical Demonology* [Wheaton: Van Kampen, 1952], 15).

[7] Robert Maynard Hutchins, ed., *Great Books of the Western World* (Chicago: University of Chicago Press, 1952), 22:434. The version reproduced above is a modernization by J. U. Nicolson from Chaucer's lilting original:

At Lucifer, though he an angel were,
And nat a man, at him wol I biginne;
For, thogh fortune may non angel dere,
From heigh degree yet fel he for his sinne
Doun in-to helle, wher he yet is inne.
O Lucifer! brightest of angels alle,
Now artow Sathanas, that maist nat twinne
Out of miserie, in which that thou art falle.

[8] John Milton, *Paradise Lost and Other Poems* (ed. Maurice Kelley; New York: Walter J. Black, 1943), 247, 324–25.

[9] The list could easily be expanded to include, e.g., the British abbot Aelfric (ca. A.D. 955–1020; cf. Leo Jung, *Fallen Angels in Jewish, Christian, and Mohammedan Literature* [New York: Ktav, 1974], 161–62), and Pope Gregory the Great (ca. A.D. 540–604).

[10] The word *foreign* is in parentheses here because, although the oracles are primarily for the benefit of Israel's people, the nation of Israel itself is not exempt from divine judgment (see Isa 22).

[11] No consensus has been reached in attempts to identify this king, although various names have been suggested: Sargon II, Sennacherib, Ashur-Uballit II, Nebuchadnezzar, Nabonidus, Alexander the Great (for details see Hans Wildberger, *Isaiah 13–27* [CC; Minneapolis: Fortress, 1997], 54–55). It is perhaps best to agree with the words of Robert H. O'Connell: "A precise identification of a particular historical figure seems unlikely" ("Isaiah xiv 4b–23: Ironic Reversal through Concentric Structure and Mythic Allusion," *VT* 38 [1988]: 417).

[12] W. S. Prinsloo, "Isaiah 14:12–15: Humiliation, Hubris, Humiliation," *ZAW* 93 (1981): 433.

[13] Wildberger, *Isaiah 13–27,* 75.

[14] Indeed, the Hebrew title of the book of Lamentations is ʾ*ēḵâ,* a lengthened form of the word translated "how" in Isa 14:4, 12.

[15] I would scan the full poem in the following concentric fashion:

A. Prologue: The Lord Confronts Babylon and Its King (vv. 3–4a)
  B. The Destroyer, Himself Destroyed, Will No Longer Disturb Others (vv. 4b–8)
    C. The King's Deceased Predecessors Meet Him, Greet Him, and Taunt Him (vv. 9–11)
      D. The King Has Been Cast Down to the Earth (v. 12)
        E. The King's Pride Knows No Bounds (vv. 13–14)
      D'. The King Has Been Brought Down to Sheol (v. 15)
    C'. The King's Deceased Predecessors Stare at Him, Ponder His Fate, and Taunt Him (vv. 16–17)
  B'. The Destroyer's Descendants, Themselves Destroyed, Will No Longer Disinherit Others (vv. 18–21)
A'. Epilogue: The Lord Almighty Destroys Babylon and Its Dynasty (vv. 22–23)

Other concentric or chiastic structures have been proposed for the stanza; cf. Prinsloo, "Isaiah 14:12–15," 435; O'Connell, "Isaiah xiv 4b–23," 407–8.

[16] The Heb. for "sacred mountain" is *ṣāp̄ôn* ("north"), often transliterated as the proper name Zaphon. It was the name of the mountain where the Canaanite god Baal resided and is referred to as "the divine Sapanu" in the Ugaritic epic of Baal (Baal I, frg. a, lines 3–4). Called Mount Kasios/Casius in Hellenistic times, it is usually identified with present-day Jebel Akra (about twenty-five miles northeast of Ras esh-Shamra [ancient Ugarit] in Syria).

[17] See A. Leo Oppenheim, *Ancient Mesopotamia: Portrait of a Dead Civilization* (Chicago: University of Chicago Press, 1964), 98: "From the point of view of Mesopotamian civilization, there was only one institution in the modern sense of the word: kingship. As a main characteristic of civilized living, it was of divine origin. . . . The royal apparel underlines the divine aspect of kingship; the horned miter with which Naram-Sin is represented and the *kusītu* garments of the Neo-Assyrian kings are similar to those worn by images of the gods."

[18] Typical is Barry G. Webb, who states that *hêlēl ben-šāḥar* (morning star, son of the dawn) is "probably the planet Venus, which seems to rival the sun in its early brightness but is soon eclipsed" (*The Message of Isaiah;* On Eagle's Wings [The Bible Speaks Today; Downers Grove, Ill.: InterVarsity Press, 1996], 83). But

while identification with Venus has reached something of a scholarly consensus, it is by no means universal. Other proposals include the sun, the moon, Jupiter (cf. Frederick C. Grant, ed., *Dictionary of the Bible* [rev. ed.; New York: Charles Scribner's Sons, 1963], 936–37), and, most recently, a comet. In the words of Donald V. Etz, "A cometary appearance seems more likely than the cyclic behavior of the sun, moon, or a planet to have been the inspiration for Isa. xiv. 12–15" ("Is Isaiah xiv 12–15 a Reference to Comet Halley?" *VT* 36 [1986]: 295).

[19] For opposing opinions on this matter cf. Johannes C. de Moor, *An Anthology of Religious Texts from Ugarit* (Leiden: E. J. Brill, 1987), 145 n. 33, which identifies the two; and J. C. L. Gibson, *Canaanite Myths and Legends* (2d ed.; Edinburgh: T&T Clark, 1978), 29 n. 1, which denies the equation.

[20] The translation is that of de Moor, *Anthology of Religious Texts,* 85–86.

[21] The translation is that of E. A. Speiser, "The Epic of Gilgamesh" (*ANET,* 93).

[22] Raymond Van Leeuwen, "Isa 14:12, *ḥôlēš ʿal-gwym* and Gilgamesh XI, 6," *JBL* 99 (1980): 173–84. He fully supports his argument from every conceivable angle, making the entire article well worth reading. He also notes, "After the present study was in press, the author discovered that *gĕwî* does in fact appear in ancient Hebrew with the meaning 'body/innards' (Sir 10:9)" (184 n. 51).

[23] Many scholars readily admit this; cf. John N. Oswalt, *The Book of Isaiah: Chapters 1–39* (NICOT; Grand Rapids: Eerdmans, 1986), 322; Wildberger, *Isaiah 13–27,* 63, 65; Prinsloo, "Isaiah 14:12–15," 438 n. 35.

[24] O'Connell, "Isaiah xiv 4b–23," 417.

[25] Brevard S. Childs, *Myth and Reality in the Old Testament* (SBT 27; London: SCM Press, 1960), 69.

[26] Robert L. Alden, "Lucifer: Who or What?" *BETS* 11 (1968): 38; cf. also, e.g., Edward J. Young, *The Book of Isaiah* (NICOT; 3 vols.; Grand Rapids: Eerdmans, 1965), 1:441; Franz Delitzsch, *Biblical Commentary on the Prophecies of Isaiah* (Edinburgh: T&T Clark, 1867; repr., Grand Rapids: Eerdmans, 1954), 1:311–12: "Lucifer, as a name given to the devil, was derived from this passage, which the fathers . . . interpreted, without any warrant whatever, as relating to the apostasy and punishment of the angelic leaders. The appellation is a perfectly appropriate one for the king of Babel." The sixteenth-century Geneva Bible contains this marginal note on "Lucifer, sonne of the morning," in Isaiah 14:12: "Thou that thoughtest thy selfe most glorious, and as it were placed in the heaven: for the morning starre, that goeth before the sunne is called Lucifer, to whome

Nebuchad-nezzar is compared." Even the KJV, which has proved to be the most influential translation in preserving the Lucifer/Satan equation, had a note on "O Lucifer" in its earliest editions: "Or, O day-starre."

[27] For additional summarizing comments concerning Isaiah's taunt song against the king of Babylon see Ronald F. Youngblood, *The Book of Isaiah: An Introductory Commentary* (2d ed.; Grand Rapids: Baker, 1993), 61–63. My original interest in the authorial intent of Isaiah's taunt song was piqued many years ago during a conversation in which Bruce Waltke described briefly the results of an exegetical exercise on Isa 14 in which he and a group of his graduate students had engaged. It is therefore with great delight and appreciation that I dedicate this study to my dear friend and colleague.

Historical Contingencies and Biblical Predictions

Richard L. Pratt Jr.

The last half of the twentieth century witnessed an explosion of interest in biblical prophecies about our future. Record sales of millennium and apocalyptic books[1] indicate that many Christians (and many non-Christians) read the Bible to find out what is yet to come and how current events fit within that chronological framework.

Recent events have only encouraged enthusiasm for this hermeneutic. Moral decay in Western culture has raised fears of cataclysmic divine retribution. Political troubles in various parts of the world have been interpreted as the initial stages of history's grand finale. As a result, North American evangelicals have become monomaniacal in their interpretation of biblical prophecy. Their greatest interest seems to be trying to discover God's plan for the future and the role today's events play within that divine program.

This study will challenge this widespread hermeneutical orientation by exploring the role of historical contingencies that intervened between OT predictions and their fulfillments. As we will see, events that took place after predictions often directed the course of history in ways not anticipated by the prophetic announcements. Sometimes future events conformed to a prophet's words; sometimes they did not. For this reason, neither prophets nor their listeners knew precisely what to expect. If the proposal I make here is correct, we can assume that the emphasis of many contemporary interpreters is misplaced and that we must find other hermeneutical interests in biblical prophecy.

I. Historical Contingencies and Theological Considerations

Before we test this proposal by the prophetic materials themselves, it will help to establish a theological framework for our discussion. Many evangelicals may find it difficult to imagine that Yahweh's prophets predicted events that did not occur. After all, the prophets were privy to the heavenly court. They received their messages from the transcendent Creator. May we even entertain the possibility that subsequent events significantly affected the fulfillments of their predictions? Does this notion not contradict the immutability of divine decrees?

By and large, critical interpreters simply dismiss these theological concerns as irrelevant. Traditional critical scholars tend to deny the possibility of prescience through divine revelation. A prophecy that gives the impression of foreknowledge actually is *vaticinium ex eventu*—a prophecy after the event. God may know the future, but humans certainly cannot. And in recent decades, process theology's repudiation of divine transcendence has challenged traditional theological concerns from another direction. For example, Robert P. Carroll urges that "talk about God knowing the future is unnecessary . . . as process theology makes so clear. The hermeneutical gymnastics required to give any coherence to the notion of God knowing and revealing the future in the form of predictions to the prophets does no religious community any credit."[2] When divinity is thought to be in process with the universe, not even God knows the future.

Despite these widespread tendencies, many interpreters of the prophets stand in continuity with historical expressions of Protestant evangelicalism and strongly affirm the immutability of God's character and eternal decrees. Historically, varying Protestant traditions have expressed different views regarding the bases and ordering of God's eternal decrees. Nevertheless, they have mostly concurred that God's character and eternal decrees are inviolable. John Calvin's assessment of the matter has been followed by many: "God so attends to the regulations of individual events, and they all so proceed from his set plan, that nothing takes place by chance."[3] In Calvin's view, God has decreed a fixed plan for the universe. This plan includes every event in history in such detail that nothing takes place by happenstance.

Evangelical scholars in the seventeenth century often echoed Calvin's language. As the Westminster Confession of Faith says, "God from all eternity did, by the most wise and holy counsel of his own will, freely and unchangeably ordain whatsoever comes to pass."[4]

Evangelical theologians in America two centuries later also used similar language. Charles Hodge, for instance, insisted that God is "immutable in his plans and purposes. Infinite in wisdom, there can be no error in their conception; infinite in power, there can be no failure in their accomplishment."[5]

As this sampling suggests, many prominent theologians in the evangelical tradition have summarized the teaching of Scripture on this subject in accordance with the views of their early forebears.[6] From eternity past, God's immutable decrees fixed every detail of history. Nothing can alter these decrees or any part of the history they determined.

In line with these formulations, we must approach prophetic predictions with full assurance that historical contingencies have never interrupted the immutable decrees of God. No uncertainties ever lay before him; no power can thwart the slightest part of his plan.[7] Yahweh spoke through his prophets with full knowledge and control of what was going to happen in the near and distant future. Any outlook that denies this theological conviction is less than adequate.

Up to this point, we have mentioned only one side of the theological framework surrounding the subject of prophecy and intervening historical contingencies. To understand these matters more fully, we must also give attention to the providence of God, to his immanent historical interactions with creation.

Just as they have maintained the doctrine of the immutability of divine decrees, evangelicals have traditionally defended the importance of God's real involvement in historical processes. Looking again to the foundational era of modern evangelicalism, we find Calvin providing a mutually agreeable summary of this doctrine of divine providence.[8] As he put it, the omnipotent God is "watchful, effective, active, . . . engaged in ceaseless activity."[9]

Beyond this, Calvin viewed divine providence as a complex reality. Providence is "the determinative principle of all things," but sometimes God "works through an intermediary, sometimes without an intermediary, sometimes contrary to every intermediary."[10] God did not simply make an eternal plan that fixed all events. He also sees that his plan is carried out by working through, without, and contrary to created means. Calvin, as many evangelicals after him, balanced his affirmation of the immutability of God's decrees with an acknowledgment of God's complex involvement in the progression of history.

The Westminster Confession also displays a deep appreciation of divine providence. The fifth chapter speaks to the issue at hand: "Although in relation to the decree of God, the first cause, all things come to pass immutably and infallibly, yet by the same providence he often orders them to fall out, according to the nature of second causes."[11] This passage acknowledges that all events are fixed by eternal decrees but also that secondary causes play a vital role in the providential outworking of those decrees.

How do secondary causes interact? The Westminster Confession affirms that they work together "either necessarily *(necessario)*, freely *(libere)*, or contingently *(contingenter)*."[12] It is important for our purposes to point out that *contingencies* are acknowledged as historical realities. Like modern evangelicals, the Westminster Assembly did not view the universe as a gigantic machine in which each event mechanically necessitates the next. On the contrary, in the providence of God, events take place freely and contingently as well.

In this sense, belief in God's immutability does not negate the importance of historical contingencies or especially the importance of human choice. Under the sovereign control of God, the choices people make determine the directions history will take.[13] If we make one choice, certain results will occur. If we choose another course, other events will follow. To be sure, God is "free to work without, above, and against [second causes] at his pleasure," but "in his ordinary providence, [he] maketh use of means."[14] That is to say, human choice is one of the ordinary ways in which God works out his immutable decrees. In accordance with his all-encompassing fixed plan, God often waits to see what his human subjects will do, and then he directs the future on the basis of what *they* decide.

Divine providence provides a perspective that complements divine immutability. Old Testament prophets revealed the word of the unchanging Yahweh, but they spoke for God in space and time, not before the foundations of the world. By definition, therefore, they did not utter immutable *decrees* but providential *declarations*. For this reason, we should not be surprised to find that intervening historical contingencies, especially human reactions, had significant effects on the way predictions were realized. In fact, we will see that Yahweh often spoke through his prophets, watched the reactions of people, and then determined how to carry through with his declarations.

II. Historical Contingencies and Predictions

Most interpreters have recognized that intervening historical contingencies play some role in the prediction-fulfillment dynamic of OT prophecy. Yet opinions vary widely on how this function should be construed. One end of the spectrum tends to restrict the significance of contingencies to a small class of predictions.[15] The other end of the spectrum gives a more central role to human choice and divine freedom.[16]

One source of confusion in the discussions of these matters is a failure to distinguish among different kinds of prophetic predictions. By and large, analyses have focused on the content of prophecies as determinative of the role of historical contingencies. We will try to bring some clarity to the discussion by distinguishing several formal features of OT predictions. We will speak of three kinds of predictions: (1) predictions qualified by conditions, (2) predictions qualified by assurances, and (3) predictions without qualifications. How did historical contingencies relate to each type of prediction?

A. Predictions Qualified by Conditions

A survey of OT prophecies uncovers a number of passages in which prophets offered predictions qualified by conditions. They explicitly made fulfillment dependent on the responses of those who listened. This qualification was communicated in many ways, but we will limit ourselves to a sampling of passages with the surface grammar of conditional sentences.[17]

Some conditional prophecies were bipolar: they declared two directions listeners might have taken—one leading to curse and the other leading to blessing. For instance, in Isa 1:19–20 we read,

> If you are ready and obey, you will eat the best produce of the land;
> but if you resist and rebel, you will be eaten by the sword.[18]
> For the mouth of Yahweh has spoken.

Isaiah made two options explicit. Obedience would lead to eating the best of the promised land; disobedience would lead to being devoured by an enemy's sword.

In a similar fashion, Jeremiah approached Zedekiah with two choices for the house of David.

> For if you thoroughly carry out these commands, then kings who sit on David's throne will come through the gates of this palace, riding in chariots and on horses, each one accompanied by his officials[19] and his army.[20] But if you do not obey these commands, declares Yahweh, I swear by myself that this palace will fall into ruin. (Jer 22:4–5)

The future of Judah's nobility depended on human actions. Great victory and blessings were in store for obedient kings, but rebellious kings would bring ruin to the palace. The prophetic prediction was explicitly qualified in both ways.

These passages introduce an important consideration. When prophets spoke about things to come, they did not necessarily refer to what the future *would* be. At times, they proclaimed only what *might* be. Prophets were "attempting to create certain responses in the community"[21] by making their predictions explicitly conditional. They spoke of *potential* and not *necessary* future events. Thus, their predictions warned of judgment and offered blessings in order to motivate listeners to participate in determining their own future. As we will see, this feature of OT prophecy is central to understanding the prediction-fulfillment dynamic.

Conditional predictions also appear as unipolar. In these cases, the prophets spoke explicitly of one set of choices and results and only implied other possibilities. Sometimes they focused on a negative future. For instance, Isaiah warned Ahaz that

> If you are not faithful,
> then you will not stand at all. (Isa 7:9)

Isaiah told Ahaz that he would face doom if he did not respond with faith in Yahweh. Isaiah did not mention any other options in the oracle.

At other times, prophets pointed to a positive future. In his famous temple sermon, Jeremiah announced,

> If you dramatically improve your ways and your actions and actually show justice to each other, if you do not oppress the alien, the fatherless or the widow, and do not shed[22] innocent blood in this place, and if you do not follow other gods to your own harm, then I will let you live in this place, the land I gave your forefathers forever and ever. (Jer 7:5–7)

The prophet told the people of Judah that their continuance in the promised land depended on their obedience. He did not spell out other contingencies.

Unipolar conditional predictions point to another important feature of OT prophecy: prophets did not always speak explicitly of all possible conditions related to their predictions. The context of Isaiah's unipolar word to Ahaz (Isa 7:9) implied that the king would be blessed if he relied on Yahweh (Isa 7:3–9). Jeremiah's words concerning the temple (Jer 7:5–7) warned of exile for disobedience (Jer 7:8–15), but this warning implied that obedience would secure continued residence in the land. Yet the explicit conditions mentioned in the oracles themselves only focused on one side of each situation. We should not be surprised, therefore, to find that in other circumstances OT prophets did not state every applicable condition to their predictions. In fact, we will see that considering unexpressed conditions is vital to a proper interpretation of prophecy.

B. Predictions Qualified by Assurances

We now turn to the other end of the spectrum, where prophets offered predictions qualified by assurances. Guarantees of different sorts accompanied prophetic oracles. We will mention three categories.

First, on three occasions in the book of Jeremiah, the prophet opposes those who hope for Jerusalem's deliverance from Babylonian dominion by revealing that Yahweh forbade intercession for the city. For instance, God declares that exile is coming for the residents of Jerusalem (Jer 7:15), but he quickly adds, "Do not pray on behalf of this people nor lift up any plea or petition for them; do not plead with me, for I will not listen to you" (Jer 7:16).

In Jer 11:11a, Yahweh announces an inescapable doom of judgment for Jerusalem. To confirm this prediction, the oracle continues, "And they may cry to me, but I will not listen to them" (Jer 11:11b). To make matters even more certain, God instructs Jeremiah once again, saying, "Not even you should pray for this people" (Jer 11:14).

Similarly, Yahweh announces the sentence of exile in Jer 14:10, and then he tells the prophet for a third time, "Do not pray for any good thing for this people"

(Jer 14:11). In addition, Yahweh insists that he will not pay attention to their fasting or to their burnt and grain offerings; he will undoubtedly destroy them (Jer 14:12). Later in the same context, Yahweh reveals his utter determination to judge by saying he will not relent "even if Moses and Samuel were to stand before [him]" (Jer 15:1).

A second type of assurance denies that Yahweh's intentions will be reversed. For the most part, these passages assert that Yahweh will not "turn back" (שׁוּב) or "repent" (נָחַם). For example, the well-known oracles of judgment in the opening chapters of Amos (1:3, 6, 9, 13; 2:1, 4, 6) repeat the same formula at the beginning of each proclamation:

> For three sins of [name of country],
> even for four, I will not turn back.

The words *I will not turn back* (אֲשִׁיבֶנּוּ) express Yahweh's determination to carry through with the sentences of each oracle. The phrase *turn back* (שׁוּב) appears frequently in the OT with God as subject to denote a change of divine disposition toward a course of action.[23] To the delight of his Israelite audience, Amos announced that Yahweh was not simply threatening the foreign nations. Yet Amos also used the same expression to make it plain that God would also not reverse himself regarding their judgment (Amos 2:4, 6).

Similar assurances occur in the books of Isaiah, Jeremiah, and Ezekiel. Isaiah confirms the promise of Yahweh's victory over all nations as "a word that will not be revoked" (וְלֹא יָשׁוּב; Isa 45:23). Jeremiah assured his listeners that Jerusalem's destruction was sure by adding, "Yahweh's anger will not turn back" (לֹא יָשׁוּב; Jer 23:20 par. 30:24). In Jer 4:28, Yahweh offers an additional assurance: "I will not relent (וְלֹא נִחַמְתִּי) and I will not turn back from it (וְלֹא־אָשׁוּב מִמֶּנָּה)." Along these same lines, Ezekiel reported Yahweh's word, "And I will not relent" (וְלֹא אֶנָּחֵם; Ezek 24:14),[24] to assure his listeners of Jerusalem's coming devastation.

A third type of confirmation appears when Yahweh takes solemn oaths. Divine oaths appear in the Prophets in the third and first persons. Frequently, the typical verbal expression נִשְׁבַּע or נִשְׁבַּעְתִּי appears. Amos declared that the northern kingdom's destruction was confirmed by oath (Amos 4:2; 6:8; 8:7). Isaiah and Jeremiah announced that Yahweh had sworn to destroy Israel's enemies (Isa 14:24; Jer 49:13; 51:14). Jeremiah insisted that the majority of Jews exiled to Egypt would die there (Jer 44:26). Twice, Isaiah confirmed Israel's future restoration by divine oath (Isa 54:9; 62:8).

Divine oaths also appear in the form "As Yahweh lives . . ." (חַי־יְהוָה) and "As I live . . ." (חַי־אָנִי). For example, Ezekiel confirmed Jerusalem's destruction with this formula (Ezek 5:11; 14:16, 18, 20; 20:3, 31, 33; 33:27). The destruction of other nations was assured by divine oath (Ezek 35:6, 11; Zeph 2:9). Judgments against certain individuals took this form in Jeremiah and Ezekiel (Jer 22:24; 44:26; Ezek 17:16, 19; 34:8). Finally, Isaiah and Ezekiel confirmed the restoration of Jerusalem by reporting Yahweh's oath (Isa 49:18; Ezek 20:33).[25]

Predictions qualified by assurances reveal two important features of OT prophecy. On the one hand, these passages make it plain that some predicted events were inevitable. With reference to these declarations, Yahweh would not listen to prayers, turn back, relent, or violate his oaths. Nevertheless, we must remember that these kinds of predictions are few in number and usually not very specific in their descriptions of the future. They assure that some events *will* take place, but they do not guarantee *how, to what extent, when,* or a host of other details. As we will see, these details are subject to historical contingencies.

On the other hand, this class of prophecies also indicates that not all predictions shared this heightened certainty. Yahweh forbade prayers in response to some oracles precisely because prayer usually had the potential to affect outcomes (Jer 26:19; Amos 7:1–6; Jonah 3:10). Similarly, Yahweh declared that he would neither "turn back" nor "relent" from some courses of action because he normally left those options open (Joel 2:14; Amos 7:3, 6; Jonah 3:9). Finally, at times Yahweh took an oath to add weight to a prediction precisely because not all predictions had this solemn status.[26]

C. Predictions without Qualifications

As we have seen, a number of passages contain explicit conditions and assurances. Now we will give our attention to a third category of passages: predictions without qualifications. These materials contain neither expressed conditions nor assurances.

From the outset, we may say without hesitation that intervening historical contingencies had some bearing on this class of predictions. The OT abounds with examples of unqualified predictions of events that did not take place. For instance, Jonah announced, "Forty more days and Nineveh will be overturned" (Jonah 3:4), but God spared the city (Jonah 3:10). Shemaiah told Rehoboam, "You have abandoned me; so, I now abandon you to Shishak" (2 Chr 12:5), but the attack was mollified (2 Chr 12:7–8). Huldah responded to Josiah's inquiry, saying, "I am bringing disaster on this place and its inhabitants" (2 Kgs 22:16), but the punishment for Jerusalem was later postponed (2 Kgs 22:18–20). Micah said to Hezekiah, "Zion will be plowed like a field" by Sennacherib (Mic 3:12; cf. Jer 26:18), but the invasion fell short of conquering the city (2 Kgs 19:20–35). In each of the examples, the predicted future did not take place. What caused these turns of events? Each text explicitly sights human responses as the grounds for the deviations. The people of Nineveh (Jonah 3:6), the leaders of Judah (2 Chr 12:6),

Josiah (2 Kgs 22:18–19), and Hezekiah (Jer 26:19) repented or prayed upon hearing the prophetic word.

These passages indicate that the fulfillment of at least some unqualified predictions were subject to the contingency of human response. Conditions did not have to be stated explicitly to be operative. As Calvin put it, "Even though [the prophets] make a simple affirmation, it is to be understood from the outcome that these nonetheless contain a tacit condition."[27]

These observations raise an important question. How should we relate the presence of tacit conditions to the well-known Mosaic criterion of false prophets in Deut 18:22?

> If what a prophet proclaims in the name of Yahweh does not occur[28] or come about, that is a message Yahweh has not spoken. The prophet has spoken presumptuously.

At first glance, this passage appears to present a straightforward test: failed predictions mark false prophets.[29] As straightforward as this interpretation may be, it does not account for the many predictions from canonical (and thus true) prophets that were not realized.

Interpreters have taken different approaches to this difficulty. Many scholars treat Deut 18:22 as a uniquely Deuteronomistic perspective that is contradicted by other biblical traditions.[30] Evangelicals usually argue that Moses' test should be taken as the general rule to which there are a few exceptions.[31]

An alternative outlook would be to assume that Moses and his audience realized unqualified predictions had implied conditions. If this dynamic was well-known, then he did not have to repeat it explicitly when he offered his criterion in Deut 18:22. In this view, Moses' test instructed Israel to expect a prediction from a true prophet to come about *unless* significant intervening contingencies interrupted.

This understanding of the Mosaic criterion may explain why so many passages highlight the historical contingencies that interrupted many fulfillments. Old Testament writers accounted for the Mosaic test of false prophets by pointing out why the predictions of true prophets sometimes did not come true. For example, the writer of Jonah explains how the king of Nineveh ordered fasting and mourning by "every person (הָאָדָם) and by every beast (וְהַבְּהֵמָה), herd (הַבָּקָר), and flock (וְהַצֹּאן)" (Jonah 3:7). The Chronicler used one of his most poignant theological terms (כָּנַע) when he said that Rehoboam and the leaders of Judah "humbled themselves" (2 Chr 12:6).[32] The writer of Kings described Josiah's ritual tearing of his robe (2 Kgs 22:11). The specificity of these passages suggests that so long as Israelites could point to significant intervening contingencies, they had no trouble accepting interrupted predictions as having originated with Yahweh.

While it seems indisputable that historical contingencies affected unqualified predictions, evangelicals have differed over the breadth of their influence. Did tacit conditions apply only to a small class of unqualified predictions? Or did conditions attach to all of these prophecies?

An answer to this question appears in the eighteenth chapter of Jeremiah, which describes the prophet's experience at the potter's house. This passage stood against the backdrop of false views concerning the inviolability of Jerusalem. Many Jerusalemites opposed Jeremiah because they believed divine protection of Jerusalem was entirely unconditional (e.g., Jer 7:4). Jeremiah 18:1–12 amounted to a rebuttal of this false security. It stated that *all* unqualified predictions, even those concerning Jerusalem, operated with implied conditions.

This chapter opens with the prophet visiting a potter's house and experiencing a symbolic event. A potter worked with ruined clay, and he reshaped it into another form (Jer 18:1–4). Immediately, Yahweh revealed the significance of this event to the prophet. The house of Israel is like clay in the hands of Yahweh, the Potter; he may do with her as he pleases (Jer 18:5–6). Yahweh elaborated further on the analogy in the following verses:[33]

> If at some time I say regarding any nation or kingdom that I will uproot, tear down, or destroy, and if that nation about which I spoke[34] repents of its evil, then I may relent[35] from the evil I planned to do to it. And if at some other time I say regarding any nation or kingdom that I will build it up and plant it, and if it does evil in my eyes—not listening to my voice—then I may relent from the good thing which I said I would do for it. (Jer 18:7–10)

Several elements in this passage point to its categorical nature. First, each sentence begins with an emphatically general temporal reference. The expressions "at some time" (רֶגַע) and "at some other time" (וְרֶגַע) emphasize that Yahweh's words apply to every situation.[36] No particular circumstances limit the protases. Second, the anarthrous expression "any nation or kingdom" (עַל־גּוֹי וְעַל־מַמְלָכָה) also points to the categorical nature of the policy. Yahweh's responsiveness applies to *all* nations. Third, these verses describe the two major types of prophetic prediction: judgment (Jer 18:7–8) and salvation (Jer 18:9–10). In terms of form-critical analysis, all prophetic oracles gravitate in one or both of these directions. Referring to these two major directions of all predictions underscores the categorical nature of the dynamic described here.[37]

The universal perspective of Jer 18:1–12 strongly suggests that *all* unqualified predictions were subject to implicit conditions. Sincere repentance had the potential of affecting every unqualified prophecy of judgment. Flagrant disobedience had the potential of negating every unqualified prophecy of prosperity.

A survey of Scripture reveals that the descriptions of God's reactions in Jer 18 are only representative. Yahweh reacted to human responses in many different ways. At various times, he completely reversed (Amos 7:1–6), postponed (1 Kgs 21:28–29; 2 Kgs 22:18–20), mollified (2 Chr 12:1–12), and carried through (2 Sam 12:22–23) with predictions. Yahweh exercised great latitude because his responses were specific to the situation and appropriate for the particularities of each event. Nevertheless, a basic pattern was always at work. The realizations of all unqualified predictions were subject to modification as Yahweh reacted to his people's responses.

Many evangelical interpreters have resisted adopting this categorical outlook. By and large they limit conditionality to predictions that exhibit two features in their content. First, the prophecy must have an imminent fulfillment. That is to say, it must refer to "the near future"[38] or to "an event which is fairly proximate in time and space."[39] Second, the prediction must depend on "some act of obedience or repentance on the part of the prophet's contemporaries"[40] or "on the free actions of the prophet's contemporaries."[41]

Those who advocate limiting conditionality in these ways have offered little support for their views from the prophetic corpus. Instead, they tend to simply point to the contents of prophecies they already believe are inviolable—such as the promise of a messiah or final judgment—or, in some cases, to modern Israel's right to the land of Canaan.[42] Predictions regarding these and related theological concerns are deemed unconditional.

The lack of argumentation makes it difficult to respond to these views; we may make only a few comments. First, it begs the question to argue that certain prophecies are unconditional because they speak of matters that are unconditionally fixed. Theological biases guide such evaluations based on a prediction's content. Second, no such limitations on conditionality appear in Jer 18:1–12. As we have seen, the language of the passage is so categorical that it would seem necessary for an absolutely unconditional prophecy to state explicitly that it is an exception to the rule. Jeremiah 18 sets no limitation of a particular time frame or subject matter. In fact, the only qualification is that historical contingencies must intervene between the prediction and its fulfillment.

In summary, we have seen that intervening historical contingencies had a bearing on all three major types of prophetic predictions. Some predictions explicitly told the original listeners that their actions would affect outcomes. A few passages assured that a prediction would be realized, but precisely how that outcome would look still remained subject to contingencies. Beyond this, unqualified predictions, the bulk of the prophetic material, always operated with tacit conditions. In all cases, significant responses had the potential of affecting to some degree how Yahweh would direct the future.

III. Historical Contingencies and Expectations

These observations raise a crucial question. If human responses could affect the way Yahweh directed history after a prediction, how did prophets or their listeners have any secure expectations for the future? Were they not cast into a sea of utter uncertainty?

The prophets themselves point us in a helpful direction. As we will see, they did not believe Yahweh was free to take history in any direction. On the contrary, they looked to past revelation to understand the parameters to which Yahweh had bound himself. To be more specific, the prophets looked to Yahweh's covenants to guide their expectations of what the future held.

It has been well established that OT prophets saw themselves as operating within the structures of Yahweh's covenants. They were emissaries of God, the great Suzerain, mediating covenant sanctions between Yahweh and his people.[43] The prophetic corpus explicitly mentions the covenant with Noah (Isa 54:9), Abraham (Isa 41:8; 51:2; Jer 33:26; Mic 7:20), Moses (Isa 63:11–12; Dan 9:11, 13; Mic 6:4; Mal 4:4), and David (Isa 9:7; Jer 30:9; Hos 3:5). No doubt, the Mosaic and Davidic covenants appear more frequently than others in the prophets' writings. The laws of Sinai formed the basis for their moral evaluations. The pervasive curses and blessings announced by the prophets corresponded to the Mosaic covenant. Even the threat of exile and the hope of restoration to the land stem from the Mosaic covenant.[44] Moreover, the intense prophetic concern with Jerusalem and its throne shows their dependence on the Davidic covenant.

To understand how Yahweh's covenants provided certain expectations for the prophets and their listeners, we need merely to recall that the language and rituals of covenants portray these events as divine oaths. It is well-known that the cutting rituals indicated explicitly in several passages (Gen 15:7–21; 17:9–14; Jer 34:18–19) as well as the common expression "to cut a covenant" (כָּרַת בְּרִית) depict covenant-making events as rites of swearing.[45] As Meredith Kline writes, "Both in the Bible and in extra-biblical documents concerned with covenant arrangements the swearing of the oath is frequently found in parallelistic explication of the idea of entering into a covenant relationship, or as a synonym for it."[46] Divine covenants were not declarations subject to revision. They were divine oaths whose invariance reflected the immutable character of God himself.

All of this is to say that whenever prophets offered predictions, they did so with the firm conviction that Yahweh would keep his covenants with Israel. It was unthinkable that he would violate the structures of blessing and curses given through these solemn oaths. Yahweh would never react to historical contingencies in ways that transgressed his covenants.[47]

This conviction provided OT prophets and their listeners with a large set of general expectations. Yahweh had sworn to accomplish certain things in history. For instance, in Noah's day Yahweh promised cosmic stability until the end the world (Gen 8:22–9:17); Isaiah acknowledged the permanence of that expectation (Isa 54:9). God promised Abraham that his descendants would possess the land of Canaan (Gen 15:18–21); this conviction remained strong in the prophetic word, even in the face of temporary exile (Amos 9:15). Yahweh revealed laws to Moses that regulated daily life and the service of the cult; the prophets affirmed these structures (Amos 2:4). God promised David that his dynasty would be permanent and victorious over all nations (Ps 89:4, 25 [MT 89:5, 26]); the prophetic word held relentlessly to these promises as well (Amos 9:11–15). The list of certainties derived from OT covenants is great.

The covenantal parameters surrounding Yahweh and his people provided a basis for many expectations, but they did not settle every question. They set limits, but much latitude existed within these boundaries. Which curses would Yahweh carry out? What blessings would he bestow, and when? Prophetic predictions drew attention to these matters. As emissaries of Yahweh, the divine king of Israel, the prophets announced how Yahweh intended to implement covenant sanctions. Special revelation gave prophets insight into how the principles of covenants applied to the present and future.

As we have seen, however, prophetic predictions based on covenant principles took several formats. How did these variations in prophetic speech bear on expectations for the future? Let us explore this matter in terms of the three major types of predictions we have already discussed.

First, *predictions qualified by conditions* specified some courses of action for Yahweh. These prophecies gave some definition to the manner in which God planned to implement covenantal oaths. For example, Yahweh voluntarily limited his options when he said to Judah, "If you are ready and obey, you will eat the best produce of the land; but if you resist and rebel, you will be eaten by the sword" (Isa 1:19–20).[48] These words indicated that Yahweh was no longer overlooking Judah's disobedience. A moment of decision had come. At the same time, however, much latitude for God remained. It was he who determined whether conditions were met. What precisely constituted obedience and rebellion? Only Yahweh knew. Moreover, only he determined the precise nature of his responses. What kind of produce would they eat upon repentance? How much? What enemy would attack? When would judgment come? How long? The prophecy did not specify. In this sense, conditional predictions narrowed the latitude with which Yahweh might deal with his people, but they did not remove all leeway.

Second, a similar assessment holds for *predictions qualified by assurances.* Once again, the manner in which Yahweh might relate to his people was somewhat restricted. When Amos announced, "For three sins of Judah, even for four, I will not turn back" (Amos 2:4), Yahweh committed himself to a course of action against Judah. Moreover, predictions qualified by divine oaths explicitly raised expectations for the prophecy to the level of covenantal certainties. For instance, Ezekiel's announcement that utter destruction would come to Jerusalem (Ezek 5:11) was as valid as Yahweh's oath to sustain the Davidic dynasty (Ps 110:4). The language of solemn oaths had the effect of equating this class of predictions with the inviolable covenants. Nevertheless, latitude remained even here. When? How? By whom? How long? These more specific questions remained unanswered for the prophets and their audiences.

Third, we may speak of expectations related to *predictions without qualifications* in at least two ways. On the one hand, Moses' criterion for true prophets in Deut 18:22 assured that unqualified announcements from Yahweh would take place in the absence of a significant intervening historical contingency. If recipients of an oracle of judgment did not repent, they could be confident that the judgment would come. If recipients of an oracle of blessing did not turn away from Yahweh, the blessing would be realized.

On the other hand, we must also ask what expectations were appropriate when intervening historical contingencies took place. Could the recipients be confident of a particular outcome? First, with regard to oracles of judgment, several passages make it clear that no specific expectations came to those who repented and sought Yahweh's favor. For instance, when Jonah announced that Nineveh would be destroyed in forty days (Jonah 3:4), the king of Nineveh called for repentance and fasting (3:7–9). Nevertheless, the king did not respond with full assurance that Yahweh would relent. Instead, he said, "Who knows (מִי־יוֹדֵעַ)? The god may turn back (יָשׁוּב) and relent (וְנִחַם)" (3:9).

Joel predicted an army of locusts was about to destroy Judah (Joel 2:1–11). He then called for repentance (2:12–13). But what was the expectation? As Joel put it, "Who knows (מִי יוֹדֵעַ), [God] may turn back (יָשׁוּב) and relent (וְנִחָם)" (2:14). Once again, the motivation for repentance was not that Yahweh was obligated to relent if they repented. No one could be sure whether he would turn back or not.

A similar situation also occurred after Nathan prophesied that Bathsheba's first child would die (2 Sam 12:14). David prayed and fasted for the child until the prophecy was realized as stated. Why did the king pray? David explained, "I thought, 'Who knows (מִי יוֹדֵעַ)? Yahweh may be merciful[49] and permit the child to live'" (2 Sam 12:22).

The similar, perhaps formulaic, character of these three responses suggests that these theological convictions were normative in Israel. Hopeful ignorance about the future was not an unusual reaction. Neither prophets nor their listeners could know for certain that human response would move Yahweh to relent from a threatened judgment. As the case of David and his son illustrates, repentance and prayer did not always result in divine favor.

Second, Dan 9 demonstrates that expectations were no higher with unqualified predictions of blessing. The Mosaic covenant stated plainly that rebellion in Israel would lead to exile and that repentance would lead to restoration (Deut 4:25–31). This basic pattern had covenantal certainty. In Jer 25:11–12 the prophet announced more specifically that the restoration of exiled Judah would take place in seventy years. Yet Daniel wrestled with Jeremiah's prophecy some sixty-six years later.[50] He surveyed his situation and prayed for Yahweh to fulfill Jeremiah's prediction (Dan 9:4–19).

Daniel's reaction to Jeremiah's prophecy raises a question. Why did Daniel pray? Why did he not simply wait for the seventy years to pass? Several interpreters have noted the similarity between Jeremiah's prophecy and an inscription of Essarhadon.[51] It would appear that seventy years was a standard sentence for rebellion against a god. E. Lipinski speaks of the designation as "*un temps de pénitence, destinée à apaiser la colère du dieu*" (a time of penitence, designed to appease divine wrath).[52]

This symbolism pressed hard against Daniel as he looked at his situation. He realized that the exiles had not responded to their seventy-year sentence as they should have. Daniel fasted in sackcloth and ashes, acknowledging Israel's sin before exile (Dan 9:4–12). He also conceded that even the punishment of exile (vv. 11–12) had not brought about repentance (9:13–14): "Yet we have not obeyed him," Daniel confessed (v. 14). The prophet cried for mercy because Israel's continuing rebellion called into question how Jeremiah's prophecy would play out.

Yahweh responded to Daniel through the angel Gabriel. Gabriel announced that Jeremiah's "seventy years" had been extended to "seventy weeks of years" (שָׁבֻעִים שִׁבְעִים), or "seven times seventy years" (Dan 9:24).[53] Yahweh multiplied the time of exile seven times according to Mosaic covenantal structures. In Lev 26 Yahweh warned that continuing sin would bring a successive increase of punishments for Israel. Each time the people refused to repent, divine curses would increase "seven times" (שֶׁבַע; Lev 26:18, 21, 24, 28), finally culminating in the exile (Lev 26:23–45). Daniel 9 extended the principle of Lev 26 and increased the exile itself seven times because the people of Israel in Daniel's day were in rebellion.[54]

From this example we may conclude that the manner in which Yahweh would interact with human responses to unqualified predictions of blessing remained uncertain. Significant intervening historical contingencies had taken place, so Daniel had no assurance how or whether the prediction would be realized. He rested assured of the basic covenantal structures, but the specifics of Jeremiah's unqualified prediction remained in question.

In summary, the original recipients of OT predictions could be confident that Yahweh would fulfill all of his covenant promises, but no particular prophecy was completely free from the potential influence of intervening historical contingencies. In this sense, those who heard and read the prophets faced a future whose precise contours remained hidden. They could hope, but the manner in which Yahweh would react to human responses remained open until the moment he acted.

IV. Conclusion

Our study of intervening historical contingencies will raise a serious question for most evangelicals. Our interpretations of biblical prophecy have been dominated by a desire to know the future and how events today fit within it, but our proposal challenges this approach. If all OT predictions are subject to variation, and most may be completely reversed, then what good are they? What value do they have if they do not tell us where we stand in relation to a fixed future?

As we have seen, with rare exception, OT prophets did not speak of what *had* to be but of what *might* be. Even the few predictions that guaranteed fulfillment did not address their timing or manner of realization. Therefore, prophetic predictions were not designed to be building blocks of a futuristic scheme into which current events fit in particular ways. To approach biblical prophecies in this manner is to misuse them.

Our study suggests that we need a shift in hermeneutical orientation toward biblical prophecy. Rather than involving ourselves in ceaseless debates over this or that eschatological scheme and how current history relates to it, we should approach biblical prophecies in ways that accord more with the role of intervening historical contingencies. At least two principal hermeneutical concerns move to the foreground. These interpretative issues parallel popular approaches to biblical prophecy, but they also differ from them.

Firstly, prophetic predictions should still cause us to deepen our interest in the future but to do so with a different emphasis. Instead of looking at biblical predictions as statements of what *must* be coming, one should view them as announcements of what *might* be coming. As has been seen, with rare exception, OT prophets did not speak of a fixed future but of a potential future. Nevertheless, the first audiences of biblical predictions still turned their thoughts toward futurity. The king of Nineveh feared what Yahweh threatened to do to his city when he heard Jonah's message (Jonah 3:6). Rehoboam and the officials of Judah gave attention to the possibility of defeat when Shemaiah predicted Shishak's victory (2 Chr 12:6). Similarly, Daniel looked forward to the restoration of Israel because of Jeremiah's seventy-year prophecy (Dan 9:2–3). These recipients of predictions did not ignore Yahweh's word because it was subject to tacit conditions. Ignorance of precisely how or whether these predictions would play out did not cast aside interest in the future. On the contrary, hearing a threat of judgment or an offering of blessing was enough to spark their interests in what Yahweh intended to do.

This interest in the potential future is understandable when we remember that prophetic predictions conveyed Israel's greatest fears and hopes. On the one hand, Yahweh often threatened to do horrible things in the world. When the prophets announced death, destruction, and exile for the people of God, faithful Israelites could hardly turn a deaf ear. Unlike today's secular minds who scoff at the possibility of divine intrusion into history, ancient Israelites believed such intrusions were real possibilities. For this reason, the dreadful thought of encountering Yahweh's anger was compelling.

On the other hand, prophetic announcements of Yahweh's blessing touched on the highest ideals and greatest desires of faithful Israelites. The prophets announced the prospect of forgiveness, safety from enemies, and prosperity beyond imagination. Unlike in our day, when hope for the human race has all but vanished, these hopes held center stage in Israel's faith. When the prophets told of the ways Yahweh offered to bring blessings to his people, interest in the future grew.

In much the same way, contemporary readers must not allow the role of intervening contingencies to dissuade them from contemplating their future. When careful study determines that a biblical prediction has implications for our potential future, we should consider what might be in store for us. The dread of judgment and the exhilaration of blessings should overwhelm us as we encounter biblical predictions of our future. Developing an intense interest in the future is one of the chief hermeneutical interests we should have toward biblical prophecy.

Secondly, our study of intervening historical contingencies suggests that we should also deepen our concerns with the implications of biblical predictions for our lives today. Unlike popular approaches, however, our approach should not speculate as to how current events fit within a fixed future. To begin with, the future is certain only to God. Beyond this, our assessments of contemporary events are too inadequate to complete such a project. Instead of looking for how actions today fit within a fixed future, we should explore how actions today *affect* the future. In a word, we should be less concerned with *foreknowledge* of the future and more concerned with the *formation* of the future.

Biblical examples already mentioned illustrate this hermeneutical interest. The king of Nineveh was not content with having some idea of what might happen to his city. He applied the prediction to that very day by trying to direct the course of the future away from the threat of judgment (Jonah 3:6–9). Rehoboam and his officials also sought Yahweh's favor in order to avert the threatened defeat

(2 Chr 12:6). Similarly, Daniel tried his best to ensure that Jeremiah's prediction of restoration would take place (Dan 9:3). In these and other examples, the recipients of predictions knew that historical contingencies could affect the realizations of the prophetic word. They responded with attempts to thwart judgment and secure blessing. Appropriate repentance, prayer, and a redirection of lifestyle became their central hermeneutical concern.

In much the same way, our focus on current events in the light of biblical prophecy should entail our efforts to form the future. The fatalism of popular approaches should be replaced by piety and activism intent on avoiding judgment and securing blessing. If we believe that human responses to biblical predictions affect the ways in which the future unfolds, we should make certain that our responses direct the future toward divine blessing. Turning away from sin, offering prayers, and working for the kingdom must become our central hermeneutical concern.

Our study of biblical prophecy opens the way for exploring a number of interesting passages. Perhaps it provides a framework for understanding why Jesus told the apostles, "Some standing here will not taste death before they see the kingdom of God come with power" (Mark 9:1). Did intervening contingencies delay the return of Christ? Maybe Peter was operating with a similar concept when he admitted that the apparent delay of Christ's return was due to the fact that God "is patient with you, not wanting any to perish, but to come to repentance" (2 Pet 3:9). Does this view explain why he then exhorted his readers, saying, "You should be holy and godly, looking forward to the day of God and speeding its coming" (2 Pet 3:11–12)? Perhaps John had this outlook as he heard Jesus announce, "Yes, I am coming soon" (Rev 22:20), and as he responded, "Amen. Come, Lord Jesus" (Rev 22:20).

If the proposal of this study is correct, we are not involved in an irrelevant academic debate. The way we handle biblical predictions will greatly affect how they are fulfilled. Our failure to respond properly may actually extend the sufferings of the church by delaying our ultimate victory. However, if we make proper use of biblical predictions, they will enhance our hopes for the future and incite us to live today in ways that will hasten the consummation of all things.

~ *Notes* ~

This paper is an edited version of the inaugural address presented to the Faculty of Reformed Theological Seminary on November 23, 1993.

[1] For example, Hal Lindsey and C. C. Carlson, *The Late, Great Planet Earth* (Grand Rapids: Zondervan, 1971) sold 3 million copies, and J. F. Walvoord and

J. E. Walvoord, *Armageddon: Oil and the Middle East* (Grand Rapids: Zondervan, 1974) sold 1.4 million copies (statistics received by telephone communication from Zondervan, October 1, 1993). More recently see the popular *Left Behind* series by Tim F. Lahaye and Jerry B. Jenkins (7 vols.; Wheaton: Tyndale House, 1996–2000).

[2] Robert P. Carroll, *When Prophecy Failed: Cognitive Dissonance in the Prophetic Traditions of the Old Testament* (New York: Seabury, 1979), 34–35.

[3] John Calvin, *Institutes of the Christian Religion* 1.16.4 (1559; ed. John Thomas McNeill; trans. Ford Lewis Battles; repr., Philadelphia: Westminster, 1967).

[4] The Westminster Confession of Faith (1647) 3.1, as found in Philip Schaff, *The Creeds of Christendom* (1877; repr., Grand Rapids: Baker, 1969).

[5] Charles Hodge, *Systematic Theology* (3 vols.; 1871; repr., Grand Rapids: Eerdmans, 1970), 1:390.

[6] For a dated but extensive discussion of the doctrine of divine immutability within the Reformed tradition, see Stephen Charnock, *The Existence and Attributes of God* (1797; repr., Minneapolis: Klock & Klock, 1977).

[7] I agree with Hodge when he says, "If He [God] has not absolutely determined on what is to occur, but waits until an undetermined condition is or is not fulfilled, then his decrees can neither be eternal nor immutable" (*Systematic Theology,* 1:540).

[8] To be sure, Calvin often described biblical accounts of God contemplating, questioning, repenting, and the like as anthropomorphisms. See Calvin, *Institutes* 1.17.12–14. See also Calvin, *Commentaries on the First Book of Moses Called Genesis* (1554; trans. John King; repr., Grand Rapids: Baker, 1979), 248–49; and Calvin, *Commentaries on the Four Last Books of Moses Arranged in the Form of a Harmony* (1563; trans. Charles William Bingham; repr., Grand Rapids: Baker, 1979), 3:334.

[9] Calvin, *Institutes* 1.16.3. Louis Berkhof reminds us that the Reformed concept of divine immutability does not deny the reality of God's intricate involvement in time and space: "The divine immutability should not be understood as implying *immobility,* as if there were no movement in God. It is even customary in theology to speak of God as *actus purus,* a God who is always in action" (*Systematic Theology* [1939, 1941; repr., Grand Rapids: Eerdmans, 1969], 59).

[10] Calvin, *Institutes* 1.17.1.

[11] Westminster Confession, 5.2.

[12] Ibid.

[13] As G. C. Berkouwer put it, "God's rule is executed and manifested in and through human activity. There are not two powers . . . each limiting the other. Yet we see men performing extraordinarily important roles in sacred history" (*The Providence of God* [Grand Rapids: Eerdmans, 1952], 100).

[14] Westminster Confession, 5.3.

[15] For example, E. W. Hengstenberg argued, "Viewing prophecies as conditional predictions nullifies them" (cited by Patrick Fairbairn, *The Interpretation of Prophecy* [2d ed., 1865; repr., London: Banner of Truth, 1964], 61). Similarly, J. Barton Payne admits to some exceptions but insists that "whether achieved by intent . . . or by the most extraordinary of coincidences . . . every inspired prophecy does come to pass" (*Encyclopedia of Biblical Prophecy: The Complete Guide to Scriptural Predictions and Their Fulfillment* [New York: Harper & Row, 1973], 59). See also C. von Orelli, *The Old Testament Prophecy of the Consummation of God's Kingdom* (trans. J. S. Banks; Edinburgh: T&T Clark, 1889), 50; and L. Berkhof, *Principles of Biblical Interpretation: Sacred Hermeneutics* (1950; repr., Grand Rapids: Baker, 1973), 148–54.

[16] For instance, Justus Olshausen urges that "none of the divine predictions are bare historical proclamations of what is to take place" (cited by Fairbairn, *Interpretation of Prophecy,* 60). Similarly, William W. Klein, Craig L. Blomberg, and Robert L. Hubbard provide a concise representation of this position: "Except for specific unconditional prophecies, . . . announced prophecy does not bind God to bring about fulfillment. God sovereignly reserves the right to fulfill or not fulfill it depending upon his own purposes and his expectations of his people" (*Introduction to Biblical Interpretation* [Dallas: Word, 1993], 306). See also Willem A. VanGemeren, *Interpreting the Prophetic Word* (Grand Rapids: Academie, 1990), 58, 60, 301.

[17] Thomas O. Lambdin reminds us that "conditional sentences in Hebrew may be virtually unmarked" (*Introduction to Biblical Hebrew* [New York: Charles Scribner's Sons, 1971], 276). See the standard descriptions of conditional sentences in GKC, 106p, 107x, 108e, 109h, 110f, 159; Joüon, 167; *IBHS,* 32.2.1, 38.2.

[18] I am emending the reading of the MT, וּמְרִיתֶם חֶרֶב תְּאֻכְּלוּ, to וּמְרִיתֶם מֵחֶרֶב תְּאֻכְּלוּ, assuming haplography and maintaining Pual vocalization. 1QIsa[a] corrects to בחרב (cf. Pesh. and Tg. Isa.).

[19] I am reading וַעֲבָדָיו *(kethiv).*

[20] The MT *(kethiv)* reads singular. LXX levels to the plural: αὐτοὶ καὶ οἱ παῖδες αὐτῶν καὶ ὁ λαὸς αὐτῶν. I have rendered הוּא "each one" to reflect the preferred singularity *(lectio difficilior).*

[21] Carroll, *When Prophecy Failed,* 33.

[22] The reading of the MT is אַל־תִּשְׁפְּכוּ (you shall not shed), which is a prohibition. I have emended the text to לֹא־תִשְׁפְּכוּ (do not shed), assuming metathesis.

[23] Deut 30:3; 2 Chr 12:12; 30:8; Job 42:10; Jer 4:28; 12:15; 16:15; 23:3; 24:6; 27:22; 29:14; 32:37; 33:11, 26; Hos 2:9; 14:4; Joel 2:14; 3:7; Zeph 3:20; Zech 1:3.

[24] Here I am following the MT. Some LXX manuscripts omit this clause by haplography.

[25] Jeremiah 22:5 combines divine oath with conditionality.

[26] Fairbairn argues that divine oaths connected to predictions were "a difference only in the mode of announcement, and one adopted in accommodation to human infirmity, not of itself indicative of any inherent peculiarity in the matter of the predictions" (*Interpretation of Prophecy,* 502). I contend, however, that qualifying a prediction by divine oath raises the prophecy to the level of covenantal certainty (see the discussion on covenantal oaths in sec. III).

[27] Calvin, *Institutes* 1.17.14. As David E. Aune observes, implicit conditions were also attached to Agabus' prophecy in Acts 21:11 about Paul's imprisonment in Jerusalem (*Prophecy in Early Christianity and the Ancient Mediterranean World* [Grand Rapids: Eerdmans, 1983], 337). The prophecy caused Paul's companions to urge him to stay away from Jerusalem (Acts 21:12). Instead of generating resignation to a predetermined future, the prophecy produced attempts to avoid the potential danger. Aune also suggests that participial constructions in NT prophecies should be rendered as conditional clauses (337).

[28] I am emending the reading of the MT, וְלֹא, to לֹא *(lectio brevior),* following the Samaritan Pentateuch.

[29] Hengstenberg urged that any exception to this straightforward reading of Deut 18:22 would render the criterion "of no value, since recourse might always be had to the excuse, that the case had been altered by the not fulfilling of the condition" (cited by Fairbairn, *Interpretation of Prophecy,* 61). See also S. R. Driver, *A Critical and Exegetical Commentary on Deuteronomy* (1895; repr., ICC; 3d ed;

Edinburgh: T&T Clark, 1973), 230; C. F. Keil and F. Delitzsch, *The Pentateuch* (3 vols.; trans. James Martin; Grand Rapids: Eerdmans, 1949), 3:397; A. D. H. Mayes, *Deuteronomy* (Grand Rapids: Eerdmans, 1979), 283; and Gerhard von Rad, *Deuteronomy* (Philadelphia: Westminster, 1966), 125.

[30] Joseph Blenkinsopp, *A History of Prophecy in Israel* (Philadelphia: Westminster, 1983), 46.

[31] See Peter C. Craigie, *The Book of Deuteronomy* (NICOT; Grand Rapids: Eerdmans, 1976), 263; Payne, *Encyclopedia of Biblical Prophecy*, 59; and J. Ridderbos, *Deuteronomy* (trans. Ed M. van der Maas; BSC; Grand Rapids: Regency Reference Library/Zondervan, 1984), 208–9.

[32] For a helpful discussion of this term in Chronicles, see Raymond B. Dillard, *2 Chronicles* (WBC 15; Waco: Word, 1987), 77.

[33] A number of interpreters view these verses as a Deuteronomistic addition. See, for instance, Siegfried Herrmann, *Die prophetischen Heilserwartung im Alten Testament* (BWA[N]T 5; Stuttgart: Kohlhammer, 1965), 162–65. Philip R. Davies goes so far as to find several layers of interpretation in these verses ("Potter, Prophet, and People: Jeremiah 18 as Parable," *HAR* 11 [1987]: 26). Davies' argument is not convincing. The basic correspondences of the analogy (Potter/Yahweh, pot/Israel) are maintained throughout the passage. For strong arguments in favor of original unity, see Helga Weippert, *Die Prosareden des Jeremiabuches* (BZAW 132; Berlin: Walter de Gruyter, 1973), 48–62, 191–209.

[34] Here I follow the MT, מֵרָעָתוֹ אֲשֶׁר דִּבַּרְתִּי עָלָיו וְנִחַמְתִּי. The LXX omits אֲשֶׁר דִּבַּרְתִּי עָלָיו by haplography.

[35] The syntax of apodoses is not thoroughly discussed in the standard grammars. Apodoses are frequently jussive, imperative, and simple future. Occasionally, modality is in view. I have rendered the apodoses of Jer 18:8, 10 modally ("I may relent," וְנִחַמְתִּי) to resolve a problem that has preoccupied interpreters. As Terence E. Fretheim says, the passage "seems to bind God to the world and to human activity in ways that compromise [his] sovereignty" ("The Repentance of God: A Study of Jeremiah 18:7–10," *HAR* 11 [1987]: 82). In my rendering, repentance and disobedience only have the *potential* of causing Yahweh to relent. As my discussion of Jonah 3 and Joel 2 indicates, no guarantees are given. The perfective apodosis of Lev 27:27 ("he may redeem," וּפָדָה) is certainly modal. Leviticus 27:28 presents an alternative course of action. Beyond this, the immediate context of Jer 18:4 supports this view. The potter is not obligated to reshape the clay. The clay will be handled "as it

seems right to do in the eyes of the potter." The sovereignty of the potter is maintained.

[36] This construction (רֶגַע ... וְרֶגַע) occurs only once in the HB. William L. Holladay views them as modifiers of the apodoses and renders them as "suddenly" (*A Commentary on the Book of the Prophet Jeremiah Chapters 1–25* [2 vols.; Hermeneia; Philadelphia: Fortress, 1986], 1:516). It seems simpler, however, to translate the adverbs "at one time" or "at some time" following Tg. Jer. (זְמַן ... וּזְמַן; cf. Ezra 9:8; Isa 26:20; 54:7–8).

[37] For a similar description of prophecies regarding individuals, see Ezek 33:13–20.

[38] Berkhof, *Principles,* 150.

[39] Walter C. Kaiser Jr., *Back toward the Future: Hints for Interpreting Biblical Prophecy* (Grand Rapids: Baker, 1989), 65.

[40] Ibid.

[41] Berkhof, *Principles,* 150.

[42] For instance, R. B. Girdlestone argued for the unconditionality of prophecies toward "the children of men as a whole," i.e., eschatological judgment (Girdlestone, *The Grammar of Prophecy: An Attempt to Discover the Method Underlying the Prophetic Scriptures* [Bible Student's Library 11; London: Eyre & Spottiswoode, 1901], 29). Kaiser argues that "the prophecies about the land are closely identified with the promise of the Seed (i.e., the Messiah) and the promise of the gospel. . . . God took completely on himself the obligation for their fulfillment" (*Back toward the Future,* 66).

[43] For general discussion of prophets as covenantal emissaries, see R. E. Clements, *Prophecy and Covenant* (London: SCM Press, 1965), esp. 23–27; James Muilenburg, "The 'Office' of the Prophet in Ancient Israel" in *The Bible in Modern Scholarship* (ed. J. Philip Hyatt; Nashville: Abingdon, 1965), 87–97; John S. Holladay, "Assyrian Statecraft and the Prophets of Israel," *HTR* 63 (1970): 29–51; Meredith G. Kline, *The Structure of Biblical Authority* (Grand Rapids: Eerdmans, 1972), 57–62.

[44] For a helpful discussion of Mosaic blessings and curses in relation to the prophets, see Douglas Stuart, *Hosea–Jonah* (WBC 31; Waco: Word, 1987), xxxii–xlii.

[45] For summaries and bibliography on these topics, see M. Weinfeld,

"בְּרִית," *TDOT* 2:253–78; associated terms such as אָלָה and עֵדוּת suggest similar concepts (Josef Scharbert, "אָלָה," *TDOT* 1:261–66).

[46] Meredith G. Kline, *By Oath Consigned* (Grand Rapids: Eerdmans, 1968), 16.

[47] My emphasis on covenantal promises is similar to the insistence in Klein, Blomberg, and Hubbard: "We still regard the prophecies that involve the major milestones in God's plan for history as unconditional" (*Biblical Interpretation,* 306).

[48] For textual comments related to this passage see n. 18 above.

[49] I am following *kethiv.*

[50] For a helpful summary of discussions regarding the identity of "Darius, son of Ahasuerus" (Dan 9:1), see Joyce G. Baldwin, *Daniel: An Introduction and Commentary* (TOTC; Downers Grove, Ill.: InterVarsity Press, 1978), 23–28. Baldwin correctly observes, "Whatever the identity of Darius, the writer had in mind the first year of the Persian empire, 539 B.C." (163–64).

[51] See the helpful summary of comparative materials and bibliography in Thomas E. McComiskey, "The Seventy 'Weeks' of Daniel against the Background of Ancient Near Eastern Literature," *WTJ* 47 (1985): 35–40.

[52] E. Lipinski, "Recherches sur le livre de Zacharie," *VT* 20 (1970): 40. Essarhadon admits that he deserved seventy years of punishment, but he praises Marduk for reducing the time to eleven years. See Essarhadon's text and translation by R. Borger in *ANET,* 533–34.

[53] McComiskey correctly warns that the "שָׁבֻעִים are not conceived of as marking precise chronological periods" ("The Seventy 'Weeks,'" 41).

[54] For a fuller discussion the "seven weeks" of years and the connection with Lev 26, see Klaus Koch, "Die mysteriösen Zahlen der judäischen Könige und die apokalyptischen Jahrwochen," *VT* 28 (1978): 443–41. See also John J. Collins, *Daniel: With an Introduction to Apocalyptic Literature* (FOTL 20; Grand Rapids: Eerdmans, 1984), 91–92. For multiples of seven as standard ancient Near Eastern expressions, see McComiskey, "The Seventy 'Weeks,'" 38–39.

Building God's House: An Exploration in Wisdom

Raymond C. Van Leeuwen

The Bible at times reveals a wonderful coherence in places unexpected. George Herbert had a marvelous sense of this in his poem "The Holy Scriptures (2)." He wrote of Scripture as a "book of stars" of which he asks,

> O that I knew how all thy lights combine,
> And the configurations of their glory!
> Seeing not only how each verse doth shine,
> But all the constellations of the story.
> This verse marks that, and both do make a motion
> Unto a third, that ten leaves off doth lie.[1]

Here I hope to honor Bruce Waltke by exploring a biblical "constellation" that connects the books of Moses, the Former Prophets, Proverbs, and some New Testament passages. The pattern that holds them together is a combination of creation, wisdom, biblical language, worship, and godly living—all themes that remind me of Bruce Waltke as Christian scholar and gentleman.

I. Building God's House in the OT

We may begin with two verses in the book of Proverbs that describe the Lord's creation of all things:

> The Lord *by wisdom* laid earth's foundation,
> made firm the heavens *by understanding.*
> *By his knowledge* the deeps were split,
> and the clouds drip dew. (3:19–20)

These four short lines describe the earth, the heavens, the waters above and below, the great cosmic spaces, and their order of separations and cycles of life-giving water. Moreover, these verses hint that this created space with its realms is like a well-arranged house with its spacious rooms. Like a house or a city, the cosmos must have its foundation "laid" (the verb *yāsad̲* is regularly used of buildings), and it must be "made firm" or solid (*kûn* is also a building term). Significantly, this cosmic "house" is built with *wisdom, understanding,* and *knowledge (ḥok̲mâ, tĕb̲ûnâ,* and *daʿat̲),* words that English readers do not usually associate with skillful building.

Yet this trio of words first appears, in the very same order, in the Exodus story of the building of God's earthly house, the tabernacle. It is, in biblical terms, a very spiritual and "wise" activity: "The Lord said to Moses, 'See, I have called Bazazel by name . . . and have filled him with the Spirit of God, *with wisdom, with understanding, and with knowledge* concerning every [sort of] work'" (Exod 31:1–3).[2]

As several scholars have pointed out, the construction of the tabernacle is modeled after God's "building" of creation, including even the pattern of Sabbath rest (Exod 31:12-17). After the commands to build the tabernacle are interrupted by the terrible tale of the golden calf, the story resumes with a repetition of the Sabbath command: human work and rest are again patterned after God's creation work and rest (Exod 35:1-3). A freewill offering of materials is taken, and then those who are "wise of heart," including the women who are "wise of heart" in spinning cloth, are called to employ their various arts and crafts and do the actual building (Exod 35:10, 25, 35; KJV gives "wisehearted").

Contrary to the argument of R. N. Whybray in *The Intellectual Tradition in the Old Testament*[3] and to much of the Western intellectual and theological tradition, such practical works are not marginal to the biblical concept of wisdom as represented in Proverbs, Israel's premier Wisdom book. Rather, the wisdom of Proverbs is eminently practical, precisely as it embodies the "fear of the Lord" in the ordinary work of life in God's world (see, e.g., Prov 1:7; 9:10). The practicality of wisdom is perhaps nowhere so clearly spelled out as in the great acrostic poem in Prov 31, the Hymn to the Valiant Woman. The Valiant Woman shows she is a "woman who fears the Lord" in the round of "secular" activities ascribed to her. She even possesses the same cloth-making wisdom found among the wise-hearted women whose work adorns the temple. The rare and precious woven goods she produces for her "house" are the same as those used in God's "house" (Prov 31:13, 19, 21–22, 24–25; cf. Exod 28:5; 35:25).[4]

Biblical wisdom to a large extent has to do with practical knowledge, with a know-how regarding the whole spectrum of human skills and activities, all in tune with the normative patterns and possibilities—and with the concrete givens—of creation. Wise activities include not only "natural" skills like nursing and weaning a child (see Ps 131:2, a metaphor for God and humans); they also include "cultural" activities like sailing (Ps 107:27, "all [the sailors'] *wisdom* was swallowed up") and that earthly work we call "agri-culture" (Ps 104:13–17; Isa 28:23–29; cf. Prov 6:6–11; 10:4–5).

The model for such human activities is God's work in creation. As the creation was made with wisdom, understanding, and knowledge, so also humans make the "micro-cosmos" of the tabernacle with God-given wisdom. In building, they are coworkers with God: "He [God] built his sanctuary like the heights [i.e., of heaven], like the earth that he established forever" (Ps 78:69 NIV). As if to emphasize this point, the description in Exod 31:1–3 of Bazazel's wisdom, understanding, and knowledge is repeated almost verbatim in Exod 35:30–31, thus reinforcing the link between the building of the tabernacle and the creation of the cosmos described in Prov 3:19–20.

The building of Solomon's temple in 1 Kings once again corresponds to the language of Prov 3:19–20 and Exod 31:1–3; 35:30–31. In fact, this important work of Solomon is a prime illustration of the wisdom for which he was famous. When Solomon sends to Hiram for cedars to build the "temple,"[5] the old king is very glad *(śāmaḥ)* and praises the Lord for giving his friend David "a wise son" (1 Kgs 5:21 [EVV 5:7]; cf. *śāmaḥ* in Prov 10:1; 15:20). Hiram agrees to bring Solomon cedar logs; in exchange, says Hiram, Solomon is "to give food [for] my *house*" (1 Kgs 5:23 [EVV 5:8]; cf. Prov 31:14–15, 27; translated as "family" in the NIV). Following the account of how Solomon provided food for Hiram's "house," we are told that "The LORD gave Solomon wisdom, just as he had promised him" (1 Kgs 5:12 NIV [MT 5:26]).

For our purposes, all these hints at the "wisdom" of Solomon's "house" building are more than confirmed by the following verse from 1 Kings, which parallels Prov 3:19–20 and Exod 31:1–3; 35:30–31: "[The Lord] filled [Hiram] with *wisdom, understanding, and knowledge* to do every [sort of] work" (1 Kgs 7:14b). Strikingly, the work of God's house is finished in "seven years" (1 Kgs 6:38), just as the creation was in seven days. In Hebrew, the summary statement of the temple's completion clearly alludes to the summary of creation in Gen 2:2: "And Hiram finished doing all the work that he did for King Solomon on the house of the Lord" (1 Kgs 7:40b; cf. 7:51).[6]

The foregoing passages presuppose a worldview in which creation is God's great temple (see Ps 29; Isa 66:1; cf. Matt 5:34–35), of which the seraphim cry, "Holy, Holy, Holy, Lord God of Hosts, the fullness of all the earth is his glory" (Isa 6:3); and the tabernacle/temple, like the creation of which it is a microcosm, has been built with wisdom, understanding, and knowledge. The Israelite temple—God's "house," where alone atonement takes place—is a localized and holy counterpart to the cosmos at large, that is, to the world that humans have corrupted and polluted. In a world under the sway of the evil one, the temple is that pure place from which God sets out to reclaim his entire world through the power of forgiveness and renewal. In the temple, God's full glory is manifest (it fills the "house"; Exod 40:34–35; 1 Kgs 8:10–11; 2 Chr 7:1–2; Rev 15:8); yet in the larger, cosmic "house," God's glory remains contested, obscured, and ignored by sinful humans. Thus Habakkuk utters the eschatological promise that someday "the earth will be filled with the knowledge of the glory of the LORD, as the waters cover the sea" (Hab 2:14 NIV). Isaiah locates that promise in the messianic kingdom of wisdom and peace (Isa 11:9).

From the foregoing parallels between creation (as the place where God means to dwell among humans) and the tabernacle/temple (as the more localized place of God's dwelling among humans), one might conclude that building a "house" with "wisdom, understanding, and knowledge" is *sacred* work, removed from the hectic world of everyday human life, work, and struggle. It is indeed sacred work, but the building of houses in imitation of God's creating—with wisdom, understanding, and knowledge—is not limited to the special task of building a temple or tabernacle.

Proverbs 24:3–4 provides a remarkable conclusion to our little collection of passages on building houses wisely:

> By *wisdom* a house is built,
> by *understanding* it is established,
> by *knowledge* its rooms are filled
> with every [sort of thing] rich, precious, and lovely.

Here the wise building of any human house, not just of a temple or tabernacle, presupposes God's wise work of creation and harmony with it—as a comparison with Prov 3:19–20 again makes clear. Thus the Lord himself is involved in godly human enterprises of the most mundane sort:

> Unless the LORD builds the house,
> its builders labor in vain.
> Unless the LORD watches over the city,
> the watchmen stand guard in vain." (Ps 127:1 NIV)

What's more, the "filling" of the human house with all sorts of good things echoes the psalmist's account of God's creation: "How many are your works, O Lord, by wisdom you made them all, the earth is filled with your creatures!" (Ps 104:24). To complete the creation, the temple, and ordinary human houses, one must fill the "house" with "furniture" and creatures appropriate for its functions.

It is into God's cosmic "house" that Wisdom, as the Lord's agent in creation, invites the simple (Prov 9:1–6). In a commentary on Proverbs,[7] I argued that this interplay of creation and "house" was a key to understanding the relationship of Prov 8, with its great account of creation, to Prov 9, where Lady Wisdom has "built her house" and subsequently invites humans into her cosmic "house" to experience her banquet of wisdom and life. This foreshadows Christ's role in creation (John 1) and anticipates Jesus' kingdom parable of the great banquet (Luke 14:15–24).

This brief account of several "leaves" in Scripture (to revert to Herbert's metaphor), which "mark" one another by their congruence in phrasing and worldview, leads me to posit several biblical-theological theses for further development and discussion among the people of God:

First, in building ordinary human houses and so-called "secular" undertakings and activities of every sort, our work should be modeled after and determined by God's work of creation in the beginning. Thus the blessing/command to "fill the earth and subdue it" (Gen 1:28) means to fill it with glory as humans image God in life and work (cf. Ps 8).

Second, all human work needs to be congruent with or "in tune with" the normative order and character of God's cosmic house in its ongoing existence. Israel's Torah, Prophets, and Wisdom writings remain faithful, normative, and divinely authoritative guides for life in God's house.

Third, the purpose of all human work is to restore, preserve, and develop the creation in ways that make it a more fitting place for God's glory to dwell. (God cannot dwell in an "unclean" temple or in a world *filled* with violence and injustice; cf. Gen 6:11–13; 1 Sam 4:21–22; Ezek 10:3–4, 18; 11:23.) This tension between those who build for God's glory and those whose cultural activities are destructive is caught in the proverb "Wise women build a house . . . but folly tears it down" (Prov 14:1).

Fourth, God's glory should be manifest in all of the creation, including the various enterprises of human culture.

Finally, the biblical imagery of this world as God's "house" underlies the parables of Jesus in which he refers to a house with servants and a master. On this point I would add a few comments.

II. Building God's House in the NT

Matthew 12:22–29 compares the coming of the kingdom of heaven (i.e., of God) to the conflict of two strong men, the owner and a thief, for mastery of a "house." Again, the "house" is this world (cf. the "field" in Matt 13:38), and the issue between Satan and Jesus is who shall be master of this world and its many kingdoms (Matt 4:8–9). Jesus' many exorcisms are his way of "cleaning house," of casting out "unclean spirits" who seek to dominate the human servants of God.[8]

This background also illuminates the Markan parable of admonition to watch and work while the owner of the house is gone (Mark 13:32–36). In the cosmic house to which the parable refers, the master gives to *each* of his servants (i.e., all human beings) "power and authority *(exousia),* each to do his own task" until the Lord of the house returns. No human task, undertaking, or work is excluded from our divinely given call to fill God's cosmic house with goods that glorify him. From family building, to business building, to house building, to evangelism, to making music and instruments to play it—all wise work for the glory of God in creation is a building of God's house, "kingdom work."

III. Building God's House Today

The temple of God in which he now dwells locally is the church, the people of God, Christ's body. This reality finds its basis and possibility in Jesus who is the builder of our world and thus our builder. The world as God's temple or house complements the church as God's house:

> Moses was faithful in all God's house. Jesus has been found worthy of greater honor than Moses, just as the builder of a house has greater honor than the house itself. For every house is built by someone, but God is the builder of everything. Moses was faithful as a servant in all God's house, testifying to what would be said in the future. But Christ is faithful as a son over God's house. And we are his house. (Heb 3:2–3 NIV; cf. 1 Cor 3:9)

How then should we live as God's building, as his "house"? First of all, our weekly worship should be the burning power-center of our cosmos, where the reality of the living God, Father and Son, is present in the Spirit who works wisdom, power, and love in those who believe (Eph 1:15–23). Here Christ and his power are present as nowhere else. Here the Holy Spirit works mightily through worship, music, and prayer as well as through the sacraments and the preaching of the word (Col 3:16; Eph 5:18–20). This corresponds to the temple worship in ancient Israel, where God dwelt among his people in grace and forgiveness.

But, as the continuation of Col 3:16 shows, the power of the Holy Spirit working in the communal life of God's people is not limited to worship! Rather, it flows over into every human activity: "And whatever you do, whether in word or deed, do it all in the name of the Lord Jesus, giving thanks to God the Father through him" (Col 3:17 NIV).[9] Since *all things* are from the Lord and for the Lord, and since they hold together in him (Rom 11:36; Col 1:15–20), our communal existence as God's house cannot be confined to the church as worshiping community.

All our "secular" activities must be done with a wisdom, righteousness, and love that reflect the Creator's own building of creation. It is here that the people of

God especially need revival; it is here that our *spirituality* is most often lacking. Our God created us "for the praise of his glory" (Eph 1:12), and we are his "workmanship, created in Christ Jesus to do good works" in all areas of life (Eph 2:10). And yet, in the common work of human culture, we Christians have often been like the "foolish man" who heard but did not *do* the words of Jesus, and so "built his house on sand" (Matt 7:26). Foolish houses—unlike those houses built by disciples who hear and do the words of Christ (Matt 7:24)—collapse under trial.

Christians have largely abandoned the shaping of North American culture to persons of passionate intensity who do not know Christ, who do not have the mind of Christ. Because Christians have failed to find unity in our one Lord, we have generally failed to develop a common Christian mind concerning life in the world. Consequently, we find ourselves unable to offer the world a viable agenda or solutions to its problems, as Joseph and Daniel once did, even though they were exiles, in a land not their own. Our public involvement is often restricted to a small number of red-button issues that mark us "godly," yet we are accomplices to many ungodly acts. We seem to applaud the pursuit of the "treasures of darkness" (Isa 45:3), as if Christ had never mentioned "mammon" (Matt 6:24). In our accommodation to the world, the church has come to tolerate the "culture of divorce," as if Jesus had never linked divorce with adultery (Matt 5:31–32). This is not how God in his wisdom made the world "in the beginning" (Matt 19:1–9).

For instance, the basic biblical agenda of righteousness and justice for the poor and needy (Gen 18:19; Ps 72; Isa 5:1–7; Jer 22:13–17; Matt 6:33; 2 Pet 3:13) seems forgotten in many evangelical churches. Like the Pharisees of old, we neglect "the weightier matters of the law—justice, mercy, and faithfulness," while the shape of our bodies suggests that we are "full of greed and self-indulgence" (Matt 23:23, 25). And often the cultural work undertaken by Christians in the realms of the arts, politics, education, and business seem shaped more by the spirit of our age than by the wisdom, word, and spirit of Christ (Rom 12:1–2). We have cause to lament and repent. We need to consider again how we *build* (1 Cor 3:9–15).

God's glory, righteousness, and wisdom are manifest in the cosmos itself (Pss 19; 93–99; 104; 148; Isa 6:3). But they must also be manifest in the activities of ordinary Christians, personally and communally. Secular society denies the objective reality of God in the world, and it tries to restrict "god" to the subjective irrelevance of individual hearts. Since this neopagan society overwhelmingly shapes the media and forms of our communal life, the church's most difficult spiritual battles may not concern what we do in worship or in private. Rather, it is in our public, civic existence that we Christians are prone to sin and fall short of God's glory (Rom 3:23). Like the godly Israelite and Christian inhabitants of the pagan empires of old, we latter-day servants of God must rediscover the more difficult spirituality of wisdom and obedience in the ordinary. We must learn, again, how to build God's house.

Notes

The Scripture quotations in this article are my own translation unless otherwise noted.

[1] George Herbert, "The Holy Scriptures (2)," in *The Complete English Poems* (ed. John Tobin; London: Penguin, 1991), 52.

[2] The word *mĕlāʾḵâ,* translated here as "work," is used both of God's creating and of tabernacle building; cf. Gen 2:2–3.

[3] R. N. Whybray, *The Intellectual Tradition in the Old Testament* (BZAW 135; New York: Walter de Gruyter, 1974).

[4] On the valiant woman and her activities, see Bruce K. Waltke, "The Role of the Valiant Woman in the Marketplace," *Crux* 35, no. 3 (1999): 23–34.

[5] Several translations, including the NIV, translate Heb. *bayiṯ* (house) as "temple" in 1 Kgs 5–8.

[6] Frequently, English translations obscure the verbal parallels that connect two or more biblical passages. In this case, translations obscure the writer's inspired allusion to the creation story. Literally, Gen 2:2 reads, "And God finished—on the seventh day—his work that he did, and rested—on the seventh day—from all his work that he did." Some ancient versions read, "And God finished—on the sixth day. . . ."

[7] Raymond C. Van Leeuwen, "The Book of Proverbs: Introduction, Commentary, and Reflections" (*NIB* 5; Nashville: Abingdon, 1997), 100–102.

[8] Contrary to the NIV, in the Synoptic Gospels, the term *unclean spirits* is not the same as "evil spirits" but is meant to remind us of Leviticus and the requirements for holiness in God's "house"—both in his tabernacle and in our daily life and world.

[9] In this context, the Greek, "giving thanks" *(eucharisteō),* may be a wordplay on the Lord's Supper, or *Eucharist.*

Wisdom of Solomon and Biblical Interpretation in the Second Temple Period

Peter Enns

I am delighted to offer this brief essay in honor of my friend and former teacher, Dr. Bruce Waltke. Bruce's many insights into the nature of wisdom in the OT have been of great benefit to me as I have attempted to follow the path of wisdom.

Over the centuries many people have grappled with the nature of biblical wisdom. The fact that the discussion continues unabated should give pause to any who would attempt to contribute to this ever-widening stream of dialogue. Perhaps, above all, we should be reminded that ferreting out the nature of wisdom is itself a matter that requires wisdom, which, as Proverbs makes clear, and as Bruce is ever fond of repeating, begins with the "fear of the Lord."

I hope with this essay to contribute to this discussion by coming at the question of the nature of biblical wisdom through somewhat of a side door. By looking in some detail at one particular example of Second Temple[1] wisdom, namely the deuterocanonical book called Wisdom of Solomon (more simply known as the Book of Wisdom), we are able to document some important developments in Second Temple wisdom in general.[2] These insights can provide a helpful perspective from which to view the nature of OT wisdom itself.

I. Introduction to Wisdom of Solomon

At the outset, a few background comments are in order. We observe, first, that although the author of Wisdom of Solomon is unknown, he nonetheless seeks to adopt a Solomonic persona (cf. Wis 7:1–14 with 1 Kgs 3:6–9). It is well-known that pseudepigraphic writing is a familiar genre of the ancient world, and Wisdom of Solomon is one celebrated example of this phenomenon. The author of this book, therefore, is conventionally referred to as Pseudo-Solomon (hereafter Ps-Solomon).

The author was likely an Alexandrian Jew who wrote this work in Greek sometime between 100 B.C. and A.D. 50.[3] Although it is difficult to pin down with precision the date of composition, it has been persuasively argued that the reign of Gaius Caligula (A.D. 37–41) serves as a reasonable setting for the composition of this work. In defense of this date, David Winston notes that many of the words Ps-Solomon uses are unattested before the first century A.D. Moreover, the clear undercurrent of persecution in the book (cf. Wis 2:10–3:19) makes good sense if this was written in Caligula's reign. In any event, what is certain is that Wisdom of Solomon is rightly categorized as Second Temple Wisdom literature, both in terms of form and content.

The book itself is nineteen chapters long. Although different outlines have been proposed, for our purposes it seems best to divide the work into two halves, chs. 1–9 and 10–19.[4] The first half has elements that certainly resemble OT Wisdom. For example, it is marked by exhortations to search out and follow wisdom, such as the following:

> Therefore I prayed, and understanding was given me;
> I called on God, and the spirit of wisdom came to me.
> I preferred her to scepters and thrones,
> and I accounted wealth as nothing in comparison with her.
> (7:7–8; cf. Prov 3:13–18)

We also find contrasts between the behavior of the ungodly and that of the righteous—a common theme in OT Wisdom literature.

> For righteousness is immortal.
> But the ungodly by their words and deeds summoned death;
> considering him a friend, they pined away
> and made a covenant with him,
> because they are fit to belong to his company. (1:15–16; cf. Ps 1; Prov 1–9)

II. Wisdom of Solomon and the Afterlife

One difference, however, between Wisdom of Solomon and OT Wisdom literature is the prominence given to the afterlife. In fact, through much of the first six chapters of the book, immortality is portrayed as the final end of all those who follow the path of wisdom.[5] For example, 3:4–8 outlines the otherworldly benefits of the righteous who, though currently undergoing suffering and persecution, will ultimately "receive great good":

For though in the sight of others they were punished,
their hope is full of immortality.
Having been disciplined a little,
they will receive great good,
because God tested them and found them worthy of himself....
In the time of their visitation they will shine forth,
and will run like sparks through the stubble.
They will govern nations and rule over peoples,
and the Lord will reign over them forever.

There is really nothing comparable to this in OT Wisdom literature, where the focus is more on mastery of this life rather than on attainment of the next life. In fact, the canonical book of Ecclesiastes is extremely skeptical about the existence of the afterlife (as can be seen, e.g., in Eccl 3:19–22 and 6:12). By contrast, it may be that Wis 1:16–2:11 was designed, at least in part, to counter such skepticism. For instance, Wis 2:1 appears to echo and critique the negative attitude of Ecclesiastes by saying,

They reasoned unsoundly, saying to themselves,
"Short and sorrowful is our life,
and there is no remedy when a life comes to its end,
and no one knows to return from Hades."

The likely reason that skepticism toward death and the afterlife will not do for Ps-Solomon is that his readers were living in a context of persecution. In short, wisdom for Ps-Solomon is not merely a means to attaining mastery of this life, but the proper means to attaining the life to come. Those who do not share this perspective he calls "ungodly." His words, in effect, are an attempt to apply the wisdom ideal to a situation that the biblical Wisdom tradition either did not address, or, as we see in Ecclesiastes, did not address adequately.

The importance Ps-Solomon places on the afterlife can be seen in yet another way, and this will help us to see more clearly the bold way in which Ps-Solomon represents a tradition that transforms biblical wisdom. He twice refers to death by using the Greek word *exodos,* in 3:2 and 7:6. The "exodus" mentioned in 3:2 refers to the faithful who die at the hands of tormentors. In 7:6, the word is used to describe the death of all people. Although it is generally ill-advised to load too much theological significance in individual words, in this case the description of death as an "exodus" is very striking in view of the Wisdom of Solomon as a whole.

III. Wisdom of Solomon and the Interpretation of Israel's History

In Wis 10–19, Ps-Solomon begins to recount Wisdom's acts of deliverance throughout Israel's history, focusing in particular on Israel's exodus from

Egypt and subsequent wandering in the wilderness. In the light of Ps-Solomon's clear purpose—giving encouragement to a people facing the possibility of death—one begins to see a possible motive behind not only his reference to death as an "exodus" in the opening chapters of the work,[6] but also his choice of Israel's exodus experience as one of the primary themes of chs. 10–19. Israel's exodus, her passage from death to life, as it were, is presented by Ps-Solomon as the prime biblical portrait of what Wisdom is doing *now* in the lives of these persecuted Alexandrian Jews—in their own passage from death to life, their own exodus. To put it another way, Ps-Solomon's treatment of death and the afterlife in the early chapters of the book is a recontextualization of the exodus of the Bible; we see in this Wisdom book an attempt to apply the lessons from Israel's history to the daily trials and struggles of a people who were asking hard questions and looking to God for answers. Whereas the canonical books of the OT often emphasize what God has done in creation (i.e., in the established order of the universe), the author of this post-canonical work seems to be saying that wisdom is to be gained not only from observing creation, so to speak, but now even more from interacting with God's past dealings with Israel. In short, the sage's "job description" now includes the exegesis of Scripture.

Although it is certainly true that in this exegesis of Scripture Ps-Solomon focuses on the complex of events surrounding the exodus, it must be admitted that the biblical material from which he draws his lessons is much broader. His application of Israel's history actually begins in Wis 10:1–14, where he relates the well-known stories of Adam, Cain, Noah, Abraham, Lot, Jacob, and Joseph. He then writes about the exodus itself (10:15–21) and the wilderness period (11:1–4). The remainder of the book moves back and forth between a number of issues centering around the exodus and around God's treatment of the Israelites in contrast to his treatment of the Egyptians.

IV. Wisdom of Solomon and Biblical Interpretation in the Second Temple Period

A. General Principles of Exposition

Before looking at some specific examples of how Ps-Solomon handles Scripture, it will be useful to identify three general principles of interpretation that he normally follows:

Firstly, *Ps-Solomon appeals to Israel's history to show the workings of divine justice.* Despite the present appearance of things—which includes the unjust suffering and death of people well before their time—Ps-Solomon is absolutely convinced about the existence of an underlying plan of God that will right all wrongs. This conviction is clearly communicated in the closing verses of each of the book's two halves:

> Who has learned your counsel,
> unless you have given wisdom
> and sent your holy spirit from on high?
> And thus the paths of those on earth were set right,
> and people were taught what pleases you,
> and were saved by wisdom. (9:17–18)
>
> For in everything *[kata panta]*, O Lord,
> you have exalted and glorified your people,
> and you have not neglected to help them at all times and in all places
> *[en panti kairō kai topō]*. (19:22)

These verses remind the faithful that God never neglects his people. It matters little what the circumstances are; he is with them *kata panta*. Nor is God's saving power relegated to a bygone era; he is with his people *en panti kairō*. And God's saving power knows no boundary; he is with his people *en panti topō*—even in death.

Secondly, *biblical characters are presented as models of virtue*. The heroic persons of the Bible are viewed by Ps-Solomon as examples for the faithful of his own day; as such, it will not do to present these figures from the past in any way other than the ideal. This is clearly seen in the historical review of Wis 10. For example, Ps-Solomon hardly mentions the fall when he speaks of Adam (Wis 10:1–2). Instead, Adam is simply described as the "first-formed father of the world" who was "delivered . . . from his transgression" and given "strength to rule all things." Likewise, in Wis 10:5 Abraham is simply a "righteous man." In the incident of the binding of Isaac, the author conveniently neglects to mention Abraham's earlier doubts about Yahweh's commitment to give him and Sarah a son in their old age (Gen 17:17–18).

The same holds true for Ps-Solomon's presentation of Lot and Jacob: in Wisdom of Solomon they are models of absolute virtue, whereas the biblical narratives paint a more nuanced portrait of them. For instance, although Lot's "righteousness" (Wis 10:6) has a clear biblical warrant in light of Abraham's persistence in pleading with the angels (Gen 18:16–33), this remains a very selective reading of the story of Genesis as a whole given Lot's own choice to settle in the disreputable "cities of the plain." Likewise, Rebekah and Jacob's deceit of Isaac (Gen 27) ought to have raised an eyebrow. But again, Ps-Solomon's Jacob is not guilty of any wrongdoing. He is, as are the others, simply "righteous" (Wis 10:10).

It is no surprise, therefore, that Ps-Solomon does not mention Moses' near fatal slip-up on the way from Midian (Exod 4:18–26) or his disobedience at

Meribah (Num 20:7–12) and his subsequent exclusion from Canaan. For Ps-Solomon, Moses is simply a "servant of the Lord" (Wis 10:16). Moreover, the people he brings out of Egypt are no longer a people prone to doubt and rebellion but "a holy people and blameless race" (10:15). In all of this, Ps-Solomon's hortatory purpose is clear: he seeks to find in these figures a biblical answer to the circumstances he is addressing.

Thirdly, *the biblical characters in Wisdom of Solomon are anonymous.* A glance at Wis 10:1–21, for example, will show that these figures are described by means of episodes in their biblical stories rather than by their names. Their names are avoided because *who they were in the past* is of little importance; what matters is *what they represent now* as models of wise conduct. To put it another way, these biblical figures have become democratized: they represent models of conduct for times, places, and people beyond the confines of the original events. For Ps-Solomon, the word of God must speak clearly to the present, stressful situation. As James Kugel puts it (commenting on a similar "catalog of heroes" in Sir 44–50), "These once-real people have become, essentially, *lessons,* whose importance can be captured in a line or two."[7]

B. Specific Examples of Second Temple Exegetical Traditions

Another important dimension of Ps-Solomon's exposition of Israel's history is the actual content of what he says. It is one thing to note his motives for adducing Israel's story (to inspire his fellow Israelites to persevere amid persecution), but it is another thing to explore what he actually says. Even a quick reading of Wis 10:1–21 will show that Ps-Solomon does not relate the content of the biblical narratives in a straightforward manner. Rather, he regularly includes elements that are not actually found anywhere in Scripture but that reflect Second Temple interpretive traditions and exegetical techniques. The following are five examples of this phenomenon:

1. Abraham as a contemporary of the Tower of Babel episode

Ps-Solomon juxtaposes the story of Abraham the patriarch and the account of the Tower of Babel in Wis 10:5:

> Wisdom also, when the nations in wicked agreement
> had been put to confusion,
> recognized the righteous man [Abraham]
> and preserved him blameless before God.[8]

That Ps-Solomon would thus connect Abraham and the Tower of Babel seems curious in that Abraham is not mentioned at all in the tower narrative, nor does his name appear in the OT until Gen 11:26, purportedly several hundred years after the Babel incident. This displacement of Abraham is not unique to

Ps-Solomon, however, but it follows an exegetical tradition seen most prominently perhaps in Josephus' *Jewish Antiquities*, where the author expounds at length on Abraham's resistance to the tower building project.[9]

How such a tradition arose is unclear. It may be that the connection between Abraham and the tower narrative served to explain other narrative gaps. In Josh 24:2, for example, it is stated that Abraham and his ancestors worshiped other gods before they left for Haran, and yet such an idea is nowhere indicated in Genesis. Early interpreters, in their attempt to construct a story to explain this inconsistency, may have created this interpretation, making Abraham not merely a resident among idolatrous people but, more specifically, an actual contemporary of the Tower of Babel episode.

Two passages in Genesis, working in tandem, may have justified such an interpretation. First, in Gen 15:7 God tells Abraham that he has taken him out of "Ur of the Chaldeans." Given that the name *Ur* is a homonym for one of the Hebrew words for fire (*ʾûr;* see Isa 31:9; 50:11), this verse can be read as a cryptic reference to Abraham's having been delivered from some Chaldean conflagration. Second, ancient interpreters linked this fire of the Chaldeans to the very fire used to burn the bricks for the Tower of Babel in Gen 11:3, a connection made even more explicit in Josephus' *Jewish Antiquities* 6.16–17.

While such exegetical maneuvering may seem far-fetched to the contemporary scholar, it is worth remembering that Ps-Solomon is not the only one to make Abraham a contemporary of the tower story. In fact, Wisdom of Solomon's brief allusion to the Abraham-Babel connection (when compared to the more detailed explanation in *Jewish Antiquities*) may suggest that the tradition needed no special introduction, reminder, or defense.

2. The Sodomites guilty of inhospitality

In Wis 19:13–17, Ps-Solomon describes the Egyptians as particularly inhospitable, ungrateful hosts to the Israelites: they received the Israelites only to turn right around and enslave them. He then adds a curious statement in v. 14: "Others had refused to receive strangers when they came to them." Who were these "others"? We find out in v. 17, where we read that the Egyptians were punished for their treatment of the Israelites by "loss of sight—just as were those at the door of the righteous man." In this passage, we see another example of Ps-Solomon's linking two seemingly unconnected events: this "loss of sight" is an allusion to the ninth plague (Exod 10:22–23); and "those at the door of the righteous man" are those who came to the house of Lot (the "righteous") demanding he hand his guests over to them and whom the angels struck blind (Gen 19:11). It is worth noting that Ps-Solomon adduces the story of Sodom's destruction to buttress his condemnation of Egypt's inhospitality. He is free to do so because, at least on one level, he understands the sin of Sodom as not specifically sexual misconduct, but rather as the Sodomites' refusal "to receive strangers"—that is, their inhospitality.

Ps-Solomon is not alone in this view, and there may even be some scriptural support for such a notion. Ezekiel 16:49–50 condemns the inhabitants of Sodom, saying Sodom "had pride, excess of food, and prosperous ease, but did not aid the poor and needy." What seems to be in view here is the Sodomites' mistreatment of other people rather than their sexual misconduct (although the latter is certainly not excluded). Moreover, Josephus' *Jewish Antiquities* 1.194 also regards the sin of the Sodomites as inhospitality, dislike of foreigners, and arrogance.

3. Giants or Cain responsible for the flood?

In Wis 14:6, Ps-Solomon seems to place the blame for the flood on "arrogant giants," no doubt alluding to the very difficult reference in Gen 6:1–4 to the "sons of God" who consorted with the "daughters of humans." The same or similar sentiment is found in 3 Macc 2:4; Sir 16:7; Bar 3:26–28; *1 En.* 6:2; and *Jub.* 5:1–11. What is particularly interesting is that Ps-Solomon seems to offer an alternate interpretation in Wis 10:4, where the blame for the flood is placed on Cain.

Why does Ps-Solomon offer two different interpretations for the same event? The answer, I would suggest here, is not that Ps-Solomon, unsure of which explanation to adopt, offered both options. Rather, it is a characteristic of ancient retellings of Scripture that the exegetical traditions incorporated in this way are not clearly (if at all) marked off from the biblical texts. The line between text and comment was often blurred. This is what we often find in Second Temple midrashic texts, when biblical events are retold again and again by different authors with some of the same interpretive embellishments. It is an example of what Kugel calls the "legendizing" of midrash.[10]

In this sense, many of Ps-Solomon's statements about the Bible are valuable witnesses not so much to how he himself "handled" Scripture (i.e., his own exegetical method) but to exegetical traditions that must have been current in his day and that influenced his understanding of Scripture.

4. The Israelites "paid" for leaving Egypt

Turning briefly to the exodus story, in Wis 10:17 Ps-Solomon describes Israel leaving Egypt with "the reward of their labors." This phrase represents a slightly different interpretation of events from that given in the Exodus account, where the Israelites are said to "plunder" (MT *nṣl;* LXX *skyleuō*) the Egyptians (Exod 12:36; cf. 3:21–22; 11:2). This shift is probably a response to polemical Greco-Roman literature that chided the Israelites for behaving in a less than "holy" fashion.[11] After all, only thieves "plunder." Ps-Solomon, standing in a well-documented tradition,[12] intends to say that the plundering was quite justified: it is a payment for years of slavery to the Egyptians. In other words, the motive that gave rise to this tradition is apologetic. However, it is not necessary to say that either Ps-Solomon or his readers had this particular apologetic motive in the forefront of their minds. Rather, it appears that this interpretation had become "attached" to the biblical account. It represented a proper, commonly accepted understanding of what the Bible says.

5. The Egyptians cast onto the shore of the Red Sea
In Wis 10:19–20, Ps-Solomon's comment on the Egyptians' death at the Red Sea is an unmistakable witness to a popular exegetical tradition.[13] He says that Wisdom "cast them [the Egyptians] up from the depth of the sea. Therefore the righteous plundered the ungodly." To say that the Egyptians were "cast up" from the sea is a clever solution to a problem posed by the biblical account. How is it that the dead Egyptians on the shore could be plainly seen by the Israelites (Exod 14:30) while elsewhere they are said have sunk "like a stone" (Exod 15:5) or "like lead" (Exod 15:10) and then been "swallowed" by the earth (Exod 15:12)? Of course, one could easily envision that first the Egyptians drowned (sunk like stone or lead) and then later their lifeless bodies washed up on shore. But early interpreters reasoned differently. For the Egyptians to be seen on the shore in Exod 14:30, they must have been cast up again after they had drowned.

Some commentators compare Ps-Solomon's handling of the above episode in Wisdom of Solomon with the Targum of Pseudo-Jonathan to Exod 15:12, which tells of a protracted debate between the sea and the land in which each refuses to accept the Egyptian dead, lest God's wrath be upon it. Only after God swears to the land that there will be no repercussions does the land swallow the dead. This interpretation is meant to reconcile Exod 15:12, which states that the earth swallowed them up, and Exod 14:28; 15:1, 4–5, and 10, in which the Egyptians are consigned to a watery grave. Whether Ps-Solomon's has in mind this tradition is impossible to tell. Nevertheless, we see again that his own apparently unique interpretation of what the Bible says must be viewed in the broader context of how other exegetes—both contemporaries and precursors—were handling Scripture.

V. Wisdom of Solomon as Second Temple Wisdom

The above examples help to illustrate the increasing importance of biblical interpretation during the Second Temple period and to sketch the broader context within which to view the interpretive activity seen in Wisdom of Solomon. It appears that Ps-Solomon's strategy was to present the biblical data in such a way as to make all Scripture speak more clearly to the ever-changing situations of the readers. This is why he portrays the heroes of Israel's past in black-and-white categories: they have become models of virtue. This is also why these heroes have become nameless figures: the past is dehistoricized in an effort to bring it more forcefully into the present. This is not to say that Ps-Solomon treats the historical events themselves lightly. In calling upon this "dehistoricized" past—one that does not emphasize the particulars of the events—Ps-Solomon is simply telling his readers that the God of Israel is still with them, that who they are now amid the changing fortunes of history must be seen in light of the never-changing God who has never failed to deliver the faithful who have gone before. Idealizing the past does not obliterate history but makes it transportable. For Ps-Solomon, therefore, the idealized past is the only proper backdrop for viewing one's present, historical situation. It is the solid rock that stands high above the ebb and flow of history. And, according to our author, it is Wisdom herself who has been God's active agent throughout Israel's history, bringing the godly through trying times. His readers, therefore, are exhorted to seek (Wis 6:12–16), honor (6:21), pray for (7:7), love (8:2), and befriend (8:18) her. Acquiring wisdom now is the key to the present, for it is Wisdom who has been active throughout Israel's past.

Ps-Solomon's portrayal of Wisdom as the primary player in Israel's history naturally leads to placing such an understanding of wisdom in the general context of the Second Temple period. We see already in Prov 8 the personification of Wisdom, who has some special status in creation either as the first of God's creations (Prov 8:22)[14] or at least as being present at creation (Prov 8:30; cf. 3:19). Proverbs 8 is one of the few expressions (and certainly the clearest) of the personification of Wisdom in the OT (see also Job 28; Prov 1, 9).

The reticence with which the OT speaks of personified Wisdom may be what motivated early interpreters to find out more about her. Hence, the nature of personified Wisdom takes on added importance in postbiblical times. Specifically, there is a well-documented postbiblical tendency to equate Wisdom with Torah. The most explicit (and probably among the earliest) text in drawing this connection between Torah and Wisdom is Sir 24:1–29.[15]

For Ben Sira, Torah is the source of wisdom, a point he makes unequivocally clear in Sir 24:23–29. First, Ben Sira places Wisdom at creation: she is the first of God's creations existing from eternity to eternity (24:9; see also 1:4, 9).[16] She then is said to make her dwelling in Israel (24:8–11). Finally, she "takes root" among God's people and grows tall and flourishes (24:12–17).

What distinguishes Sir 24:1–29 from Wis 10:1–21 is that Ps-Solomon deals with specific instances of Wisdom's participation in Israel's history, whereas Ben Sira mentions only her presence at creation and gives a vague notion of her presence in Israel. But this distinction only pertains to Sir 24:1–2, for Ben Sira turns to the topic of Wisdom's participation in Israel's history in great detail in Sir 44–50 (which is very similar to Wis 10:1–21), where the author recounts the deeds of "famous men" (44:1) whose lives stand as permanent examples of righteous lives, righteous because they exemplify the wisdom ideal (see 44:2–6).[17]

Scripture, specifically Torah, has become the depository of wisdom. The role of wisdom, as G. T. Sheppard puts it, has moved from "mundane advice to Wisdom's recital of her participation in Israel's traditions."[18] In Wisdom books like Proverbs, Job, and Ecclesiastes, we find scarcely a single, clear scriptural allusion. Starting with Ben Sira and Wisdom of Solomon, however, we see books of Wisdom that are steeped through and through with references to biblical figures and events.

This fact does not make these two books any less a part of the Wisdom genre. Rather, it is the nature of wisdom itself that has shifted. Whereas the sages of the Hebrew Bible were concerned with observing patterns in the created order as the basis for godly conduct—"exegeting the world" so to speak—Ben Sira and Ps-Solomon were concerned with observing the nature of God's activity by exegeting the Book: the sage's repertory of knowledge now includes Scripture. Wisdom of Solomon, therefore, is not simply a commentary on Scripture but a search for wisdom, a search for God's overarching, eternal plan, on the basis of Scripture. God's eternal wisdom is to be learned from the Bible, for it is Scripture that is the depository of wisdom.

VI. Conclusion

In the light of the above, we can see why biblical interpretation gained such importance in the Second Temple period. Simply stated, Scripture is God's wisdom. It is rich in meaning and invites—even demands—that one search for that meaning. It is little wonder, then, that the exegetical traditions witnessed to in Wisdom of Solomon came to be so closely associated with the biblical text. Scripture must be properly interpreted in order for it to serve as a guide for living. A biblical passage is of little use if its meaning is unclear. But when it is "interpreted," its meaning becomes clear. The presence of these exegetical traditions in Wisdom of Solomon are not mere legends or artistic embellishments. They are, rather, the fruit of sagely activity that treated the Bible as a gift from God for a standard of faith and conduct with, at least for Ps-Solomon, eternal consequences. It is wisdom that is contained, yet hidden, in the text. It is to meet the challenge of bringing God's wisdom to God's people that biblical interpretation became a wisdom activity in the Second Temple period.

Notes

All Scripture quotations are taken from the NRSV unless otherwise noted.

[1] The phrase *Second Temple period* is preferred to the phrase *intertestamental period* because it covers a broader time period than that implied by *intertestamental.* At least one example of "intertestamental" Wisdom literature, Wisdom of Solomon (the topic of this essay), may well have been written around the time of Christ.

[2] There are a number of other examples of Wisdom literature from this period, most notably Ecclesiasticus (also known as Sirach). This well-known deuterocanonical book shows many of the same tendencies as Wisdom of Solomon does, and so it will come into our discussion at certain points. Still, our focus will be on Wisdom of Solomon.

[3] With a few exceptions, it is nearly universally accepted that Wisdom of Solomon was written originally in Greek and is not a translation. A succinct summary of the various positions may be found in David Winston, *The Wisdom of Solomon* (AB 43; Garden City, N.Y.: Doubleday, 1979), 17 n. 16, with more detailed treatments in B. J. Lillie, "A History of the Scholarship on the Wisdom of Solomon from the Nineteenth Century to Our Time" (Ph.D. diss., Hebrew Union College, 1982), 108–48; and W. P. Berwick, "The Way of Salvation in the Book of Wisdom" (Ph.D. diss., Boston University, 1957), 36–41. For discussions on the language and style of Wisdom of Solomon and its affinities with Greek literature, see Winston, *Wisdom of Solomon,* 15–16 nn. 4–14; and J. M. Reese, *Hellenistic Influence of the Book of Wisdom and Its Consequences* (AnBib 41; Rome: Pontifical Biblical Institute, 1970), 1–31.

[4] The discussion concerning the structure of the book essentially centers around the question of whether it should be considered a two- or three-part work. Bruce M. Metzger is one of many who has argued for a two-part division, 1:1–9:18 and 10:1–19:22 (*An Introduction to the Apocrypha* [New York: Oxford University Press, 1957], 68–73). A. G. Wright likewise has a two-part division but makes the division at 11:2 rather than at 10:1 ("The Structure of the Book of Wisdom," *Bib* 48 [1967]: 165–84). Three-part divisions have been proposed by P. Heinisch in *Das Buch der Weisheit* (EHAT 24; Münster: Aschendorffsche Verlagsbuchhandlung, 1912), xiv, and by Winston in *Wisdom of Solomon,* 9–12.

[5] An excellent study on death and immortality in Wisdom of Solomon is M. Kolarcik, *The Ambiguity of Death in the Book of Wisdom 1–6: A Study of Literary Structure and Interpretation* (AnBib 127; Rome: Pontifical Biblical Institute, 1991).

[6] It is interesting to observe that Jesus' death is referred to as a "departure" *(exodos)* in Luke 9:31.

[7] James A. Kugel and Rowan A. Greer, *Early Biblical Interpretation* (Philadelphia: Westminster, 1986), 49.

[8] "Confusion" *(synchythentōn)* is a clear reference to the Tower of Babel story, where God is said to confuse the language of the people and then scatter them over the face of the earth. (See LXX of Gen 11:7, 9, where the same Greek root is used.) Wisdom of Solomon 10:5b would thus suggest that Abraham's resistance to the building effort, as he was guided by Wisdom, is what "preserved him blameless before God."

[9] In addition to Josephus, *Jewish Antiquities* 6–7, this popular tradition is also found in *Gen. Rab.* 38.13; 44.13; *b. Pesaḥ.* 118a; *Deut. Rab.* 2.29; *Cant. Rab.* 1.55; 8.9; *Midr. Teh.* 118.36–38. Winston mentions *Gen. Rab.* 38.6 and *S. ʿOlam Rab.* 1, both of which make Abraham a contemporary of the tower episode but do not mention the fire (*Wisdom of Solomon*, 214). Géza Vermès discusses the tradition in some length in *Scripture and Tradition in Judaism* (StPB 4; 2d ed.; Leiden: E. J. Brill, 1973), 85–90. See also G. W. E. Nickelsburg, "Good and Bad Leaders in Pseudo-Philo's *Liber Antiquitatum Biblicarum*," in *Ideal Figures in Ancient Israel* (ed. J. J. Collins and G. W. E. Nickelsburg; SBLSCS 12; Chico, Calif.: Scholars Press, 1980), 51–52.

[10] See J. Kugel, "Two Introductions to Midrash," *Proof* 3 (1983): 131–55, esp. 151; repr. in *Midrash and Literature* (ed. G. H. Hartman and S. Budick; New Haven: Yale University Press, 1986), 77–103.

[11] Winston, *Wisdom of Solomon*, 220.

[12] This interpretive tradition is quite early, appearing in *Jub.* 48:18, Philo's *De vita Mosis* 1.141, and Ezekiel the Tragedian's *Exagoge* 162–66. *Jubilees* was written in the first half of the second century B.C., Philo lived from 30 B.C. to A.D. 45, and the *Exagoge* is likely a late second-century B.C. document.

[13] The Egyptians' death at the Red Sea is also referred to in a number of rabbinic texts as well as in Philo's *De vita Mosis* 2.225.

[14] The Hebrew root *qwn* in Prov 8:22 is open to several meanings in addition to "create," including "beget" and "acquire."

[15] For a study of wisdom and law in Sirach, intertestamental literature, the Dead Sea Scrolls, and the Apostle Paul, see E. J. Schnabel, *Law and Wisdom from Ben Sira to Paul: A Tradition History Enquiry into the Relation of Law, Wisdom, and Ethics* (WUNT 2/16; Tübingen: J. C. B. Mohr [Siebeck], 1985). See also R. Wilken, ed., *Aspects of Wisdom in Judaism and Early Christianity* (Notre Dame: University

of Notre Dame Press, 1975); J. Blenkinsopp, *Wisdom and Law in the Old Testament: The Ordering of Life in Israel and Early Judaism* (Oxford: Oxford University Press, 1983); G. Boccaccini, *Middle Judaism: Jewish Thought 300 B.C.E. to 200 C.E.* (Minneapolis: Fortress, 1991), 81–99; and Winston, *Wisdom of Solomon,* 33–38. Many rabbinic passages assume the equation of Torah and Wisdom while referring specifically to Prov 8:22: e.g., *Mek. Shir.* 9:123, which cites Prov 8:22 as a proof text that Torah is a possession of God. See also *Gen. Rab.* 1:4; *Lev. Rab.* 11:3; 19:1; *Cant. Rab.* 5:11.

[16] Ben Sira certainly models his discussion of wisdom after Proverbs 8 (P. W. Skehan, "Structures in Poems in Wisdom: Proverbs 8 and Sirach 24," *CBQ* 41 [1979] 365–79). In contrast to Ben Sira, however, Ps-Solomon presents wisdom as having a role in the act of creation itself (Wis 7:22; 8:4, 6).

[17] In this context, one thinks, too, of the catalog of heroes in Hebrews 11. A. Schmitt cites a number of examples of *historische Beispielreihe* in antiquity, including biblical, apocryphal, pseudepigraphal, Hellenistic and classical Greek literature ("Struktur, Herkunft und Bedeutung der Beispielreihe in Weish 10," *BZ* 21 [1977] 1–22).

[18] G. T. Sheppard, *Wisdom as a Hermeneutical Construct: A Study in the Sapientializing of the Old Testament* (BZAW 151; Berlin/New York: de Gruyter, 1980), 6.

Sophia Christology: The Way of Wisdom?

Karen H. Jobes

In an age when medical technology is making it possible for people to choose the gender of their baby at conception, it may seem reasonable to some that people should also be entitled to choose the gender of their god. Within the last few decades some Christians, who have the intention of presenting the gospel as relevant to the social issues of our times, have rediscovered the ancient conceptualization of Jesus as the incarnation of God's wisdom, appealing to, among other things, Paul's references to Christ as "the power of God and the wisdom of God" (1 Cor 1:24). Because the Greek word for *wisdom* is the feminine noun *sophia*, and because wisdom was personified as a woman in the OT book of Proverbs, the identification of Jesus as the incarnation of the female, preexistent Wisdom-Sophia has provided feminist theologians with an effective means of "re-gendering" the gospel of Jesus Christ for modern society. As Roman Catholic theologian Elizabeth A. Johnson expresses it,

> The combination Jesus Christ/Sophia leads to a healthy blend of female and male imagery that empowers everyone, and works beautifully to symbolize the one God who is neither male nor female, but creator of both, delighter in both, savior of both, and imaged by both.[1]

Although some feminist theologians have renounced the Christian faith as hopelessly androcentric,[2] others wish to uphold the historic Trinitarian confession of Christianity and to reclaim within it neglected elements that validate the co-equal status of women and men in Christ's redemptive work.[3] Sophia Christology claims to have rediscovered in the NT itself an early understanding of Jesus as the incarnate Wisdom-Sophia of God that was presented to show the feminine principle of God as an acceptable complement to the masculine metaphors of son and king.[4] This earliest understanding of the identity of Jesus in feminine terms—so it is claimed—was later suppressed and eventually supplanted by the masculine language for Christ that has dominated Christianity for two thousand years.

The apologetic and evangelistic concerns of this agenda are expressed, for instance, by James M. Robinson when he writes,

> Perhaps such a Wisdom Christology, precisely because of the non-exclusivity of its beginnings, would be useful in our society today, when to leave a male deity at the top of our value structuring seems often more like the deification of the omnipotent despot of the ancient Near East than an honoring of God, more a perpetuation of patriarchalism than a liberation of women and men. If we, like Jesus, can be inspired by the feminine aspect of God, we may be able to bring good news to our still all too patriarchal society.[5]

The re-gendering of Christ as Sophia has found appeal not only among theologians with feminist concerns, but also among the laity of the church, as evidenced by the Re-imagining Conference held in November 1993 in Minneapolis.[6] This conference, which was later denounced by several participating denominations, was billed as an opportunity to re-imagine Christianity in terms that are more suitable to the spiritual needs of women. For example, the traditional Christian sacrament of the bread and wine of Holy Communion was replaced by a ritual that substituted milk and honey with a prayer offered to "Our maker Sophia."[7]

Johnson observes that Jesus' historical maleness has been used in ways hurtful to women to "reinforce an exclusively male image of God," an image that has been further used to "legitimize men's superiority over women in the belief that a particular honor, dignity, and normativity accrues to the male sex because it was chosen by the Son of God 'himself' in the incarnation."[8] Moreover, she argues that if traditional Christology were correct in its conceptualization of the necessary maleness of the Savior, the possibility that women can be saved would be jeopardized:

> If maleness is essential for the christic role, then women are cut out of the loop of salvation, for female sexuality is not taken on by the Word made flesh. If maleness is constitutive for the incarnation and redemption, female humanity is not assumed and therefore not saved.[9]

Since the NT gospels clearly do not exclude women from the redemption Christ achieved on the basis of their gender, Johnson sought a theological basis for woman's redemption by finding a female aspect in Christ's incarnation. For her and others, this theological basis is found in Sophia as God's wisdom incarnate in Jesus.

The evangelical church must address both the soteriological and social concerns raised by feminist theology if it hopes to effectively engage the intellectual claims of our times with the gospel of Jesus Christ. Sophia Christology is offered as a rediscovery of a very early apostolic understanding of Jesus reflected in the NT and rooted in the Wisdom traditions of Judaism. But does it indeed provide a biblical basis for a feminine aspect to the incarnation? Does Wisdom-Sophia in the Jewish tradition provide the basis from which an identification of Jesus and Sophia could later be developed? And is a female aspect to the incarnation necessary as a theological basis for the redemption of women? These are some of the concerns that this article seeks to answer.

I. The Hellenistic Background of Sophia Christology

The revival of interest in Sophia in the present day as a means of relating Christian faith to the values of our society parallels the apologetic use of Sophia by the Jews during the Hellenistic age (ca. 300 B.C.–A.D. 200), although the Jews of that day were not concerned with issues of gender. When God's covenant people found themselves in exile scattered among the pagan nations, they faced a problem not unlike that faced by the global Christian church today: how to relate their faith to the surrounding pagan culture—a culture that was largely apathetic at best, or hostile at worst, to their basic convictions—and how to do so in a way that would give them sufficient intellectual and social standing to make their faith viable and attractive in the marketplace of ideas.

Wisdom-Sophia provided a point of contact for their apologetic purposes. Greek philosophers generally understood wisdom as knowledge needed for living toward life's highest good. But the Jewish people themselves held claim to the reputedly wisest man who ever lived, King Solomon (1 Kgs 3:12),[10] whose writings were preserved in the books of Proverbs, Song of Songs, and Ecclesiastes. Employing these writings, Jewish apologists elaborated on the teachings of Solomon to urge that true wisdom was to be found in the knowledge of Yahweh, the One, True, Living God who had created all.

Drawing from the resulting body of Wisdom literature, proponents of Sophia Christology have identified various texts as representing a development of the Jewish Wisdom tradition inherited by NT writers, who used it to describe the preexistence of Jesus Christ. This trajectory of thought begins in the OT with Proverbs, is developed in the deuterocanonical books of Sirach and Wisdom of Solomon, reappears among early Christians in the reconstructed Q document, and culminates in the NT with the identification of Jesus as God's Wisdom-Sophia incarnate in the writings of Matthew, Paul, and John.

A. The Hebrew Proverbs

One of the claims of Sophia Christology is that the Jewish Wisdom tradition provides a more inclusive point of contact between Christianity and other religions because the book of Proverbs itself inscripturated universal principles of wisdom that were not unique to ancient Israel.[11] It is true, of course, that the book of Proverbs does lack explicit concern with Israel's covenant relationship to Yahweh, including the Torah as Yahweh's law revealed at Sinai and Israel's election; nevertheless, it is also clear that the book presumes that particular socioreligious background by presenting its teachings as those of Yahweh's theocratic king, Solomon. Bruce Waltke, whom we are honoring with this work, defines *wisdom* in Proverbs as designating "a fixed, eternal, religio-social order, an order that God created, established and upheld. Its synonyms are 'law,' 'commandment,' 'fear of God.'"[12] Even if Proverbs shares the social function, genre, literary conventions, language, and even some precepts with ancient Near Eastern Wisdom literature more broadly, its teaching nevertheless presumes the covenant relationship with Yahweh, the only source of genuine wisdom.

Wisdom-Sophia first appears as a female personification in Prov 1:20–33 in the instructions a father is giving to his son. The father exhorts his son to turn from the deceptive Strange Woman, or harlot, whose way leads to death, and to instead embrace Wisdom-Sophia, whose way leads to life. Lady Wisdom is introduced as a mediatrix of Yahweh's revelation with the highest authority.[13] Throughout Proverbs, the literary device of female personification vividly represents the two ways set before Israel: to embrace Wisdom is to enter into and abide in an exclusive covenant relationship with Yahweh; to pursue the harlot is to turn away to others gods and forfeit righteousness and life (cf. Deut 30:19).

But why does Proverbs present Wisdom as a woman and not as a man? As Waltke points out, the answer lies in linguistics, not in the history of religions.[14] The feminine grammatical gender of the Hebrew noun for *wisdom—ḥoḵmâ* (occasionally *ḥoḵmōṯ*)—facilitated the female gender of the literary personification, but grammatical gender must never be used to implicate sexual gender.[15] However, female personification provided a vehicle for a subsequent understanding of Wisdom-Sophia as a female consort of Yahweh. For polytheistic groups wanting to embrace Israel's religion, this presented an opportunity for identifying Wisdom-Sophia as a goddess, but for monotheistic Judaism it presented an apologetic problem.

Proverbs 8:22–36 presents an exegetical crux for Sophia Christology, which takes the personified Wisdom-Sophia to be an active agent of creation who can later be identified as the preincarnate *Logos* of John 1:1:

The LORD brought me forth as the first of his works,
before his deeds of old;
I was appointed from eternity,
from the beginning, before the world began....
[B]efore the mountains were settled in place,
before the hills, I was given birth....
Then I was the craftsman at his side.
I was filled with delight day after day,
rejoicing always in his presence,
rejoicing in his whole world
and delighting in mankind....
For whoever finds me finds life
and receives favor from the LORD.
But whoever fails to find me harms himself;
all who hate me love death. (Prov 8:22–23, 25, 30–31, 35–36 NIV)

The primary support for the active role of Wisdom-Sophia in creation is taken from the phrase, "I was the craftsman at his side." The Hebrew word translated in the NIV as "craftsman" occurs only twice in the OT, and it can be pointed to read either "craftsman" (taking it as the noun *ʾāmōn*) or "favored child" (taking it as the Qal passive participle, *ʾāmûn*).[16]

Although most English translators today support the translation "craftsman," those who produced the ancient Greek translation (the Septuagint, or LXX) during the Hellenistic era adopted neither pointing but instead seem to interpret rather than translate the Hebrew. They used a Greek participle *harmozousa,* which means "to be in harmony with," "to fit together with," possibly introducing Stoic influence.[17] Exactly what the translators intended by this rendering is a matter of considerable debate. However, three other Jewish translators of antiquity—Aquila, Symmachus, and Theodotion—each took the Hebrew word to mean that Wisdom was God's child *(tithenoumenē)* who frolicked beside him as he created the universe.[18] So understood, the now-grown woman (Wisdom-Sophia personified elsewhere in Proverbs) is not a craftsman in the act of creating but a witness to the moment of creation and to all of history since. In such an understanding, the teachings of Yahweh's Wisdom-Sophia are to be accepted by all people, both Jew and Greek, as trustworthy and true because of "her" longevity and cosmic vantage point, not because she was an agent of creation.

B. The Greek Translation of Proverbs

The Septuagint text of Proverbs was probably translated early in the Hellenistic period and contributes to our understanding of how Wisdom-Sophia was understood by the Jews of the Greek-speaking Diaspora. Moreover, it is this Greek translation of Proverbs that provides the specific lexical basis from which Sophia

Christology has taken its name, for the translators of Proverbs rendered the feminine Hebrew noun *ḥoḵmâ* most often, though not always, with the Greek word *sophia* (wisdom), which in Greek also happens to be a grammatically feminine noun. The common gender of the Hebrew and Greek nouns facilitates carrying the female personification of Wisdom into the Greek translation.

When the various Greek translations of the Hebrew Scriptures were produced, significant changes were sometimes introduced to prevent a misunderstanding of Israel's theology when their Scriptures were read in the new polytheistic context of Hellenism. Feminist theologians who refer to Proverbs seldom recognize the differences between the Hebrew version and its Greek translation, which must be considered an important step in any development of the Jewish Wisdom tradition in the Hellenistic period. A given expression might be completely unambiguous in the monotheistic context in which the original text was produced, but in translation that same expression might possibly be misconstrued by a culture that did not share Israel's religious assumptions. Thus a comparison of the Hebrew Proverbs with its Greek translation yields insight into how the Jewish translator of the Hellenistic period understood the role of Wisdom.

In a recent study of the Greek translation of Proverbs, Johann Cook finds that one of the translator's primary interests was to warn the reader of the inherent dangers of foreign wisdom, such "wisdom" that would have tempted the Jews under the increasing pressure of Hellenization.[19] While comfortably using Greek style and rhetoric, the translator nevertheless does not accommodate the message of Proverbs to Greek ideas about wisdom; on the contrary, the translator amplifies the warnings implicit in the Hebrew text against compromise and apostasy.

Because the Greek word for *wisdom* is feminine, as is the Hebrew, the Greek translation is able to preserve the literary personification of Wisdom as a woman. However, in the creation poem of Prov 8:22–36 Cook finds the most conspicuous difference between the Hebrew text and its Greek translation to be that the Greek makes God the explicit subject of creation and makes no reference at all to Wisdom-Sophia in this regard.[20] In four verses (Prov 8:23–25, 31) the Greek translator has intentionally changed the verb to eliminate any possible ambiguity that would suggest Wisdom-Sophia as a hypostasis responsible for creation. Moreover, in 8:25 the Hebrew reads, "Before the mountains had been shaped, before the hills, I [Wisdom-Sophia] was brought forth," whereas the Greek explicitly changes the verb to the third person and active voice with God as the subject: "Before the mountains were settled, before the hills he begets me." Any ambiguity about Wisdom-Sophia's activity in creation is resolved by showing her as a passive witness, possibly to avoid reading the literary personification as a reference to the Greek hypostasis of Wisdom.

On the other hand, the Greek translation of v. 22 exalts the privileged place

Wisdom-Sophia holds in relationship to Yahweh as his special creation for his redemptive work in the world ("The Lord created me as the beginning of his ways, for the sake of his works"). As Cook notes, the translator takes pains to protect God as the sole agent of creation but underlines the superiority of the Jewish Wisdom tradition with respect to other cultural systems that vied for the hearts of people.[21]

Therefore, rather than embracing a Greek concept of Sophia, with its constellation of Greek cultural connotations, the Jewish translator of the Greek version of Proverbs appears to be upholding the idea that true wisdom is to be found only in Yahweh's revelation to Israel. The teachings of Solomon represented in literary personification are to be trusted by all peoples because they are cosmic in scope and as old as creation itself.

C. Sirach

The book of Sirach, also known as Ecclesiasticus, is a second composition of Hellenistic Judaism important to the development of Sophia Christology. Originally written in Hebrew in Jerusalem ca. 180 B.C., it was translated into Greek in Alexandria some fifty years later. Apparently Sirach was an important religious book to Hellenistic Jews; today it is included in the collection of books known as the Apocrypha or deuterocanonical literature.

Sirach is clearly dependent on the book of Proverbs, and it endorses a wisdom that is rooted in the revelation of Yahweh to Israel. Like Proverbs, Sirach affirms that the fear of Yahweh (not Astarte, or Isis, or Plato!) is the source of wisdom (Sir 1:14). Moreover, in a time when many different voices competed for the right to define wisdom, Sirach emphasized that obedience to Yahweh is life's highest good and that the practice of the Torah (Law) is the way of wisdom:

> Whoever holds to the law will obtain wisdom. (Sir 15:1)
>
> The whole of wisdom is fear of the Lord, and in all wisdom there is the fulfillment of the law. (Sir 19:20)
>
> The wise will not the hate the law, but the one who is hypocritical about it is like a boat in a storm. (Sir 33:2)

Chapters 1 and 24 of Sirach clearly depend on ch. 8 of Proverbs. The personification of Wisdom-Sophia in Sir 24:1–33 is so similar to Prov 8 in structure, theme, and even wording that it is most likely a deliberate development of the Wisdom motif found there.[22] Like the Greek translator of Prov 8:22, the author of Sir 24 agrees that Wisdom-Sophia had no active role in creation but that she has been created by God to serve his purposes throughout the whole world. He further particularizes Wisdom by identifying the dwelling place of Yahweh's Wisdom-Sophia on earth as in Jerusalem—not in Athens or Alexandria:

> Then the Creator of all things gave me a command,
> and my Creator chose the place for my tent.
> He said, "Make your dwelling in Jacob,
> and in Israel receive your inheritance."
> Before the ages, in the beginning, he created me,
> and for all the ages I shall not cease to be.
> In the holy tent I ministered before him,
> and so I was established in Zion. (Sir 24:8–10)

Immediately following this literary personification of Wisdom-Sophia, Sirach explicitly identifies her with Israel's covenant law: "All this is the book of the covenant of the Most High God, the law that Moses commanded us as an inheritance for the congregations of Jacob" (Sir 24:23). Sirach then develops the implications of such an exclusive concept of wisdom for Israel's new socio-political setting in a polytheistic and pluralistic culture. Contra Johnson, who finds a universalizing tendency in the Jewish Wisdom-Sophia that escapes the temple and priesthood,[23] Sirach stresses a conservative stance, calling for a wisdom that is centered on Torah with its particular expression in the Jerusalem temple and priesthood, not in natural theology prompted by Greek ideals.[24]

D. The Wisdom of Solomon

A quite different portrayal of Wisdom-Sophia is found in the apocryphal book Wisdom of Solomon, a pseudonymous work possibly composed as late as the Roman period under the emperor Caligula (A.D. 37–41).[25] The remarkable similarities between Wisdom of Solomon and the works of Philo, the Jewish philosopher of first-century Alexandria, show that the author of Wisdom of Solomon (hereafter Ps-Solomon) was attempting to relate the teachings of Solomon to Greek philosophical concepts.

The nature of Solomon's Wisdom-Sophia as transformed by Greek philosophical categories is clearly portrayed in ch. 7 of Wisdom of Solomon:

> I [King Solomon] learned both what is secret and what is manifest,
> for wisdom, the fashioner of all things, taught me. . . .
> For wisdom is more mobile than any motion;
> because of her pureness she pervades and penetrates all things.
> For she is a breath of the power of God,
> and a pure emanation of the glory of the Almighty;
> therefore nothing defiled gains entrance into her.
> For she is a reflection of eternal light,
> a spotless mirror of the working of God,
> and an image of his goodness.
> Although she is but one, she can do all things,

> and while remaining in herself, she renews all things;
> in every generation she passes into holy souls
> and makes them friends of God, and prophets. (Wis 7:21–22, 24–27)

Over against the ancient Greek translations of Proverbs and Sirach, Ps-Solomon understands Wisdom-Sophia to be the "fashioner *(technitis)* of all things" (v. 22), giving her a more independent role in creation. Furthermore, she is one who "pervades and penetrates all things" (v. 24), giving her a pantheistic quality comparable to the Stoic concept of *logos.* Ps-Solomon does not merely develop the same thought found in the Greek versions of Proverbs; rather, he presents Wisdom-Sophia in terms of a Stoicising neoplatonism that would have been unacceptable to the Jewish translator of the Proverbs into Greek.[26]

The more active role of Wisdom-Sophia in creation and her existence as a "pure emanation of the glory of the Almighty" (v. 25) move Wisdom of Solomon away from the orbit of biblical Judaism as Ps-Solomon attempts to harmonize Jewish Wisdom tradition with the concepts in Greek philosophy of that day. Rather than being identified as the Torah of Yahweh's covenant (as in Sirach), Wisdom-Sophia in Ps-Solomon's work is portrayed as a hypostasis, a supernatural entity that occupies an intermediary role between God and creation.[27]

This attempt to relate monotheistic Judaism to Greek culture took what was originally a literary personification of Wisdom-Sophia in the Scriptures of Israel and used it as an apologetic vehicle for reconciling Jewish Wisdom with Greek thought. As David Winston points out, Wisdom-Sophia "was the perfect bridge between the exclusive nationalist tradition of Israel and the universalist philosophical tradition which appealed so strongly to the Jewish youth of Roman Alexandria."[28] Moreover, by relating the particularism of Israel's tradition to a universalist philosophy, Israel's religion could also be related to other parochial religions whose particulars were understood to be an expression of those same universals. As Elisabeth Schüssler Fiorenza observes, "The apologetic and missionary needs of Hellenistic Judaism compel the author of the Wisdom of Solomon to incorporate concepts and materials of the Isis myth and cult into his theological reflection."[29]

Wisdom-Sophia could function as the perfect bridge between the parochial claims of Judaism and the cosmopolitan culture of the Greco-Roman world because Ps-Solomon portrayed her as a divine emanation in terms comparable to those used to describe the divine principle of the *logos* of Stoicism. The *logos* was the Stoic conception of an all-penetrating divine essence that pervades and orders the universe and reaches into each person's mind, making each human being a fragmentary part of the cosmic consciousness. Following Philo, Ps-Solomon understands Torah as a particular expression of the divine Wisdom-Sophia that is in harmony with the cosmic order and communicates virtues to humanity. Therefore, Ps-Solomon allows that what the Greeks called *logos,* the Jews also knew previously as *sophia.*

Such an apologetic may have had evangelistic interests. Ben Witherington reads Ps-Solomon as attempting "to forge a new but risky marriage of mainly Jewish ideas with some Greek ones . . . in order to show his audience that whatever is really of worth that they might be seeking in Hellenistic religion or culture can in fact be found in Judaism."[30] However, by portraying the revelation given to Israel in the language of universal religion, the exclusive claims of monotheistic Judaism were put at risk of compromise by allowing them to be read within the context of a pantheistic cosmology and anthropology that rejected the particular and exclusive claims of Yahweh.

Sophia Christology understands Proverbs, Sirach, and Wisdom of Solomon to form a trajectory in the development of Wisdom-Sophia that was later used by NT writers to explain the preexistence of Christ. However, Sirach and Wisdom of Solomon present two quite different ways of relating the Jewish faith to the Graeco-Roman culture, for they reflect the deep conflict that divided the Jews of that period over the appropriate response to Hellenization. Whereas Wisdom of Solomon represents "a marriage between Judaism and Hellenism," Sirach is a "conservative backlash against Hellenization."[31]

The above observations lead to the following question: which, if either, Wisdom tradition is reflected in the NT?

II. Sophia Christology in the New Testament

A. Background

"The figure of divine wisdom in Prov 8 and in the Wisdom of Solomon is theologically identical to what the New Testament describes as the *Logos,* or 'Son' of God."[32] Too often sweeping statements such as this one are accepted and allowed to stand as the foundation for today's Sophia Christology. They are questionable on at least two points. As just argued above, the concept personified by Wisdom-Sophia in Prov 8 in both its Hebrew and Greek versions and in Wisdom of Solomon are *not* the same. Furthermore, contrary to the above quote, the New Testament as a whole does not so identify Jesus as the *logos.* The identification is found only in John's gospel and then only in the Prologue (see discussion on John below).

Studies of the fuller corpus of Hellenistic texts show that there was not one but perhaps as many as five different castings of Wisdom-Sophia in Judaism at the turn of the era.[33] The Wisdom-Sophia so often identified with Jesus is a modern construct made up of a pastiche of images taken out of context. Most of the passages cited come from texts that present fundamentally different, and probably incompatible, portrayals of wisdom and its relationship to Yahweh, creation, and humanity. In effect, feminist theologians approach the NT after first having constructed a Sophia who is a divine hypostasis, co-eternal with God and an agent of creation. Johnson argues that Wisdom-Sophia at the time of Jesus was understood as "a personification of God's own self. . . . The wisdom literature . . . presents the divine presence in the woman's *Gestalt* of divine Sophia."[34] For Johnson, this means that

> whoever espouses a wisdom christology is asserting that Jesus is the human being Sophia became; that Sophia in all her fullness was in him so that he fully represents and manifests all that God is in creative and graciously saving involvement in the world; therefore that his very deity is the deity of Sophia, since Sophia is God's gracious goodness reaching out to and active in the world.[35]

Schüssler Fiorenza, herself an early influence in the development of Sophia Christology, recognized that Wisdom-Sophia was a ubiquitous religious motif but that there was no single basic wisdom myth present in the many different portrayals of Wisdom-Sophia in Jewish, Jewish-Hellenistic, and Gnostic writings. Such a basic myth "is a systematic reconstruction and reflects more the concern of the reconstructing scholar than that of the texts."[36] Rather than finding a unified understanding of Wisdom-Sophia, she sees "reflective mythology" in the Hellenistic texts, which is

> a form of theology appropriating mythical language, material, and patterns from different myths, and it uses these patterns, motifs, and configurations for its own theological concerns. Such a theology is not interested in reproducing the myth itself or the mythic materials as they stand, but rather in taking up and adapting the various mythical elements to its own theological goal and theoretical concerns.[37]

Schüssler Fiorenza goes on to describe the theological concerns of Jewish interpreters in the Hellenistic period as

> the post-exilic community's problem of theodicy and its missionary interests in the face of the renewed Isis cult, Philo's concern for the transcendence of God, or the gnostic's longing for salvation. The mythological elements found in these writings should not be reduced to one basic myth but should be seen in their different functions within distinct theological contexts.[38]

Today feminist theologians are doing reflective theology when they appropriate the language and literary images of Hellenistic Wisdom-Sophia but take them up and use them for their own theological goals and concerns, specifically that of finding a female face for God. Such gender concerns are a thoroughly modern use of Wisdom-Sophia.

In 1970 M. Jack Suggs published a work in which he argued that the source document Q understands Jesus in his prophetic role as a child of Wisdom-Sophia but that Matthew's gospel develops the association by actually identifying Jesus as Wisdom-Sophia incarnate.[39] Subsequently, the title Sophia-Jesus began to be used by feminist theologians as a reference to the feminine aspect of the incarnate God. This usage marks a curious step in the development of Sophia Christology, since it involves the confusion of a literary device, the personification of Wisdom-Sophia, with a historical person, Jesus of Nazareth. Even if one were to agree with Johnson that Wisdom-Sophia was a personification of God himself, one cannot achieve gender parity by identifying Sophia with Jesus. Such parity might be achieved only if Jesus, like Wisdom-Sophia, was also a literary device, merely a male personification of God himself. Then one could perhaps argue that after two thousand years of using male personification, the church should now use the alternative female personification in the interests of gender equity. This possibility seems to be suggested in Johnson's comment that "the figure of personified Wisdom offers an augmented field of female metaphors with which to interpret the saving significance and personal identity of Jesus the Christ, and the choice of metaphors matters."[40]

Human gender is a part of the created order and has no metaphysical correlate in the Godhead. God is neither male nor female. But this does not mean that we can choose language of either gender when speaking of him. For when God entered creation in the historical incarnation of Jesus, he disallowed the popular theory that *all* language about God is necessarily metaphorical and that, therefore, a female metaphor is as appropriate as a male metaphor. God did not simply step into the narrative world of the gospel texts; he stepped into human history. Jesus is not a metaphor for God's presence, but God in the flesh. Commenting on the frequently repeated claim that "Jesus was the ultimate 'parable' or 'metaphor' for God," Oxford theologian Janet Martin Soskice writes,

> Such a statement may be appropriate from a pulpit, but is out of place in a work whose object is to clarify the function of metaphor and parable within a text. In such a context, to say that Jesus was a metaphor or a parable is either to have an odd Christology or, more likely, poorly conceived definitions of metaphor and parable.[41]

The female personification of Wisdom-Sophia in the canonical Wisdom books is a literary device used to characterize God's revelatory acts in both creation and redemption; "she" has neither metaphysical reality nor historical embodiment. Jesus Christ should not be renamed Sophia-Jesus because he is *not* merely an idea in the history of religions recently made passé by feminist ideology; according to the witness of the NT, he is the Lord of history to whom all social movements must someday give an account.

This is not to say, however, that first-century concepts of Wisdom-Sophia were unimportant to discussions about the person and work of Jesus Christ. The apostles had to understand and interpret the unique historical event of the life, death, and resurrection of Jesus in categories of religious thought and symbols that existed during and immediately after his lifetime. Jesus himself may have referred to certain aspects of his person or work by using well-known categories of the Jewish Wisdom tradition. In fact, given how ubiquitous the category of Wisdom was within the ancient world, it would be surprising indeed if it had not played a role in emerging christology.[42] But not just *any* idea associated with Wisdom in the Hellenistic world can be equated with God's truth as revealed in Christ. Concepts of Wisdom found in books such as Wisdom of Solomon—books that would not have been considered canonical by the Jews at the time of Christ—cannot be quickly identified with biblical wisdom.

The apostle Paul related wisdom not to Christ's incarnation in general, but specifically to Christ's crucifixion (e.g., 1 Cor 1:21–24, 30; cf. Fee's article in this volume). Feminist theologians find Wisdom-Sophia had no role in atonement in the literature of Hellenistic Judaism, even though atonement was an assumed precondition for attaining wisdom in the writings of ancient Israel. The later Hellenistic development of Wisdom-Sophia in the Diaspora, far from temple and sacrifice, is congenial to those who today eschew the very concept of sin and atonement as an outdated idea that is not central to the message of Christianity. Theologian Nancy Cocks has been quoted as saying, "The idea that Jesus Christ substituted for humankind on the cross and atoned for what we do is seen by some feminists as abusive. It suggests that those in power are able to punish those with less power. Sophia is a more inclusive way of looking at God."[43] Unfortunately, such a Sophia Christology offers a Christianity eviscerated of the heart of the gospel: the cross of Jesus Christ. For the sake of a well-intentioned but misguided inclusiveness it offers religion but no reconciliation to God.

B. The Prologue of John's Gospel

The first-century understanding of Jesus as Sophia is said to reach its fullest biblical form in the high christology of John's gospel, most especially in the Prologue (John 1:1–18). Johnson writes, "The figure of divine Sophia shines through the Logos terminology; at the point of fullest development they are theologically identical. . . . Jesus is Sophia incarnate; Jesus is Logos incarnate."[44] The full equivalence of Sophia and Jesus is allegedly presented in the Prologue, where the *logos* that has become incarnate in the human person of Jesus is understood as synonymous with *sophia.* This claim of synonymy is supported by the observation that everything said of the *logos* in the Prologue, with the exception of identity with God and the incarnation in flesh (v. 14), had already been said of Wisdom-Sophia in previous Jewish writings.[45] Some scholars even identify the original form of the Prologue as a hymn to Sophia that was later applied to Christ.[46]

However, if the development of Wisdom-Sophia in Hellenistic Jewish writings provided such a fine fit with the apostolic understanding of Jesus that culminates in the high christology of John's gospel, it is certainly strange beyond comprehension that the Greek word *sophia* does not occur *once* in John's gospel or in the Johannine Epistles.[47] This conspicuous absence raises the question of whether the author (whom I will refer to as John, following tradition) is intentionally distancing his christology from associations with Wisdom-Sophia because the use of that category to interpret the preexistence of Jesus had already developed in directions the evangelist refused to go. If so, the full flowering of that trend may be seen in the second-century emergence of a distinctively gnostic form of Sophia Christology. This suggests that the Wisdom-Sophia trajectory found in Wisdom of Solomon was developed even further by those who sought to accommodate Jesus Christ to Greek philosophy.

What is undeniably clear is that John's Prologue does *not* say that in the beginning was Sophia, and Sophia was with God, and Sophia was God; nor does it say that Sophia became flesh and dwelt among us. If John meant to identify Jesus with the personification of Wisdom-Sophia as directly and fully as feminist theology claims, his choice of words could not have been more confusing. So thoroughly absent is Wisdom-Sophia in the Fourth Gospel that Wayne Meeks concludes, "In the Fourth Gospel there is no trace of the usual feminine Sophia; she has become entirely the masculine Logos, the Son of Man."[48]

The question of why the Prologue identifies Jesus Christ with the *logos* instead of with *sophia* is generally answered by claiming that *sophia* and *logos* were used so interchangeably that they were virtually synonymous and that John chose the masculine noun *logos* instead of its feminine synonym *sophia* because Jesus was male. In this way, some feminist interpreters attribute male chauvinism as the motive for the replacement of earlier feminine categories by the male metaphors later adopted at Nicea as the foundational statements of christology. Probably such an understanding unfairly projects male chauvinism onto the NT writers, because the same shift from the feminine *sophia* to the masculine *logos* is found in the works of Philo, who was not a Christian and whose writings predate the Gospels.[49] Thus, even before the Christian era there apparently was a shift away from using Wisdom-Sophia to describe God's relationship to the universe. This previous shift suggests that any chauvinism perceived by modern eyes was not motivated by the peculiar issues of christology in the church nor by the maleness of Jesus. It may rather imply that ancient writers, such as Philo, recognized Wisdom-Sophia to be merely a literary personification that derived its feminine aspect simply from the grammatical gender of the word (as do all literary personifications in languages where nouns have gender) and not from any metaphysically feminine aspect of God.

Moreover, the two terms *sophia* and *logos* were certainly not synonyms in the lexical stock of *koinē* Greek. In Jewish Wisdom writings they were sometimes used to refer to related concepts, but in no case is *sophia* (wisdom) explicitly identified with the *logos* of God.[50]

Even if one were to accept the premise that *sophia* and *logos* were completely synonymous concepts for the author of John's Prologue, the argument that the masculine noun was chosen because Jesus was male completely overlooks the fact that Jesus is described with feminine nouns elsewhere in John's gospel. In the predicate nominative construction of John 14:6, Jesus says, "I am the way and the truth and the life," where *all three* nouns are feminine *(hodos, alētheia,* and *zōē).* This example is particularly interesting because Truth, like Sophia, was a hypostatized female entity in classical Greek thought,[51] yet John does not fear using that feminine noun in explicit identification with Jesus. Therefore, John's avoidance of *sophia* in reference to Jesus suggests that it was something other than the feminine gender that disqualified its use. Moreover, his use of feminine metaphors elsewhere is evidence that male chauvinism was not his motivation. The predicate nominative in John 14:6 further implies that connotations associated with *truth* at the time the Fourth Gospel was written were more compatible with Jesus' identity than were those associated with *wisdom.* In light of this, John's complete avoidance of the word *sophia* as an identifier for Jesus demands that we must consider the possibility that he was unwilling to take the very step that modern Sophia Christology has taken—namely, to claim that Wisdom-Sophia is the preexistent feminine divine being who became incarnate in Jesus.

Given the complete absence of the word *wisdom* in John's gospel, the recent commentary entitled *John's Wisdom* by Witherington represents a bold application of the Wisdom motif to this gospel. According to Witherington, "recognizing that Jesus is being portrayed as God's Wisdom, indeed Wisdom incarnate . . . is *the key* to understanding" John's presentation of Jesus (emphasis original).[52] His argument is not limited to the Prologue, where allusions to Wisdom have long been recognized, but is based on perceived textual parallels between motifs, symbols, and patterns used throughout the gospel with what is said of Wisdom-Sophia in various Jewish Wisdom texts. For instance, Witherington observes that Jesus is characterized in the seven statements as bread, light, the door, life, and the true vine. According to Witherington, "*All* of these things are said at one point or another to come from or characterize personified Wisdom" (emphasis original).[53] However, his conclusion that therefore Jesus is Wisdom-Sophia incarnate is questionable. His own supporting example from Wis 7:26 actually states that Wisdom-Sophia is *but a reflection* of eternal light, not the light itself as is claimed for Jesus.

Furthermore, surely the terms *wisdom* and *life,* as well as *light* and *vine,* were too ubiquitous in religious discourse to be used today as compelling evidence for John's direct dependence on or specific reference to any one of them. It is questionable whether most of the parallels Witherington cites between what is said of Jesus and what had previously been said of Wisdom-Sophia constitute true literary parallels. Moreover, perceived literary parallels alone do not necessarily constitute a relationship of equivalence but rather possibly one of negation or supercession. For instance, the two statements "Sophia is the light of the world" and "Jesus is the light of the world" are syntactically parallel, but they need not be understood as equating Sophia and Jesus; rather, the second can be understood as a negation and denial of the first. Although Witherington's work offers many excellent insights, he presses the identification of Jesus with Wisdom beyond what the nature of the parallels can bear.

But previous to Witherington's work, other scholars had also observed parallels between what is said of the *logos* in the Prologue and what is said of Wisdom elsewhere. For example, Raymond Brown has summarized the numerous parallels between Wisdom-Sophia and Christ in John's Prologue:[54]

- She existed with God from the beginning.
- She was an emanation of God's glory, and Jesus also revealed God's glory.
- She is a reflection of the eternal light of God.
- She descended from heaven to dwell with humanity.
- She ascended to heaven after being rejected by humanity.
- She teaches the things that are above.
- She speaks in first person, just as Jesus did, saying, "I am . . ."
- She leads people to life and immortality.
- She offers her blessings in the symbols of food and drink.
- She calls those who listen to her children.

Observe, however, that these alleged parallels between the *logos* and Wisdom-Sophia are offset by some significant contrasts. For instance, in Prov 8 Wisdom-Sophia was created by God and witnessed the creation of the universe; the *logos* was not only with God, but *was* God, and was the agent of all creation. Jesus was not a child of Wisdom-Sophia as some theologians would claim; rather, the preexistent Christ created the Wisdom-Sophia found in Prov 8 and all that she represents. In Wisdom of Solomon, Wisdom-Sophia is "a reflection of eternal light" (Wis 7:26); in the Prologue the *logos* is the light itself. Sophia Christology would argue that these differences develop and advance Wisdom-Sophia in Christian thought, but such significant contrasts could also make the point that the *logos* in John's Prologue is a completely different entity. Moreover, Sophia Christology makes much of parallels between John's Prologue and Hellenistic Jewish Wisdom writings, but it gives lesser consideration to the parallels with the creative and prophetic word of the Lord in the OT.

Given that the Prologue exhibits parallels with both Jewish Wisdom tradition and ancient Israel's prophetic tradition, it would be a mistake either to ignore one or to pit one over against the other. The author apparently intended a more diffused use of his background material. Even the parallels with the Wisdom corpus cited by Brown are gleaned from several different texts—Proverbs, Job, Baruch, Sirach, Wisdom of Solomon, and Enoch—each of which presents different views of Wisdom-Sophia when read in context (e.g., differences between Sirach and Wisdom of Solomon as discussed above). Therefore, it appears that John has neither any single text in mind as the background for the Prologue nor a unified concept of Wisdom-Sophia; rather, he is alluding to a kaleidoscope of ideas generally associated with Wisdom-Sophia. But the question is, were they indeed intended to identify Wisdom-Sophia with the preexistent Christ (as has been maintained), or were they rather intended to contrast his excellence over anything previously attributed to Wisdom-Sophia? The observation of parallels does not so readily admit the identification of Jesus with Sophia as assumed by Sophia Christology.

If feminist theologians are correct that Wisdom-Sophia actually was one of the earliest conceptualizations for the preexistent Christ in the first century, then the allusion made to the Wisdom motif in the Prologue could, in fact, be read as a correction of errant Sophia theology. In other words, we can construe much of the evidence presented for identifying Jesus with Sophia as exactly the opposite: the Prologue is, in fact, a polemic against viewing Jesus Christ through the lens of Jewish Wisdom as refracted by Greek philosophy—an apology for presenting him as the one who subsumes and supersedes all previous ideas of Wisdom. The relevant dialectic would then be represented by the following set of questions and answers: Who is the active agent in creation? Not Wisdom-Sophia, but Jesus the incarnate God, Creator and Sustainer of all things. Who is the light of the world? Not Wisdom-Sophia, but Jesus Christ, the genuine Light. Who is the source of life? Not Wisdom-Sophia, but the resurrected Jesus Christ, who is truly and eternally alive.

If this reading of John's Prologue is correct, it represents not a development of the Wisdom motif but a marked discontinuity between Johannine christology and the previous Wisdom-Sophia traditions. The personification of Wisdom-Sophia in Proverbs as a metaphor for God's purposes in relation to creation, humanity, and salvation may have been properly understood in its original historical setting in monotheistic Israel, but the use of Wisdom-Sophia had developed nonbiblical connotations in polytheistic Greek culture, even among the Jews. Toward the end of the first century, in a culture greatly enamored of wisdom, John needed to exhort his readers to look to Christ as life's highest good, not to the wisdom of the world. Only in Jesus Christ will everything that Wisdom was thought to offer—and much more, even eternal life—be found.

C. Summary

In summary, I have argued that Sophia Christology is methodologically and exegetically flawed at several points:

1. The exegesis of Prov 8:30 that casts Wisdom-Sophia in an active role in creation is mistaken. Wisdom personifies the creative and redemptive reach of God into this world that was first expressed in his verbal word, Torah, and that finds its ultimate expression in the cross of Christ.

2. The Jewish Hellenistic texts do not present a unified concept of Wisdom-Sophia. The Sophia identified with Jesus is a modern construction made of images gathered from many disparate texts.

3. The apologetic use of Wisdom-Sophia by the Hellenistic Jews and possibly by the early Christians was a way to recommend the monotheistic faith to a polytheistic culture enamored of wisdom. Gender concerns were not in view, and the feminine personification of *sophia* was completely governed by the grammatical gender of first the Hebrew and then the Greek noun for *wisdom*. Modern feminists have latched onto the language of *sophia* and then have reconstructed it to address gender concerns when it had no such purpose in late-Jewish/early-Christian usage.

4. Sophia Christology confuses a literary personification with an actual person and justifies it by the erroneous assumption that all language for God is necessarily metaphorical.

5. The identification of Jesus with Sophia is primarily based on observing parallels between NT texts and Jewish Wisdom texts. This methodology is questionable because even genuine parallels do not necessarily imply a relationship of identity; they may instead imply a relationship of negation and supercession.

6. In the canonical texts, Wisdom-Sophia was not a universalizing impulse used to embrace peoples of many religions; such use today tends to compromise the exclusive claims of the gospel of Jesus Christ.

7. The accusation that the earliest Christian understanding of Jesus as Wisdom-Sophia was later masculinized by chauvinistic orthodoxy is a projection of modern prejudices back on patristic history. The "masculinization" of *sophia* is found in non-Christian writings that predate the NT.

8. Some of the NT passages quoted to support Sophia Christology, such as 1 Cor 1:22–24 and John 1:1, may be understood instead as resisting, not supporting, the identification of Jesus with Wisdom-Sophia.

III. Is There Another Way?

Regardless of how one evaluates the modern feminist movement, Sophia Christology raises a theological question that should be of interest and concern to Christians who still believe that vicarious atonement is central to the gospel of Jesus Christ: Can a male savior save women? As Jay Wesley Richards points out, this question finds its impulse not in feminism but in historic Christian orthodoxy.[55] The Cappadocian father Gregory of Nazianzus (d. 389) argued that what is not fully assumed in the incarnation is not redeemed. This axiom arose in the context of his argument with Apollinaris over the question of whether Jesus had a human mind. Gregory argued that if the incarnate Christ did not have a fully human mind, he would not have an essential property of human nature, and therefore he would not be qualified to save human beings.

Feminist theologians, such as Johnson, apply this axiom to gender. If female gender is not assumed in the incarnation, can female human beings be saved by a male savior?[56] Feminist theologians tend in at least two directions at this point. Some deny the need for atonement altogether. Others who seek to work within historic orthodox Christianity articulate Sophia Christology in terms that attempt to find in the incarnation a female aspect in which woman's salvation can be theologically grounded. Although there is neither time nor space to enter into this debate fully, I offer here a few preliminary observations on an issue raised by Sophia Christology that deserves to be developed further elsewhere.

Throughout, the NT teaches that women are indeed redeemed by Jesus Christ, but no verse is more to the point than Gal 3:28, where Paul writes with startling certainty, "There is no longer male and female; for all of you are one in Christ Jesus." And so the question I would pose is not, *Can* a male savior save women? but rather, *How* can a male savior save women? How can we affirm the historic formulation of the necessity of Christ's full humanity and ground the redemption of women in a savior who did not embody femaleness, if gender is an essential property of humanness?[57] The incarnation of Christ as a male human being raises important questions about the relationship of human gender to essential human nature.

The question raised by feminist theologians presumes an understanding that gender is an essential property of humanness. This presumption creates a pressure to somehow find gender parity in the incarnation by identifying a female counterpart to Jesus' maleness. Another possibility offers itself: the efficacy of the male savior for both male and female human beings necessarily implies that gender be a contingent, rather than an essential, property of humanness. In other words, Christ's vicarious atonement implies that men and women are united by our human nature more than we are divided by our gender differences.

Perhaps it is natural to think of one's gender (as opposed, for instance, to the color of one's eyes) as so constituting one's being that it must be an essential property. Many of us may not be able to imagine ourselves embodied as the opposite gender, or as genderless beings, and may therefore conclude that gender is in fact an essential property of humanness. In addition, the fact that every human being does exist in this world as either male or female (even if one changes one's sexual identity) can also be viewed as implying that gender is an essential property of humanness. But this confuses the properties essential to individuation with the properties essential to humanity as a kind. My femaleness may be an essential property of myself *as an individual*, but it is nevertheless a contingent property of my humanness.

I would therefore argue that "genderedness" is an essential property of humanness but that maleness and femaleness as such are contingent properties. If so, then both male and female embody the essential properties of humanness, making both equally normative as human beings. Therefore, the incarnate Christ had to have gender to be fully human, but his maleness was a contingent property of his humanness. Jesus therefore fully exemplifies essential humanity for both women and men, although incarnated as male.

The fact that there is not "male and female" in Christ means the female human being is united with Christ no differently than is the male human being; it also means our essential humanity is more constitutive of our metaphysical existence than is our gender. The contingent property of gender may nevertheless be a part of our eternal identities because the resurrected Christ apparently retained his gender, at least in appearances in this space-time continuum. If the efficacy of Christ's atonement for women necessarily implies that gender is a contingent property, then the male must not be thought of as the paradigm human being from which the female is metaphysically derivative and secondary. The way one understands the relationship between human gender and essential human nature has far-reaching implications for both theology and practice.

To consider the gender of Jesus as a contingent property is not to say that his maleness is unimportant, nor is it to say that androgynous or female concepts and language may be applied to him. If gender is a contingent property of humanness, then it is true that a female savior could in principle have saved both men and women. But God stepped into human history as a *man*, and the significance of that choice must be respected. Nevertheless, when God became fully human with male gender, he equally dignified and honored the female gender because no man was involved in the conception of Jesus Christ at all. *All* of Jesus' fully human nature came from a woman, his virgin mother, Mary. Thus, the virgin birth also necessarily implies that the female fully embodied the essential humanness communicated to the male person of Jesus Christ necessary for his salvific role.

Sophia Christology is a modern impulse that appropriates ancient language and uses it for contemporary purposes. Its search for a female aspect of God is misguided and unnecessary both as the theological basis for women's salvation and as an apologetic for evangelism in a gender-conscious society. In a world still filled with voices competing to define life's highest good, the exclusive claims of the Word who was God and became flesh and dwelt among us rises above the cacophony as the one and only way of true wisdom.

Notes

The author wishes to acknowledge and thank Moisés Silva, the Mary Rockefeller Distinguished Professor of New Testament at Gordon-Conwell Theological Seminary, as well as Robert Gundry, the Kathleen Smith Professor of Religious Studies, and Jim Taylor, Professor of Philosophy, both at Westmont College, for their helpful critique of this paper at various stages.

The Scripture quotations in this article are taken from the NRSV unless otherwise noted.

[1] Elizabeth A. Johnson, "Jesus, the Wisdom of God: A Biblical Basis for Non-androcentric Christology," *ETL* 61 (1985): 294.

[2] For example, Mary Daly, *Beyond God the Father: Toward a Philosophy of Women's Liberation* (Boston: Beacon, 1973).

[3] See Harold G. Wells, "Trinitarian Feminism: Elizabeth Johnson's Wisdom Christology," *ThTo* 52 (1995): 330–42.

[4] Elisabeth Schüssler Fiorenza, *In Memory of Her: A Feminist Theological Reconstruction of Christian Origins* (New York: Crossroad, 1987), 132.

[5] James M. Robinson, "Very Goddess and Very Man," in *Images of the Feminine in Gnosticism* (ed. Karen L. King; Philadelphia: Fortress, 1988), 123.

[6] "Sophia Emerges as Metaphor for God among Feminist Theologians" *Vancouver Sun*, 4 April 1994, A4.

[7] Work on women's spirituality from a feminist perspective is vast and varied. See, e.g., Rosemary Radford Ruether, *Sexism and God-Talk: Toward a Feminist*

Theology (Boston: Beacon, 1983); Patricia Wilson-Kastner, *Faith, Feminism, and the Christ* (Philadelphia: Fortress, 1983); Gail Paterson Corrington, *Her Image of Salvation: Female Saviors and Formative Christianity* (Louisville: Westminster John Knox, 1992); Catherine Mowry LaCugna, ed., *Freeing Theology: The Essentials of Theology in Feminist Perspective* (San Francisco: HarperSanFrancisco, 1993); Maryanne Stevens, ed., *Reconstructing the Christ Symbol: Essays in Feminist Christology* (New York: Paulist Press, 1993); Susan Cole, Hal Taussig, and Marian Ronan, *Wisdom's Feast: Sophia in Study and Celebration* (Kansas City: Sheed & Ward, 1996).

[8] Elizabeth A. Johnson, "Redeeming the Name of Christ," in *Freeing Theology: The Essentials of Theology in Feminist Perspective* (ed. Catherine Mowry LaCugna; San Francisco: HarperSanFrancisco, 1993), 119–20.

[9] Johnson, "Redeeming," 120.

[10] For a discussion of the role of Solomon in Israel's Wisdom tradition see R. B. Y. Scott, "Solomon and the Beginnings of Wisdom in Israel," in *Wisdom in Israel and in the Ancient Near East* (ed. M. Noth and D. Winton Thomas; VTSup 3; Leiden: E. J. Brill, 1955).

[11] The issues surrounding the origin of the book of Proverbs and its relationship to Canaanite and Egyptian Wisdom traditions are complex. See M. Noth and D. Winton Thomas, eds., *Wisdom in Israel and in the Ancient Near East* (VTSup 3; Leiden: E. J. Brill, 1955); R. N. Whybray, *Wisdom in Proverbs* (London: SCM Press, 1965); Gerhard von Rad, *Wisdom in Israel* (trans. James D. Martin; Nashville: Abingdon, 1972); James L. Crenshaw, *Studies in Ancient Israelite Wisdom* (New York: Ktav, 1976); Leo G. Perdue, *Wisdom and Cult: A Critical Analysis of the Views of Cult in the Wisdom Literatures of Israel and the Ancient Near East* (SBLDS 30; Missoula, Mo.: Scholars Press, 1977).

[12] Bruce Waltke, "Lady Wisdom as Mediatrix: An Exposition of Proverbs 1:20–33," *Presb* 14 (1988): 1.

[13] Ibid.

[14] Ibid.

[15] This point is sometimes lost on English speakers because the English language does not include grammatical gender for nouns. For instance, Spanish speakers would never think of *la casa* (a feminine noun meaning "house") as something female, but were *casa* to be personified in Spanish, it would be natural to portray it as a woman.

[16] Most English translations read "craftsman," but Martin Hengel takes "favorite child" as the preferred pointing (*Judaism and Hellenism* [Philadelphia: Fortress, 1974], 153).

[17] Cited in Hengel, *Judaism and Hellenism,* 162. See also G. Gerleman, "The Septuagint Proverbs as a Hellenistic Document," *OtSt* 8 (1950): 26. For an extended discussion of the Greek word that concludes with an opposing view, see Johann Cook, *The Septuagint of Proverbs: Jewish and/or Hellenistic Proverbs? Concerning the Hellenistic Colouring of the LXX Proverbs* (Leiden: E. J. Brill, 1997), 230.

[18] In the christological debates of the fourth century, the Arians used the LXX version, while those whose view became the orthodox Christian position preferred the text of Aquila, Symmachus, and Theodotion.

[19] Cook, *Septuagint of Proverbs,* 292.

[20] Ibid., 224.

[21] Ibid., 246.

[22] Ibid., 235; Patrick W. Skehan and Alexander A. Di Lella, *The Wisdom of Ben Sira* (AB 43; Garden City, N.Y.: Doubleday, 1987), 331–38.

[23] Elizabeth A. Johnson, "Wisdom Was Made Flesh," in *Reconstructing the Christ Symbol: Essays in Feminist Christology* (ed. Maryanne Stevens; New York: Paulist Press, 1993), 97.

[24] Leo G. Perdue, *Wisdom and Cult: A Critical Analysis of the Views of Cult in the Wisdom Literatures of Israel and the Ancient Near East* (SBLDS 30: Missoula, Mo.: Scholars Press, 1977), 190, 193.

[25] David Winston, *The Wisdom of Solomon* (AB 43; Garden City, N.Y.: Doubleday, 1979), 23.

[26] Cook, *Septuagint of Proverbs,* 239.

[27] Winston, *Wisdom of Solomon,* 34.

[28] Ibid., 37. Even if one dates Wisdom of Solomon earlier in the Ptolemaic period, the point would still stand.

[29] Elisabeth Schüssler Fiorenza, "Wisdom Mythology and the Christological Hymns of the New Testament," in *Aspects of Wisdom in Judaism and Early Christianity* (ed. Robert L. Wilken; Notre Dame: University of Notre Dame Press, 1975), 31.

[30] Ben Witherington III, *Jesus the Sage: The Pilgrimage of Wisdom* (Minneapolis: Fortress, 1994), 103.

[31] Ibid., 112.

[32] Ruether, *Sexism,* 117.

[33] See James D. G. Dunn, *Christology in the Making* (Philadelphia: Westminster, 1980), 168. Johnson lists five similar views in "Jesus," 271–73.

[34] Johnson, "Jesus," 274–75.

[35] Ibid., 280.

[36] Schüssler Fiorenza, "Wisdom Mythology," 33. Dunn also finds methodological problems when concepts about wisdom from different contexts are interpreted as equivalents; see Dunn, *Christology,* 170.

[37] Schüssler Fiorenza, "Wisdom Mythology," 29.

[38] Ibid., 33.

[39] M. Jack Suggs, *Wisdom, Christology, and Law in Matthew's Gospel* (Cambridge: Harvard University Press, 1970).

[40] Johnson, "Redeeming," 122.

[41] Janet Martin Soskice, *Metaphor and Religious Language* (Oxford: Clarendon, 1985), 56.

[42] For various views on the use of wisdom in the development of christology, see Dunn, *Christology,* 163–209; Marinus de Jonge, *Christology in Context* (Philadelphia: Westminster, 1988), 79–82, 189–99; Rudolf Schnackenburg, *Jesus in the Gospels* (Louisville: Westminster John Knox, 1995), passim.

[43] "Sophia Emerges," *Vancouver Sun,* A4.

[44] Johnson, "Jesus," 288–89.

[45] R. Bultmann, *The Gospel of John* (trans. G. R. Beasley-Murray; Oxford: Blackwell, 1971), 22; C. H. Dodd, *The Interpretation of the Fourth Gospel* (Cambridge: Cambridge University Press, 1953), 274; Raymond E. Brown, *The Gospel According to John* (AB 29; Garden City, N.Y.: Doubleday, 1966), cxxii–cxxiii, 523.

[46] J. R. Harris, *The Origin of the Prologue to St. John* (Cambridge: Cambridge University Press, 1917), 6; J. Painter, "Christology and the History of the

Johannine Community in the Prologue of the Fourth Gospel," *NTS* 30 (1984): 460–74; Schüssler Fiorenza, "Wisdom Mythology," 17–41; John Ashton, "The Transformation of Wisdom: A Study of the Prologue of John's Gospel," *NTS* 32 (1986): 161–86.

[47] This observation emerged out of conversation with Robert H. Gundry and has also been raised as an objection to seeing Sophia Christology in the Johannine corpus by Andreas J. Köstenberger in his review of Ben Witherington III, "John's Wisdom: A Commentary on the Fourth Gospel," *JETS* 42 (1999): 154.

[48] Wayne A. Meeks, "The Man from Heaven in Johannine Sectarianism," *JBL* 91 (1972): 72.

[49] Dunn, *Christology,* 171; C. K. Barrett, *The Gospel According to St. John* (2d ed.; Philadelphia: Westminster, 1978), 154; Robert M. Grant, "The Christ at the Creation," in *Jesus in Myth and History* (ed. R. Joseph Hoffman and G. A. Larue; Buffalo, N.Y.: Prometheus, 1986), 159.

[50] See Dunn, *Christology,* 219. Witherington attempts to establish the synonymous use of *logos* and *sophia* by observing their occurrence in synonymous parallelism in Wis 9:1–2. But even if they were used interchangeably there, such parallelism does not establish similar interchangeability in John 1:1, especially since, as noted above, *sophia* does not occur in John's Prologue. See Ben Witherington III, *John's Wisdom* (Louisville: Westminster John Knox, 1995), 53.

[51] For example, Sophia is found in the poetical works of Empedocles and Parmenides, cited in LSJ.

[52] Witherington, *John's Wisdom,* 20.

[53] Ibid., 22.

[54] Brown, *John,* cxxii–cxxvii.

[55] Jay Wesley Richards, "Can a Male Savior Save Women? Gregory of Nazianzus on the Logos' Assumption of Human Nature," *Christian Scholar's Review* 28 (1998): 42–57.

[56] Johnson, "Redeeming," 120.

[57] Of course it should be noted that the issue of race raises the same question. Can a non-Chinese Jesus save the Chinese? Is gender a more or less essential property of humanness than race?

Wisdom Christology in Paul: A Dissenting View

Gordon D. Fee

When I did my doctoral studies in the 1960s, the phrase "Wisdom Christology" was rarely heard. Although the roots of the idea go back much earlier[1]—such language was tentatively used as early as 1947 by C. H. Dodd[2]—the term has picked up momentum since the 1970s, so that it has now become coin of the realm in the New Testament guild. This is evidenced especially by the prominent billing it is given in J. D. G. Dunn's recent comprehensive study of Pauline theology.[3] But the catalog of those who speak thus of Paul's christology is large and includes, in addition to Dunn, many scholars of considerable reputation. It is therefore with some apprehension that I offer a dissenting voice; nonetheless, I will do so in this essay, in part because I am convinced that the evidence brought forward in support of it is tenuous at best and in part because the logic of the argument in its favor seems flawed in both its major and minor premises.

What I offer here is another reading of the texts involved (the Wisdom literature and Paul's letters) with the suggestion that such a reading of these texts—independently of each other and on their own terms—does not support the many assertions being made about the influence of Jewish Wisdom on Paul's christology. I will begin with a brief overview of the issues, the texts, and the methodology.

I. Overview

A. The Issues

It is interesting that even though the phrase Wisdom Christology[4] is now so commonplace, it emerges at only one point in the discussions of Paul's theology: on the issue of preexistence,[5] and especially in the interest of tracing out the origins of this idea. That is, even though a great deal is said about Wisdom in the Jewish texts, and even though Paul has much to say about Christ in his letters, the only place these two literary traditions intersect is on the matter of Christ's preexistence. Furthermore, this issue is most often brought forward at only one point in discussions of preexistence, namely, Wisdom's role in creation, where assertions are made over and again to the effect that "the ultimate source of this doctrine [Christ as Wisdom] is Prov. 8 where Wisdom is conceived as pre-existent and as God's agent in creation."[6]

B. The Texts

Although God is said to have created "all things in wisdom" (Ps 104:24; LXX 103:24 πάντα ἐν σοφίᾳ ἐποίησας; cf. Prov 3:19), the crucial texts from the Jewish Wisdom tradition are those where Wisdom is personified and pictured as present with God when he created. These texts are basically three:[7] Prov 8:22–31 (in light of 3:19); Sir 24:3–22; and Wis 6:1–10:21 (esp. 7:12, 22; 8:4–5; 9:1–9). On the Pauline side the crucial texts are 1 Cor 8:6 (in light of 1:24, 30) and Col 1:15–17 (in light of 2:3).

C. The Methodology

My concerns here go in two directions: First, as will be pointed out, there is no *significant* linguistic correspondence—indeed, if any *linguistic* correspondence at all—between Paul and these texts. The question, then, is how one determines *conceptual* influence in such cases. After all, we have abundant evidence that Paul both cites and "echoes" the Hebrew Bible in a variety of ways. But what is missing in the case of preexistent Wisdom as the agent of creation is not only verbal correspondence between Paul and the Wisdom tradition at this point, but also clearly identifiable echoes from these texts as well.

Second, the method used to establish the links between Paul and the Wisdom tradition on these matters takes a form of logic that goes like this:[8]

> *Major premise:* In the Jewish Wisdom tradition, personified Wisdom is pictured as the divine agent of creation.
>
> *Minor premise:* The Jewish Paul specifically calls Christ the Wisdom of God (1 Cor 1:24) and sees him as the agent of creation (8:6).
>
> *Conclusion:* Therefore, when Paul speaks of Christ as the agent of creation, he is both relying on this tradition and putting Christ in the role of Wisdom.

As with many such syllogisms, however, when there are questions about how one reaches a given conclusion, the problem often lies with one or both of the premises. And so it is in this case. The minor premise is especially suspect, as exegesis of these passages on their own terms seems to make certain. But there are flaws in the major premise as well, especially as to what one means by "agent of creation." Together these flaws make the whole argument tenuous—or at least so it seems to me. Here is another case where "it is very doubtful whether a set of weak arguments adds up to one powerful one."[9]

II. Another Look at the Pauline Texts

Instead of beginning with the major premise—as is normally done in the conventions of scholarship—I wish to begin the discussion with the minor premise, looking closely at the primary texts in 1 Corinthians and Colossians. The problem with starting with the role of Wisdom lies with the inherent danger (and, from my perspective, the fundamental error) of reading too much into Paul and, as is often the case, of not paying close enough attention to his own argumentation in context.[10] We begin, therefore, with the key text, 1 Cor 8:6, and its alleged support in 1:24, 30.

A. 1 Corinthians 8:6

At issue in this section of 1 Corinthians is an ongoing argument between Paul and the Corinthians over their insistence on the right to attend festive meals in pagan temples.[11] Apparently Paul has already forbidden such practice (5:9), but in their return letter, they have argued vigorously for their right (ἐξουσία) to continue attending (8:9). Their argument can be reconstructed with a measure of confidence from Paul's citations from their letter: "We all have knowledge" (8:1)[12] that "an idol has no reality" since "there is only one God" (v. 4); therefore since food is a matter of indifference to God (v. 8), it matters neither what we eat nor where we eat it (v. 10).

Paul's response to this specious reasoning is especially noteworthy. For even though he will eventually condemn their *theology*—as a radical misunderstanding of the demonic nature of idolatry (10:14–22)—he begins by appealing to the nature of Christian *love,* which should forbid their casual destruction of the faith of others (8:2–3, 9–13). But even at this early stage in the argument he offers a preliminary correction to their theology per se (vv. 5–6, in response to their basically correct assertions in v. 4). In doing so, he acknowledges the "subjective reality"[13] of idolatry in the form of the "gods many and lords many" of the Greco-Roman pantheon and the mystery cults (v. 5). But before spelling out in v. 7 the consequences for "weaker" believers, for whom the subjective reality of idolatry still outweighs the objective reality being denied by those "in the know," Paul does an even more remarkable thing: he insists that their understanding of the "one God" needs to be broadened to include Christ as well (v. 6); and he does so because, at the end of the day, the attitudes and actions of the "knowing ones" who assert their "rights" serve potentially to destroy the work of Christ in others (vv. 10–13).

Our interest lies in v. 6, where in nicely balanced clauses Paul affirms,[14]

(1) ἀλλ᾽ ἡμῖν	εἷς θεὸς	ὁ πατήρ,					
	ἐξ	οὗ	τὰ τάντα	καὶ	ἡμεῖς	εἰς	αὐτόν,
(2) καὶ	εἷς κύριος	Ἰησοῦς Χριστός,					
	δι᾽	οὗ	τὰ τάντα	καὶ	ἡμεῖς	δι᾽	αὐτοῦ,
(1) But for us	one God	the Father,					
	from	whom	all things	and	we	*for*	him,
(2) and	one Lord	Jesus Christ,					
	through	whom	all things	and	we	*through*	him.

This is clearly a Christian restatement of the Shema (Deut 6:4: "Hear, O Israel: The Lord our God, the Lord is one"), with *God* now referring to the Father and *Lord* referring to the Son.[15] Because Paul's interests here are pastoral, he identifies the "one Lord" as none other than the historical Jesus Christ, the one who died for all, especially those with a weak conscience (v. 11). Thus, over against the "gods many" of paganism, the Shema rightly asserts—as the Corinthians themselves have caught on—that there is only one God; and typical of Paul's Jewish monotheism, the one God stands over against all pagan deities at one crucial point: creation. Thus God the Father is ἐκ/εἰς (from/for) in relation to everything that exists; he is its source and goal (or purpose) of being, although the final phrase ("we for him"), noticeably Pauline, moves easily from creation to redemption, where God is the goal of his people in particular.[16]

The surprising moment comes in line 2. Over against the "lords many" of paganism, there is only *one* Lord, Jesus Christ, whose relation to creation is that of mediator. Thus the Father has created all things through the agency of the Son, who is also—and now Paul's second point is being established—the agent of their redemption ("and we through him"). The whole, therefore, typically for Paul, encloses the work of the Son within that of the Father; that is, the two διά phrases regarding the one Lord's role as agent of creation and redemption are (logically) framed by the ἐκ and εἰς phrases regarding the Father as the ultimate source and goal of all things—both creation and redemption.

For our present purposes, three additional things must be noted about this passage. First, although the *conceptual* frame for this construction can be found elsewhere in the NT,[17] there is nothing quite like this use of prepositional phrases apart from Paul himself. Indeed, the only other known use of this specific scheme of prepositions in all of ancient literature is in Rom 11:36, where the full phrase ἐξ αὐτοῦ καὶ δι᾽ αὐτοῦ καὶ εἰς αὐτὸν τὰ πάντα (from him and through him and for him [are] all things) appears in a doxology without this christological modification.[18] It is of significant theological interest that in the Romans doxology *God* is the one "through whom" are all things, while in Col 1:16 *Christ* is the one "for whom" are all things. As Richard Bauckham has recently argued in a slightly different way, this interchange of prepositions indicates full identity of Christ with God.[19] My point here is simply to note that this formulation is a uniquely Pauline construct in the NT and in Paul's Jewish heritage; furthermore, as we will note later, there is nothing even remotely like it in the Jewish Wisdom tradition.

Second, this assertion is striking because at one level it is unnecessary to the present argument, since nothing *christological* is at stake. That is, Paul is not trying to demonstrate Christ's creative agency here; he simply assumes it by assertion. Nonetheless, at a deeper level this is precisely the assertion that will make both the theological and ethical dimensions of the argument work. By naming Christ as the "one Lord" through whom both creation and redemption were effected, Paul not only broadens the Corinthians' narrow perspective on the Shema but at the same time anticipates the role Christ is to play in the argument that follows (esp. 8:11–12; 10:4, 9, 16–22),[20] where everything hinges on their ongoing relationship to Christ himself. What is important for our present purposes is (1) Paul's deliberate use of κύριος for Christ, language that in the Septuagint was substituted for the divine name of the one God; and (2) the *presuppositional* nature in these passages of the *historical person,* Jesus Christ, as preexistent and as the personal agent of creation itself. There is simply nothing like this to be found in Jewish Wisdom or anywhere else in Paul's heritage.

Third, there is nothing inherent in this passage nor in its surrounding context that would suggest that Jewish Wisdom lies behind Paul's formulation. At issue in the present context is behavior predicated on *gnosis*, not *sophia*. An insistence that Wisdom nonetheless lies behind Paul's formulation will have to remain in the category of scholarly discovery, not Pauline disclosure. And one should not expect a reader of Paul's text, including the Corinthians themselves, to catch such subtlety. This leads us directly to the texts that are understood to be presupposed in Paul's present formulation.

B. 1 Corinthians 1:24, 30

Those who read 8:6 as a Pauline construct based on personified Wisdom's role as "agent of creation" invariably turn to these two passages in the argument of 1 Cor 1:10–4:21, usually in terms like "at this point we need to recall that Paul in fact already explicitly identified Christ as God's Wisdom—in 1 Cor 1.24 and 30."[21] But such an understanding of 1:24 is highly questionable, especially if one reads the passage on its own terms, without a prior agenda.

It must be noted at the outset that it is especially doubtful whether *wisdom* is a truly Pauline word at all and whether, therefore, Paul ever thinks of Christ in terms of Jewish Wisdom.[22] The linguistic data tell much of the story: The noun σοφία and its cognate adjective σόφος occur 44 times in the Pauline corpus—twenty-eight in 1 Corinthians, twenty-six of these in chs. 1–3,[23] and most of them pejorative! Of the remaining seventeen, one occurs in a similarly pejorative way in 2 Cor 1:12, while ten occur in Colossians and Ephesians, where the "heady" nature of the false teaching being addressed again calls forth this language. This means that in the rest of the corpus this word group appears only five times, only one of which is the noun (Rom 11:33), where it echoes OT usage referring to God's attribute of wisdom. These statistics, therefore, not to mention the argument itself, indicate that wisdom is actually a Corinthian thing and that Paul is trying to counter it by appealing to God's foolishness[24] as evidence that the gospel that saved them is not to be confused with σοφία in any form![25]

Indeed, Paul's assertion of Christ as "God's power" and "God's wisdom" in 1:24 (note Paul's order) is not a christological pronouncement at all,[26] as though Paul were reflecting either a Dynamis or Sophia Christology.[27] Rather, he is taking the *Corinthians'* word, however they understood it, and demythologizing it by anchoring it firmly in history—in a crucified Messiah, God's "foolishness" and "weakness," whereby that same Messiah turned the tables on all human schemes and wisdom that try to "find out God." After all, the presenting statement in v. 18 makes clear that the issue is *salvation* through the *message of the cross,* which divides all humankind into those perishing and those being saved. For the former the cross is "folly and weakness." Paul now asserts that for "those who believe" the message of a crucified Messiah is the precise opposite: not "folly and weakness" but "power and wisdom." "Christ the power of God and the wisdom of God," therefore, is shorthand for "God's true power and wisdom, that belong to him alone, are to be found in the weakness and sheer folly of redeeming humankind by means of the cross," which by God's own design is intended to nullify the wisdom of the wise (hence the citation of Isa 29:14 in v. 19). If Jewish Wisdom were to lie behind this at all, the use of δύναμις and σοφία here would seem most likely to echo a passage like Job 12:13,[28] having to do with God's attributes of "power and wisdom." These divine attributes, Paul argues with the Corinthians, have been put on full display in the ultimate oxymoron of a "crucified Messiah."

This understanding is further confirmed by v. 30. Having reaffirmed that God has made Christ to be "wisdom for us," Paul immediately qualifies it in such a way that the Corinthians could not have imagined that he had personified Wisdom in mind. "Wisdom for us" is again clarified in terms of Christ's saving work—righteousness/justification, sanctification, and redemption,[29] three nouns that appear later as "saving verbs" (6:11) or as metaphor (6:20).

Finally, in 2:7 Paul argues again that wisdom can indeed be found in the gospel he preached; but it is a (formerly) "hidden wisdom" that is so contradictory to mere human wisdom it can only be known by the revelation of the Spirit (v. 10), which the whole context and v. 12 in particular (by use of χαρίζομαι) indicate is to be found in the cross. Again, if there is Jewish background to this idea at all, it is to be found in Jewish apocalyptic, not Jewish Wisdom.[30]

This means that when Paul refers to Christ in 8:6 as our "one Lord, Jesus Christ, through whom are all things and we through him," it is altogether unlikely that he now is thinking christologically of something that he historicized in 1:18–31. To argue so would require significant *linguistic and conceptual* evidence, which is exactly what is lacking in this passage. Conceptually,[31] God created all things not through Christ as Wisdom but through the one Lord whom the Corinthians know historically as Jesus the Christ. This seems to be made certain by the fact that the designation employed for the "one God" is *Father,* which implies not Wisdom Christology but the "Son of God" Christology that explicitly dominates the text to which we turn next. And linguistically, as we will note momentarily, there is not a single tie of any kind between Paul and the Jewish Wisdom texts.

C. Colossians 1:15–17

When we turn from 1 Corinthians to Colossians, we find very much the same thing. Here Paul refers to the preexistent *Son*[32] as the divine agent of creation in a deliberately programmatic way at the beginning of a letter[33] to a church where some false teaching has emerged with the damaging effect of diminishing both the person and work of Christ.[34] Thus a sentence that began as thanksgiving to God the Father for redemption in "his beloved Son" (vv. 12–14) now proceeds—in what appears to be a two-stanza hymn[35] (vv. 15–20)—to exalt the Son by picking up the two sides of his agency in creation and redemption expressed in creed-like fashion in 1 Cor 8:6. Our interest lies in the first strophe (vv. 15–17), which is a considerable elaboration on the δἰ οὗ τὰ πάντα of line 2 in 1 Cor 8:6.[36]

(a)	ὅς ἐστιν	εἰκὼν	τοῦ θεοῦ	τοῦ ἀοράτου,	
(a')		πρωτότοκος	πάσης κτίσεως,		
(b)	ὅτι	ἐν αὐτῷ	ἐκτίσθη	τὰ πάντα	
(b¹)					ἐν τοῖς οὐρανοῖς καὶ ἐπὶ τῆς γῆς,
(b²)					τὰ ὁρατὰ καὶ τὰ ἀόρατα,
(b³)					εἴτε θρόνοι εἴτε κυριότητες
(b⁴)					εἴτε ἀρχαὶ εἴτε ἐξουσίαι,
(b')	τὰ πάντα	δἰ αὐτοῦ καὶ εἰς αὐτὸν	ἔκτισται		
(c)	καὶ	αὐτός ἐστιν πρὸ πάντων			
(c')	καὶ	τὰ πάντα ἐν αὐτῷ συνέστηκεν			

The strophe is expressed in three pairs of parallels, with a considerable expansion of the first line of the second pair. Together these lines emphasize the Son's supremacy over the whole created order, especially over the powers. The first doublet affirms the two essential matters: the Son as the εἰκών (image) of the otherwise invisible God, thus using *Pauline* language to emphasize that the Father is revealed in the Son (cf. 2 Cor 4:4–6); and the Son as the πρωτότοκος of every created thing, which points to his holding the privileged position of "firstborn"—both heir and sovereign with regard to creation.

The ὅτι that begins the *b* lines, typical of many psalms, gives reasons for exulting in the one who is the "image" of God and holds primacy over creation. The two lines are synonymous and together emphasize that "all things" were created "in him," which is elaborated in the second line in terms of both "through him" and "for him." Line *b'* begins as a direct echo of 1 Cor 8:6; its second half, however, now asserts that God's "firstborn" Son is also the *goal* of creation, the one for whom all creation exists and toward whom it points. Thus two (διά, εἰς) of the three all-encompassing prepositions in Rom 11:36 are found here and attributed to the Son. The ἐκ, which belongs to the Father alone, is conceptually present in the divine passive (ἐκτίσθη, were created), but even that is moderated (remarkably so) by the assertion that all things were created *in him* (i.e., in the Son).

Finally, line *c* reemphasizes what was implied in lines *a'*, *b*, and *b'*: that the Son *is*—not was—*before* all things, where the Greek preposition bears the same ambiguity (temporal and spatial) found in the English word *before*, thus emphasizing both his existence prior to the created order and his having the position of primacy over it because he is the agent of its existence. In the final line *(c')* his role as the preexistent creator of all things is furthered by emphasizing that they are currently "held together" in and through him.

The linguistic ties between this passage and 1 Cor 8:6, not to mention 2 Cor 4:4, suggest that the same christological point of view lies behind both of them, especially so since the next stanza (vv. 18–20) spells out in similar detail the καὶ ἡμεῖς δι' αὐτοῦ (and we through him) of the earlier passage. The Colossians passage simply spells out in greater detail what is already presupposed in 1 Corinthians.

But here in particular, Dunn has argued for "a sequence of correlation [between Paul and personified Wisdom that] can hardly be a matter of coincidence." Indeed, he asserts that Paul's language in this passage (and in 1 Cor 8:6) offers "classic expressions of Wisdom christology."[37] But despite this assertion, there is an almost complete lack of both linguistic and conceptual ties to this tradition. Dunn's "sequence of correlation" consists of basically five points (including Christ's role in creation, the controversial point that will be picked up in the next section). Let me first address the other four:

1. Dunn points out that the same term "image [εἰκών]" is used of both personified Wisdom (Wis 7:26)[38] and of Christ (Col 1:15). Indeed, C. K. Barrett makes bold to say that "*image* is a word that belongs to the Wisdom literature"; he then cites Wis 7:26 as evidence.[39] But this is a plain overstatement of the case, since this use in Ps-Solomon is in fact the *only* occurrence of the word with this sense in the literature.[40] Furthermore, Paul and Ps-Solomon scarcely reflect truly parallel uses of language; for personified Wisdom is not "the εἰκών of *God*," but is merely "an image of his *goodness*" (εἰκὼν τῆς ἀγαθοτήτος αὐτοῦ), one of the clear concerns of this author. Paul, on the other hand, is intending something very much like what he says in 2 Cor 4:4–6: that God is now to be known not through personified Wisdom but in his beloved Son (Col 1:13), who alone bears the true image of the Father to whom Paul has been giving thanks (v. 12).

2. Wisdom is further alleged to be called "God's 'firstborn' in creation." But this is quite misleading, since Paul's word (πρωτότοκος) does not occur at all in the Wisdom tradition—at least not in Paul's sense.[41] Not only do the texts brought forward (Prov 8:22, 25) have totally different words in the LXX, but also their point (the fact that Wisdom is the first of God's "creations" so that she might be present to frolic as he creates all else) is something radically different from Paul's use of πρωτότοκος here, where Christ *as Son* holds the rights of primogeniture with regard to every created thing, since they were all created *through* him and *for* him.

3. It is further argued that when Sir 1:4 speaks of Wisdom as "before all things," this correlates with what Paul says here of the Son. But this is particularly dubious, since Sirach's phrase has an altogether different word and he means something almost the opposite of Paul. Sirach says that "Wisdom was *created* before all things [προτέρα πάντων]," which Skehan and Di Lella (correctly) translate "before all things else."[42] Paul, on the other hand, says that the Son ἐστιν πρὸ πάντων (*is* before all things), by which he means that the Son through whom all things were created *is* "before them" both by virtue of his preexistence temporally as well as by his primacy of rank. Therefore this is not a correspondence of any kind.

4. Finally, Paul's assertion that "in him [the Son] all things hold together [συνέστηκεν]" is alleged to correspond to Wis 1:6–7, where the author refers to "*that which* holds all things together [τὸ συνέχον]," referring in this case specifically to the Spirit of the Lord. This one is a bit tricky, since it is related to a very complex issue regarding the translation of v. 6: When Ps-Solomon says that "wisdom is a kindly spirit," does the author mean to equate a personified Wisdom with the Spirit of the Lord, or (which seems far more likely) does he refer to the "spiritual" quality of wisdom? In any case, he does not in fact say that "Wisdom holds all things together";[43] rather he says it is the Spirit who does.

These various strands of a questionable use of parallels, therefore, hardly constitute the kind of "sequence of correlation" asserted by Dunn. Indeed, there are no certain linguistic ties in the Colossian passage with the Wisdom literature at all, certainly not of a kind to allow the use of such a term as Wisdom Christology.[44] What Paul's sentences point to instead is a Son of God Christology, which may have some distant echoes conceptually to things said about Wisdom in the earlier literature, but even this is doubtful. A case of clear *literary* or *conceptual* dependence of Paul on this literature needs to be demonstrated for us to entertain the idea of a Wisdom Christology in Paul. So we turn next to these texts themselves to see whether they actually posit personified Wisdom as the agent of creation, which is the sticking point.

III. Is Wisdom the Agent of Creation?

When one turns from Paul to examine the Wisdom tradition itself more closely (the major premise), one is surprised to find how much mileage is made on what appears to be far more vapor than petrol. At issue first is whether, by the various personifications of Wisdom found in Prov 8:22–31, Sir 24:3–12, and Wis 6:1–10:21, their authors have a divine hypostasis in view—that is, an actual divine (or quasidivine) being who exists alongside (or in relationship with) God in some unique way.[45] Or are these merely literary moments in which the feminine nouns *(ḥokmâ, sophia)* are made powerfully present through means of the literary device of personification? The significance of this is, as Dunn's own work demonstrates, that one may draw quite different conclusions if Wisdom is more a literary device than a divine hypostasis.

Although there has been considerable debate on this matter, the consensus of those who have worked closely with these texts—without our agenda in view—is that in Proverbs and Ben Sirach, we are dealing with a literary device, pure and simple.[46] On the other hand, the personification of Wisdom in Ps-Solomon seems to move much more toward some kind of hypostasis, so that the consensus here is to be found in the following oft-quoted definition: "a quasi-personification of certain attributes proper to God, occupying an intermediate position between personalities and abstract beings."[47] The nature of this "intermediate position," however, is taken by scholars each in their own way, depending on the degree to which they perceive the author to regard Wisdom as both personified and separate from her originator.[48] The point to make here is that if Paul were in fact dependent on this tradition, which seems doubtful at best, it is not at all clear that he would have understood Wisdom in terms of *personal preexistence in the same way that he so considered Christ.*[49]

At issue finally in this discussion is the relationship of Wisdom to creation.

And it is crucial here to note again that, despite some attempts at finding other echoes of Wisdom in Paul, this is the one point at which the whole enterprise seems to have found its origins and continues to find support in the literature. Thus it is to these texts in particular that we now turn.

I begin by noting that, in contrast to repeated assertions to the contrary, it is doubtful whether anywhere in the tradition it is explicitly stated that personified Wisdom was the *mediating agent* of creation. In none of the passages brought forward to defend such a view does one find language similar to that found in Paul; that is, these authors do not come close to saying that God created τὰ πάντα διὰ σοφίας (all things through Wisdom).[50] Rather, Wisdom is personified as present in another sense, namely as the attribute of God that is manifest through the masterful design exhibited in creation.

A. Psalm 104:24

This way of speaking about creation finds its first expression in the exalted poetry of Ps 104:24 (LXX 103:24). After reflecting on the heavens, the earth, the living creatures on the earth, the sun, and the moon, the author bursts forth, "How many are your works, O Lord! In wisdom you made them all." Wisdom here is "neither instrument nor agent but the attribute displayed by Yahweh in creating."[51] My contention in what follows is that all of our subsequent authors are guided by this same theology, so that even when they express in a heightened personified way Wisdom's presence with Yahweh at creation, she as such is never the *agent* but instead the attribute made manifest in God's own creative work. Nor is it likely that Paul would himself have understood such language in terms of personal agency, so it would never have occurred to him to identify the historical, now exalted *kyrios,* Jesus Christ, with a mere literary personification.

B. Proverbs 8:22–31

This literary interpretation of wisdom is most evident in Prov 8, the passage from which all others take their lead. For example, Prov 3:19 affirms that "in wisdom the Lord laid the earth's foundations"; that this does not mean Wisdom personified is made plain by the rest of the quatrain: "by understanding he set the heavens in place; by his knowledge the deeps were divided, and the clouds let drop the dew." When Wisdom is later personified in a literary way in the marvelous poetry of 8:22–31,[52] she is pictured as *present* at creation, precisely because of what is said in 3:19, but not as its mediator: "I was there when [God] set the heavens in place, when he marked out the horizon on the face of the deep" (8:27). Thus Prov 8:22–26 asserts in a variety of ways that Wisdom was the first of God's creation, emphasizing her priority in time, so that her being *present* with God when he alone created the universe would thus reflect—as it actually does—God's wise blueprint. This, then, is the point picked up in vv. 27–31, which further depict Wisdom as present at creation, again in the sense of 3:19.

Those who think otherwise find their hope in the ambiguous Hebrew term ʾāmōn in v. 30, which is assumed to lie behind the Greek τεχνῖτις/τεχνίτης (fashioner, designer) in Wis 7:21 (7:22 NRSV); 8:6; 14:2, which meaning is then read back into the Hebrew of Proverbs. In another context the author's poetry might be stretched to mean "that [he] sees Wisdom as pre-existing and probably as having an active role in the work of creation."[53] But this assumes a more hypostatic view of Wisdom than can be demonstrated in Proverbs, not to mention that it fails to take the point of the poetry seriously in the context of Prov 8 itself. To be sure, Wisdom is the "master worker" at God's side, but she is not the *mediator* through whom creation came into being. Rather, to our author the whole created order is so full of evidences of design and glory that God's wisdom, now personified in a literary way, can be the only possible explanation for it. It needs only to be pointed out that this falls considerably short of Paul's understanding of Christ's role in creation.

C. Sirach 24:1–22

The next appearance of these ideas is in "The Praise of Wisdom" in Sir 24:1–22. While creating his own (equally magnificent) poem, Sirach at the same time remains absolutely faithful to the understanding of his predecessor in Proverbs, on whom he is obviously dependent. For Sirach, who delights in the literary personification of Wisdom, God alone is nonetheless the sole Creator of all things, including Wisdom herself ("Before the ages, from the beginning, he created me," 24:9 [ἀπ' ἀρχῆς ἔκτισέν με]; cf. v. 8, "my Creator").

Those who find preexistent, personified Wisdom as having a role in creation appeal to v. 3 ("I came forth from the mouth of the Most High, and covered the earth like a mist," NRSV).[54] But that is surely to come to the text with an agenda in hand, not to read it on its own terms.[55] This passage reflects Sirach's view that Wisdom is there "before the ages," since "from the first, he created [Wisdom]" (24:9), and it is Sirach's own interpretation of "the Spirit of God . . . hovering over the waters" in Gen 1:2. His referent is not to her creative agency but to her having "sought a resting place" (v. 5), which took place historically *not* in creation but in her presence with Israel in the exodus!

D. Wisdom of Solomon 6:1–9:18

That brings us, then, to the Wisdom of Solomon, which by everyone's reckoning has the crucial texts (found in the adulation of and prayer for wisdom in 6:1–9:18).[56] But here especially one needs to read what the author says in the context of the entire poetic narrative. Ps-Solomon's concern seems ultimately to be semi-apologetic (both toward the Greeks as well as for the Jewish community's encouragement), since the opening section (1:1–6:11), allegedly written by one who is himself a king, is framed by appeals to "the rulers of the earth," variously called "kings" or "despots." This opening appeal also sets forth his basic agenda: that "living well" (doing justly and living righteously) is rewarded by immortality, whereas death awaits those who are evil. The way one lives well in this sense is to emulate Solomon and his own request for wisdom, a theme that is taken up in the crucial central section of the narrative (6:1–9:18; "If you delight in thrones and scepters, O monarchs over the peoples, honor wisdom, so that you may reign forever," 6:21 NRSV),[57] where "Solomon" sets out "to tell you [the monarchs] what wisdom is and how she came to be" (6:22 NRSV).

One can easily trace the author's progression of thought in this central section. He begins with Solomon's adulation of (now personified) Wisdom (6:12–21), which he proposes to describe (vv. 22–25). But before doing so the author reminds his readers of Solomon's ordinary humanity (7:1–6) and also of the great things that happened to him when he received wisdom (vv. 7–21), the secret to which he now hopes to "pass on liberally" (v. 13 NJB). That leads to his "eulogy of Wisdom" (7:22–8:1), which the NJB note describes as "the peak of OT writings on Wisdom." Because of Wisdom's undoubted greatness—both for understanding and uprightness, which alone leads to immortality—the author returns to Solomon's own love for Wisdom (8:2–18), who knows that he could never have it unless it be given by God (vv. 19–21). Thus this author's own version of "In Praise of Wisdom" concludes with Solomon's prayer for Wisdom (9:1–18).

The rest of the narrative is an intriguing mixture of reflection on God's goodness to Israel in its history—especially in the exodus, with several antitheses between this goodness received and its opposites that befell Israel's opponents. What is fascinating structurally is that this narrative begins with Wisdom playing the leading role (10:1–11:3), from Adam (10:1–2) to the exodus (10:15–11:3). But after the first antithesis—a contrast between Israel's gift of water from the rock and the water that punished their enemies (11:4–14)—the rest of the poetry takes the form of personal address to God, while Wisdom fades altogether from view (except for a cameo appearance as the "artisan" of boats in 14:2, 5).[58] It is in this last section in particular, all of it addressed to God and quite apart from reference to wisdom of any kind, that the author's "theology" in true Jewish fashion emerges over and again: namely, that it is their God who is the sole Creator and Ruler of all that is (11:17, 24–25; 13:3–5; 16:24).

My reason for rehearsing this narrative and its structure is that it must affect the way one reads the eulogy of Wisdom in the brief central section. Our author's concern with wisdom is not theological per se but practical and ethical. Only by having wisdom will rulers rule well, and only by having wisdom will people live well. This concern leads to his expansive praise of Wisdom and her "works." At issue is whether agency in the original creation of the world is seen by the author as part of these works. As indicated, and quite in keeping with the traditions to which he is indebted and despite his enthusiasm for Wisdom's greatness, he sees Wisdom as only *present* at creation, not as its divine agent.

This comes out especially in the crucial texts in 9:1–2, 9, at the beginning of Solomon's prayer. Precisely because he is now praying for Wisdom—not describing her—and thus addressing God in the second person, he says of God, "you who have made all things by your word [τὰ πάντα ἐν λόγῳ σου]," thus reflecting the Genesis narrative by way of the loaded Greek term *logos,* while adding in the parallel, "and by your wisdom [τῇ σοφίᾳ σου] have formed humankind to have dominion over the creatures you have made." This is so obviously not a personification, either of a divine *logos* or divine *sophia,* that even the NJB with its bias toward personified Wisdom translates these in the lowercase. The only way one can find hypostatic Wisdom as the agent of creation in this passage is by bringing to the text a prior disposition to do so and by misreading the parallelism so as to make *logos* and *sophia* interchangeable. Our author's obvious concern is not with Wisdom's role in creation as such but with her role in God's "equipping or constructing" (κατασκευάζας) human beings for their life in the world that God created by his word. And because the world is so wondrously arrayed by the God who created it, he goes on to add in v. 9 (NRSV), "With you is wisdom, she who knows your works and was present when you made the world." This is a straightforward reflection of Prov 8:27–31.

This is precisely the role Wisdom plays in the other texts brought forward to support her agency in creation, where the author says of her, for example, that she is "the fashioner [τεχνῖτις] of all things" 7:21 (7:22 NRSV), which in context has nothing to do with creating as such but with the design of the world as it exists (including the elements, the cycles of nature, the natures of animals and of human beings). So also in 7:24, where Wisdom is said to "pervade and penetrate all things," Ps-Solomon is not at all interested in her *creative* role but in her obvious place in the world as he knows it—a world created by the God whose attribute is wisdom. This is also the case, finally, in 8:4–7, where Solomon expresses his desire for Wisdom. Why? Because evidence of her "work is everywhere," be it in wealth (v. 5), intellect (v. 6), or uprightness (v. 7). That she is described in the present tense in v. 6 as "the fashioner of what exists" is not a theological statement about original creation; it is a typical personification of her role in making the present world work well.

E. Conclusion

Where, then, does this overview of the texts from the Wisdom literature leave us?

Hardly with the kind of statements on which Paul could have built his theology of Christ's preexistence. It is never quite certain even in Ps-Solomon that the author thought of Wisdom as a hypostasis with existence and being apart from God; nor do the texts themselves ever explicitly spell out a *mediating* role for her in creation. And what is most lacking in all of this material is a verbal or conceptual linkage between Wisdom and creation of the kind explicitly found in Paul with reference to Christ. On the contrary, Wisdom is regularly referred to as "created" before all other things (Prov 8:22; Sir 24:9), a motif never applied to Christ. Instead, in keeping with the Genesis narrative—and its later echoes in the OT[59]—God created by *speaking* "all things" into existence (or by fashioning everything with "his hands"). Wisdom is present only because creation so obviously proclaims God's wisdom in design and sustenance.

When we return to 1 Cor 8:6 from this material, what we see is not similarity but contrast. Paul asserts that along with the one θεός, "the Father," there is an (uncreated) one κύριος, who is distinguished in *strictly personal terms based on his incarnation in human history* as "Jesus the Christ." Thus Paul does not understand Christ as agent of creation in some nebulous way akin to Wisdom's presence with God at creation; rather it is Jesus Christ, the Son of God himself, who is not simply present at creation but the actual agent of creation. "All things" came to be "through him." This understanding is made certain by the fact that in the final phrase about the "one Lord" (καὶ ἡμεῖς δι' αὐτοῦ), Paul uses the same preposition to refer to Christ's historical work of redemption.[60] Nothing like this is even hinted at in the Wisdom literature.

I realize that some might see this exercise as undercutting the concept of preexistence in Paul's view of Christ.[61] But not so; my point is first of all a purely academic one, to call into question personified Wisdom as the *source* of Paul's understanding and thus to challenge the use of terms like *transferring, adopting,* and *adapting* as being applied to Wisdom when referring to Paul's christology because of the highly suspect nature of the data themselves. Second, I want to point out that the use of Wisdom to diminish the aspect of preexistence in Paul's theology (cf. Dunn) is equally suspect. Wisdom is of virtually no—or very little—help in understanding Paul's view of the preexistent Christ; and if hypostatic Wisdom must be barred from the front door, it does no good to bring a diminished view of preexistent Wisdom in through the back door, as Dunn and others try to do.[62]

IV. Some Concluding Observations about Method

If my reading of these texts is close to what both Paul and the Wisdom writers intended, then the question remains, Why have so many read these texts in a different way? The possibility remains, of course, that my reading is simply a poor one. But another very real possibility is that scholarship at this point was driven by a need to discover the *origins* of Paul's high christology. The way forward seemed to be the "discovery" that personified Wisdom played a similar role to Christ's in Paul's own Jewish heritage, so the transfer of ideas from Wisdom to Christ was an easy, natural one.

But that raises for me several questions about method. My first concern arises out of the fact that one cannot find elsewhere in Paul a single trace of influence from Wisdom, neither in his theology in general[63] nor in his christology in particular. That is, how at the end of the day does the term Wisdom Christology fit Paul at all, if this very questionable "correspondence" is the only significant christological relationship between Paul and the Wisdom tradition? It is true, of course, that Paul is quite ready to use texts from this tradition where they support his own theology, especially those passages that display the folly of human beings trying to "match wits" with God. This is how he cites Job, for example, in the two certain citations of this book—in 1 Cor 3:19 (of Job 5:13) and Rom 11:35 (of Job 41:3)—whereas his only citation of Proverbs (22:8 in 2 Cor 9:7) is precisely as one might expect: to reinforce a very practical expression of Christ's love.

But at issue here is the use of the term Wisdom Christology, when in fact these texts say any number of things about Wisdom not found in Paul's language or patterns of thought. Paul, on the other hand, says a great deal more about Christ, both his person and work, that has no connection—or at least no perceptible one—with anything that is said of Wisdom. I would think that this fact alone would cause the New Testament guild to back away from such language and use more modest terms.

The greater methodological issue, of course, has to do with what Samuel Sandmel some years ago caricatured as "parallelomania," which (in my terms) is a tendency to turn every *linguistic* correspondence between a Jewish or hellenistic document and Paul's writings into a *conceptual* parallel and every alleged "parallel" into an "influence" or "borrowing." In this case the issue is slightly different, since *linguistic* parallels of any useful kind are lacking. The methodological concern, therefore, has to do with how one goes about establishing *conceptual* parallels in such a case.

Here in particular is where Paul's use of the OT should perhaps play a role in one's method, since Paul uses these documents in at least three ways: *(a)* by direct citation, *(b)* by clear allusion, and *(c)* by intertextual echo. Direct citation is easy enough; and it must be noted here again that Paul does not cite either Sirach or the Wisdom of Solomon, and when he cites Proverbs, it is for purposes other than christological ones. Clear allusion is also easy to see, such as in the argument of 1 Cor 10:1–13, where what happened to "our fathers" serves as warning to the Corinthians not to test Christ by idolatrous practices as some of them did, who then fell in the desert.

On the other hand, the identification of "intertextual echo" is much less certain. Richard Hays and I, for example, find Paul's use in Phil 1:19 of the exact language from the LXX of Job 16:13 and the similar kinds of historical settings of Phillipians and Job to be compelling reasons for interpreting Paul in light of Job.[64] Others however are less sure here. I find the same kind of phenomena to be present in Phil 2:15–16, which has a series of linguistic echoes from the Pentateuch with reference to the story of Israel. Similarly, the debate over whether "all his holy ones" who accompany Christ's Parousia in 1 Thess 3:13 refers to angels or the Christian dead seems to me to be settled conclusively by the specific echo of the language of Zech 14:5 (LXX) in a similar apocalyptic context.

But what about echoes or allusions where there is no linguistic correspondence at all, as is the case in the present matter? This is not to say that conceptual allusions may not exist in Paul's use of the OT. Take, for example, the possibility that there is a conceptual allusion to Adam in the description of Christ in Phil 2:6. I am less enamored with this option than many others are; but I am open to the possibility precisely because one can imagine that those who know the biblical story well—as Paul's readers in this case would—might hear such an echo even if Paul did not intend such himself.[65] But that kind of possible allusion to a well-known biblical narrative is the very thing lacking in this case.[66] That is, the biblical narrative of creation itself does not make reference to wisdom at all, and when later writers bring that concept in, they do so in such a way that is not central to their concerns. This is where the issue of "what one is looking for" comes into the methodological discussion. Those who find Wisdom behind 1 Cor 8:6 in particular, and somewhat less so in Col 1:15–17, are not reading Paul on his own terms, it would seem; instead, they are especially interested in the question of where this idea came from. When one starts with that kind of question, one is far more apt to find what one is looking for than otherwise.

All of this is to say, finally, that the most fruitful way to approach the question of origins almost certainly does not lie with such nebulous findings based on a questionable methodology. More likely it lies with Paul's *kyrios* Christology, which is not only firmly established in Paul himself, but also provides the key to much of his christology. Preexistence in Paul is an easy step back in time, if you will, from Christ's having been exalted to God's right hand, thus fulfilling Ps 110:1 (see esp. Rom 8:34),[67] as well as Christ's assuming Yahweh's role in all kinds of OT texts and phrases through the title "Lord." Here, at least, one is on *terra firma* with regard to Paul's own use of texts and allusions.

But that is for another essay. For now I trust that my friend and colleague, Bruce, will find these ruminations worthy of further reflection.

Notes

I am pleased to offer these musings in honor of my dear friend and colleague, Bruce Waltke, with whom I have team-taught both biblical exegesis and biblical theology for the past decade. Bruce is a man of great integrity and personal piety, whom students and colleagues alike have learned to treasure. My wife Maudine and I have especially enjoyed the friendship of Bruce and his wife Elaine over these years, one of the highlights of which has been regular evenings out for dinner and a concert by the Vancouver Symphony. Without his knowing what I was about, I was able to discuss the basic concerns of this essay with Bruce and found him to have the same reservations about personified Wisdom that I have carried for many years; so it is appropriate that I should offer this study in his honor.

[1] Especially in Hans Windisch, "Die göttliche Weisheit der Jüden und die paulinische Christologie," in *Neutestamentliche Studien für Georg Heinrici* (ed. H. Windisch; Leipzig: J. D. Hinrichs, 1914), 220–34. For a convenient overview of this history see E. J. Schnabel, *Law and Wisdom from Ben Sira to Paul: A Tradition History Enquiry into the Relation of Law, Wisdom, and Ethics* (WUNT 2/16; Tübingen: J. C. B. Mohr [Siebeck], 1985), 236–63. For a brief, helpful overview see E. Elizabeth Johnson, "Wisdom and Apocalyptic in Paul," in *In Search of Wisdom: Essays in Memory of John C. Gammie* (ed. L. G. Perdue et al.; Louisville: Westminster John Knox, 1993), 263–83.

[2] See C. H. Dodd, "The History and Doctrine of the Apostolic Age," in *A Companion to the Bible* (ed. T. W. Manson; Edinburgh: T&T Clark, 1947), 390–417. Dodd broaches the subject with due caution: "It seems probable also, though the proof is not complete, that some teachers, independently of Paul, had associated [Christ's] authority as the revealer of God with the OT idea of the divine Wisdom" (409). But then he cites 1 Cor 1:24 quite out of context to the effect that Paul considered Christ to be the Wisdom of God. He finally asserts, without giving the evidence, that "in Col 1:15–19, without mentioning the word 'wisdom,' he [Paul] uses language which can be traced *in every point* (except the one word 'fullness') to Jewish Wisdom theology" (italics mine). Nonetheless, when starting his next paragraph, Dodd is content to put the term in quotes ("This 'Wisdom-Christology' made it possible for Paul to give a more adequate account of what was meant by calling Christ the Son of God"). I have not found an earlier use, but further research is needed.

[3] J. D. G. Dunn, *The Theology of Paul the Apostle* (Grand Rapids: Eerdmans, 1998), 266–81. Cf. his earlier *Christology in the Making* (Philadelphia: Westminster, 1980), 176–96.

[4] How to capitalize *wisdom* in this study is problematic. I have capitalized it when referring to the Jewish sapiential tradition and, following the lead of the NJB, when I intend its personification; it is lowercase when it refers simply to an attribute of God or when it is used synonymously with understanding or knowledge. I refer to the deuterocanonical Wisdom of Solomon as Ps-Solomon except when the reference is followed by chapter and verse numbers (e.g., Wis 1:6), for the sake of clearer distinctions between the book and the concept.

[5] It is of some interest at this point to note that Dunn uses Wisdom Christology in order to diminish the concept of *personal* preexistence in Paul. See, e.g., on 1 Cor 8:6: "Is there then a thought of pre-existence in 1 Cor. 8.6 . . . ? Of course there is. But it is the pre-existence of divine Wisdom. That is, the pre-existence of God. . . . Whether the subtlety of the theology is best expressed as 'the pre-existence of Christ' *simpliciter* is another question" (*Theology*, 274–75).

On the other side—and the list is long here—are those who find in Wisdom Christology support for a more traditional understanding of preexistence in Paul; see *inter alios* M. Hengel, "Jesus as Messianic Teacher of Wisdom and the Beginnings of Christology," in *Studies in Early Christology* (Edinburgh: T&T Clark, 1995), 95–117; Hengel, *The Son of God* (Philadelphia: Fortress, 1976), 48–51; S. Kim, *The Origin of Paul's Gospel* (WUNT 2/4; Tübingen: J.C.B. Mohr [Paul Siebeck], 1981), 114–23; Ben Witherington III, *Jesus the Sage: The Pilgrimage of Wisdom* (Minneapolis: Fortress, 1994), 295–333; E. J. Schnabel, "Wisdom," in *DPL*, 967–71.

It has also become an especially crucial construct in the Roman Catholic feminist theology of Elizabeth A. Johnson (see "Jesus, the Wisdom of God: A Biblical Basis for Non-Androcentric Christology," *ETL* 61 [1985]: 261–94 [esp. 276–89]).

[6] The citation is from A. M. Hunter, *The Gospel According to St. Paul* (Philadelphia: Westminster, 1966), 68, and is used here because of its brevity and clarity. But whether in brief or at length, this encapsulates the position held by a large number of scholars who have either written on the subject or who are (as is Hunter here) dependent on those who have.

[7] They are also discussed in the essay in this volume by Karen Jobes, who was kind enough to let me read her paper when I was at the beginning of my research for an examination of the concept of incarnation and preexistence in Paul presented at the Incarnation Summit, Dumwoodie, N.Y., at Easter 2000, and to be published with the other papers under an Oxford University Press title. While working on that paper, I experienced dis-ease over the matter at hand and included my reservations as part of that presentation. Although these studies have

quite different concerns, in both cases I go over much of the same exegetical ground, so that there is some repetition (and reproduction) in the two exegetical sections of the two papers—after all, I have scarcely changed my mind on these matters over the six-month period between working on the two essays!

[8] By imposing a logical syllogism on the discussion, I do not mean to caricature those with whom I differ. In fact, I have gone over the arguments several times with painstaking care to make sure that this proposed syllogism fairly represents the actual "steps" in the argumentation. See Dunn, e.g., who begins his argument (*Theology,* 267–69) with a brief look at the two key Pauline texts (1 Cor 8:6; Col 1:15–20); he then turns to examine personified Wisdom in the Jewish Wisdom texts (ibid., 269–72), stating unequivocally, "Clearly, then, Paul was attributing to *Christ* the role previously attributed to divine Wisdom" (270). I doubt whether this is clear at all (see sec. II.B).

[9] See I. H. Marshall, *1 and 2 Thessalonians* (NCB; Grand Rapids: Eerdmans, 1983), 35, about Trilling's arguments for the inauthenticity of 2 Thessalonians.

[10] See also N. T. Wright, "Poetry and Theology in Colossians 1.15–20," *NTS* 36 (1990): 445–58 [452]. Although his concern is slightly different, he questions whether starting with Wisdom is the best procedure.

[11] For the full argumentation in support of this perspective see Gordon D. Fee, "Εἰδωλόθυτα Once Again: An Interpretation of 1 Corinthians 8–10," *Bib* 61 (1980): 172–97; cf. Fee, *The First Epistle to the Corinthians* (NICNT; Grand Rapids: Eerdmans, 1987), 357–63. The objection to this point of view presented by Bruce Fisk ("Eating Meat Offered to Idols: Corinthian Behavior and Pauline Response in 1 Corinthians 8–10," *TJ* 10 [1989]: 49–70) is flawed at several key points in both his lexical analysis and his theological presuppositions about Corinth and Paul, which will be pointed out in a forthcoming publication.

[12] There is every good reason to believe that the Corinthians came to this view of *knowledge*, as they did of *wisdom* in 1:10–4:21, by way of their experience of the Spirit, since these two are the first items Paul picks up in his listing of Spirit manifestations in 12:8. In fact, chs. 1–4, 8–10, and 12–14 constitute the three largest blocks of argumentation in this letter, and in each case a part of Paul's argument with the Corinthians takes the form, "If anyone thinks that he/she . . ." ("is wise" 3:18; "has knowledge" 8:2; "is spiritual" 14:37). See Fee, *Corinthians*, 10–15.

[13] This is my own term for the nature of Paul's argumentation. In 10:14–22 he asserts, in effect, that despite "idols being nothing," they nonetheless have an

objective reality as the habitation of demons. In the present argument (ch. 8), besides v. 5 where he affirms that for pagans there are "gods many and lords many," he acknowledges in v. 7 that some with weak consciences do not have the "knowledge" of the others. This surely does not mean that they did not understand the truth that God is one and therefore that idols have no reality as gods; rather, because they had long attributed reality to the idols, when the "weak" became believers they were unable to shake themselves free from these former associations with pagan worship—which is why it would be so deadly for them to return to the temples for festive meals that honored a "god" (vv. 11–12).

[14] Translations throughout are my own, unless otherwise noted.

[15] To be sure, Paul does not here use "son" language in referring to Christ. But since he has just referred to God as Father, this is one of those certain places where Paul's presuppositions allow us to identify Christ as Son, just as he assumes God as Father when he speaks only of the Son. The evidence for this is writ large in his letters; in the present letter, see 1:3, 9, where in v. 3 "God" is "our Father," while in v. 9 the God who has already been so designated has called believers "into fellowship with his Son, Jesus Christ." Only sophistry of the worst kind would deny the same relationship being in view in 8:6 simply because Paul does not use "son" language. Of the large literature on this matter, see esp. Larry W. Hurtado, "Son of God," in *DPL,* 900–906; cf. Hurtado, "Jesus' Divine Sonship in Paul's Epistle to the Romans," in *Romans and the People of God* (ed. Sven K. Soderlund and N. T. Wright; Grand Rapids: Eerdmans, 1999), 217–33.

[16] Because of this, and because he is enamored with the text as a pre-Pauline creed, K.-J. Kuschel, in his *Born before All Time? The Dispute over Christ's Origin* (trans. J. Bowden; London: SCM Press, 1992), 285–91, argues that this passage has to do only with soteriology (as did J. Murphy-O'Connor before him; see "I Cor. VIII, 6: Cosmology or Soteriology?" *RB* 85 [1978]: 253–67). But that is to misread the passage in context; the analogy for Pauline usage here is Rom 11:36, not 2 Cor 5:18, as argued by Kuschel. What seems to make this creational reading of 8:6 certain is the identical use of τὰ πάντα δι᾽ αὐτοῦ in Col 1:16, which Kuschel gets around by denying Pauline authorship of Colossians (a circular argument that assumes what is questionable; see n. 33 below). Compare the critique in Dunn, *Theology,* 268 n. 5.

[17] Most notably Heb 1:1–2, where God has "appointed the Son" as "heir of all things, *through* whom also he made the universe."

[18] In Dunn's commentary on Romans (*Romans 9–16* [WBC 38B; Dallas: Word, 1988], 701), he notes that "the use of prepositions like [these three] when

speaking of God and the cosmos . . . was widespread in the ancient world and typically Stoic." But apart from the three Pauline texts (Rom 11:36; 1 Cor 8:6; Col 1:16–17) he lists only six others, none of which contains another instance of all three prepositions occurring together. In his *Theology* (269) Dunn has further suggested regarding one of the texts (Philo, *Cher.* 125–27) that it serves as an illustration of one who has made "a similar division in the 'by, from, and through' formulation, between the originating role of God . . . and the instrumental role of the Logos." While this is partly true, Philo's context and concerns are quite different from Paul's; and he does not come close to Paul's formulation as such. In fact, he would be mortified to think that Paul would use διά to refer to the "one Lord," since such a usage by Cain ("I have gotten a man through God") is to Philo an abomination ("even in these last two words he erred") and is the cause of the discussion that leads to the distinction between "by" (not "from") and "through."

[19] Richard Bauckham, *God Crucified: Monotheism and Christology in the New Testament* (Grand Rapids: Eerdmans, 1999), 37–40.

[20] It should be noted here that Dunn would have us see an allusion to Wis 11:4 (where Wisdom is associated with "the water [that] was given them out of the flinty rock") in the reference to Christ as the "spiritual rock" that "followed" Israel in the desert in 10:4. While one need not doubt the association with Wisdom in Ps-Solomon (see Wis 11:1), it is in fact at this point in the poetry that the author begins to address *God* (as the "you" makes plain; see esp. in context Wis 10:20 and 11:26). This author is simply too Jewish at the core for him to address Wisdom and say, "When they were thirsty, they called upon you [Wisdom], and water was given them. . . ." All such addresses in this book are toward God alone. Thus the role of Wisdom is left a bit ambiguous here, although it is likely that Wisdom is to be understood as the divine instrument behind the various favors from God in the desert. But this is a far cry from Paul's bald assertion that "the rock that followed them *was* Christ," where he is picking up a rabbinic tradition that had the rock accompanying Israel in the desert, since Moses struck it twice: once at the beginning of the wilderness experience (Exod 17:6) and once toward the end (Num 20:11). For details see Fee, *Corinthians*, 447–49.

[21] Dunn, *Theology*, 274. This is an invariable in all such discussions, because without it no one could possibly have seen "Wisdom" as lying behind 8:6. In fairness to Dunn, as over against many others, he at least recognizes that Paul turns divine wisdom into the proclamation of Christ crucified; but even so, he treats v. 24 altogether as a christological, rather than soteriological, statement.

[22] Contra Witherington, e.g., who (typical of many) is bold here: "[Paul]

saw Christ as Wisdom come in the flesh (cf. 1 Cor 1:24)." Ben Witherington III, "Christology," in *DPL*, 103.

[23] And the remaining two (6:5; 12:8) seem clearly to hark back to the issue raised here. In 6:5, the question "Can it be that there is no one *wise* enough to adjudicate between brothers?" is straight irony, predicated on the Corinthians' own position as it has emerged in chs. 1–3. In 12:8, in Paul's listing of Spirit manifestations in the community, he begins with the two that played high court in Corinth (λόγος σοφίας; λόγος γνώσεως) so as to recapture them for the vital life of the Spirit within the community ("for the common good," 12:7).

[24] His foolishness is seen, first, in his saving through a crucified Messiah (1:18–25); second, in his choosing the Corinthian "nobodies" to be among his new eschatological people (1:26–31); and third, in his calling them through Paul's preaching in personal weakness (2:1–5). For details see Fee, *Corinthians,* ad stet.

[25] In fact Paul asserts categorically that "in the wisdom of God" (as attribute) the world through wisdom (διὰ τῆς σοφίας) did not know God; it seems altogether unlikely that he would then turn about and say that Christ is Wisdom and, by implication, suggest that one can know God through Wisdom after all.

[26] That is, a pronouncement about Christ's *person* as over against his *work* (soteriology). I grant that in the final analysis one can scarcely do justice to Paul's theology if person and work are separated. But in the present case, the question is whether these statements are saying something fundamental about who Christ is or about what he accomplished on the cross. That is, in saying Christ is the "power of God," is this a christological referent about Christ's embodying God's power in his person, or is it a shorthand way of referring to the effectiveness of the cross as God's power for salvation to those who believe (v. 18)? The answer lies with the obvious point of the passage, which is to eliminate Corinthian boasting in wisdom altogether by pointing to Christ's humiliating *death* (not to Christ as embodying preexistent Wisdom) on a Roman gibbet as the ultimate expression of divine wisdom; and only the Spirit can reveal it as such.

[27] In fact (*pace* J. A. Davis, *Wisdom and Spirit: An Investigation of 1 Corinthians 1.18–3.20 against the Background of Jewish Sapiential Traditions in the Greco-Roman Period* [Lanham, Md.: University Press of America, 1984]), nothing in the argument suggests that those in Corinth enamored with "wisdom" had any interest at all in the Jewish Wisdom tradition, since the contrast "wisdom/folly" belongs on the Greek side of the equation, with "power/weakness" on the Jewish side, as vv. 20, 22–24 make plain.

[28] LXX παρ᾽ αὐτῷ σοφία καὶ δύναμις, αὐτῷ βουλὴ καὶ σύνεσις ("with him are wisdom and strength; he has counsel and understanding," NRSV). The significance of this text is not so much that Paul would be echoing it as that these two words occur together in an expression of Jewish Wisdom in which wisdom is not personified—very much the same way it is found in Prov 3:19–20 ("The Lord in wisdom laid the earth's foundations").

[29] Witherington (*Sage*, 310–11) tries to circumvent this by (1) making the ἐν Χριστῷ Ἰησοῦ instrumental (a possible but unusual sense for this phrase), (2) making the relative clause, toward which the whole sentence is pointing, parenthetical, and (3) thus turning the three nouns, which sit in apposition with σοφία, into predicate nouns with "you are." Thus, "But from God *you* are through Christ (who was made Wisdom for us by God), righteousness and sanctification and redemption" (both italics and comma in the original). Rather than the "natural sense of the grammar" as he asserts, this looks like a "translation" intended to get around the plain implications of the text.

[30] On this matter see Gordon D. Fee, *God's Empowering Presence: Holy Spirit in the Letters of Paul* (Peabody, Mass.: Hendrickson, 1994), 97–101, and especially the discussion of the relationship of Paul to the Wisdom of Solomon in the final chapter, "The Pauline Antecedents," 911–13.

[31] For the missing linguistic evidence, see the argument in section II.C.2 below.

[32] The contextual point that must be made here, and one that is seldom noted in the literature because of our fascination with the hymn as allegedly pre-Pauline, is that the *grammatical*—and therefore contextual—*antecedent* of all the pronouns, beginning with the relative pronoun in v. 14, is "God's beloved Son" at the end of v. 13. A new sentence does not begin until the final clause in v. 16; and even here all the pronouns that follow have "the beloved Son" as their antecedent. In fact, the term *Christ* does not occur in the entire passage (vv. 9–23) and does not emerge until v. 24, where Paul picks up on his own role as messenger of the gospel.

[33] I will not belabor here the historical difficulties I have with the rejection of the Pauline authorship of Colossians. One wonders how a pseudepigrapher would have had access only to the semiprivate letter to Philemon among the letters of Paul and used only its incidental data as the basis for a letter like this written in Paul's name. To accept Philemon as written by Paul and yet reject Colossians seems historically illogical. See further Fee, *Presence*, 636 n. 4.

[34] For a convincing presentation that the "false teaching" was a syncretism of

the gospel with folk religion (including magic and belief in intermediate beings), see C. E. Arnold, *The Colossian Syncretism: The Interface between Christianity and Folk Belief at Colossae* (Grand Rapids: Baker, 1996).

[35] But see Wright, "Poetry and Theology," who prefers to see it simply as a poem.

[36] While not all may agree with my structural arrangement, my concern here is simply to have a convenient display of the whole passage so as to comment briefly on its relevant parts.

[37] Dunn, *Theology*, 269; the whole of his presentation here rebutted appears in 268–70, concluding with "Clearly, then, Paul was attributing to *Christ* the role previously attributed to divine Wisdom." "Clear," it would seem, as with beauty, is surely in the eye of the beholder!

[38] In this and in the following cases, Dunn also draws on several references from Philo, assuming Philo to be representative of a Wisdom tradition similar to Ps-Solomon. But as noted below (n. 49), what appears to be the best reading of the evidence puts Ps-Solomon and Philo in Alexandria basically as contemporaries. Their relationship, therefore, is unlikely to be literary; it is rather the reflection of a common milieu. What cannot be demonstrated in any way is Pauline dependence on Philo. Nonetheless I shall also examine the Philo materials here, since the issue could be argued not in terms of direct dependency but of a point of view that is "in the air," as it were.

[39] C. K. Barrett, *Paul: An Introduction to His Thought* (Louisville: Westminster John Knox, 1994), 146–47.

[40] It is elsewhere found in Sir 17:3 and Wis 2:23 with direct reference to Gen 1:27, and in Ps-Solomon in several instances referring to idols (Wis 13:13, 16; 14:15, 17; 15:5) and once in a metaphorical way (17:21) referring to darkness.

[41] In fact the only other occurrences are in a textual variation of Sir 36:17 and as a plural in Wis 18:13 referring to the slaughter of Israel's firstborn. Dunn also gives two references to Philo as supporting this "parallel" (*Ebr.* 30–31; *QG* 4.97); but these are especially dubious. In the first instance Philo speaks of God's having union with knowledge, who "bore the only beloved son who is apprehended by the senses, the world which we see" (LCL 3.335); "knowledge" is then equated with wisdom, at which point Philo "cites" Prov 8:22 in his own way: "God obtained me first (πρωτίστην) of all his works." But that is not remotely related to Paul's use of πρωτότοκος, which has to do not with the Son's being created first but with his having the role of firstborn, heir, and sovereign over all creation. The other passage exists only in an Armenian translation, which has been

rendered in English as "And who is to be considered the daughter of God but Wisdom, who is the first-born mother of all things." It would be of great interest to see what Philo's Greek actually looked like in this instance. But in any case this helps very little, since the Wisdom literature itself does not use this language, and to argue for dependence of Paul on Philo is more than most would wish to do. What it does point out is that such a view existed in Alexandria at the turn of the Christian era; but what is of interest is that it fails to make its way into Ps-Solomon.

[42] See Patrick W. Skehan and Alexander A. Di Lella, *The Wisdom of Ben Sira* (AB 39; Garden City, N.Y.: Doubleday, 1987), 136.

[43] Dunn also appeals to several instances in Philo where he says the same thing of Logos; but that is to assume what must be proven, not simply asserted: namely that Logos and Sophia are interchangeable ideas for the author of Wisdom of Solomon (on the basis of 9:1–2; but see the interpretation of this text offered below).

[44] It should be noted that Col 2:3 ("in whom [Christ] are hidden all the treasures of wisdom and knowledge") is sometimes brought forward as supporting the view that this passage reflects an alleged Wisdom Christology (in somewhat the same way 1 Cor 1:24 is said to support such a view of 1 Cor 8:6). But that will hardly do in this case, since Paul does not refer to Christ as "wisdom," but, vis-à-vis all lesser "powers," as God's (now revealed) "mystery," in whom the divine attributes of "wisdom and knowledge" are found as treasures. This is several leagues short of referring to Christ as personified Wisdom, present as agent at creation. Indeed, it is most unlikely that anyone would have found a reference here to Wisdom Christology who was not looking for it in the first place.

[45] A point made by Dunn (*Christology,* 168–76; cf. *Theology,* 270–72) that has seemed to fall on deaf ears. My disagreement with Dunn is in his finding a Wisdom motif at all in the Pauline texts, when there does not appear to be one.

[46] For Proverbs, see the commentary by R. B. Y. Scott, *Proverbs and Ecclesiastes* (AB 18; Garden City, N.Y.: Doubleday, 1965), 69–72, to which one might now add the forthcoming commentary by the honoree of this *Festschrift;* for Sirach, see the commentary by Skehan and Di Lella, *Ben Sira,* 332. This is also affirmed by David Winston (*The Wisdom of Solomon* [AB 43; Garden City, N.Y.: Doubleday, 1979], 34), who sees Philo and Ps-Solomon in contrast to Proverbs and Sirach at this very point.

[47] W. O. E. Oesterley and G. H. Box, *The Religion and Worship of the*

Synagogue (London: Pitman, 1911), 169, and cited, e.g., by Winston, both in his commentary (see n. 46, above) and in his contribution to the Gammie Memorial volume ("Wisdom in the Wisdom of Solomon," in *In Search of Wisdom: Essays in Memory of John C. Gammie* [ed. L. G. Perdue et al.; Louisville: Westminster John Knox, 1993], 150); cf. R. Marcus, "On Biblical Hypostases of Wisdom," *HUCA* 23 (1950–1951): 159, who in turn is cited by Witherington, *Sage,* 109. But see also the cautions raised by Dunn, *Theology,* 272.

[48] This ambivalence can be found especially in Winston, who in his commentary cites the Oesterley-Box definition but in the footnote goes on to aver, "In Philo and Wisd ... where Sophia is considered to be an eternal emanation of the deity, we undoubtedly have a conception of her as a divine hypostasis, coeternal with him" (34). This would seem to go beyond Oesterley-Box by some margin. Winston's commitment both to a much more hypostatic understanding, as well as to this preexistent hypostasis as being God's agent of creation, can be found in the introduction (59), where he asserts, "The central figure in Wisd is Sophia, described as an 'effluence' or 'effulgence' of God's glory, and his agent in creation (7:25–6; 8:4; 9:1–2)." The reference in 7:25–6 is to Sophia: "while remaining in herself she renews all things *(ta panta kainizei).*" But in the commentary on this passage he does not so much as mention creation—for good reason, one might add, since it simply is not in the text. The same ambivalence is to be found in the attempt to distinguish between wisdom as God's attribute and Wisdom in the NJB, especially in its handling of the three occurrences of σοφία in Wis 1:4–6, as well as in 3:11. The consistent use in that translation of the capitalized Wisdom in 6:9–10:21 can only be described as prejudicial.

[49] After all, the author of the Wisdom of Solomon, who may well have been an older contemporary of Paul himself (Winston, e.g., dates the work within the reign of Caligula [37–41 C.E.]), is most likely merely heightening the effect of the personification, rather than thinking of an actual being distinguishable from God. As will be pointed out below, the latter seems to be an unfortunate misreading of our author's text, not to mention his theology.

[50] The closest thing to it in the LXX is Ps 103:24 (EVV 104:24), πάντα ἐν σοφίᾳ ἐποιήσας, which is not only in a nonwisdom passage but also reflects what the Wisdom tradition does indeed affirm: that "God in his own wisdom created" things so that they reflect his wisdom of design and purpose—which scarcely amounts to mediation.

[51] Quoting Scott, *Proverbs,* 70, who applies these words to the companion passage in Prov 3:19.

[52] See ibid., 70–71; Scott argues convincingly that this poem is written by the same author as 3:19.

[53] Witherington, *Sage,* 44.

[54] Compare ibid., 95; Witherington appeals to H. Ringgren, *Word and Wisdom: Studies in the Hypostatization of Divine Qualities and Functions in the Ancient Near East* (Lund: Ohlssons, 1947), 108–9.

[55] Compare Skehan and Di Lella, *Ben Sira,* 332–33, who do not so much as mention a view that reads this passage as Wisdom's having a role in creation itself.

[56] One of the problematic features of "dependency" on the part of Paul with regard to Ps-Solomon is, of course, its date. If Winston is correct that it should be dated during the reign of Caligula (see n. 49), then there seems almost no chance that Paul, who had become a follower of Christ by this time, would have known about this work—or given it the time of day, had he known of it. But since this dating (which I think is to be preferred for the reasons Winston sets forth) is much debated, I have chosen to enter this discussion on the playing field and under the assumed rules by which the game has been played by others.

[57] Unless otherwise noted, this and other translations will be from the NRSV from this point on, in part because in keeping with its translation style it tends to be close to the Greek text and in part because it consistently translates σοφία in the lowercase (just as in Proverbs and Sirach), thus not prejudicing the reader toward any view of personification.

[58] While some would see this text as supporting a view of Wisdom as agent of creation, that is to make too much of almost nothing. Verse 5 offers the author's perspective on the personification of v. 2, and it has nothing to do with creation of the world as such: "It is your will that works of your wisdom [in this case, ships!] should not be without effect." Here the usage is simply in keeping with the whole sapiential tradition.

[59] Thus in Ps 33:6, "By the word of the Lord were the heavens made, their starry host by the breath of his mouth."

[60] Some (e.g., E. J. Schnabel, "Wisdom," *DPL,* 970) see here a second "transfer" to Christ of personified Wisdom's role in the Wisdom tradition, namely a soteriological one. But this rests on an even shakier understanding of the relevant texts.

[61] This is because for them the predicate for the "origins" of the idea of preexistence is so integrally tied to an alleged preexistent Wisdom.

[62] A further way that personified Wisdom has been "found" in Paul stems from Eduard Schweizer's influential study, in which he argued for a double "sending" formula in Wis 9:10–17 as "background" for Paul's words in Gal 4:4, 6, about the Father's having sent the Son and the Spirit ("Zum religionsgeschichtlichen Hintergrund der 'Sendungsformel' Gal 4,4f., Rm 8,3f., Joh 3,16f., 1 Joh 4,9," *ZNW* 57 [1966], 199–210). I have had previous occasion to call much of this study into question, regarding both the "formula" itself as well as the way Schweizer (and others following him) uses the Spirit material (see Fee, *Presence,* 911–13).

[63] I am well aware of the long history of trying to find Ps-Solomon behind Paul's pneumatology, but as I pointed out in *Presence* (911–13), that is a demonstrably wrong use of sources.

[64] See Richard B. Hays, *Echoes of Scripture in the Letters of Paul* (New Haven: Yale University Press, 1989), 21–24; cf. Gordon D. Fee, *Paul's Letter to the Philippians* (NICNT; Grand Rapids: Eerdmans, 1995), 130–32.

[65] My hesitation in this case is due both to the lack of any linguistic parallels at all (*pace* Dunn's and others' wanting to make μορφή equal to εἰκών) and to the fact that the case of Christ in this passage and the case of Adam in the Genesis narrative are simply not parallel. See the discussion in Fee, *Philippians,* 209–10, esp. n. 73; Dunn's (now more moderated) view can be found in *Theology,* 282–88.

[66] Here I have the same difficulty with Dunn's (and others') allusions to Wisdom in 1 Cor 8:6—where both linguistic and certain conceptual echoes are missing—as he does with various attempts to find it (and other motifs) in Phil 2:6–11; see Dunn, *Theology,* 282 n. 68.

[67] So I have argued in a preliminary way in my contribution to the Incarnation Summit (see n. 7 above); see now esp. Bauckham, *God Crucified,* 29–31.

The Wisdom of Marriage

Roger R. Nicole

> "For this reason a man will leave his father and mother and be united to his wife, and the two will become one flesh." This is a profound mystery—but I am talking about Christ and the church.
>
> ~ *Eph 5:31–32*

Marriage today is in trouble—both outside and inside the church. The nature and significance of the relationship are in the melting pot of debate, and, as a result, consensus is lacking about the ethic of married life. What wisdom, we may ask, does the Bible yield to help us in these matters? As a tribute to my honored colleague, Bruce Waltke, I here set out the beginning of an answer to some of the questions that arise in this debate. Consider the following three facts from the teachings of Jesus, Paul, and John.

First, when Jesus was asked a question about marriage and divorce, he referred to the original institution: "He who made them *from the beginning* . . . and said . . ." and "Moses permitted you to divorce your wives because your hearts were hard. But it was not this way *from the beginning*" (Matt 19:4, 8; Mark 10:6 RSV). The teaching here is that marriage is to be managed according to God's original purpose in creation, that is, as a *unitive relationship of climactic significance,* one in and for which permanence is always to be sought.

Second, when Paul discussed the mutual responsibilities of Christian spouses, he appealed not only to God's original institution of marriage as explained in Gen 2:24, but also to the fact that Christian marriages are to be lived out in the Lord (Jesus) and as service to the Lord (cf. Col 3:18–24) and that the marital relationship itself is meant to mirror the relationship between Christ and his church (Eph 5:21–33). The teaching here is that married believers must seek to rise to the height of their calling—namely, to embody for all to see the way in which the

Savior and his people love and affirm each other and, by the harnessing of their mutual affection, to honor and exalt each other.

Third, when John in Revelation wrote of God's goal for the church, racked as it was (and still is) by the hostility and opposition of a fallen and demonized world, he described it as a marriage, the marriage of the Lamb (see Rev 19:7–9), thus relaying to us both what his angelic instructor told him and what he saw himself. In the book of Revelation images are explained by other images, and the bride, the Lamb's wife, is explained as the holy city, the new Jerusalem (21:2, 9–10). But this does not cancel out the huge significance of John's presenting the consummation of church history as the Lamb's marriage to his perfected and now flawless bride, with the accompanying beatitude, "Blessed are those who are invited to the wedding supper of the Lamb" (19:9). What is envisaged here is evidently the full realization and enjoyment of a sin-free relationship, one that is in no way tarnished by the distorting and disfiguring influences of a perverted world. In this respect the *first* marriage, that of Adam and Eve, and this, the *last* marriage, that of the church and the Lamb, are alike and stand in contrast to every other marriage that has ever been. From this fact—plus the status of marriage itself as the first created relationship, plus the significance of the eschatological marriage as the end to which the whole plan of grace in history is the means—the full dignity of Christian marriage, and the valuation and expectation that undergirds its ethic, begins to come clear.

Thus the two basic concerns of the Bible regarding human marriage are set before us: the importance of unity for the marriage relationship and the need for the human marriage to mirror the future marriage between Christ and the church. In this article we first offer a few comments on the nature of marital unity, and then we proceed to develop, via a biblical theology, the idea of the heavenly marriage as an image for the earthly marriage. Following an exploration of the implications of this patterning relationship, we conclude with a few general thoughts.

I. The Principle of Unity

Marriage is about unity, the unity of a man and a woman. Unities of being and purpose are central to the biblical revelation of God and his work. The texts quoted have already pointed to two great and glorious unities, with two more presupposed as their background. When set in order, these unities appear as follows:

The unity of the Father, the Son, and the Holy Spirit as one God with one nature—a single essence, or being, as theologians have expressed it—and one will. This Trinitarian unity is an eternal fact: God is, was, and always will be the Three-in-One, and there only ever has been, or will be, one single divine purpose that embraces everything. Within this unity the Father initiates, the Son and Spirit submit, and the mutual responsiveness of all three persons, co-equal in divinity, is affirmed.

The unity of the full, undiminished divine nature with the full, sinless human nature in the one person of Jesus Christ the God-man. This incarnational unity, which began in Mary's womb, is now an everlasting reality. When the gospel narratives tell of Jesus' making decisions and acting on them, they show us everything that is involved both in divine and in human resolving, inseparably joined—fused, we might say, without being con-fused. This justifies the church's historic testimony to Jesus' two wills, one human and one divine, constantly (not alternately!) operating together within the unity of his one incarnate person (cf. Matt 26:39, 42; Heb 10:7, 9). The two unities, Trinitarian and christological, thus set forth are presupposed by the two that now follow.

The unity here and now of God's redeemed people in and from every age. This is the universal church, filled with the glorious company of people who—without losing their individuality—are brought, tuned, adjusted, and integrated together into a single, harmonious, dedicated entity. In the language of Paul, they are the Israel of God (Gal 6:15–16); the "one new man" (Eph 2:15); the building (Eph 2:19–21), body (Eph 1:22–23), and bride of Christ (Eph 5:25–27; Rev 21:9–10); the community that Paul pictures as God's olive tree (Rom 11:16–24) and that Jesus speaks of as the one flock of which he is the shepherd and as branches in the vine, which is himself (see John 10:14–16; 15:1–8).

The unity here and now of the God-man with the church, that is, with every person who belongs to the church and with all of them together. This unity, as we have seen, will be most fully realized and enjoyed at the eschatological wedding of the Lamb.

These unities—of the Godhead, of the person of Christ, of the church, and of Christ and the church—form the frame within which the theology of what I shall call *covenantal marriage* is to be explored and within which its divinely ordained unity is to be understood.

What this essay aims at can now be stated more clearly. Its goal is to sharpen our focus on the nature and purpose of God's institution of human marriage in light of the eschatological marriage between Christ and his church. The hypothesis to be explored is that, over and above the ideal of monogamous unity founded on committed loyalty, which Gen 2:24 announces as built into the created order, the coming certainty of the heavenly marriage reinforces this pattern for earthly marriage as a sign of what is to be and so finally establishes the creation ideal as having permanent significance and fixed validity. In making this case the OT will be read canonically in the Christian sense of that word, namely, as embodying God's planned preparation for all that was to be revealed as reality in Christ; on this basis the Edenic and eschatological marriages will be linked up in a relatively direct way.

II. The Marriage of Christ and the Church as the Climax of History

When one wishes to understand a person's purpose in any specific endeavor, the way of wisdom is to focus on the beginning and the end. A builder's aim, for instance, will be discernible both from the blueprint and from the final edifice, though intermediate stages in the process of construction may exhibit ancillary or temporary features that momentarily obscure what he has in mind. It will be urged that, similarly, in the intervening time between the fall of humanity and the *eschaton,* God has sanctioned provisional adjustments for our "hardness of heart," while yet his ideal and goal remain intact.

We now begin at the beginning, with a careful look at Gen 1–3.

A. Marriage in Eden

Following the layout of Gen 1, we perceive that God's work of creation manifests a progression from large-scale inanimate matter to fine-tuned, complex animal creatures. In the sixth and final creative day, the climax of God's creative activity is achieved in the creation of humanity made *in the image and likeness of God;* nothing is, or ever could be, higher than that. Adam was created first and Eve afterward (Gen 2:7, 22; 1 Tim 2:13). The creation of Eve was apparently delayed for a while so that Adam could perceive his own need by viewing animals filing before him in pairs and then appreciate God's care for him by his providential response to that need.[1]

Immediately after the creation of Eve, God instituted human marriage as a fitting apex to all this creative work and as the means of human fulfillment (Gen 2:18) as well as of human reproduction (Gen 1:28). It is this chronological sequence that permits us to identify the purpose of the divine creative activity: human marriage, as a basic form of human relationship, is the goal of creation.

Adam and Eve fell from this exalted position by a lapse that defies rational explanation, as is related in Gen 3. This fall, far from being a minor defection, was an act of fundamental and even blasphemous defiance, in the form of direct disobedience to God's express commandment. It involved discontent with the place God had given humanity, unbelief in doubting the motives of God's prohibition, selfishness in seeking to secure personal advantage without regard to anyone else, and arrogant pride in the attempt to capture the prerogatives of God himself. A radical and pervasive corruption like a sinister cancer has invaded all of our beings and faculties.[2] The standard name for it is original sin.

The impact of the fall is seen at once in the breakdown of relationships. We read that the transgression of the primitive pair worked itself out in the following ways:

Their fellowship with God was breached. Eve certainly, and Adam presumably, blindly accepted the serpent's accusation that God had lied in threatening death to the disobedient when he was in fact concerned to maintain his own supremacy and, so it would seem, to encourage Adam and Eve to exercise reverent restraint within the frame of free choices that he had given them. When next God visited them in Eden, they fled from him. In 3:16–19 God uttered the curses for their disobedience and expelled them from the garden.

Their personal intimacy was lost. Their former nakedness (2:25) had reflected their unselfconscious mutual openness and transparency. Now they felt a need for some concealment not only from God but also from each other (3:7, 10–11).

Their marriage relationship broke down. Cowardly Adam shifted the blame to Eve and indirectly to God who had created Eve. The battle of the sexes, in which blame is a primary weapon, had begun, as had the bad habit of always trying to excuse oneself. Such attitudes undermined the harmony of their relationship and set them at a distance from each other, leading to a struggle for control. God himself indicated as much when he said to the woman, "Your desire will be for your husband, and he will rule over you" (3:16). As the New Geneva Study Bible notes, "The harmony, intimacy and complementarity of the pre-Fall marriage . . . are corrupted by sin and marred by domination and enforced submission."[3]

Their relation to the physical order was dislocated. Things that would have been easy and pleasant would now be recalcitrant and painful. God specified the woman's pain in childbirth and the man's toil and sweat in securing his living (3:16–19).[4]

The fall thus constituted a victory and a beachhead for Satan in his ongoing rebellion against God (2 Cor 11:3, 14). But instead of abandoning humanity to its deserved misery, God—on the very day of the fall, in the conclusion of his curse on the serpent—adumbrated his great plan of redemption in Christ: the woman's offspring would crush the serpent's head, though his heel would be struck in the process. Genesis 3:15 has therefore rightly been called the *Protoevangel,* the beginning of the gospel. From Gen 4 to Rev 22, the costly redemption God had planned for human relationships is, in one way or another, the theme of the whole Bible.

The drama of redemption, then, has two major phases: before Christ and after his birth. Both phases include direct instruction—positive and negative—regarding marriage: condemning violation of the marital bond and commending proper observance of it by lifelong monogamous fidelity. Both also speak of God's relationship to his covenant people in terms of close fellowship of a marital type. In the study that follows we pursue a basic three-part pattern: with reference to the major periods in biblical history, we will consider (1) statements of prohibition, (2) statements of positive commands, and (3) the language of covenant used to describe the relationship between God and his people.

B. Marriage in the Old Testament

1. The Patriarchal Period

Before ever the divine law was codified in Moses' time, God blessed married life, the family relationship, and marital faithfulness. In Noah's ark the principle of monogamy, implied in the creation of one wife for Adam, was again exhibited in that there were four men in the ark and one wife for each of them (Gen 7:13). Later, God specifically came to the help both of the unjustly dismissed Hagar (Gen 16) and of the falsely accused Joseph who resisted the temptation to adultery (Gen 39).

Negatively, although the meaning of the beginning of Gen 6 remains cryptic, it is apparent that the frightful corruption that affected humanity was traceable, at least in part, to some deviation from the divinely established sexual order. This demanded eliminating the human population with the exception of those who were in Noah's ark. Polygamy, seemingly instituted by Lamech, a descendant of Cain, is presented in a pejorative way by virtue of its origin with a macho murderer (Gen 4:19–24). All the polygamous homes of Genesis were dysfunctional at least in some respects. Even Abraham and Isaac are brought under reproach for dissimulating their marriage to safeguard their lives at the risk of damaging Sarah's and Rebekah's honor (Gen 12:17–20; 20:1–18; 26:1–11). Adultery, however, is condemned as "a wicked thing and sin against God" (Gen 39:9). Incest is viewed as so grievous as to involve the loss of the honor of primogeniture (Gen 35:22; cf. 49:4). And homosexuality is condemned in no uncertain terms in the destruction of Sodom (Gen 13:13; 18:4).

Positively, we find that marriage is commended in the words of its initiation: "A man shall leave his father and mother and be united with his wife" (Gen 2:24). This statement, let us recall, is ascribed by Jesus to God himself (Matt 19:5).[5]

God's intimacy with humans, even after their expulsion from the garden of Eden, is manifested by Enoch's closeness to God (Gen 5:22, 24; Heb 11:5). It is also apparent in God's revealing his purpose for Sodom and Gomorrah (Gen 18:17) to Abraham, his friend (Jas 2:23). Jacob also experienced the closeness of God in dramatic ways (Gen 28:10–17; 32:22–32), and he was blessed with the knowledge that his God was with him constantly (Gen 28:15; 31:3; 46:4). Of course this intimacy does not rise to the level of what could be called a "marriage union," though it points in that direction. While marriage is not expressly called a "covenant" *(bĕrîṯ)* it was undoubtedly the most common form of covenant in the patriarchal age, being marked by a mutual pledge as were all covenants.[6]

2. Moses

God's revelation on the place of marriage and on his relation to his people was deepened by the inscripturation of the law.

Negatively, we observe a strong condemnation of adultery, emphasized in both the seventh and the tenth of the Ten Commandments. Violation of this law was punishable by death for both culprits (Lev 20:10). No Israelite was to become a shrine prostitute. The earnings of such could not be brought to the sanctuary because that would defile it (Deut 23:17, 18). Incest, defined carefully in Lev 18, was punishable by death in the most severe cases (Lev 20:11, 12). Male homosexuals also were to be executed (Lev 18:22; 20:13). Bestiality was punishable by death (Exod 22:19; Lev 18:23; 20:15, 16; Deut 27:21). God severely punished the original inhabitants of Canaan because of their immoral sexual practices (Lev 18:24–28; 20:23). In short, sexual relations outside marriage, whatever their form, are very firmly ruled out. Idolatry was condemned not only because it violated the proper worship of God, but also because it frequently involved sexual immorality (Exod 32:6, cf. 1 Cor 10:7–8).[7]

A slight opening for divorce was provided in the Mosaic legislation (Deut 24:1–4) "because [their] hearts were hard," as Jesus averred (Matt 19:8; Mark 10:5). This enactment, which is clearly designed to protect cast-off women against further exploitation by their one-time husbands, certainly makes it plain that a man had at times a right to divorce his wife; but it does not specify either whether a wife had a similar right or what the circumstances were that warranted the separation.[8]

In any case, the legislation of Deuteronomy was able to safeguard the rights of a divorced party and possibly to establish the demand for a reimbursement of the original dowry. In this sense it firms up rather than weakens marriage.

Positively, provision was made for men to defer military service by as much as one year to ensure the stability and happiness of engaged or newly married couples (Deut 24:5). Levirate marriage was established as a proper routine in order to preserve inheritance laws (Deut 25:5, 6). A man was not absolutely compelled to comply, but he was put to shame for his refusal (Deut 25:7–10).

While the structure of society still reflects a patriarchal pattern, the place and rights of women (esp. wives) are safeguarded in the Mosaic law much more fully than was done in the surrounding Near Eastern civilizations. Unfortunately, the Jewish practice often failed to implement the Mosaic ideal. The loose conduct of Samson (Judg 14–16) and the abominable events related in Judg 19–21 regarding the Levite concubine are evidence of this situation. On the other hand, the description of the wife of "noble character" in Prov 31:10–31 manifests the high esteem of womanhood that had been established in Israel, at least among serious people.

God's relationship to Israel was not at this stage presented directly as that of a husband to his wife, yet idolatrous tendencies and practice were sharply condemned as "playing the harlot" (see Exod 34:15–16; Lev 20:5–6; Judg 2:17), just as one is jealous when one's spouse is unfaithful.[9]

3. The Prophets

The prophets were people raised up by God in keeping with his promise (Deut 18:15–20), in order to reassert the principles of the law, to protest against inadequate obedience, and to challenge Israel in the light of future developments.

Negatively, the prophets raised their voice against adultery. Jeremiah and Ezekiel particularly emphasize the wickedness of this deed, which Ezekiel called "defil[ing one's] neighbor's wife" (Ezek 18:6) and described "a detestable offense" (Ezek 22:11; "an abomination" KJV). Malachi speaks of marriage as a covenant and quotes God himself as saying, "I hate divorce" (Mal 2:16).

Positively, the prophets called men to be faithful to the wife of one's youth (Mal 2:15). With this goes the affirmation that God's relation to his people is like that of a husband to his wife. This parallel is exhibited strikingly in the writings of the prophet Hosea in the eighth century B.C. His experience with his unfaithful wife, Gomer, parallels that of Yahweh with idolatrous Israel. This experience, which dominates the whole book of Hosea, is a theme frequently echoed in later prophecies. We find a brief allusion to it in Isaiah (1:21) and in Micah (1:7), but a much greater emphasis is placed on it by Jeremiah (2:20–25; 3:1–3, 6–10; 13:25–27) and Ezekiel (16:15–43; 23).[10]

C. Marriage in the New Testament

1. Christ's Teaching

Our Lord made it very clear that he did not intend to repudiate the law but rather to bring about its fulfillment (Matt 5:17–20). This is particularly evident in his teaching about marriage.

Negatively, he made it plain that the seventh commandment does not merely prohibit the physical violation of the marriage commitment, but also tells us that God frowns on impure thoughts and looks (Matt 5:27–30). Jesus' willingness to associate with the adulterous woman of John 8:1–11 did not reflect a condoning of her behavior; rather it showed that God is willing to receive all those who repent and believe.

Similarly, Jesus discussed divorce in the light of God's basic purpose in marriage, and he revealed, as we have seen, that a provision of the law regulating divorce (Deut 24:1–4) was a concession "because [their] hearts were hard" (Matt 19:8; Mark 10:5) rather than an embodiment of the fundamental purpose of marriage. Clearly, the same should be said of the exclusionary clause in Matt

5:32: "except for marital unfaithfulness." That clause implies a breakdown in a commitment that was meant to be lifelong, "till death do us part"!

Jesus taught, however, that the exclusive bond of human marriage in this world would cease to be perpetuated in the *eschaton* (Matt 22:30); this is not because marriage is not aligned with God's intent but rather because in eternity all the purposes of each couple's union will be fulfilled in the supreme marriage, that of Christ to the church, in which they will share.

Positively, Christ embodied the fulfillment of the great OT passages where God is presented as the husband of his people. This was already perceived by John the Baptist (John 3:29). Jesus called himself "the bridegroom" (Mark 2:19–20), and some of his parables announce the coming culmination as a marriage feast (Matt 22:2; 25:1). Thus our Lord endorsed the teaching of the OT prophets and, in effect, asserted his deity by claiming for himself the title—*bridegroom*—that was given to Yahweh in the OT.[11]

2. The Teaching of the Apostles

In an age of rampant sexual looseness, the apostles, following the lead of Jesus Christ their Lord, were adamantly hostile to anything that weakened or undercut the marital bond. They explicitly condemned adultery (Rom 2:22; 13:9; 1 Cor 6:9; Heb 13:4), prostitution (1 Cor 6:15–16), fornication (Acts 15:20; Eph 5:3; Col 3:5; 1 Thess 4:3), homosexual activity (Rom 1:26–27; 1 Cor 6:9; 1 Tim 1:10), and incest (1 Cor 5:1, 5). Purity, which is a combination of single-minded steadiness, self-respecting restraint, and God-honoring passion, must be the goal.

In the book of Revelation, evil is personified as the great prostitute (Rev 17) who shares the divine condemnation with the beast and the false prophet (Rev 19:2, 20). She is in total contrast to the bride of the Lamb (Rev 19:7–8), who is radiant, holy, and without stain or wrinkle or any other blemish (Eph 5:26–27). The contrast makes its own point.

Positively, the apostles emphasized the goodness, dignity, and propriety of believers' marriages (1 Cor 9:5; Heb 13:4). They spoke strongly of blessing on the Christian home and family (1 Cor 7; Eph 5:33–6:9; Col 3:18–21; 1 Pet 3:1–7). They sanctioned sexual asceticism only for a limited time (1 Cor 7:5) or on an emergency basis (1 Cor 7:29). Marriage is forbidden only by deceiving spirits and demons (1 Tim 4:1–3).

The apostolic perspective is illuminated by the prospect of the second coming of Christ, that momentous event to which more than three hundred NT passages refer. Eschatological expectation shapes all of the apostles' ethical and relational teaching. They are always looking ahead to Jesus' forthcoming reappearance and to the joys that await Christians then. This is the prospect that the book of Revelation presents pictorially as the marriage of the Lamb.

D. The Marriage of the Lamb

About this marriage, which is the true climax of human history, we can say at least the following things. The bride is the company of all God's redeemed people from the worlds of both Testaments (cf. Rev 21:12, 14) now brought together in perfect unity so that they constitute one body in Christ with one will and purpose common to all, namely to endorse and execute the will of God. The bridegroom is the mediator of the new covenant, the great Son of God, the God-man, Jesus Christ, the Savior and lover of our souls, who has blessed the bride in countless ways during the period between his two comings and who now presents her to himself in a glorious, because glorified, condition. The unity of the church that Jesus had in view in his high priestly prayer of John 17 was certainly not a unity of essence nor of centralized organization or mechanical uniformity in this world; it was a unity of mind and heart and purpose in which all are perfectly one—at one, that is—in seeking to do the will of God and so glorify and please him (Rom 12:1–2). This is how it will be to perfection at the Parousia, when the work of grace is done and the wedding takes place.

In the *eschaton* we shall know and enjoy the fulfillment of our request to a degree utterly unimaginable at present. Totally free from the individualistic, isolating, and irresponsible anti-God down-drag of sin, we shall spontaneously seek and find full togetherness—in other words, full unity—with Christ and with each other in Christ, while Christ gives himself to each of us simultaneously and to all of us corporately in a way that goes beyond anything we have known of him previously. After all, he loves us, and this is his wedding day.

It is worth observing that the abiding unity with Christ in will and purpose that will be enjoyed by the church in the divine marriage is, from one standpoint, a *perfect submission*—indeed, one could say a perfect subordination, since all the initiative will be Christ's—as well as being, from another standpoint, a *perfect consensus.* It is against this background that the question of how our earthly marriages should reflect and witness to the coming divine marriage is to be explored.

It is tempting to say, in light of all we have reviewed, that the Lamb's marriage in Rev 19 and 21 is just a metaphor for our entry upon a celestial condition that is best defined and described in other terms. Tempting, yes, but surely wrong. For similarly here the Lamb's future marriage is the archetypal reality that Christian marriage must reflect in its own partial and derived way. Paul indicated this when he inserted into his overview of the married couple's proper relationship the statement "But I am talking about Christ and the church" (Eph 5:32). On earth, in the sequence of created time, marriages existed long before the realities of which they are scaled-down, adapted, and limited reproductions were made known. What is decisive here, however, is not temporal priority in the order of knowing but the eternal purpose of God in the order of being (Eph 1:4;

1 Pet 1:20). The first person of the Trinity was always the Father and the second person, the Son, was always destined for the eschatological consummation (Eph 1:10). When these things were revealed through Christ's earthly ministry and the apostolic teaching that followed it, God's purpose adumbrated in the OT positives and negatives on marriage and the family became clear at last: there was an eternal, normative divine design that these temporal relationships were meant to reflect.

III. Implications for Christian Marriage

We have seen that, in the economy of God, the foreordained future marriage between Christ and the church sets a pattern for human marriages. God, it appears, planned from the start that the relationship between him and his servants should be covenantal in character, each party being committed to the other in unqualified *loyalty and love;* and when God countered the entry of sin by turning his covenant of innocency for innocents into one of grace for sinners, the gift and expectation of reciprocated loyalty and love remained unchanged. The present form of the covenant partnership centers on the relation between Christ, the mediator of all life and all grace, and the community that consists of all who trust him as their Savior, Lord, lover, friend, life, and hope. In this relationship Christ reconciles, pardons, supports, enriches, and protects, while the church bows to him in worshipful obedience. We have to ask, then, How should this pattern be followed in the mutual attitudinal relations of Christian husbands and wives?

In Eph 5:21–33, Paul works out a substantial answer to that question. A full exegesis cannot be attempted here, but note the following points:

The relationship should incorporate mutuality. This whole passage of household instruction (wives and husbands, 5:22–33; children and parents, 6:1–4; slaves and masters, 6:5–9) specifies the mutual submission required of all Christians: submission in Christ, under Christ, out of reverence for Christ, expressing the neighbor-love taught by Christ (5:21). The submission required, then, is mutual and so has nothing to do with seeing oneself as an inferior and observing a chain of command from a top person to a bottom person, but it has *everything to do with relating to others in a way of love, that is, with a purpose of respecting them, doing them good, being at their service, and seeking to make them great in God's sight.* All the details of the passage must be understood within this parameter.

The relationship should incorporate headship. Paul declares that the husband's position as head of the wife corresponds directly to Christ's position as head of the church (which is Christ's body, says Paul). But Christ's headship over the church, authoritative as it truly is, is a headship of *responsible, active, enriching love.* Paul spells this out in glowing terms and then tells husbands to love their wives "in the same way" (5:28 NRSV). All the details of married life must be brought within this parameter.

When these guidelines are followed, the consciousness of loving and being loved will dominate the relationship; and the basis on which the husband and wife discharge their roles as *responsible leader and reliable supporter*, respectively, will be their shared sense of co-equality before God and before each other as persons of equal need who live by receiving equal forgiveness and grace. This path leads to joyful marriage.

IV. Concluding Thoughts

Some thoughts of a more general sort may now be offered as a conclusion.

First, in reflecting on how the passages requiring submission of wives to husbands apply today, it may be right to ask whether part of the reason why God says what he does through Paul and Peter (1 Cor 11:3; 14:34; Eph 5:22–23; Col 3:18; 1 Tim 2:11; 1 Pet 3:1–6) might be the same as the reason why, according to Jesus' explanation, he permitted divorce in Moses' day: namely "because of your hardness of heart." If so, the commandment to submit would be more a remedy and protective safeguard against emergencies than a fundamental expression of the nature of marriage. The point then would be that the command implies that the wish and intention to submit are presently somewhat lacking and that when the archetypal blueprint of marriage becomes reality, namely at the wedding feast of the Lamb, this will not be the case. To the extent that it is the case in earthly marriages at present, they do not yet match the divine model and so need this remedial command for formational purposes, to help them on their way.

In any case, the command to submit is temporary only, for in the *eschaton*, when the Lamb's marriage takes place, the will of all will correspond totally to the will of Christ, and nothing outside this identity of desire and purpose will be in anyone's mind, so that nothing about submission will need to be said, or felt, or thought. This identity of purpose will match that within the Trinity, where there is one will common to the three persons as one aspect of their shared essence. Granted, in the Trinitarian economy (the functional pattern of divine joint action) the Son does the Father's will and the Holy Spirit does the will of both; but to say this is only to spell out the formal shape of their common will and is not to affirm an intrinsic hierarchy of nature or a tritheistic distinctness of being in place of those personal distinctions within the divine unity that the NT displays and teaches.

Second, God's concern for the institution of human marriage, and his hostility to all that disrupts it, must be emphasized today, as he himself emphasizes it in the Bible. Both Testaments contain drastic threats against fornicators, the promiscuous, homosexuals, adulterers, users of prostitutes, and other pursuers of disordered sex, which in all its forms is seen as a threat to marriage. The flood in the days of Noah, the burning of Sodom and Gomorrah, and the divine command to wipe out the Canaanites (see, e.g., Deut 7:2) are instances of God's curse on sexual immorality. The way in which, under God's providence, entire civilizations (Egyptian, Babylonian, Persian, Greek, Roman) collapsed after centuries of glory seems in part bound up with their increasing sexual license, and it leaves us facing the question whether this is not a serious threat to Western culture at the present time.

Third, Satan labors to undermine sexual sanity in order to trivialize, disfigure, and ultimately demolish God's great idea and purpose in human marriage, as we have sought to think it through in the foregoing pages. Today, erotica, coarse language, pornography, promiscuity, prostitution, nudism, pedophilia, rape, and other perversions—not to speak of the spirit of sexual titillation and indulgence that marks so many of our public spectacles, our TV programs and advertising, our popular songs, our contemporary literature, and our magazines and newspapers—combine to drag sex into the gutter. All of this constitutes a kind of satanic sneer at God's lofty purpose. Surely Christians should deliberately stand apart from all this, seeing it for the devilish reality it is.

Fourth, when couples distressed by a dysfunctional marriage have recourse to counseling in hope of achieving a better relationship, it seems clear that an appeal to a hierarchic and distorted concept of the marital union is not likely to improve matters. By contrast, an appeal for an effort to realize consensus where opposition reigned before and an appeal to love rather than a demand for subordination may touch the root of the problem and thus open avenues of better understanding, mutual consideration, and more cooperative living. This is what the theology of marriage that we have sketched out would recommend.

Appendix
Submission and Domination: A Creation Ordinance?

My assertion above (in sec. II.A)—that the domination of wives by husbands referred to in Gen 3:16 is not a creation ordinance but a curse following sin—does not go unchallenged. To my knowledge, six lines of argument are advanced to support the view that wifely submission in some form was a feature of the Edenic age before the fall and is somehow a measure of healthy married life today. All of these, singly or in combination, appear inadequate and indeed counterproductive. They are as follows:

1. "Adam was formed first, then Eve" (1 Tim 2:13). This is true, but anteriority (prior existence) cannot be held to imply authority over the later arrival, for if it did, *(a)* animals, having been created before humans on the fifth and sixth days, would have authority over us (Gen 1:28 states the opposite); *(b)* primogeniture would give authority over one's siblings (but the careers of younger brothers like Jacob, Joseph, David, and Solomon, to mention only a few, show the contrary); *(c)* parents, being always older than their children, would have permanent authority over them (but this is negated in Gen 2:24; Luke 12:51–53; 14:26; 18:29–30); and *(d)* an older wife would have permanent authority over her younger husband. Having examined this line of reasoning, it appears that the idea of authority following from anteriority is quite mistaken.

2. Adam was not deceived as Eve was when she sinned (1 Tim 2:14). Again, this is true, but it is hard to see how this fact bears on our question. Both Adam and Eve were culpable for yielding to temptation, and Adam—who had heard the prohibition directly from the mouth of God (Gen 2:17) and had experienced God's gracious providence overwhelmingly in the creation of Eve—was particularly culpable. But if the counterargument is that *(a)* Adam was more guilty because he was morally mature and discerning in a way that Eve was not; *(b)* that Eve's immaturity had already led to the necessary arrangement of her assuming a quasi-infantile subordinate role and Adam's assuming a quasi-parental, dominant role; and *(c)* that all marriages should reflect this, then the reply must be that Gen 2–3 gives no hint of such an arrangement.

3. "Man did not come from woman, but woman from man; neither was man created for woman, but woman for man" (1 Cor 11:8–9). In the verses preceding these, Paul has stated that women can pray and prophesy in the congregation (provided they are "covered"), and he goes on to stress the mutual dependence of the sexes, saying "as woman came from man, so also man is born of woman" (1 Cor 11:11–12). Yet he is not saying anything here that bears on the larger question of whether husbands should dominate their wives. However true it is that *(a)* Eve was created from and for Adam, *(b)* as Christ is the head of the male Christian so the Christian husband is head of the Christian woman who is his wife, and *(c)* Paul on God's behalf wants the distinction and difference of the sexes kept clear when women minister (see 1 Cor 11:3–16), he is not discussing the domination of wives by their husbands. The fact that Paul does not require the husband to regulate the public praying and prophesying of his wife is an omission that here speaks volumes. And should Paul be taken to mean that what is extracted from another must therefore always be submissive to that other, it would then follow that all males except Adam must be subject to women (their mothers, out of whose womb they came) while no woman except Eve was ever actually required to be subject to a man—which is absurd in itself and the opposite of what the argument was invoked to prove.

4. Eve's description as Adam's "helper" (ʿēzer) implies subordination (Gen

2:18, 20). Not so! This noun is used nineteen more times in the OT, and fifteen of these (more than seventy-five percent) are references to God as helper (Exod 18:4; Deut 33:7, 26, 29; Pss 30:2; 33:20; 70:5; 115:9–11; 121:1–2; 124:8; 146:5; Hos 13:9). The cognate word *help (ʿezrâ)* refers to God's help twenty-seven times out of sixty-four. Certainly no subordination of any sort can be inferred from the use of "helper" to describe Eve.

5. Adam named Eve, calling her "woman," and giving someone a name implies dominion over that person. First, *woman* (Gen 2:23) was not Eve's personal name; Adam was designating her species, as part of the task God had delegated to him. Adam gave Eve her personal name after the fall and the curse, showing by it, as it seems, his confidence in God's promise (Gen 3:15). Second, though the giving of a name may be an indicator of an already established dominion (see, e.g., Dan 1:6–7), it does not create dominion where there was none before. Neither the angels nor Jesus' earthly parents gained dominion over Jesus by virtue of having named him.

6. "Because you listened to your wife, . . . 'cursed is the ground because of you'" (Gen 3:17). Advocates of a husband's right to dominate his wife sometimes argue that in this verse God is reproaching Adam for inverting the ordained order of authority by listening to his wife, instead of insisting that she should listen to him! But it is clear that Adam's error was to listen to *any* voice that suggested disobedience to God's express command. The idea of Adam's right to domination is being read into the text when this argument is used; it cannot be read out of the text, for it is not there.

In view of the weakness of all these arguments and because there is no mention of subordination, submission, or domination in Gen 1–2 or 5:1–2, I conclude that there was no such thing before the fall. The subordination of women to men was a result of the curse of Gen 3:16, not a continuation of a regime already present in Eden.

Notes

The Scripture quotations in this article are taken from the NIV unless otherwise noted.

I desire to express here my gratitude to my dear friend Dr. James Packer, who has done a great service in editing, simplifying, supplementing, and, at times, gently toning down what might otherwise have been less effective. I am still responsible for the ideas expressed, but I desire to give him credit for a considerable improvement of my work.

[1] Thus Eve appears as the supreme climactic product of God's work of creation. As Matthew Henry wrote, "If man be the head, she is the crown; a crown to

her husband, the crown of the visible creation. The man was dust refined, but the woman was dust double-refined . . ." (*An Exposition on the Old and New Testaments* [3 vols.; London: Partridge & Co., 1854], 1:9).

[2] See Gen 6:5; Jer 17:9; Rom 3:10–15; Eph 2:1; Titus 1:15. A moving exposition of this may be found in G. Campbell Morgan, *The Crises of the Christ* (London: Revell, 1903), 19–61.

[3] *New Geneva Study Bible* (Nashville: Thomas Nelson, 1995), 14. Compare Derek Kidner's comment that "the phrase *your desire shall be for your husband* (RSV), with the reciprocating *he shall rule over you,* portrays a marriage relation in which control has slipped from the fully personal realm to that of instinctive urges passive and active. 'To love and to cherish' becomes 'To desire and to dominate.' While even pagan marriages can rise above this, the pull of sin is always toward it" (*Genesis: An Introduction and Commentary* [TOTC 1; London: Tyndale, 1967], 71). It is widely asserted that in Eden before the fall, Eve was submissive to Adam in the terms of Gen 3:16 and that this wifely subordination was and remains a fundamental feature of marriage as instituted by God. But that view overlooks the fact that this pattern of domination is first mentioned in Gen 3:16 as the climax of God's penal curse on Eve. See Appendix.

[4] Note that God's curse against Eve and Adam is not a divine commandment but rather a prophecy of what would happen in human history. It goes without saying that anything designed to alleviate female suffering in childbearing or male travail in cultivating the ground and earning a living must be welcomed as provided by a gracious divine providence against the background of the continuing curse.

[5] It is remarkable that this text affirms that the husband leaves his parents. Of course, the wife also leaves hers, and the independence of the new home is thus established. In the patriarchal age, a dominant place was given to males in the genealogies and the narratives of events, yet not so as to disparage women.

[6] The word *covenant* (Heb. *bĕrîṯ;* Gk. *diathēkē*) is found more than two hundred times in the OT and at least twenty times in the NT.

[7] Preferably, Israelites married other Israelites; union with foreigners was discouraged (Exod 34:15–16; Deut 7:3; Josh 23:12)—although Esau, Judah, Moses, Solomon, and Boaz married foreigners—because foreigners' allegiance to other gods might turn the Jewish spouse toward idolatry.

[8] The strict interpretation of Shammai, that "something indecent" (Deut 24:1) related to a severe sexual disorder, appears to have been endorsed by Jesus

(Matt 5:31–32) over the loose view of Hillel, that any displeasure of the husband would be a sufficient ground for divorce (e.g., his irritation at her lack of skill as a cook).

[9] See the very apt development of this point in Raymond Ortlund Jr., *Whoredom: God's Unfaithful Wife in Biblical Theology* (Grand Rapids: Eerdmans, 1996), 25–45. See also R. Abma, *Bonds of Love: Methodic Studies of Prophetic Texts with Marriage Imagery* (Assen: Van Gorcum, 1999), x, 281.

[10] See the detailed examination of these passages in Ortlund, *Whoredom.*

[11] My colleague Dr. Simon Kistemaker called my attention to the fact that Jesus' words in John 14:2 (NRSV)—"I go to prepare a place for you"—are the bridegroom's words at one moment in the Jewish marriage liturgy and that the apostles would very probably have understood them in that light.

Biblical Wisdom, Spiritual Formation, and the Virtues

Jonathan R. Wilson

Three of the liveliest areas of discussion in the larger field of theology are biblical wisdom, spiritual formation, and the virtues. Interest in biblical wisdom developed as scholars wrestled with a conundrum in OT theology. In an earlier era, biblical theology of the OT focused on "the God who acts."[1] This approach easily incorporated the law and history of the OT, but it had difficulty incorporating the Wisdom literature. G. Ernest Wright gave voice to this problem, noting that "in any attempt to outline a discussion of Biblical faith it is the wisdom literature which offers the chief difficulty because it does not fit into the type of faith exhibited in the historical and prophetic literatures."[2] Of course, scholars like nothing better than unsolved problems, so increasing attention has been given to the OT Wisdom tradition.[3]

At the same time, various authors have directed the attention of evangelicals to the tradition of spiritual formation.[4] As we will see, this return to classical Christian spirituality must be clearly distinguished from the rise of market-driven, consumer spirituality. Finally, in the field of Christian ethics, many scholars seeking a genuinely *Christian* ethics rooted in theology have drawn increasingly on the resources of the virtue tradition.[5] Previous to this, many scholars have approached Christian ethics as a subset within the larger field of general ethics: the issues and approaches of Christian ethics are given by the discipline of ethics. In contrast to that general approach, some theologians are seeking to describe the practical force of Christian convictions by drawing on the virtue tradition. These theologians, then, are not "virtue ethicists" of a Christian variety in contrast to virtue ethicists of, say, an Aristotelian variety; rather, they are theologians drawing critically on the resources of the virtue tradition in order to display the practical force of Christian convictions.[6]

In this essay I will draw these three developments into conversation with one another.[7] At times I will show how these three are mutually illuminating; at other times, I will argue that attention to biblical wisdom untangles some of the knots in the virtue tradition and grounds spiritual formation in biblical revelation. I will structure my presentation around four issues: cosmic teleology, the process of becoming mature, the embodied nature of morality, and the communal setting for human flourishing.

I. Cosmic Teleology

When I say "cosmic teleology," I mean the purpose, the goal, of the cosmos. We are used to arguing about the origin of the cosmos and the presence (or absence) of design in the cosmos. Here I want to bring to our attention the question of cosmic purpose or goal: for what and toward what is the cosmos moving? This, of course, begs other questions, such as whether the cosmos is moving or being moved and whether the cosmos is moving anywhere at all. As we pursue an answer to my first question, we will also find answers to these other questions.

In much of the virtue tradition, reflection is directed toward the human community and often toward a particular conception of the *polis* ("city," "political community"). In much contemporary spirituality, the concern is narrowed even further, to the individual. Such spirituality is guided not by a thirst for God but by a narcissistic preoccupation with the self turned in.[8] Since the "incurved self" is a classic Christian definition of sin, much contemporary spirituality perpetuates sin.

This narrowing of virtue and spirituality to merely human concerns confines teleology to human purposes, humanly defined. It does not attend to God's purposes, divinely revealed. That divine teleology is identified in biblical wisdom and is incorporated into some accounts of the virtues and spirituality, though not always in direct conversation with biblical wisdom. Biblical wisdom begins, continues, and ends with the fear of the Lord (Prov 1:7). Wisdom is deeply concerned with human life and issues of character, but those concerns have a larger setting. That larger setting is God's redemptive purpose for all creation.[9] When we turn to the virtues, then, we need to look to accounts like that of Thomas Aquinas, which is set within the context of the vision of God. Likewise, we must be careful to draw on spirituality that sees God, not the self, as the primary agent and end of spiritual formation.

When our accounts of virtue and spirituality are directed by the cosmic teleology of biblical wisdom, we begin to understand ourselves as participants in God's cosmic work. Virtues, spirituality, and wisdom do not simply better human life, they bring human life into alignment with God's redemption of all creation. That cosmic setting helps guide a recovery of a fully Christian doctrine of creation, turns us from the ever-present threat of anthropocentrism to biblical theocentrism, and qualifies every Christian account of the virtues, spiritual formation, and biblical wisdom.

II. Becoming Mature

Each of these traditions is concerned at some level with the process by which we become mature. "Becoming mature," however, depends on context. Aristotle's *Nicomachean Ethics,* for example, understands maturity as the ability to function as a citizen of the Greek *polis,* namely Athens. Some contemporary spirituality (but not all) seeks to enable us to live as citizens of Western liberal democracy and late capitalism. Biblical wisdom, in contrast, calls us to formation as a people capable of living according to God's intentions for human life and ultimately for all creation.

The best way to identify this issue is to recognize that "becoming mature" is always teleologically oriented. That is, becoming mature presumes a vision of what maturity will look like. Biblical wisdom teaches us that this vision, or *telos,* is the "fear of Yahweh" (Prov 1:7 NJB). This vision calls us to rethink the virtues theologically from the beginning. The virtues that sustain the Greek *polis*—or "America," or Western civilization—may not be and often are not the virtues that conform us to the fear of Yahweh. Becoming mature in accordance with biblical wisdom leads to good citizenship in the kingdom of God, not in the modern nation-state.[10] Furthermore, becoming mature according to biblical wisdom leads to "self-fulfillment" only as we receive a new self by participating in God's redemptive work in the cosmos.

Therefore, as we work with the virtues and contemporary spirituality, we must constantly guard against their errors and weaknesses and correct them with biblical wisdom. The virtue tradition tends to be socially conservative, and contemporary spirituality often merely helps us live with the status quo. By contrast, being fully formed in biblical wisdom leads us to fear Yahweh, who loves justice and is a friend of the poor and oppressed.

Another problem with becoming mature concerns the very possibility of arriving at the *telos.* For Aristotle and much of the virtue tradition, becoming virtuous was impossible for women, slaves, and men of low social status. One of the lingering conundrums of Aristotle's ethics is that one must be virtuous to become virtuous.[11] By contrast, biblical wisdom calls all to the possibility of wisdom. To be sure, much of the Wisdom teaching appears to come from a court setting. But by its content and by its inclusion in the canon, wisdom is offered to all. Against the backdrop of Aristotle's exclusion of women, it is all the more striking that the book of Proverbs includes the mother as a teacher of wisdom and that it concludes with a description of the virtuous woman.

What is missing from much of the virtue tradition and contemporary spirituality is the reality of God's grace. Concern for the virtues can easily slide into Pelagianism, and contemporary spirituality is often a form of self-salvation. Over against these, biblical wisdom calls us to discipline and effort (Prov 2:1–5), but it recognizes that in the end wisdom is a gift from God: "For the LORD gives wisdom, and from his mouth come knowledge and understanding" (Prov 2:6). Maturity comes as a gift from God, because in the very quest for wisdom, if it is rooted in the fear of Yahweh, we participate in God's work in our world.

III. The Embodied Life

One of the rediscoveries of our time is the embodied nature of our lives as human beings. For many years, perhaps centuries, the influence of the Enlightenment has led to a "disembodied self." That is, we have acted as if human life is essentially about the life of the mind.[12] As Christians we have separated spirit from body and have lived as if our faith were only concerned with "spiritual matters" separated from bodily life.[13]

Among many intellectual currents, the retrieval of the virtues and some contemporary spirituality has brought into focus the significance of embodied life. Since the virtues are not merely about inward dispositions, but also about how those dispositions are displayed in our actions, we must attend to our bodies for a full account of morality. Moreover, the best contemporary Christian spirituality has been concerned with bodily discipline as an essential aspect of our becoming mature, not merely with bodily discipline as a possible consequence of our becoming "spiritually" mature.

This renewed concern with our embodiment illuminates biblical wisdom and draws our attention to a neglected emphasis in the Wisdom literature. Think, for example, of the description of Job's bodily suffering (Job 2:7–8) in light of Satan's challenge to the Lord: "Stretch out your hand and strike his flesh and bones, and he will surely curse you to your face" (Job 2:5). Or remember the significance of "bodily" pleasures in the narrative of Ecclesiastes. Then turn to any chapter in the book of Proverbs, and note the significance of the body for wise living. Food, labor, sleep are all arenas for wise—and foolish—behavior.

When we recover the significance of our embodiment, three important insights follow. First, we recognize that we must collapse the distance between the material and immaterial life of humankind.[14] Physical concerns are also spiritual concerns, and spiritual concerns are also physical. Perhaps to remind ourselves of this reality and to overcome our recent errors we should speak only of persons. Thus, we should say that the transformation of the whole person is the goal of the virtues, spiritual formation, and biblical wisdom. Here these three do not correct one another; rather, they mutually reinforce one another and correct the dualism that has reigned for too long.[15]

The second insight that follows from our recovery of embodiment is that our lives are concerned with the everyday. Too often we have thought that ethics is solely concerned with "moral quandaries" or "boundary situations." Challenging this, the virtue tradition teaches us that ethics is concerned with the whole of life, with ordinary, everyday living.[16] Too often we have thought that "spirituality" had to do only with Sunday worship, times of prayer, a quiet time of Bible reading. Against this way of thinking, the recent recovery of spiritual formation teaches us that Sunday worship is training for the rest of the week, that prayer is a way of life, and that "quiet times" are nothing unless we live them out in our everyday relationships.

Biblical wisdom provides biblical grounding and guidance for this "everydayness" of our lives. In the book of Proverbs, for example, eating, drinking, laboring are all subject to the guidance of wisdom. Wisdom itself is described in the first verses of the book by terms that cover all kinds of human dealings. Human insight, information, and shrewdness are all aspects of wisdom.[17] This everydayness of life is given theological grounding by the integral relationship between wisdom and creation (Prov 3:19–20; 8:22–31; Job 28, 38–39). Living wisely means living in accordance with God's intention for the redeemed creation in our everyday lives.

The third insight to be gained from our embodiment is the necessity of habituation. Again, the virtues, spiritual formation, and biblical wisdom agree. Virtuous living, spiritual maturity, and wisdom can only be gained by disciplined habituation. Although some contemporary spirituality seems to promise a quick fix for our lives, at its best spiritual formation calls us to persistent practice. Here we may deepen our understanding of "becoming mature" by recognizing that though maturity is a gift of grace, it is also strenuous effort on our part. Too often in our society, followers of Jesus Christ triumph over vice, resist temptation, and turn from folly to wisdom, only to find that vice, temptation, and folly have not gone away. Like weeds in a garden, they continue to grow. We fail to recognize that our whole being, including our bodies, has been habituated in sin from birth. New birth is the beginning of a lifetime of habituation in the righteousness of Christian virtues, spiritual formation, and wisdom. We do not "conquer our bodies"; rather, our bodies are redeemed, though only partially in this age, by habituation in right living.

IV. The Community of Wisdom

One of the constant refrains of contemporary life is the turn from the errors of individualism to the promise of community. In our time, we are recognizing more clearly than ever the destructiveness of the hyper-individualism of late modernity.[18] We may be greatly helped in our attempt to recover from individualism by the resources of the virtue tradition, spiritual formation, and biblical wisdom.

In the virtue tradition, the community, not the individual, is the locus of virtue and the inculcation of virtue. Likewise, Christian spiritual formation draws on the Christian community through the ages. The best writing on Christian spirituality turns to the classics of previous times in order to free us from captivity to this present age. Only then may we live in accordance with God's intentions rather than in accordance with the selves that have been shaped by our own times. Adding to these insights, biblical wisdom locates our becoming mature in the instruction of parents, the friendship of the wise, and, for many, the influence of a godly spouse.[19]

The home is the first school of virtue, spiritual formation, and wisdom. In faithfulness to God's command (Deut 6:7–9), the parents in the book of Proverbs teach their children wisdom. As we can observe time after time, when that formation is lacking, other habits take hold. Then the quest for maturity becomes much more difficult and treacherous. In Christian homes, training in wisdom should be the primary and explicit goal of parenting. That training includes portraying the desirability of wisdom, correcting folly, and instructing in wisdom. It includes all of life, from table manners to working for justice, because all of these matters concern our life in community and our participation in God's redemption.

Friendship is another form of community that teaches wisdom (Prov 13:20; 27:17).[20] Virtue, wisdom, and spirituality never arise in a vacuum. Rather, they come as we live with others who seek after them. If we chose companions who love material things or the counterfeit "pleasures" of folly, we will become like them. Everyone is being formed toward an implicit or explicit *telos*. Everyone is walking on the way somewhere. Folly calls us to the way that leads to death; wisdom calls us to the way that leads to life. One of the surest tests of the way in which we are walking is to ask who our companions are. We may deceive ourselves, but when we observe the lives of our friends we may see more clearly the shape of our own lives. That is the lesson of wisdom.

Finally, those who are married should seek in that expression of community a call to wisdom. In that closest of human relationships, wisdom should be a way of life. By recognizing the influence of a spouse upon one's quest for wisdom, the OT adds significantly to the virtue tradition. As I have noted, the book of Proverbs corrects Aristotle's denial of virtue in women. In its recognition of the mother's instruction in wisdom and of spousal, especially wifely, encouragement toward wisdom, the book of Proverbs adds another dimension of community.

In addition to calling us to life in the *polis* (city), wisdom calls us to life in the *oikos* (household). Much of our life today, and much of the virtue tradition, sets the *polis* and the *oikos* in tension with one another. The virtues that sustain the nation-state and capitalist economy are often at odds with the virtues that sustain family life and other forms of communal life.[21] For biblical wisdom, there is no separation between *polis* and *oikos*, and thus there is no tension between the two and no conflict between two sets of virtues. This is because for biblical wisdom, the *polis* and the *oikos* are both situated within the one people of God. Thus, for biblical wisdom and for Christians, *polis* identifies the public life of the church, not the life of the nation-state. Formation in virtue, spirituality, and wisdom is always formation for life among the people of God.

V. Biblical Wisdom, Spiritual Formation, and the Virtues

In the preceding discussion, I have brought together these three themes in mutual correction or illumination. By way of concluding this essay, I will extend my presentation to a more radical conclusion. To this point, I have simply proposed that these three be brought into conversation with one another. Now, I will propose that such coming together radically transforms biblical scholarship by biblical wisdom, Christian education by spiritual formation, and theology by the virtues.

The connections that I am making between each of these is somewhat artificial. Any one of my themes could serve as the transformative key for biblical scholarship, Christian education, and theology. Moreover, I have implicitly argued that, properly understood, biblical wisdom, spiritual formation, and the virtues are after the same thing. However, the scheme I am using takes advantage of natural affinities that exist among the various themes and practices under consideration.

If biblical scholarship is transformed by biblical wisdom, it will have a new *telos*. Grammatical, lexical, historical, cultural, and other "technical" studies will still be needed, but they will no longer be self-sustaining or self-justifying. Transformed by wisdom, these studies and all biblical scholarship will be directed toward the *telos* of wisdom, orienting human life toward God's redemptive intention for creation. Biblical scholarship will be driven to set before us the fear of the Lord and the call to live by seeking wisdom. Biblical scholarship will, by the grace of God, take on the role of Dame Wisdom calling us to life.

If Christian education is radically transformed by spiritual formation it will address the whole person in relationship. Its *telos* will be human participation in the life of the Triune God. Thus transformed, Christian education is not something alongside education in science, history, or any other discipline. Rather, Christian education as spiritual formation becomes the characteristic of all our learning as we are caught up into the life of God that pervades the universe. By the Spirit we come to know Christ and be formed in him, "in whom are hidden all the treasures of wisdom and knowledge" (Col 2:3).[22]

If theology is transformed by the virtues it will seek to incorporate the whole person into the life of the redeemed community. Theology will not abandon doctrine; the primary claim of virtue theologically understood is that doctrine entails not merely right thinking but right living as well. Doctrine is not something separable from the community of the redeemed; it is one of the constitutive elements of that community.[23] Since it is partly constitutive of the community, its work is not completed until our lives are incorporated into the community that participates in the *telos* of creation.

Of course, the account that I have sketched here is programmatic. It falls short of describing the particulars of transformation in any substantive way. That is because we will only find out what that transformation looks like as we do it. But if such a program is adopted, then biblical scholarship, Christian education, and theology will not go on their way as discrete disciplines, each pursuing its own *telos*. Rather, these three come together as different practices pursuing the same *telos*. That coming together will, of course, be troublesome; we will be meddling in one another's affairs. But such coming together will also be one way of practicing the reconciliation that God has accomplished in Jesus Christ; it will be our scholarly participation in the one *telos* of God's creation. Such is the way of biblical wisdom, spiritual formation, and the virtues.

Notes

The Scripture quotations in this article are taken from the NIV unless otherwise noted.

[1] One classic expression of this approach is G. Ernest Wright, *The God Who Acts: Biblical Theology as Recital* (SBT 8; London: SCM Press, 1952).

[2] Wright, *God Who Acts*, 103.

[3] An early work is Gerhard von Rad, *Wisdom in Israel* (trans. James D. Martin; London: SCM Press, 1972). More recently, see Roland Murphy, *The Tree of Life: An Exploration of Biblical Wisdom Literature* (2d ed.; Grand Rapids: Eerdmans, 1996); Derek Kidner, *The Wisdom of Proverbs, Job, and Ecclesiastes* (Downers Grove, Ill.: InterVarsity, 1985); and, pertinent to the topic of this essay, William P. Brown, *Character in Crisis: A Fresh Approach to the Wisdom Literature of the Old Testament* (Grand Rapids: Eerdmans, 1998), and Benjamin W. Farley, *In Praise of Virtue: An Exploration of the Virtues in a Christian Context* (Grand Rapids: Eerdmans, 1995). It is fitting that Bruce Waltke is one of the leading evangelical scholars of OT wisdom. I am indebted to him for introducing me to the

study of Wisdom in a seminar on the book of Proverbs and for supervising my Regent thesis, "The Place of the Book of Proverbs in Old Testament Theology" (M.C.S. thesis, Regent College, 1980).

[4] Here again scholars at Regent College—James Houston, Eugene Peterson, and J. I. Packer—have been at the forefront of this renewal.

[5] Of course, among Catholics, attention to the virtues has a long and unbroken history. Among Protestants, scholars such as Stanley Hauerwas, Gilbert Meilaender, and Charles Pinches have given increasing attention to the virtues; see Stanley Hauerwas, *Character and the Christian Life: A Study in Theological Ethics* (2d ed.; San Antonio: Trinity University Press, 1984); Gilbert Meilaender, *The Theory and Practice of Virtue* (Notre Dame: University of Notre Dame Press, 1984); Stanley Hauerwas and Charles Pinches, *Christians among the Virtues: Theological Conversations with Ancient and Modern Virtues* (Notre Dame: University of Notre Dame Press, 1997); and Jonathan R. Wilson, *Gospel Virtues: Practicing Faith, Hope, and Love in Uncertain Times* (Downers Grove, Ill.: InterVarsity Press, 1998).

[6] I did not make this point clearly enough in *Gospel Virtues.* Although I was trying to make this point in the chapter "Can Virtue Be Christian?" I still left the impression that my account was simply a variety of virtue ethics generally. Stanley Hauerwas pointed this out to me when I was writing the book, but I still did not get it at the time.

[7] Many of the issues that I discuss in this essay could be directed toward specialists in these fields. In this essay, however, I will seek to address nonspecialists. My intention here is to lay out a program that could bring specialists in these fields into fruitful conversation with one another. No doubt my treatment will not satisfy specialists; I hope that dissatisfaction stirs further attention to the interconnections among biblical Wisdom, spiritual formation, and the virtues.

[8] L. Gregory Jones, "A Thirst for God or Consumer Spirituality? Cultivating Disciplined Practices of Being Engaged by God," *Modern Theology* 13 (1997): 3–28.

[9] By this formula, I intend to indicate that "creation" in itself is not a sufficient setting for biblical wisdom. Because we live as fallen creatures, who are not yet fully redeemed, in a fallen creation, only God's redemptive work in creation is a sufficient setting for biblical wisdom. This redemptive work is not sufficiently acknowledged in most accounts of Wisdom theology that set it in the context of creation.

[10] For a sustained critique of the modern nation-state by a complex

Christian thinker, see the work of George P. Grant, conveniently collected in *The George Grant Reader* (ed. William Christian and Sheila Grant; Toronto: University of Toronto Press, 1998).

[11] Aristotle, *Nicomachean Ethics* 2.14.1105a.

[12] One of the most significant challenges to this separation is the analytical work of G. E. M. Anscombe, *Intention* (Ithaca: Cornell University Press, 1958).

[13] This separation may be seen clearly in theology and in the life of the church. In theology we have failed to develop a doctrine adequate to the challenges of a culture formed by scientific materialism. In the church, we have often spoken of "winning souls" in a way that implied that the gospel is not good news for the whole person. We have been so successful in this that my students typically think eternal life is about the postmortem survival of their spirits. When I talk about the physical resurrection and life in a new heaven and new earth (Rev 21–22), they accuse me of heresy!

[14] I am leaving open the precise understanding of humankind taught by Scripture and the Christian tradition. For two different recent accounts, see John W. Cooper, *Body, Soul, and Life Everlasting: Biblical Anthropology and the Monism-Dualism Debate* (Grand Rapids: Eerdmans, 1989), and Warren S. Brown, Nancey Murphy, and H. Newton Malony, *Whatever Happened to the Soul? Scientific and Theological Portraits of Human Nature* (Minneapolis: Fortress, 1998).

[15] This has important consequences for theology, which has often reflected the belief that doctrine was merely concerned with right thinking, such that an entire system of theology could be written without reference to right living. Right living and right thinking are both integral to right doctrine. Theology is for life.

[16] For a brief development of this point, see Wilson, *Gospel Virtues,* 19–25.

[17] See Derek Kidner's wonderfully compact description of this "rainbow" of wisdom in *Proverbs: An Introduction and Commentary* (TOTC; Downers Grove, Ill.: InterVarsity Press, 1964), 36–37.

[18] Two of the most powerful analyses of the consequences of individualism are Charles Taylor, *Sources of the Self: The Making of the Modern Identity* (Cambridge: Harvard University Press, 1989), and Alasdair MacIntyre, *After Virtue: A Study in Ethical Theory* (2d ed.; Notre Dame: University of Notre Dame Press, 1984); see also Jonathan R. Wilson, *Living Faithfully in a Fragmented World: Lessons for the Church from MacIntyre's "After Virtue"* (Valley Forge: Trinity, 1998), and *Gospel Virtues,* 27–29.

[19] I am delighted to acknowledge that I am indebted to Bruce Waltke for this list. However, he is not responsible for the way that I develop my account.

[20] Here some accounts of the virtues must be corrected by Christian convictions. For example, Aristotle denies the possibility of virtuous friendship between those who are not equals (*Nicomachean Ethics* 1159b). For a correction of Aristotle and an account of friendship between God and humans, see L. Gregory Jones, *Transformed Judgment: Toward a Trinitarian Account of the Moral Life* (Notre Dame: University of Notre Dame Press, 1990).

[21] See the account of this difference in John Milbank, *Theology and Social Theory: Beyond Secular Reason* (Oxford: Basil Blackwell, 1990), 364–438, and Reinhard Hütter, *Suffering Divine Things: Theology as Church Practice* (trans. Doug Stott; Grand Rapids: Eerdmans, 2000), 163–64.

[22] See my elaboration of this view in *Gospel Virtues*, 72–95.

[23] This claim cries out for elaboration that cannot be provided here. For a powerful and complex account of this claim see Hütter, *Suffering Divine Things.*

The "Double Knowledge" as the Way of Wisdom

James M. Houston

> To know God, and yet know nothing of our wretched state breeds pride: to realize our misery and know nothing of God is mere despair: but if we come to the knowledge of Jesus Christ we find our true equilibrium, for there we find both human misery and God.
>
> ~ *Blaise Pascal*

Bruce Waltke, my dear friend and colleague of over twenty years, has long inspired me as an example of a humble man who knows himself before God, a godly man whose quest has been to know Jesus Christ better. He thus exemplifies the way of wisdom that our church fathers have pioneered for us in his sustaining a proper synthesis of the knowledge of God and the knowledge of ourselves. For years Bruce, as a true seeker of wisdom, has given himself to the intensive study of one verse of the book of Proverbs each day.

In my first profession as a geographer, I was always chastened by one of those proverbs in particular: "The eyes of a fool are on the ends of the earth!" (Prov 17:24). That seemed to me the final condemnation of my profession, until I began to see how Augustine interpreted such "curiosity." It is strange, says Augustine in his *Confessions,* how one has the tendency to look speculatively and outwardly on the external world rather than to focus inwardly upon knowing oneself before God. Such is the fool's outlook that this proverb is describing. This same proverb begins by saying, "A discerning person keeps wisdom in view"; and it is the aim of this paper to trace, however sketchily, a tradition of wisdom, the "double knowledge," spelled out consistently by the wise people of the church right up until the seventeenth century.[1] We have become spiritually impoverished by its neglect since then. Perhaps we are now ready to recover its importance. This paper reflects my hope that this is so.

I. The "Double Knowledge" in the Early Church Fathers

The Delphic maxim "Know thyself" was cited so frequently in antiquity that it has often been assumed to contain the whole substance of classical philosophy. An early fragment of the writings of Heraclitus discussed it, Aristotle discoursed fully about it, and later Plutarch expounded on it. Indeed, it became basic to the philosophy and ethics of the Stoics. To summarize much classical scholarship on the maxim, seven injunctions have been interpreted from it:

1. Know your own measure: that is, do not be blinded by ambition and flattery.
2. Know what you can and cannot do: that is, do not overestimate your own ability.
3. Know that your place is to be virtuous, neither high-minded nor of low self-esteem.
4. Know the limits of your wisdom by not claiming too much knowledge of others.
5. Know your own faults by getting beyond the blinding effect of self-love.
6. Know that you are human and mortal, while your soul is divine and immortal.
7. Know that your self is your real self, so control your body and senses.[2]

Self-knowledge was thus viewed as the beginning of philosophy, an elitist pursuit that is difficult indeed! Various procedures were prescribed by various teachers: avoidance of flattery (Lucian), personal purification (Philo), friendship (Aristotle), and the study of the rationality of the cosmos (the Stoics). Augustine, the Christian apologist, shows what is lacking in all these efforts in his meditation on 1 Cor 2:11:

> You, Lord, are my judge. For even if "no man knows the being of man except the spirit of man which is in him" (1 Cor 2:11), yet there is something of the human person which is unknown even to the "spirit of man which is in him." But you, Lord, know everything about the human person; for you made humanity. . . . What I know of myself I know because you grant me light, and what I do not know of myself, I do not know until such time as my darkness becomes "like noonday" before your face (Isa 58:10).[3]

Clement of Alexandria (ca. 150–215) was one of the first church fathers to counter polemically the Greek understanding of the maxim "Know thyself." This he does in his *Stromata,* or *Miscellanies.* It was Clement's belief that one of the Greek sages learned the idea from Abraham, and he affirmed that the maxim expressed "many things": "that one is mortal, born a human being, . . . yet is of no account."[4] Clement also interpreted self-knowledge in terms of the *imago Dei,* an idea that Ambrose was later to reaffirm. Clement was aware that classical literature was replete with types of self-ignorance. An exaggerated self-estimate, for instance, demonstrated that one was self-ignorant. Alcibiades and Alexander the Great, with their vast ambitions, were the stock examples of those who did not know themselves, nor did flattery help them. It was Diogenes who said of Alexander the Great, "you are your own worst enemy," for Alexander ignored the reality that his own character did not match up with his military victories. On the other hand, there is "the little-minded man," so Aristotle observed, who does not know and accept the potential he has to develop. Cicero advised his brother likewise to make the best of what abilities he did have, by fuller self-understanding. The Stoics, as we saw, made the maxim the very foundation of their philosophy and ethics. The tendency to relate the four cardinal virtues to the admonition to "Know thyself" also became distinctly marked in the neoplatonists. All of this was familiar to Clement, and it formed the background for his own statements.

Origen (ca. 185–254), pupil of Clement, often criticized what he saw as the philosophers' misunderstanding of wisdom, their being unaware of its salvific and transformative purpose. Instead, they worshiped what their own minds had construed. The pagan Celsus, to whose anti-Christianity Origen responded, had accused the Christians of banishing all wisdom. Origen replied that in knowing the "will" and "spirit" of the Scriptures lay the supreme criterion of judgment, which must overcome all personal opinions. For him the Christian should not separate "wisdom from knowledge," for both implied self-understanding before God.[5] Origen was the first to use Song 1:7 as a challenge to the Christian seeking self-understanding, in the light of being made "in the image and likeness of God." Our primary concern, said Origen, should be to "be still and know that I am God" (Ps 46:10), for without self-concern as a form of self-knowledge, we become foolish indeed. Such teaching impressed his pupil Gregory Thaumaturgus to testify of Origen, "He taught us to be wise and to be with self, and to wish to know ourselves."[6]

This "double knowledge"—knowledge of God and of oneself in the light of God—was taken further by Ambrose (ca. 339–97) and further still by Augustine. For Ambrose, the Psalter, along with the book of Deuteronomy, was the primary source for self-understanding before God.[7] Both books heighten one's sense of the beauty and dignity of the human being as well as provide cathartic realism about the sinfulness of women and men before God, to which the philosophers were seemingly oblivious. Ambrose highlighted ideas stressed by the early church fathers: (1) knowing that we are created in God's image; (2) knowing that we are sinners in need of repentance; and (3) knowing that we are immortal. Yet as Tertullian (ca. 160–220) had recognized, the mission of Christ was not to make the soul know itself, but to make the soul safe by a knowledge of the resurrection in Christ. Ambrose, too, was deeply aware of this.

Mentored by Ambrose, Augustine (354–430) took the theme of the "double knowledge," the way of the wise, to a new intensity. In *Soliloquies,* his opening prayer is "I desire to know God and the soul . . . and nothing more."[8] His book *Confessions* was written with this prayer in mind, and he introduces the book by saying, "Can anyone become the cause of his own making? Or is there any channel through which being and life can be drawn into us other than what you make us, Lord?"[9] Only God who made us truly knows us; only God who truly knows us can enable us truly to know ourselves. Augustine wrote for his friends—*servi Dei,* servants of God—who formed an oasis of wisdom for the mutual cultivation of the Christian life in a wilderness of paganism. Elected a bishop, Augustine realized he needed to examine deeply and prayerfully his own life before God to sustain his identity and his responsibilities as a shepherd of the church. Scripture tells us that "out of [the heart] are the issues of life" (Prov 4:23 KJV), and *Confessions* was quite succinctly the story of Augustine's heart, his "feelings," or *affectus.*[10] Indeed, he looked at himself with ferocious honesty and transparency, and few, other than the psalmists, have ever disclosed themselves so openly. In a passage that was to deeply affect Petrarch at a later period, Augustine himself marvels at how people could pull back so readily from self-understanding before God: "People are moved to wonder by mountain peaks, by vast waves of the sea, by broad waterfalls on rivers, by the all-embracing extent of the ocean, by the revolutions of the stars. But in themselves they are uninterested."[11]

Augustine explored his emotions and attitudes exhaustively, leading his readers into wisdom by his new method of *confessio.* And yet he concludes that "man is a vast deep, whose hairs you, Lord, have numbered, and in you none can be lost (Matt. 10:30). Yet it is easier to count his hairs than the passions and emotions of his heart."[12] Like the prodigal son, we all wander far from our own hearts: "You were there before me, but I had departed from myself. I could not even find myself, much less you."[13] Echoes of Augustine's neoplatonism can be heard here, but his conversion had already revolutionized his attitudes, so that *confessio* now means for him "accusation of oneself, praise of God."

Exposure of one's soul was a traditional theme among even pagan philosophers. But it was most unusual to insist, as Augustine did, that one could never sufficiently search one's own heart so as really to know one's own personality, just as it was unique to Christians to maintain that only God the Creator could ever introduce one truly to oneself. Augustine shrank from the dangers of complete self-exposure, but with that he was also drawn to trust God more than he could ever dare trust himself: "I know myself less well than I know you. I beseech you, my God, show me myself so that to my brothers who will pray for me I may confess what wound I am discovering in myself."[14] Augustine was always mindful of how vulnerable he was to temptation whenever he remained so ignorant of himself. He realized how foolish it was to put confidence in what appears at present as one's own best intentions:

> My mind on examining myself about its strengths does not regard its findings as easy to trust. What lies within is for the most part hidden unless experience reveals it. No one should be complacent in this life which is called a "total temptation" (Job 7:1). Anyone who could change from the worse to the better can also change from the better to the worse. There is one hope, one ground of confidence, one reliable promise—your mercy.[15]

If his *Confessions* is not exactly an act of therapy, neither is it a mere reminiscence of Augustine's past life. Augustine was only too aware that "the past twistings of my mistaken life" were a shameful memory to have, since "without you, what am I to myself but a guide to my own self-destruction?"[16] Nor for him was *memoria* like the Platonic *anamnesis*, bringing to consciousness the latent retention of things known in an earlier celestial existence. Rather *memoria* was the consciousness of God, deep within one's soul, associated with what we call "the unconscious ('the mind knows things it does not know it knows'), with self-awareness, and so with the human yearning for true happiness found only in knowing God."[17] At the root of memory itself was God, so that at the very foundation of the person—to use modern language—there was God. "We show most clearly the image of God in our fullest self-presence."[18] This awareness could stir us to recollection, as the prodigal son experienced "in the far country." Such awareness is grounded in the realization that we have been created "in the image and likeness of God," although that identity has been forfeited by sin. As Augustine explored in depth "the fields and vast palaces of memory," as well as its "broad plains and caverns," he became the "Western originator of the notion of autobiographical memory"—not just as a literary device, but as expressive of theological anthropology.[19] Memory was thus given a critical role both in sustaining personal continuity and in creating self-knowledge.[20] Indeed, in medieval Christendom, memory became so central a feature of thought about human life that in place of one who had "self-knowledge" and "self-expression"—meaningless terms in medieval society—one was rather "a subject-who-remembers" and who in remembering also felt, thought, and judged before God.[21]

But Augustine, having in this way enhanced the importance of memory, then belittled it, since memory (so he insisted) is no container for God. God is not a place or an item in the mind. Although God exists in the mental activity by which a mind desires to know him, he also transcends the seeker after him. Yet ironically Augustine had sought for God externally even while God was already present to him inwardly.[22] Recognizing this, however, Augustine then concluded practically that memory helps us gain wisdom through the review of one's own experiences in the light of the narrative of the Scriptures, upon which we should constantly reflect as a "medicine for the mind."[23]

In all the speculative complexity of Augustine's psychology, more fully elaborated in the second half of his treatise *De Trinitate,* the unity and content of the "double knowledge"—knowledge of God and of oneself—lay in faith and reflection upon the Scriptures.[24] The ongoing distinction between knowledge *(scientia)* and wisdom *(sapientia),* already made by the early fathers, was now further elaborated by Augustine to the effect that knowledge was reasoning that was used as an end in itself, whereas wisdom was a remembering as related to higher ends, indeed to the love of God; and this was the wisdom of Christ. Augustine, then, would have viewed modern academic theology of the post-Enlightenment sort as being merely *scientia,* factual knowledge that has no healing or transformative power, whereas *sapientia* was seen as life-giving, corresponding to what today we are calling "spiritual formation": "that we may be refashioned to the image of God; for we follow the Son by living wisely."[25] Augustine saw *sapientia* as a fruit of faith, quoting the biblical aphorism "Unless you believe, you will not understand." Whether we explore knowledge of oneself or knowledge of God, both are grounded upon faith, he argued.

Augustine went further, setting forth a realistic understanding of the role of the will. Plato had argued that a weak will was related to a poor vision or understanding and that a better understanding would cure it. But for a sinner like Augustine or Paul, *akrasia* (that is, what we would call lack of self-control and, in that sense, weakness of will) was no curable philosophical problem; it was a stubborn reality of everyday living, not changed or brought under control by any thoughts or urgings in the mind: "For I have the desire to do what is good, but I cannot carry it out. For what I do is not the good I want to do; no, the evil I do not want to do—this I keep on doing" (Rom 7:18–19 NIV). Since the will belongs so intimately to the essence of my being and can only be altered and strengthened by the almighty action of God, then the very essence of Augustinian—and indeed all Christian—piety must ever lie in a sense of dependence, in one's inmost being, upon God.[26] Such, then, was Augustine's understanding of the "double knowledge" of God and ourselves. True self-knowledge comes only through knowledge of God; knowledge both of self and of God comes only through the Bible; and only true self-knowledge will bring about the dependence upon God of which true godliness consists.

II. The Augustinian "Interior Man" of the Middle Ages

The Augustinian concept and language of inwardness has been a crucial inheritance of Western culture, both in its use and misuse. Gregory the Great (ca. 540–604) is fully in line with Augustine when he says, "The art of arts is the guidance of souls . . . [and for this] it is first necessary to know oneself."[27] As a pope who had preferred to be a contemplative, Gregory was well aware of what the desert fathers referred to as "the moral slough of busyness": giving "thought to a multitude of concerns, without knowing [one's] self."[28] And in the twelfth-century blossoming of individuation, in what is sometimes called the "first Renaissance of the West," the early Cistercians especially cultivated the "double knowledge" much further. Thus Bernard of Clairvaux (1090–1153) wrote a remarkable series of admonitions to his former pupil (now known as Pope Eugene III), including the following:

> What does it profit you if you gain the whole world [i.e., of knowledge] and lose one person—yourself? Even if you were a wise man your wisdom would lack something if it did not benefit you. How much would it lack? Everything, I feel. Although you know every mystery, the width of the earth, the height of the heavens, the depth of the sea; if you do not know yourself, you are like a building without a foundation; you raise not a structure but ruins. Whatever you construct outside yourself will be but a pile of dust blown by the wind. Therefore, he is not wise, whose wisdom is no benefit to himself. The wisdom of a wise man will benefit him and he will be the first to drink from the water of his own well. Therefore, let your consideration begin and end with yourself.[29]

We catch here the echoes of Augustine's own words and those of Proverbs already alluded to: "the eyes of the fool are on the ends of the earth." To the medieval contemplative, this was the vice of *curiositas,* externalizing one's interest and focusing on things around and about one instead of fixing one's gaze upon God. Activism also has this tendency to blind one to oneself, noted Bernard. He writes, "If you apply all your experiences and knowledge to activity and have nothing for consideration, do I praise you? I do not."[30] The focus for deep reflection, both for Augustine and for later medieval contemplatives, was the truth of the *imago Dei:* how much it means to say that we were created in the image of God and how unlike him we are now as sinners. So Bernard confesses,

> As for me, as long as I look at myself, my eye is filled with bitterness. But if I look up and fix my eyes on the aid of the divine mercy, this happy vision of God soon tempers the bitter vision of myself. . . . It reveals [God] to us as listening compassionately to our prayers, as truly merciful. . . . In this

way your self-knowledge will be a step to the knowledge of God; he will become visible to you according as his image is being renewed within you.[31]

Bernard followed Origen's exegesis of Song 1:7: "If you do not know yourself, O most beautiful among women, then go away and follow the flocks of your friends." Bernard saw these words as a starting point for a discussion on self-knowledge. The God-given self-recognition of which Bernard was speaking—more so than mere introspection or psychological knowledge—would be the entry point for much proper self-humbling, while self-ignorance would lead to moral instability and lack of concern for one's heavenly vocation. Self-deception, coupled with human pride in refusing to acknowledge God as God, was the cause of the fall; but humble, God-given self-knowledge would enable one to grasp the underlying orientation, or *telos,* of one's being. A necessary corollary of such self-knowledge would then be awareness of one's sinful and wounded nature.[32] Bernard thus displayed pastoral realism about the vital role self-knowledge should play in spiritual formation.

The bridal mysticism that meditation on Song of Songs fostered throughout the late Middle Ages, rooted as it was in continuing Augustinian spirituality, sustained an ongoing interest in the "double knowledge." Following the theme of Song 1:7, the anchorites in *Ancrene Wisse* were warned against forgetting their espousal to Christ, lest they fall into temptation.[33] Recognition of the dichotomy between self-knowledge and *curiositas* intensified in the fourteenth century, as is illustrated by *Piers Plowman*'s Dreamer, who sees wonders with his mirror in Middlerd but is distracted and deceived in self-ignorance. Walter of Hilton's *Scale of Perfection* teaches likewise that "a soul which wants to have knowledge of spiritual things must first have knowledge of itself."[34] There were devotional manuals, or *florilegia,* on that theme in the fifteenth century that quoted extensively from Walter, Julian of Norwich, and other mystics.[35] It was a theme very familiar to Catherine of Siena in her letters of counsel and her *Dialogues.*

The "double knowledge" was strongly developed by Teresa of Avila (1515–82), both in her *Life* and in *The Interior Castle.* Unlike the false spiritualities of the *dejados* (self-abandoned ones) that caused concern to the Spanish Inquisition, Teresian self-knowledge was set forth as a polemic against introspection for its own sake. As Rowan Williams points out, "*The Interior Castle* is among other things an attack against interiority as an ideal in itself and this opening emphasis on self-knowledge [in the book] should alert us to this fact. We enter the castle, and if our eyes are open, what we actually see is God. . . . By seeing God we see more clearly who we are."[36] Thus the self-knowledge advocated in the first three of Teresa's seven mansions is about encountering God appropriately in order to enter with increasing intimacy into the knowledge of his love in the remaining four series of mansions. This is where some contemporary feminist commentators, who see Teresa as a token exponent of their cause, completely misunderstand her interpretation of self-knowledge, for her purpose is not to assert herself but rather to deepen her humility before God.[37]

III. Luther and Calvin on the "Double Knowledge"

In his early lectures (1515–16) on the epistle to the Romans, Martin Luther (1483–1546) continued the tradition of the cognition of oneself through the knowledge of God in his word. Self-understanding before God was for him "the science of the sciences." He understood this intertwining unity, on the basis of the doctrine of justification, as consisting of four steps. First, faithful people, in a way wholly at odds with the false self-estimation of the proud, know they are sinners. Second, they believe that the triune God absolutely corresponds to himself and so is unlike humankind. Third, through God's approaching people outside of his own relationship to himself, their being is changed. Fourth, by knowing God's truth, people are enabled to know themselves truly as being justified by God's grace.[38] Soon after, Luther—reflecting on Ps 51 (1516–17), where God "desires truth in the inward man" (v. 6)—interpreted the righteous as those who are accusers and judges of themselves before God and thus are truly justified by God, whereas the unrighteous will defend and justify themselves, thus placing themselves under the judgment of God. Thus when people truly know themselves, they confess they are stupid, blind, fallen, wretched, false, and indeed nothing. Then it is known that God is wise, all-seeing, good, and truthful. In his second series of lectures on the Psalms, in 1532, Luther said more explicitly that Ps 51 instructs the theological knowledge of man and also the theological knowledge of God. "A man should know himself, should know, feel, and experience that he is guilty of sin and subject to death; but he should also know the opposite, that God is the Justifier and Redeemer of a man who knows himself this way."[39]

Luther was aware that there are other forms of knowing that assume self-knowledge of a sort—the knowledge, for instance, of lawyers, physicians, and even parents. But these "discuss man differently from the way a theologian does,"[40] that is, for the theologian (which means the Christian), self-knowledge is not abstract but personally inspired by God, so that it becomes real *coram Deo,* "in the realized presence of God."

John Calvin (1509–64), in the opening sentence of his *Institutes of the Christian Religion* (1559), writes, "Nearly all the wisdom we possess, that is to say, true and sound wisdom, consists of two parts: the knowledge of God and of ourselves." [41] He made it even clearer that these are inseparable in his French version of 1560, where he states simply, "In knowing God, each of us also knows himself."[42] Oddly, William Bouwsma attributes this to a "formula he had taken from Cicero."[43] It is much more likely that Calvin was consciously following the traditional Augustinian approach, perhaps influenced by his use of Bernard, to focus the outlook and demonstrate the orthodoxy of the Reformed position. But with the Renaissance and the reaction to late medieval scholasticism, the nature of knowledge was being radically critiqued in ways that challenged Calvin to use Augustine's insight doctrinally with new clarification. He urges his readers, then and now, to reconsider the exercise of the "double knowledge" in three ways.

First, he makes it obvious that existentially our self-awareness before God will always give us more realism about the human condition—our sin, guilt, shame, and need. This is why humility is interpreted by the medieval writers as the consequence of the "double knowledge." As one sets oneself toward God in an appropriate way as a sinner, in the light of divine holiness, knowledge of God and effective self-knowledge grow together. As Calvin puts it, "There exists in man something like a world of misery, and ever since we were stripped of the divine attire our naked shame discloses an immense series of disgraceful properties."[44] Coming to such an experimental depth of self-understanding, one is then motivated to seek more and more the knowledge of God in grace. In this emphasis Calvin indicts the Schoolmen's speculative theology, which lacked such motivation. As P. Lobstein says, "The knowledge of God is not something purely theoretical, but a practical experience, engaging the whole human personality, soliciting all the energies of the conscience and heart, putting in motion all the spiritual faculties."[45]

Second, "double knowledge" makes sense of the world around us as being created by God, and therefore it leads us to know appropriately how we too should relate to the world. Calvin still lived within the medieval consciousness of "the great chain of being," with humankind as a microcosm of the universe.[46] So "knowledge of ourselves" could be, and was, used by Calvin as synecdoche (a part for the whole) signifying all man's knowledge of creation.[47] One thus sees oneself as part of the created order, and one looks out to the world and appreciates it as God's creation. Calvin often asserted we have a *sensus divinitatis,* by which we discern the Creator within his creation. Calvin did not really help us to define exactly this mode of knowledge of God, but the universality of religion, the servile fear of God, and the troubled conscience are all phenomena indicative of its reality.[48] *Con-scientia* in particular, as a "knowing with, or conjoint knowing," reinforces the significance of the "double knowledge" within us, which no human being entirely lacks.

Third, after reflecting on God as Creator in the first book of his *Institutes,* Calvin moves on (in the second book) to another form of the knowledge of God, which is given through the full revelation of God as Savior and Redeemer. Here Calvin commentators divide and project their own reading upon Calvin. Hegelian, liberal theologians like F. C. Baur in the nineteenth century, or like Alexandre Ganoczy today, interpret the two forms of knowledge—through creation and in redemption—as a dialectic of thesis/antithesis. Like Augustine in his strong anti-Pelagianism, Calvin too saw that there is a radical human-divine opposition, which is overcome only by the mediation of Jesus Christ. But it is provisional, a consequence of sin, not intrinsic to God's nature; for his covenant with humankind, manifested fully through the incarnation, rests on God's hypostatic union with human reality in the person of Jesus and involves the vitalizing union of all Christians with the risen Christ through the Holy Spirit.

Writes Calvin of the incarnation, "The Word was therefore made flesh; he who was God likewise became man so that the very same one might be both man and God, not by confusion of substance, but by unity of person."[49] And in *Institutes* 3.1, he dwells on the "in-Christ" relationship within which the Spirit imparts the gifts of Christ to us.

But as our self-knowledge through God is relational, so too knowing God is having knowledge of him as a person, not just knowledge "about him." It requires then appropriate personal dispositions and responses Godward that are only possible for us through the Holy Spirit. Paul declares, "Who among men knows the thoughts of a man except the man's spirit within him? In the same way no one knows the thoughts of God except the Spirit of God" (1 Cor 2:11 NIV). Nor can anyone respond in faith to God's thoughts without the Spirit's presence and help. Calvin covered these points by his strong Trinitarian construal of divine grace, whereby all is from the Father through the ministry of the incarnate Son and the indwelling Spirit. For Calvin, the Trinity is not an abstract doctrine but is expressive of the being and action of the living God himself, who is self-revealed in and through Christ:

> We are persuaded that there is for us no other guide and leader to the Father than the Holy Spirit, just as there is no other way than Christ; and that there is no grace from God save through the Holy Spirit. Grace is itself the power and the action of the Spirit . . . : through grace God the Father, in the Son, accomplishes whatever good there is; through grace He justifies, sanctifies, and cleanses us, calls and draws us to himself, that we may attain salvation. . . . Therefore, we believe in the Holy Spirit, acknowledging him, with the Father and the Son, to be our one God, holding as sure and firm that the work and power are his . . . because we have received him in faith.[50]

True as it is to label Calvin's thought christocentric, it is truer still to describe it as Trinitarian. It is clear that by structuring the *Institutes* upon the

Trinity, he intended to emphasize that the divine self-disclosure in saving grace is essentially Trinitarian. For it is in Christ that the Father is disclosed, and it is by the Holy Spirit that one receives the knowledge of God. It is then the Father, through the Son, acting by the Spirit who first gave the word and who now renders the word effective. Self-knowledge is then given by the Spirit within the frame of faith-knowledge of God and is expressed by the Spirit-prompted responses of faith in repentance, cross bearing, perseverance, and prayer. For Calvin is fully aware that authentic human response is only made possible by the indwelling Spirit of God.

Thus Calvin spells out the "double knowledge" in positive terms; and throughout his career as theologian and expositor we find him wrestling with its obstacles, such as a malfunctioning conscience, temptation, anxiety, weakness, indecisiveness, and weak will, as well as imperfection and pose. Further investigation of such obstacles, however, falls outside the limits of this essay.

IV. The Modern Loss of the "Double Knowledge"

Just as Augustine had developed the "double knowledge" more than his predecessors had, so Calvin had been more self-conscious than those before him of the need for an "informed conscience." But it was really the Epicureans, and then the Stoics, who developed the role of conscience in moral life in a way that set a standard for the West. The Greek assumption of man's rational ability to be knowledgeable about moral actions went unchallenged, and Thomas Aquinas implicitly embraced it when he defined conscience as the ability to apply moral principles to particular cases. Then the later Calvinists, notably the Puritans in England, developed the process of "the examination of conscience," and of dealing with "cases of conscience," during the seventeenth century. William Perkins (1558–1602) was a pioneer in this approach, writing *A Treatise of Conscience* in 1596. Later Perkins gave a more exhaustive series of lectures in Emmanuel College, Cambridge, published posthumously as *Cases of Conscience* in 1606. He preserved Calvin's twofold knowledge of God—natural and revealed—but he laid no emphasis on the "double knowledge." Self-knowledge, as he describes it, is simply the ability to know oneself better than the Catholic priest does or the allegedly interceding saints do, for one can and should pray directly to God without any intermediary.[51] The Christian also has "the infallible knowledge that one is a child of God."[52] That the Holy Spirit gives knowledge through the Scriptures is all Perkins says about the informing of conscience on these matters. Moreover, conscience, according to Perkins, has two faculties, understanding and will, so that rational moral endeavor ("duty") was now given much more prominence than before.

William Ames (1576–1633) went further than Perkins in giving place to the rational conscience, in light of the admonitions to examine ourselves (2 Cor 13:5) and to judge ourselves (1 Cor 11:31). In his treatise *Conscience with the Power and Cases Thereof* (1632), Ames makes no suggestion that the knowledge of God empowers us to know ourselves, as Calvin insists so strongly. Rather, he was more confident that everyone has the ability to examine oneself. Ames followed, as Perkins had also done, the humanist Pierre de la Ramée (Ramus) in his dialectic of idea and act as devices to develop a theology that reflected experience. Calvin had a clear conviction that proper self-examination is hindered by self-love and that self-knowledge happens as a gift of grace; Ames, however, distinguished God's judgment and knowing one's own state as distinct acts and had no problem regarding the possibility of the latter. All in all, Ames had confidence that "he knows that he knows." The Trinitarian spirituality of Calvin seems to be wholly missing in Ames's theology.[53]

Richard Baxter (1615–91) tells us that he was one of those tortured souls of the seventeenth century who, like John Bunyan, spent seven years in doubt about his salvation. Later, in 1659, he wrote a full treatise on the text of 2 Cor 13:5 ("Examine yourselves to see whether you are in the faith; test yourselves," NIV), entitled *The Mischiefs of Self-Ignorance and the Benefits of Self-Acquaintance.* Calvin, one suspects, would have simply referred to "the benefits of Christ" for the justified believer. Pastorally, Baxter had much practical advice to give as an amateur physician as well as a pastor, but theologically he mixed some Stoicism with Christian faith; indeed, he quotes Seneca at length. In another treatise, the *Right Method for a Settled Peace of Conscience and Spiritual Comfort* (1653), he appears to confuse theological certainty with personal sincerity, a cultural tendency of the century that again had Stoic influences. The new reliance on introspection as definitive for self-knowledge, which these examples illustrate, shows that the conscious quest for the "double knowledge" was almost over in Christendom.

The French Catholic bishop Jacques-Bénigne Bossuet (1627–1704) was perhaps the last to write a treatise *(De la connaissance de Dieu et de soi-même)* on the subject. This is not, however, in any sense an Augustinian study. Rather it is a Socratic venture of self-understanding, used as a polemic against quietism. Thus his perspective is wholly humanistic; he says, "Wisdom lies in knowing God and knowing oneself. From the knowledge of self we rise to the knowledge of God" (a statement neither Augustine nor Calvin would ever have made). Very different was mathematician and philosopher Blaise Pascal (1623–62), who said instead, "Know proud man what a paradox you are to yourself. Down then feeble reason; and let this foolish nature keep silence! Know how much more than merely man is man, and learn from your Master your true condition of which you are wholly ignorant. Listen to God."[54]

When the poet Alexander Pope declares that "the proper study of mankind is man," he is registering an intellectual sea change that René Descartes, John

Locke, and the subsequent Enlightenment project brought about in a very thorough way. No longer was it the goal to know God in order to know ourselves. There began "the satanic questioning," as Michael Buckley calls it, as to whether the Christian God is not the enemy of humanity, such that humanity will never realize and know itself without the "death of God," which became the conclusion of Friedrich Nietzsche.[55] Moreover, Locke had given a radical re-direction to epistemology since, under his influence, knowledge of objects began to vaporize into knowledge as theories about the process of knowing.

In 1744, John Mason, an educator for the young, wrote *A Treatise on Self-Knowledge,*[56] calling it "an important science" that should not be neglected. Mason is clearly inspired by Richard Baxter's treatise *The Mischiefs of Self-Ignorance and the Benefits of Self-Acquaintance,* yet he is critically impatient with Baxter for not including the broader classical authors that Mason incorporates into his text. Clearly, Mason considered himself a devout Christian in that he advocated the need for prayer for self-understanding, but he had no theological discernment about his own syncretism. His treatise is much closer to Baxter's than to Bossuet's work, but it too breaks away from the Christian "double knowledge."

V. The Contemporary Challenge

In his recent study on the origins of atheism in the modern world, Buckley argues cogently that the self-contradiction of theological communication creates alienation within the religious life. This then contributes to modern *a-theism*—not the actual denial of God's existence but the assertion of his irrelevance as we seek to know about him. When the belief that God is personal becomes merely data that is communicated impersonally, as began to happen in the Renaissance and has since been standard procedure in Western theology, arguments for "God" become abstractly inferential. Again, when one insists upon doctrines without reference to personal experience, the gap created between reason and experience is too great for the doctrines to be credible. In the concluding sentence of his remarkable book, Buckley states, "The origin of atheism in the intellectual culture of the West lies thus with the self-alienation of religion itself."[57]

The modern person has embraced a disengaged instrumentalism that leaves her self-ignorant, even when she thinks she has learned to know herself exhaustively by psychoanalysis.[58] To such, Anatole France ironically responded earlier this century, "Be ignorant of yourself." This, France thought, was more fruitful than embracing the Socratic self-confidence of the maxim "Know thyself"! For in being "disengaged" and yet also "expressive," human identity becomes "stultified," "shallow," even "banal." And where "personal resonance" disappears, an ethic of "authenticity," to be gained by withdrawal within oneself, also becomes mirage-like, self-deceptive, and unreal. What appears in all this is that those who do not seek to know God will not know themselves either.

Within as well as outside the church, the pervasiveness of a-theism in Buckley's sense intensifies. That is to say, much of our communication of what we offer as God's truth does not vitalize personal life and relationships. It seems to have lost its relevance. So what promise might the reinterpretation of the "double knowledge" give us in renewal of hope?

Clearly, the knowledge of God and of ourselves is indicative of personal relationships. The *imago Dei* is expressive of God's eternal intent that we enjoy fellowship with him in his triune being as his covenant partner. As Karl Barth has argued, the proposition "I am in encounter" expresses the true humanness of our humanity—as between God and humanity, elected by God to be his covenant partner, and as between human persons, male and female—just as it is expressive of the eternal relations within the triune God of grace, the ground of all created relationality. The "I-Thou" relationship is the denial, then, of any individualism.

In expounding this, Barth uses a "recursive" method by which to establish the definitional character of the "I" that is always a property of "I-Thou," that is to say, reciprocal and self-referential within each relationship.[59] In human relationships, so he explains, recursiveness operates in several ways, with increasing degrees of complexity. (1) One sees the other, who sees that the other is also seeing himself or herself, an event that, in the miracle of the babe's first recognizing its mother, we think of as personal "attestation." (2) Recursion develops with mutual speech and listening with the other as we interact in misunderstanding as well as in understanding. (3) In mutual assistance there is a further level of recursion, as we treat each other with respect, fairness, empathy, and much else. By such recursive interchange we come to "understand" one another. We can begin to say, "I know that person, and I am also known too." (4) But there is also a fourth level, where I can say, " I am known of God," for by divine election, God has called me to be his covenant partner. All my true knowledge of him is then grounded upon this reality of divine initiative. This is God's grace, giving promise of endless recursive responses since his loving fellowship is inexhaustible. It is like walking through an infinite corridor of mirrors, each imaging and reflecting in endless recession.[60] The Father is always calling us further into the recursive experiences of being known of him by his Spirit, which bring us increasing self-knowledge in the light of his ongoing self-revelatory action and of his final revelation of himself in his Son. Our knowing God, says the Apostle Paul, is precisely a matter of being known of God (Gal 4:9). Our willingness to allow God to reveal himself to us steers us away from imagining or re-imagining him in terms of our own wishes (which is viewing him idolatrously) and from speculating like

Augustine about *vestigia trinitas* within ourselves, or any other fancied correspondence between us and God that the Bible does not teach. So says Barth most helpfully; but not everyone listens to him.

This requiem for a lost knowledge of God and of ourselves, which we have here reviewed, is heard today, even while postmodern critics are asking us afresh, Can we *really know?* Such a question challenges us deeply to revise our communication of theology where we are still presenting it as speculative, abstract, rationalistic, and thus eventually a-theistic. "Knowing God" is expressive of the Christian's whole covenant life before the self-revealed God who is Father, Son, and Holy Spirit; it is not at all the fruit of our own instrumental epistemology. Only as we re-learn the "double knowledge" from the Bible, which leads us to it, shall we be made "wise unto salvation."

Notes

[1] An important historical survey of the "double knowledge" is given by Pierre Courcelle in *Connais-toi toi-même de Socrate à Saint Bernard* (Paris: Etudes Augustiniennes, 1975), 77–82.

[2] This is summarized from the helpful survey of Eliza Gregory Wilkins, *"Know Thyself" in Greek and Latin Literature* (New York: Garland, 1979), 12–77.

[3] Augustine, *Confessions* 10.7 (trans. Henry Chadwick; Oxford: Oxford University Press, 1991).

[4] Clement of Alexandria, *Stromata* 5.4 (*ANF* 2:234).

[5] See Henri Crouzel, *Origen* (San Francisco: Harper & Row, 1989), 112–19.

[6] Quoted by Wilkins, *"Know Thyself,"* 39.

[7] See Courcelle, *Connais-toi toi-même,* ch. 8.

[8] *The Soliloquies of St. Augustine* (trans. Rose Elizabeth Cleveland; Boston: Little, Brown & Co., 1910), 10.

[9] Augustine, *Confessions* 1.10.

[10] Peter Brown, *Augustine of Hippo* (London: Faber & Faber, 1967), 163–81.

[11] Augustine, *Confessions* 10.15.

[12] Ibid., 4.22.

[13] Ibid., 5.2.

[14] Ibid., 10.62.

[15] Ibid., 10.48.

[16] Ibid., 4.1.

[17] Ibid., 10.12 n. 12.

[18] Charles Taylor, *Sources of the Self: The Making of the Modern Identity* (Cambridge: Harvard University Press, 1989), 124.

[19] William F. Brewer, "What Is Autobiographical Memory?" in *Autobiographical Memory* (ed. D. C. Rubin; Cambridge: Cambridge University Press, 1986), 26.

[20] Brian Stock, *Augustine the Reader: Meditation, Self-Knowledge, and the Ethics of Interpretation* (Cambridge: Harvard University Press, Belknap Press, 1996), 13.

[21] Mary J. Carruthers, *The Book of Memory: A Study of Memory in Medieval Culture* (Cambridge: Cambridge University Press, 1990), 182.

[22] Augustine, *Confessions* 10.38.

[23] Stock, *Augustine,* 227.

[24] For Augustine's understanding of self-knowledge, see Rowan Williams, "The Paradoxes of Self-Knowledge in *De Trinitate* X," *Collectanea Augustinia* (1992).

[25] Augustine, *De Trinitate* 7.2, 5.

[26] See Taylor, *Sources,* 139.

[27] Quoted by R. W. Southern, *Saint Anselm: A Portrait in a Landscape* (Cambridge: Cambridge University Press, 1990), 234.

[28] Gregory the Great, *Pastoral Care IV* (trans. Henry Davis, S.J.; New York: Newman, 1950), 27.

[29] Bernard of Clairvaux, *Five Books on Consideration: Advice to a Pope* 2.3.6 (trans. Elizabeth T. Kennan; Kalamazoo: Cistercian, 1976).

[30] Ibid., 1.5.

[31] Bernard of Clairvaux, *On the Song of Songs II,* 36.6 (trans. Kilian Walsh; Kalamazoo: Cistercian, 1976).

[32] See Michael Casey, *A Thirst for God: Spiritual Desire in Bernard of Clairvaux's Sermons on the Song of Songs* (Kalamazoo: Cistercian, 1987), 154–57.

[33] *Anchoritic Spirituality:* Ancrene Wisse *and Associated Works* (trans. Anne Savage and Nicholas Ward; New York: Paulist, 1991), 85.

[34] J. A. W. Bennett, "Nosce te ipsum: Some Medieval Interpretations," in *J. R. R. Tolkien, Scholar and Storyteller: Essays in Memoriam* (ed. Mary Salu and Robert T. Farrell; Ithaca: Cornell University Press, 1979), 138–58.

[35] See Walter Hilton and Julian of Norwich, *Of the Knowledge of Ourselves and of God: A Fifteenth-Century Spiritual Florilegium* (Fleur de Lys Series 17; ed. James Walsh and Eric Colledge; London: Mowbray, 1961).

[36] Rowan Williams, *Teresa de Avila* (London: Geoffrey Chapman, 1991), 116.

[37] Likewise, some Jungian interpreters wholly distort Teresa's pastoral nurture of her sisters. See Robyn Wrigley, "Symbolism and Mystical Truth in Teresa of Avila" in *Alive to the Love of God: Essays Presented to James M. Houston by His Students on His Seventy-Fifth Birthday* (ed. Kenneth N. Pearson; Vancouver: Regent College Publishing, 1997), 347–62.

[38] Joachim Ringleben, "Die Einheit von Gotteserkenntnis und Selbsterkenntnis: Beobachtungen anhand von Luthers Römerbrief-Vorlesung" (Neue Zeitschrift für Systematische Theologie und Religionsphilosophie 32 [1990]), 133.

[39] *Luther's Works* (ed. Jaroslav Pelikan; St. Louis: Concordia, 1955), 12:311.

[40] Ibid., 12:312.

[41] John Calvin, *Institutes of the Christian Religion* 1.1.1, 7 (MacDill, Fla.: MacDonald, n.d.).

[42] Ibid.

[43] William Bouwsma, *John Calvin: A Sixteenth-Century Portrait* (New York: Oxford University Press, 1988), 160.

[44] Calvin, *Institutes* 1.1.1, 7.

[45] Quoted by Edward Downey, *The Knowledge of God in Calvin's Theology* (Grand Rapids: Eerdmans, 1994), 19.

[46] See Arthur O. Lovejoy, *The Great Chain of Being: A Study of the History of an Idea* (Cambridge: Harvard University Press, 1936).

[47] Downey, *Knowledge of God*, 21.

[48] Ibid., 53.

[49] Quoted from the 1536 edition of Calvin's *Institutes of the Christian Religion* by Philip Walker Butin, *Revelation, Redemption, and Response: Calvin's Trinitarian Understanding of the Divine-Human Relationship* (New York: Oxford University Press, 1995), 17.

[50] Ibid., 29.

[51] William Perkins, *The Workes* (ed. John Leggett; Cambridge: University of Cambridge Press, 1606), 2:280, 282.

[52] Ibid., 3:360.

[53] See the suggestive article of David Foxgrover, "Self-Examination in John Calvin and William Ames," in *Later Calvinism: International Perspectives* (ed. W. Fred Graham; vol. 22 of *Sixteenth-Century Essays and Studies,* ed. Charles G. Nauert Jr.; Kirksville, Mo.: Northeast Missouri State University Press, Sixteenth-Century Journal Publishers, 1994), 451–69.

[54] Quoted by Étienne Gilson, *The Spirit of Mediæval Philosophy: Gifford Lectures 1931–1932* (trans. A. H. C. Downes; London: Sheed & Ward, 1936), 227.

[55] Michael J. Buckley, "Modernity and the Satanic Face of God," in *Christian Spirituality and the Culture of Modernity* (ed. Peter J. Casarella and George P. Schner; Grand Rapids: Eerdmans, 1998), 100–122.

[56] John Mason, *A Treatise on Self-Knowledge: Showing the Nature and Benefit of That Important Science, and the Way to Attain It: Intermixed with Various Reflections and Observations on Human Nature* (orig. pub. London, 1745; repr., Haverhill, Mass.: William B. Allen, 1812).

[57] Michael J. Buckley, S.J., *At the Origins of Modern Atheism* (New Haven: Yale University Press, 1987), 363.

[58] See Rowan Williams, " 'Know Thyself': What Kind of an Injunction?" *Philosophy, Religion, and the Spiritual Life* (Royal Institute of Philosophy Supplement 32; ed. Michael McGhee; Cambridge: Cambridge University Press, 1992), 211–27.

[59] Karl Barth, *Church Dogmatics* (ed. Geoffrey W. Bromiley and T. F. Torrance; Edinburgh: T&T Clark, 1960), III/2, 246–47.

[60] See the helpful study of Barth's analogy of relations in David K. Miell, "Barth on Persons in Relationship: A Case for Further Reflection?" *SJT* 42, no. 4 (1989): 541–55.

Select List of Publications by Bruce K. Waltke

listed chronologically in separate categories

I. Books and Commentaries (Authored)

Creation and Chaos: An Exegetical and Theological Study of Biblical Cosmogony. Portland, Oreg.: Western Conservative Seminary, 1974.

With R. K. Harrison, G. Fee, and D. Guthrie. *Biblical Criticism: Historical, Literary, and Textual.* Grand Rapids: Zondervan, 1978.

Micah: An Introduction and Commentary. Pages 135–207 in *Obadiah, Jonah, Micah.* TOTC. Leicester: Inter-Varsity Press, 1988.

With Michael O'Connor. *An Introduction to Biblical Hebrew Syntax.* Winona Lake, Ind.: Eisenbrauns, 1990.

Micah. Pages 591–764 in vol. 2 of *The Minor Prophets: An Exegetical and Expository Commentary.* Edited by Thomas Edward McComiskey. Grand Rapids: Baker, 1993.

Joshua and *Micah.* Pages 233–60 and 822–32 in *New Bible Commentary: Twenty-First Century Edition.* Fourth edition. Edited by D. A. Carson et al. Downers Grove, Ill.: InterVarsity Press, 1994.

Finding the Will of God: A Pagan Notion? Gresham, Oreg.: Vision House, 1995.

Biblical Theology. Grand Rapids: Zondervan, forthcoming.

Commentary on Genesis. Library of Biblical Interpretation Series. Grand Rapids: Zondervan, forthcoming.

Proverbs. NICOT. Grand Rapids: Eerdmans, forthcoming.

II. Books (Edited)

Consulting OT Editor. *Expositor's Bible Commentary: With the New International Version of the Holy Bible.* Edited by Frank E. Gaebelein. 12 vols. Grand Rapids: Zondervan, 1976–1981.

Associate Editor. *Theological Wordbook of the Old Testament.* Edited by R. Laird Harris. 2 vols. Chicago: Moody, 1980.

Associate Editor. *The New International Dictionary of Old Testament Theology and Exegesis.* Edited by Willem A. VanGemeren. 5 vols. Grand Rapids: Zondervan, 1997.

III. Journal and Magazine Articles

"Old Testament and Birth Control." *CT* 13 (November 8, 1968): 3–6.

"Palestinian Artifactual Evidence Supporting the Early Date of the Exodus." *BSac* 129 (January–March 1972): 33–47.

"Creation Account in Genesis 1:1–3, Part I: Introduction to Biblical Cosmogony." *BSac* 132 (January–March 1975): 25–36.

"Creation Account in Genesis 1:1–3, Part II: The Restitution Theory." *BSac* 132 (April–June 1975): 136–44.

"Creation Account in Genesis 1:1–3, Part III: The Initial Chaos Theory and the Precreation Chaos Theory." *BSac* 132 (July–September 1975): 216–28.

"Creation Account in Genesis 1:1–3, Part IV: The Theology of Genesis 1." *BSac* 132 (October–December 1975): 327–42.

"Creation Account in Genesis 1:1–3, Part V: The Theology of Genesis 1 (Continued)." *BSac* 133 (January–March 1976): 28–41.

"The Date of the Book of Daniel." *BSac* 133 (October–December 1976): 319–29.

"Reflections from the Old Testament on Abortion." *JETS* 19 (winter 1976): 3–13.

"1 Corinthians 11:2–16: An Interpretation." *BSac* 135 (January–March 1978): 46–57.

"The Book of Proverbs and Ancient Wisdom Literature." *BSac* 136 (July–September 1979): 221–238.

"The Book of Proverbs and Old Testament Theology." *BSac* 136 (October–December 1979): 302–317.

"The Relationship of the Sexes in the Bible." *Crux* 19, no. 3 (September 1983): 10–16.

"Is It Right to Read the New Testament into the Old?" *CT* 27, no. 13 (September 2, 1983): 77.

"The Redeemed and the Righteous." *The Canadian Baptist* 131, no. 1 (January 1985): 6–12.

"Cain and His Offering." *WTJ* 48, no. 2 (fall 1986): 363–72.

With Walter C. Kaiser Jr. "Shared Leadership or Male Headship?" *CT* 30, no. 14 (October 3, 1986): 12-I, 13-I.

"Hermeneutics and the Spiritual Life." *Crux* 23, no. 1 (March 1987): 5–10.

"The Authority of Proverbs: An Exposition of Proverbs 1:2–6." *Presb* 13, no. 2 (fall 1987): 65–78.

"Evangelical Spirituality: A Biblical Scholar's Perspective." *JETS* 31 (March 1988): 9–24.

"Lady Wisdom as Mediatrix: An Exposition of Proverbs 1:20–33." *Presb* 14 (spring 1988): 1–15.

"The First Seven Days: What Is the Creation Account Trying to Tell Us?" *CT* 32 (August 12, 1988): 42–46.

"*The New International Version* and Its Textual Principles in the Book of Psalms." *JETS* 32 (March 1989): 17–26.

"Aims of OT Textual Criticism." *WTJ* 51 (spring 1989): 93–108.

"Relating Human Personhood to the Health Sciences: An Old Testament Perspective." *Crux* 25, no. 3 (September 1989): 2–10.

"Lord Sabaoth Is His Name." *Tabletalk* (February 1990): 33–34.

"Old or New? Which Testament Takes Priority?" *Tabletalk* (June 1990): 30.

"The Date of the Conquest." *WTJ* 52 (fall 1990): 181–200.

"Harold Bloom and 'J': A Review Article." *JETS* 34, no. 4 (December 1991): 509–20.

"The Literary Genre of Genesis, Chapter One." *Crux* 27, no. 4 (December 1991): 2–10.

"Superscripts, Postscripts, or Both." *JBL* 110, no. 4 (winter 1991): 583–96.

"1 Timothy 2:8–15: Unique or Normative?" *Crux* 28, no. 1 (March 1992): 22–23, 26–27.

"Introducing Proverbs." *Journal of the Christian Brethren Research Fellowship* 128 (September 1992): 5–11.

"The Fear of the LORD." *Journal of the Christian Brethren Research Fellowship* 128 (September 1992): 12–16.

"Does Proverbs Promise Too Much?" *Journal of the Christian Brethren Research Fellowship* 128 (September 1992): 17–22.

"Psalm 49: Responding to an Unethical Society." *Stimulus* 1, no. 3 (August 1993): 13–18.

"How I Changed My Mind about Teaching Hebrew (or Retained It)." *Crux* 29, no. 4 (December 1993): 10–15.

"He Ascended and Sitteth: Reflections on the Sixth Article of the Apostles' Creed." *Crux* 30, no. 2 (June 1994): 2–8.

"Exegesis and the Spiritual Life: Theology as Spiritual Formation." *Crux* 30, no. 3 (September 1994): 28–35.

"How We Got the Old Testament." *Crux* 30, no. 4 (December 1994): 12–19.

"What Is Wisdom?" *Tabletalk* (January 1995): 24–30.
"How to Know God." *Tabletalk* (February 1995): 28–36.
"The Genre of Wisdom." *Tabletalk* (March 1995): 14–52.
"Wealth and Poverty." *Tabletalk* (April 1995): 41–42.
"Does Proverbs Promise Too Much?" *Tabletalk* (May 1995): 29–30.
"Characteristics of Wise Parents." *Tabletalk* (June 1995): 35–36.
"An Introduction to Ecclesiastes." *Tabletalk* (August 1995): 28–29.
"The Message of Ecclesiastes." *Tabletalk* (September 1995): 26–27.
"The Role of Women in the Bible." *Crux* 31, no. 3 (September 1995): 29–40.
"Grammar School of Suffering." *Tabletalk* (October 1995): 30–31. Reprinted on pages 319–36 in *Andrews University Seminary Studies* 34, no. 2 (autumn 1996).
"Reflections on Retirement from the Life of Isaac." *Crux* 32, no. 4 (December 1996): 4–14.
"The Role of the Valiant Woman in the Marketplace." *Crux* 35, no. 3 (September 1999): 23–34.

IV. Articles in Works of Composite Authorship

"Old Testament Texts Bearing on the Problem of the Control of Human Reproduction." Pages 7–24 in *Birth Control and the Christian: A Protestant Symposium on the Control of Human Reproduction.* Edited by Walter O. Spitzer and Carlyle L. Saylor. Wheaton, Ill.: Tyndale, 1968.
"The Samaritan Pentateuch and the Text of the Old Testament." Pages 212–39 in *New Perspectives on the Old Testament.* Edited by J. Barton Payne. Waco: Word, 1970.
"The Textual Criticism of the Old Testament." Pages 211–28 in vol. 1 of *Expositor's Bible Commentary: With the New International Version of the Holy Bible.* Edited by Frank E. Gaebelein. 12 vols. Grand Rapids: Zondervan, 1976–1981.
"A Canonical Process Approach to the Psalms." Pages 3–18 in *Tradition and Testament: Essays in Honor of Charles Lee Feinberg.* Edited by John S. Feinberg and Paul D. Feinberg. Chicago: Moody, 1981.
"An Evangelical Christian View of the Hebrew Scriptures." Pages 105–39 in *Evangelicals and Jews in an Age of Pluralism.* Edited by Marc H. Tanenbaum, Marvin R. Wilson, and A. James Rudin. Grand Rapids: Baker, 1984.
"Historical Grammatical Problems." Pages 69–129 in *Hermeneutics, Inerrancy, and the Bible.* Edited by Earl D. Radmacher and Robert D. Preus. Grand Rapids: Academie, 1984.
"Oral Tradition." Pages 117–35 in *Inerrancy and Hermeneutic: A Tradition, a Challenge, a Debate.* Edited by Harvie M. Conn. Grand Rapids: Baker, 1988.

Repr. from pp. 17–34 in *A Tribute to Gleason Archer.* Edited by Walter C. Kaiser Jr. and Ronald Youngblood. Chicago: Moody, 1986.

"Biblical Authority: How Firm a Foundation." Pages 84–96 in *The Evangelical Round Table: Evangelicalism: Surviving Its Success.* Edited by David A. Fraser. St. Davids, Penn.: Eastern College Press, 1987.

"Creation Myths." Pages 542–46 in *Baker Encyclopedia of the Bible.* Edited by Walter A. Elwell. Grand Rapids: Baker, 1988.

"Kingdom Promises as Spiritual." Pages 263–87 in *Continuity and Discontinuity: Perspectives on the Relationship between the Old and New Testaments: Essays in Honor of S. Lewis Johnson Jr.* Edited by John S. Feinberg. Westchester, U.K.: Crossway, 1988.

"The Phenomenon of Conditionality within Unconditional Covenants." Pages 123–39 in *Israel's Apostasy and Restoration: Essays in Honor of Roland K. Harrison.* Edited by Avraham Gileadi. Grand Rapids: Baker, 1988.

"Theonomy in Relation to Dispensational and Covenant Theologies." Pages 59–86 in *Theonomy: A Reformed Critique.* Edited by William S. Barker and W. Robert Godfrey. Grand Rapids: Academie, 1990.

"Psalms 2 and 4." Pages 86–92 in *The Making of the* NIV. Edited by Kenneth L. Barker. Grand Rapids: Zondervan, 1991.

"The Fear of the Lord." Pages 17–33 in *Alive to God: Studies in Spirituality Presented to James Houston.* Edited by J. I. Packer and Loren Wilkinson. Downers Grove, Ill.: InterVarsity Press, 1992.

"A Response." Pages 347–359 in *Dispensationalism, Israel, and the Church: The Search for Definition.* Edited by Craig A. Blaising and Darrell L. Bock. Grand Rapids: Zondervan, 1992.

"Samaritan Pentateuch." Pages 932–40 in vol. 5 of *The Anchor Bible Dictionary.* Edited by David Noel Freedman. New York: Doubleday, 1992.

"Love, Justice, and the Allocation of Limited Medical Resources." Pages 75–91 in *Questions of Right and Wrong: Proceedings of the 1993 Clinical Bioethics Conference.* Edited by Edwin C. Hui. Vancouver, B.C.: Regent College Publishing, 1994.

"Old Testament Textual Criticism." Pages 156–86 in *Foundations for Biblical Interpretation: A Complete Library of Tools and Resources.* Edited by David S. Dockery, Kenneth A. Mathews, and Robert B. Sloan. Nashville: Broadman & Holman, 1994.

"The Dance between God and Humanity." Pages 87–104 in *Doing Theology for the People of God: Studies in Honor of J. I. Packer.* Edited by Donald Lewis and Alister McGrath. Downers Grove, Ill.: InterVarsity Press, 1996.

"Circumcision." Pages 143–44 in *The Complete Book of Everyday Christianity: An A-to-Z Guide to Following Christ in Every Aspect of Life.* Edited by

Robert Banks and R. Paul Stevens. Downers Grove, Ill.: InterVarsity Press, 1997.

"Micah, Theology of." Pages 936–40 in vol. 4 of *The New International Dictionary of Old Testament Theology and Exegesis.* Edited by Willem A. VanGemeren. 5 vols. Grand Rapids: Zondervan, 1997.

"Proverbs, Theology of." Pages 1079–94 in vol. 4 of *The New International Dictionary of Old Testament Theology and Exegesis.* Edited by Willem A. VanGemeren. 5 vols. Grand Rapids: Zondervan, 1997.

"The Reliability of the Old Testament Text." Pages 51–67 in vol. 1 of *The New International Dictionary of Old Testament Theology and Exegesis.* Edited by Willem A. VanGemeren. 5 vols. Grand Rapids: Zondervan, 1997.

"Old Testament Interpretation Issues for Big Idea Preaching: Problematic Sources, Poetics." Pages 41–52 in *The Big Idea of Biblical Preaching: Connecting the Bible to People.* Edited by Keith Willhite and Scott M. Gibson. Grand Rapids: Baker, 1998.

"Preaching the Old Testament: An Exposition of Proverbs 26:1–12." Pages 175–76 in *The Big Idea of Biblical Preaching: Connecting the Bible to People.* Edited by Keith Willhite and Scott M. Gibson. Grand Rapids: Baker, 1998.

With David Diewert. "Wisdom Literature." Pages 295–328 in *The Face of Old Testament Studies: A Survey of Contemporary Approaches.* Edited by David W. Baker and Bill T. Arnold. Grand Rapids: Baker, 1999.

V. Contributions to Dictionaries and Encyclopedias

About 30 articles in *The Zondervan Pictorial Encyclopedia of the Bible.* Edited by Merrill C. Tenney. 5 vols. Grand Rapids: Zondervan, 1975.

About 30 articles in *International Standard Bible Encyclopedia.* Fully revised. Edited by Geoffrey W. Bromiley et al. 4 vols. Grand Rapids: Eerdmans, 1979–1988.

Several articles in *New Dictionary of Christian Ethics and Pastoral Theology.* Edited by David J. Atkinson and David H. Field. Downers Grove, Ill.: InterVarsity Press, 1995.

Several articles in *Evangelical Dictionary of Biblical Theology.* Edited by Walter A. Elwell. Grand Rapids: Baker, 1996.

We want to hear from you. Please send your comments about this book to us in care of the address below. Thank you.

ZondervanPublishingHouse
Grand Rapids, Michigan 49530
http://www.zondervan.com